D0426350

FATAL
CROSSROADS

FATAL
CROSSROADS

THE UNTOLD STORY OF THE
MALMÉDY MASSACRE AT
THE BATTLE OF THE BULGE

DANNY S. PARKER

DA CAPO PRESS
A Member of the
Perseus Books Group

Editorial production by the Book Factory
Designed by Cynthia Young.

Cataloging-in-Publication data for this book is available from the Library of Congress.
ISBN: 978-0-306-81193-7

Published by Da Capo Press
A Member of the Perseus Books Group
www.dacapopress.com

Da Capo Press books are available at special discounts for bulk purchases in the
U.S. by corporations, institutions, and other organizations. For more information,
please contact the Special Markets Department at the Perseus Books Group,
2300 Chestnut Street, Suite 200, Philadelphia, PA 19103, or call (800) 810-4145,
ext. 5000, or e-mail special.markets@perseusbooks.com.

Maps by Gaadt Studio

10 9 8 7 6 5 4 3 2 1

For Sarah and Wade

CONTENTS

LIST OF MAPS

ACKNOWLEDGMENTS

This book emerged from a larger seventeen-year project on the life and times of Jochen Peiper. However, after reviewing the mass of writing, my editor, Bob Pigeon, realized that we had a separate and very dramatic story of the Malmédy massacre—and one not completely told.

Special thanks to Will C. C. Cavanagh, an English subject at the time living in Waimes, Belgium, who helped me over a two-year period to interview many civilian witnesses in the Ardennes. The many Belgians who thoughtfully invited us into their homes to relive disturbing events touched us deeply. In particular, my discussions with Robert Pfeiffer and Peter Lentz were vitally important, as both boys—now men—were witnesses to the massacre and its aftermath. Other local interviews for which I am thankful include Joseph Dejardin, Joseph Pothen, Armand Reutsch, Marthe and Ida Martin, and Madeleine Warand-Lejoly. In La Gleize, Gerard Gregoire and his daughter Marie France suggested contacts, and Erik Wuite helped with one last-minute interview. I also appreciate the warm welcome from Marcel and Mathilde Schmetz at the Remember Museum as well as their willingness to search out local information.

I am particularly indebted to John Bauserman, whose book on the Malmédy massacre remains a singular accomplishment. Over the long gestation of my work John always helped with sources and his own personal interviews as well as to examine the mass of evidence from the tragic and deeply complicated sequence of events at Baugnez. Also, George Gaadt, who knows the Malmédy story intimately, has been of considerable help and has contributed maps and illustrations. Similarly, I appreciate Belgian historian Henri Rogister, whose research on the massacre supplemented my own. Dr. Donald Goldstein and the University of Pittsburgh assisted with photographic sources.

I interviewed many individuals from the 285th FAOB: Ted Paluch, Bill Summers, Bobby Werth, Al Valenzi, Tom Bacon, Stephen Domitrovitch, Harold Billow, Warren Schmidt, George Fox, and Robert Mearig. I corresponded with several more. Their stories highlight the human spirit amid adversity. In 1999 I was able to walk with Bill Merriken and others, tracing his epic trek to escape the killing field. Sadly, Bill died before this project was complete, but here I preserve his poignant tale. In 2007 I accompanied Ted Paluch back to Baugnez in a particularly revealing odyssey. Ted and I remain good friends.

At the U.S. National Archives (NARA) I had a great deal of help. Richard Boylan, Paul Brown, Amy Schmidt, and the late John E. Taylor were instrumental in helping me over a decade to wade through the mountain of documents and papers (over thirty-eight thousand pages) dealing with the Malmédy investigation. Other thanks go to Patricia Spayd and Bill Warnock for their unselfish willingness to help at NARA. After spending many weeks in the nation's capital at the archives, I am indebted to the staff and regulars at the Hotel Tabard Inn, my home away from home. There, revelry is defined.

At the U.S. Army Military History Institute I received assistance from Dr. Richard J. Sommers and David A. Keogh. I extend thanks to the late John Toland and his daughter Tamiko for making all of his private papers and taped interviews available to me at both the Franklin D. Roosevelt Library and the Library of Congress. At the latter I had assistance from Ronald E. Cogan, Jeff Flannery, and Bryan Cornell. Locally, Yayi Rickling at Brevard Community College was always of help.

In England, Gen. Michael Reynolds, the author of his own important account of the Kampfgruppe Peiper, always lent a hand when I asked. John S. D. Eisenhower graciously made available his personal papers at the Eisenhower Library as well as agreed to a pleasurable afternoon discussing his father's remembrances of the episode. Particular note also must be made of Professor Emeritus James Weingartner at Southern Illinois University, the author of the seminal work on the trial, *Crossroads of Death: The Story of the Malmédy Massacre and Trial*, who shared freely from unique sources.

One person to whom I owe a heavy debt is my very professional Austrian interpreter and translator living in Washington, DC, Helmut Thiess. Together we conducted some key interviews in Germany. Helmut became a close friend, only to die tragically in the midst of the long research. I miss his wise counsel and like to think he would be proud of what he helped me create. In Germany, we were ably assisted by Dr. Jens Westemeier, who was instrumental in making many contacts and setting up interviews. We developed a real friendship over the years of work from which this book emerged. Timm Haasler and Hans Weber, experts on Kampfgruppe Peiper, helped with many details essential in piecing together the story from the German side. Finally, Mike Smeets, a Dutch historian, also shared freely from his sources and interviews.

I greatly appreciate the Waffen SS veterans who faced me with openness even when our views did not match. Hans Siptrott, Arndt Fischer, Gerhard Walla, Reinhold Kyriss, and Rolf Reiser all told stories from firsthand presence. Werner Ackermann and Manfred Thorn gave extensive interviews of their experiences in Peiper's panzer regiment. Several witnesses preferred to remain anonymous; to those not mentioned I give my thanks. Thanks also to Wolf Mauder, who introduced me to several unique sources. To those on the German side, who may feel betrayed by my conclusions, I express my gratitude; I've made a sincere effort to be objective.

I have benefited from helpful readers. Ann Hamilton Shields helped review the writing with critical comment throughout. More than this, during my last three years of work Ann became the project research assistant in Germany and contributed hundreds of selfless hours as well as interviews assisted by her husband, Mo. Moreover, her friends, Sarah and Edith, provided expert translation on short notice. Another careful reviewer was Ms. Terry Hirsch, to whom a number of corrections owe their origin.

Early on, Clyde Taylor, my literary agent with Curtis Brown Ltd., professed confidence in this project. Tragically, Clyde died suddenly in early 2001—a painful loss. Fortunately, Kirsten Manges and, later, Katherine Fausset, also with Curtis Brown, stepped in to take over. At DaCapo Press, thanks to Andrea Schultz for the vision to take the project on and to Robert Pigeon, my patient editor who saw an opportunity to create a special book on Malmédy. Finally, within the closing stages, project editor Lori Hobkirk and copy editor Josephine Mariea provided much-needed polish.

At home my family has endured my years of work with this difficult subject with as much cheer and understanding as can be reasonably expected. Any writer knows that means a lot.

—*Danny S. Parker*
Cocoa Beach, July 2011

Prisoners of War are in the power of the hostile Power, but not of individuals or corps who have captured them. They must at all times be humanely treated and protected, particularly against acts of violence, insults and public curiosity.

—Article Two of the *Convention Relative to the Treatment of Prisoners of War*, signed July 27, 1929, at Geneva, Switzerland, by forty-six nations, of which Germany was one.

BAUGNEZ·BELGIUM·1944
DECEMBER 17.1944·CROSSROADS
285TH FIELD ARTILLERY OBSERVATION BATTL.

BIRDSEYE — ROUGH SKETCH — GEORGE S.GAADT·II

Prologue

The last shot echoed from the crossroads and reverberated beyond the Belgian hills before fading slowly like a hushed sonic wave, signaling something from afar. It echoed with a seeming hesitation, booming from the nearby pine forests and resounding across the hillsides in cold air. The wavering thunder took several seconds to fade, seeming to pull the world along into a new silence—cold, lonely, and dying in a whimper.

As far away as two miles downhill in Malmédy, the shots were heard. Armand Reutsch, a young nineteen-year-old amateur photographer in town, along with his sister Agnes could plainly hear the shots from their house by the railroad. Although the occasional sound of distant shotgun blasts was familiar in the Ardennes, as hunting wild boar and deer was a long winter tradition in the region, Reutsch knew from experience that these were not from a hunter's shotgun or rifle. And even more odd were other strange events in Malmédy the day before. Did Reutsch know more?

At daybreak the day before, Saturday, December 16, giant explosions had rocked the town of six thousand. Twenty died, including two American soldiers and one of the community's most popular young women. No one knew the source of the explosions; the whole thing was quite mysterious. Some people said it was another of Adolf Hitler's threatened new secret weapons. With his futuristic V-2 rockets slamming into the nearby industrial city of Liège every week, the townspeople could dismiss the rumors easily. Yet others tagged the source as a big WWI-style German rail gun lobbing huge artillery shells. Even so, why were the Germans turning such a weapon on a sleepy Belgian settlement?

Nestled in the Amblève River valley, Malmédy was a simple medieval market town. By World War II the Ardennes region had become something of a European resort, and before 1939 many traveled to nearby Spa to take the cure of its healing waters.[1] But summer holidays were not on the minds of anyone in Belgium in 1944, engulfed with the rest of Europe in a cataclysmic war. By mid-December, however, the tiresome conflict seemed to be receding at last. On June 6 the Allies had landed in Normandy, France, and had liberated that country by summer's end. In September the Allies had driven the Germans out to the border after four long years of occupation. Since then, the fighting front before the Ardennes had become quiescent.

Although everyone in the town was very aware that the German army was only forty kilometers to the east, the military activity along the border became so torpid that autumn that American soldiers lucky enough to be posted there had taken to calling it the "ghost front." And even less happened behind the lines. Now liberated, the citizens of Malmédy looked forward to resuming the bacchanalian annual carnival, the *Grantés haguétes*. And for the few American GIs, the watered-down beer and friendly Belgian girls were the big draw.

On Sunday, December 17, 1944, however, rumors abounded. Some of the locals said the Germans were coming back, and their pronouncement could hardly be taken lightly: Malmédy had been part of Germany until its repatriation to Belgium after World War I. Because the region had been invaded numerous times, everyone there was always aware of their war-minded neighbors to the east.

But that Sunday all things German were quite distant from the wistful dreams of Armand Reutsch. Armand fancied himself as a lazy bachelor. Thanks to an indulgent mother, he did not rise from his warm covers until just before the late morning Mass. He walked dutifully toward the cathedral, past slate-roofed houses under the gray, sullen sky. He noted the frozen mist in the air—to be Belgian was to learn to appreciate the winter shades of gray. He pulled his wraps tightly; the temperature was just above freezing. On the street he joined others making their way to the cathedral, and soon they were all inside. During the late Mass the priest dutifully intoned the Eucharistic Prayer as the parish strained to ignore the grinding noise of clanking tanks on the cobblestone street. To be sure, they were American tanks, somebody said from the 7th Armored Division. But why were they slithering through town on a Sunday?

The only Americans in Malmédy that December—the 291st Combat Engineers, who worked the quarry near the Reutsch home, and the 44th Evacuation Field Hospital, down in the center of town—hardly inspired a vision of war. They had a casual manner, and Armand, who was fascinated by images of Hollywood movie stars, had made friends with several of them since their arrival. Although their demeanor was easy, Armand suspected their friendly way also had much to do with his attractive younger sister. Now, as the tanks rolled through the town that Sunday, he wondered what the American cowboys were up to. By the time the congregation emerged through the thick wooden doors onto the steps of the cathedral, the tanks were gone. It was puzzling.

Yet the recent past of Armand Reutsch reflected the political confusion that made American soldiers uneasy in Malmédy. During the previous two years Reutsch had been a member of the Hitler Youth in Eupen-Malmédy. Although such information set off all kinds of alarms for American intelligence ears, membership in that organization was obligatory for young men in the region during the occupation, which was considered German territory. Indeed, only a written note, excusing them due to pressing farm chores, could let someone off from attending Sunday meetings in Malmédy. Although he was more interested in amateur photography than National Socialism, Reustch still participated in the marches, the singing, the terrain exercises, and the like.

Still, even being an unwilling member of the Hitler Youth had its implications, for in October 1944 Armand and two hundred others were impressed into a construction detail improving Westwall fortifications in Kall, which was on the other side of the German border. By November 18 the Belgian youths received rifle training and were told that they would take an oath the following day. A German-army noncommissioned officer taking note of their poor enthusiasm iced the mood: "Wait until you really encounter the enemy," he complained, "You will run away and be beaten badly." That was enough for Reutsch; he, along several others, deserted that night and headed back home to Belgium. Three days later an American intelligence detachment apprehended Reutsch while he was crossing the border at Hollerath.[2] After a detailed interrogation, they released the Belgian youth to return home. Thankful to be back in Malmédy, Reutsch had nothing more to do with the National Socialist sympathizers anymore. Instead, he hung out with the Americans and again embraced his hobby of photography.

That Sunday, after the tanks had rolled through the town, Armand and Agnes returned to their home across the railroad and prepared to go out again that afternoon. They were to attend the christening of their new niece, an event to which their parents had already departed. Armand slipped on his coat and gloves and paused at the door. Just then he heard a loud boom followed right away by an even louder bang. Agnes looked up, somewhat startled, "What was that?"[3] Armand instinctively turned his gaze up the hill. "Big guns," he whispered. There were more muted explosions and gunfire, and then all became silent again. The quiet seemed ominous. They both huddled by the door, hoping their parents might soon return. "I'm not going anywhere," he told his sister. Later—maybe half an hour—he heard the shooting start again, only this time it was different.

From a distance, the sound was like a series of crackling pops, spaced so closely that they blended into a rattle. Armand knew the sound instantly; he had heard it many times watching wartime newsreels in occupied Belgium. German machine guns—*Hitlersäge*, or Hitler's Saw—had a distinct ripping sound produced by bullets spurting out the barrel of the MG 42s at sixteen hundred rounds per minute. German machine guns here? A silent pause. Now there were single reports punctuating the gray afternoon, reverberating through the north valley. Was there a battle for the town being fought just up the hill? Armand and Agnes waited. Yet just as soon as the noise started, it ended. Days would pass before Armand and his sister would know what they had heard.

At the crossroads where it originated no one really paid attention to the final shot. Out in a grassy field, over 130 young men lay sprawled on the cold ground.[4] They were a long way from their homes: Elizabethtown, Pennsylvania, or Baltimore, Maryland, or Bedford, Virginia. Many were dead; others lay dying. Some bullets had pierced two or three men, and blood, clothing, and bone fragments had sprayed like a gruesome mist over the twisted tangle of bodies. Some pleaded for help, others called for mother or God. There were the quiet sighs of those dying; the collective sound was "almost like a lowing."[5]

Preceded by a long gun barrel, a dark panzer lumbered past the crossroads, its deck covered in pine boughs. "You dirty bastards will cross the Siegfried line!" chided an accented voice.[6] The loud metallic grinding of tank tracks drowned out the moans of the dying. A few of the vehicles fired into the knots of bodies lying in the frozen field. Then something more frightful began: Men with pistols came to the field where the wounded were lying, giving "mercy shots" to those who showed signs of life. Footsteps grew closer. "*Da kriegt noch einer Luft*" ("Here's one still breathing.")[7] More voices . . . a kick and a muffled grunt. Curses—even laughter. Individual shots and more silence. This went on for a time, with more steps and shots. There were other sounds too horrible to recount.

One of the men lying in the field was William Hite Merriken. He was a staff sergeant with the 285th Field Artillery Observation Battalion, which sounded much more soldierly and martial than Bill Merriken felt as he lay out there in the muddy field. He was wounded and cold. Most of all, he was scared. Even though the twenty-one-year-old could see nothing with his head pressed to the frozen ground, his hearing was acute. After the continuous gunfire ended, he could hear enemy voices. Merriken felt the two bullets burning in his back. A warm wet liquid—his own blood—was slowly spreading across his shirt. Unsure of his nearness to death, he dared not move.

A wounded man next to him—Max Schwitzgold—was in obvious pain. At Merriken's side when the shooting began, the wounded GI had flopped on top of him during the initial volley of gunfire.[8] Now, the pained soldier was only partially conscious and thrashing in agony. As the man on top of him moaned, Merriken could hear other men screaming—a horrifying warble—and he knew the enemy would see Schwitzgold moving. There were Germans off to his left. "Are you hurt?" a voice called out in English. An anguished reply: "Yes! I'm in pain." Another pause. Then a pistol shot.

Merriken knew the Germans would soon hear the wailing man on top of him; perhaps he could save them both. "Be quiet. Be still," Merriken whispered urgently. But the boy was delirious. He moaned uncontrollably. The measured sound of footsteps grew near once more and Merriken recognized the two voices. He could not understand them, but their intent was clear. They were right over him now. Although not particularly religious, Bill Merriken did as many do when faced with their end: he silently intoned a prayer. He thought of his aunt and uncle who had raised him in Bedford, Virginia, believing he would never see them again. He imagined how they would learn of his death just eight days before Christmas 1944 by a lonely crossroads somewhere in Belgium. The serenity of resignation flooded past. His face was buried in his arms as he waited for the end. He smelled the damp earth.

There was a deafening blast and a concussion of air. His entire body lurched from the impact of a bullet as it tore into his knee after passing through the wounded soldier's body. With his mouth on his right arm, Merriken bit hard. Not a sound came from his lips, and the weight of the GI's form kept his leg from involuntarily jerking. The young soldier was silent now—a 9mm slug fired into his temple. The two enemy soldiers didn't bother with Merriken. Covered in blood, he presented a ghastly sight. "Tot" (dead), one sighed in dismissal. They walked away.

Surrendered to fate, Bill Merriken's mind had become as clear as the cold water flowing though the Warche River just two miles away in Malmédy. He held his breath so as not to create vapor in the winter air. When he did breathe, he took a slow, deliberate, and shallow draft. The footsteps and voices receded. He inhaled slowly. Merriken felt as if his soul had somehow detached from his body. He floated free of this terrible scene. So this is how it felt to die, he thought. He prayed, not for himself, but that "somebody would get out to tell of what they had done." After a long time, the enemy soldiers left the field, satisfied that all had been put out of their misery. Yet Bill Merriken felt somehow protected; he just lay there in peace for what seemed like hours.

After a time the steady rumble of vehicles ceased and the voices faded. Now he could hear only the wind stirring the naked tree branches. His body numb from the cold, Merriken wondered if perhaps he was already dead. Suddenly, he heard someone yell off to his right. "Let's make a break!" the voice implored. Someone else was alive! *What the hell*, Merriken thought to himself. He saw himself a dead man with nothing to lose. He thrust himself up off the ground with numb hands. He shoved hard and somehow stood up. He could see again, but he felt dizzy. Merriken staggered as feeling returned. His right leg buckled out from under him; the bullet had shattered his knee. In spite of shooting pain, he tried to orient himself. From the field he could see the clapboard café by the crossroads and some other buildings near that. A few flakes of snow swirled through the cold air. There were olive drab–clad bodies lying all about him, but some of the men rose crazily from the tangle of arms and legs on the ground. He struggled to keep his balance on one foot. Like flushed rabbits, the men scattered quickly in every direction, with most heading northwest. Foreign voices buzzed excitedly—there were still some Germans! Out of his peripheral vision, he could see at least a dozen Americans sprint west toward a patch of trees—they were really moving. Still, Merriken's first step convinced him that he would never make it to the woods; he nearly collapsed from the pain. More gunfire—they were shooting at those trying to escape. Some fell.

Hopping awkwardly on a single foot, Bill Merriken headed almost straight to the north toward the rear of the café. His vision of the scene bounced crazily with his staggered gait. A machine gun stammered to life and tracers whizzed by, the bullets kicking up the muddy ground around him. He limped along, expecting gunfire to cut him down as he crossed the field. How he made it, he would never know. Dragging his right leg, he hobbled painfully behind the café, where a wall concealed him from direct view from the crossroads. Ahead, he saw a two-story stone house on the north side of the dirt road. As he limped away from the field, he could see two or three Americans banging to get in the door. As Merriken drew closer, someone inside quickly slammed the door closed. The unwelcome men ran off toward the rear of the house. But where would he go?

Breathing hard, Merriken stumbled toward a small shed in front of the house. He was desperately looking for any place to hide. There was more shooting and then some shouting just behind him, but he did not look back. He dragged himself to the edge of a thick hedge line by the dirt road that he recognized as the ubiquitous hedgerows the farmers in the region used as a ready fence for the cows. Now the barrier separated him from potential refuge. He had to get across quickly to the house; he could hear running footsteps drawing closer.

Bill glanced to his right and saw a dark-uniformed soldier running up from the crossroads. As he hobbled toward the hedge, the German soldier on the other side spotted him, obviously in pursuit of the Americans running to the west. The two were only twenty feet apart and nearly face-to-face. As Merriken lurched toward the hedgerow thicket, the uniformed man pulled out a pistol and aimed it directly at him. He pulled the trigger, so close that Merriken could hear the hammer drop. *Click.* It misfired! The German soldier ran and cursed as he fumbled with the pistol.

While the German was preoccupied, Merriken threw himself into the bushes, awkwardly emerging out the other side and falling headlong into a ditch. He crawled across the dirt road and headed for a small lean-to woodshed fifty yards to the left of the two-story farmhouse.[9] He reached the entrance, exhausted and in burning pain. On elbows, he slowly squirmed inside. To his relief, there were no animals. He hid himself next to a large pile of firewood as best he could.

The woodshed was nothing more than a dilapidated lean-to, but through the cracks in its weathered wooden slats, Merriken could see outside. Off to the east he could see the path from the crossroads; to the west the road disappeared into a copse of pines. The two-story house with the attached barn was nearby. Less than five minutes had gone by when Merriken saw the black-capped German, his pistol still drawn, trotting back down the road from the west. The enemy soldier stopped, looking about where he and Merriken had encountered each other, as if searching for a wounded quarry. He paused to turn about in the road 180 degrees, searching for where the American might be hiding. After a few long minutes, Merriken could no longer see the man hunting for him.

Merriken decided that perhaps his luck had finally run out. He could clearly hear an increasing bustle of German activity nearby— engines, clanking tracks, shouts, and voices. Only the gathering darkness held any promise of escape. How would he evade the enemy? He was too weak to run, and his oozing wounds hurt like hell. "I'll bleed to death," Merriken whispered to himself. For over an hour he listened to

German voices outside, clenching his teeth and locking his arms on his chest to prevent himself from chattering in the cold. Loss of blood left him fading with the twilight as he stared out of the wooden slats toward the field and the bright torch of the burning café—the enemy had set it afire to flush out hapless men hiding there. When Bill Merriken fell asleep, it was dark and cold. He was totally exhausted and nearly without hope.

That evening, several miles down the road at a spacious two-story house in Malmédy where they had established a command post, Gustav Berle, Joe Thiele, and Armand Demers were discussing the most disquieting reports from headquarters.[10] The three men were intelligence operatives with U.S. 205th Counter-intelligence Corps. In recent days they had received unnerving signs of something unusual from their double agents who were operating across the German border. Their informants had told them of many German trucks, troops, and even tanks just across the border. They dutifully forwarded the reports to the U.S. V Corps headquarters, but no one seemed inclined to act.

Then, the day before, Saturday, December 16, early in the morning huge artillery shells mysteriously fell on Malmédy. Although the shells had landed in the town marketplace, fairly distant from the command-post house, they leveled several buildings and damaged the American evacuation hospital there. Even though distant, the concussion shook the ancient building to its foundation. Only large-caliber rail guns could do something like this—but in the Ardennes? The civilians in town had been understandably rattled. Joe Thiele, a quiet, bespectacled schoolteacher from Wisconsin, had even gone out among the villagers that morning while the shells were still falling to assure them that the Americans were staying. They listened, but in his own mind he wasn't so sure whether the GIs in town might bug out.

On Sunday night, December 17, Berle, Thiele, and Demers held a hasty meeting. Discussing the incoming reports, they decided to bury their files and IDs and wear unmarked civilian clothes until things quieted down. Earlier that day they sent their female Polish domestic servants to the safety of nearby Stavelot. On the road the servants became meshed in a gaggle of Belgian refugees clogging the roads. "The

Germans are coming," those fleeing all said. The foreboding rumble of distant artillery fire punctuated the cold night air along with the snap of ice falling from the trees outside. Unknown American soldiers had parked a halftrack outside their building facing broadside to block the road. They piled chairs and tables on the balcony of the building and installed a Browning automatic rifle. They took turns sleeping.

Sometime later that night a lone jeep with its headlights blacked out suddenly roared up to the halftrack. It arrived so abruptly that the guard on the armored vehicle involuntarily fired off a round from its .50-caliber machine gun. "Stop!" someone cried out. Confusion reigned as the jeep screeched to a halt. A flashlight from the halftrack revealed three shivering GIs. One had a bad chest wound, his field jacket soaked with blood. The other two appeared unwounded, although nearly hysterical, both speaking at once to the three surprised agents. They said something terrible had happened at the crossroads just to the south.

Within hours the two unwounded men were driven to nearby Spa, Belgium, to appear before Lt. Col. Oliver B. Seth, the Inspector at the U.S. First Army headquarters. At 7:30 P.M., the first witness, Pfc. Homer D. Ford, a military policeman who had survived the shooting along with several artillery observers, gave General Courtney Hodges and the U.S. First Army leaders unsettling news. Already shaken by the ferocity of the surprise German winter attack, Hodges now pondered a shocking new wrinkle: *the enemy was executing prisoners!*

Other survivors from the crossroads began appearing later that night. Having escaped at dark, Pvt. James P. Mattera ran headlong down the road, stumbling into a roadblock the 291st Engineer Combat Battalion set up just outside of Malmédy. "What's the password?" a nervous sentry demanded, pointing his rifle at the trembling GI. "I'm from Lancaster County," Mattera blurted out in frustration, "Forget the password . . . outfit wiped out . . . the Germans are coming!" More reports started coming in as additional survivors were picked up—some wounded, most suffering from exposure, and all in shock.

By the following morning the report had percolated from the U.S. First Army headquarters all the way to Gen. Dwight D. Eisenhower, the Supreme Head of the Allied Expeditionary Forces (SHAEF).

Just outside Paris, within the intelligence section of Eisenhower's expansive Versailles headquarters, word of the incident rattled off a clicking telegraph:[11]

> FROM: First US Army AC of S G-2
> TO: CG, SHAEF Main, CG 12 Army Group Main,
> CO 12 Army Group TAC
> B-394, 18 December 1944
>
> SS troops vicinity L 8199 captured U.S. soldier,
> traffic MP with about 200 other U.S. soldiers.
> American prisoners searched. When finished,
> Germans lined up Americans and shot them with
> machine pistols and machine guns. Wounded
> informant, who escaped. More details follow later.

Bill Merriken awoke with a start sometime that Sunday night. A nightmare, he thought, but slowly he realized the whole thing was real. It was dark now, and he was still in the woodshed by the crossroads. He shivered, reaching behind his back to cautiously probe his wound. There seemed to be less fresh blood. The gooey red fluid from the wound had caked and glued to his uniform, but he was weak and in pain. Everything smelled of burning wood. Peering from the east side of the shed, he could see that the café at the corner was still ablaze, burning brilliantly in the night, its flames illuminating the crossroads in an eerie glow. While he looked on, enemy vehicles occasionally appeared before turning the corner and sputtering on past the crossroads. Then came a strange roaring-buzzing sound: a German jet—a pilotless V-1 robot bomb, climbed steeply into the starless sky before disappearing into the night. Minutes later another of Hitler's "secret weapons" snarled overhead. The unworldly racket faded into the crackle of the flames from the café. Merriken wondered if the Germans were launching the "buzz bombs" from just beyond the crossroads.

A phantom interrupted his idle thoughts—did he see something move? He rubbed his eyes. Then, just out of the corner of his vision in the orange glare of the fire, he spied a dark shape warily approaching along the road from the other side. Although weak, he groped for a shaft of firewood from the dirt floor. The dark shape rose up and headed for the shed's entrance. His heart racing, Bill Merriken clutched his weapon like a baseball bat.

He would not go down without a fight.

CHAPTER 1

"Like a Storm Wind"

Deep in the heavily forested rolling hills of the Ardennes in Belgium, a crucial act in a five-year drama was about to unfold quietly on the evening of Friday, December 15, 1944. Adolf Hitler, the founder of German National Socialism and totalitarian leader of its Third Reich, prepared to unleash his offensive plan to win the war at the last moment.

Since 1939 Hitler, Germany's undisputed Führer, had been waging a brutal war of conquest and racial genocide across Europe. The great conflict stretched from the Atlantic shores of France to the frozen steppes of Russia. By autumn 1944, after five years of devastating war, Hitler's forces had been thrown back to the German border along Luxembourg and Belgium. The massive Soviet offensives in Russia in the summer of 1944 gobbled up an entire German army group. In the following months Hitler's military capacity suffered one body blow after another. With the collapse of their Italian ally and the D-Day landings in France, Germany appeared trapped in an impossible military position. The final Allied and Soviet knockout thrust to the heart of the Third Reich could not be far away.

On the other side of the battle, Allied morale in the west was high as Christmas 1944 drew near. Working together with the Soviets to defeat Hitler, the Americans and British believed they were on the cusp of victory. They had landed on the Normandy beaches in June, broken out of the coastal area at the end of July, and then only logistical exhaustion had left them breathlessly halted on the German border.

Seeing the September front slowly congeal along the German border, Gen. Dwight D. Eisenhower, the head of SHAEF, saw the dense Ardennes forest as a godsend. He decided to defend the Ardennes lightly in order to concentrate his most powerful forces to the north and south of the mountain terrain, where he thought they might advance most quickly into Germany. He placed his First Army under Gen. Courtney Hodges to the north of that nearly impassable terrain, within striking distance of the city of Aachen and the industry-rich region of the German Ruhr. The U.S. Third Army, led by dashing American Gen. George S. Patton, would attempt to punch beyond the Alsace-Lorraine on the French border to the south and then slice into Germany via the back door.

The hope was that perhaps the enemy armies would collapse, and forces under Gen. Bernard Law Montgomery, Gen. Courtney Hodges in the center, or impetuous Gen. George S. Patton in the south would suddenly spring free and plunge deep into the heartland of Hitler's Germany, ending the bitter war. In spite of valiant efforts—Montgomery's audacious parachute operation at Arnhem in September and Patton's grinding offensive in the Lorraine—the German forces opposite their Allied enemies kept finding ways to deny a breakthrough. Although the U.S. First Army captured the major Germany city of Aachen in October, conquest of the nearby heavily wooded Hürtgen forest, which separated American armies from the Rhine River, turned into a bloody fight that was horrifyingly reminiscent of Passchendaele in World War I.

Meanwhile, the Ardennes salient separating the two U.S. armies was cold and quiet. Taking its name from the ancient *Arduenna Silva*, the Ardennes had been a vast forest since Roman times. The Allied front twisted some eighty-five miles through terrain deeply incised by rivers, a landscape reminiscent of Vermont's Green Mountains.[1] Even though the Ardennes and Losheim Gap had served as a major point of entry for German offensive attacks to the west both in 1914 and 1940, watching from Versailles, Eisenhower was inclined to discount the risk that they would use it again. After all, those earlier German incursions had come during good summer weather. But now, with the dismal northern European autumnal weather—rains punctuated by snow, making winding icy roads nearly impassable—Eisenhower could hardly conceive his teetering enemy might consider any major attack, much less one in the Ardennes.[2]

For an experience of fighting in a similarly difficult terrain, Eisenhower only had to look at the bloody inconclusive fighting his VII Corps had suffered in the Hürtgen Forest earlier that autumn. Not only would the Germans not likely attack in the Ardennes, he thought, but so unpromising was the terrain, there was little reason to waste troops badly needed elsewhere.

However, inspired by the stalled Allied advance on the German border at the end of summer and realizing that he must somehow regain the initiative, Hitler decided to launch his last great attack in the west—and the only major German offensive launched in the dead of winter. The strategy was entirely the Führer's brainchild. He announced his dramatic plan on September 6. "I have made a momentous decision," he said as he stabbed a finger across a field map. "Here out of the Ardennes! Across the Meuse and onto Antwerp!"[3] With this great Belgian port seized and lines of Allied communication lanced, much of the British and American armies would be without supplies and left to wither into collapse. Further, knowing that a purely military solution now exceeded his grasp, Hitler sought a sudden, blazing victory in the west that would so shock the Allies that they would sue for a separate peace. At that point he could then turn his armies to the east to settle accounts with the Russians, whom he sarcastically referred to as the *Untermenschen.*[4]

Meanwhile, Eisenhower and Gen. Omar Bradley referred to their light defense of the Ardennes as their "calculated risk." Only six American divisions, three of which were relatively green, held the eighty-five-mile Ardennes front, and although the other three divisions were veteran units, they had been bled white in the bloody October battles in the Hürtgen and sent to the Ardennes to rest and refit.

Nine days before Christmas 1944 the tired American soldiers along the frozen Ardennes front seemed no closer to the end of the war than they had been in September. For the typical soldier each day was an effort for shelter: Improve the foxhole or bunker and find fire to stay warm in the cold and wet misery.[5] For American GIs this was the "Ghost Front"—an area where nothing seemed to happen.

Along the Ardennes front the Americans were only facing, at best, low-strength skeletal German Volksgrenadier battalions. For the most part both sides were content not to irritate the other during the cold and rainy autumn. They both fired artillery mainly for registration and conducted patrols warily to capture green American soldiers or Germans eager to surrender. Interrogation showed what everyone already knew: nothing to report.

However, at the beginning of December, amid draconian security restrictions, the Eifel Hills east of the Ardennes saw the staged arrival of Germany's strongest remaining forces. Just a few miles beyond the meandering German border that stretched from Monschau along the twisting Our and Sauer Rivers to Echternach, three of Hitler's armies stealthily moved across the band of thick firs and silence that separated them from unsuspecting American forces. While German night-fighter aircraft swooped low over the forested hills to drown out noise, panzer companies and infantry-laden halftracks secretly eased into camouflaged positions under the pine trees lining the roads. Meanwhile, eighteen divisions—over 250,000 men, 2,623 artillery pieces, and 717 tanks and assault guns—rolled slowly over muddy roads matted with straw into final attack positions.[6]

All the while Allied intelligence officers debated the interpretation of clues they had gathered that showed the Germans moving tank forces to the Ardennes. To the G-2 men, a major German counteroffensive thrown through those wooded brambles made no strategic sense. The sparse and tangled road network and the difficult terrain made the idea of a game-changing German counteroffensive there seem a far-fetched folly. Thus, with a strong eye toward a cunning enemy deception to take Allied attention off the more important terrain north and south of the Ardennes, U.S. intelligence officers, particularly with Gen. Omar Bradley's 12th Army Group, reasoned that there was no danger. And Lt. Gen. Courtney Hodges, the U.S. First Army Commander, was too preoccupied with improving the slow progress of his forces to capture the Roer dams beyond the dense woods in the Elsenborn area. On the 16th he was having himself fitted for a better hunting rifle, and pushing the logistics people to make sure each man got some hot turkey at the front line on Christmas Eve.

Commanding from his opulent Versailles villa, Gen. Dwight D. Eisenhower pondered the cold, gray Parisian skies through the wrought-iron casement windows. The sky seemed sullen, ominous. The Trianon palace, with its timeless buildings, ornate décor, and sculptured courtyards, made for a distinctly fashionable setting for Allied headquarters for SHAEF. That afternoon of December 16, Eisenhower would meet over the worrisome infantry replacement situation with Gen. Omar Bradley. However, on that Saturday, there were other big events, namely that Gen. Eisenhower was being promoted to five-star general, the U.S. Army's highest rank. As usual, Eisenhower was up at 6 A.M. for a breakfast of sausage topped with hominy grits. At the end of his meal he received a note from Fldm. Bernard L. Montgomery requesting holiday leave and reminding Ike he owed him money on a bet fourteen months before that the war would be over by Christmas. "While it seems certain you will have an extra five pounds for Christmas," Eisenhower quipped, "you will not get it until that day."[7]

Later, Eisenhower and Gen. Walter Bedell Smith, his SHAEF office manager, followed along to the Louis XIV chapel at Versailles. To celebrate Eisenhower's promotion, the chef at the Trianon had prepared Ike's favorite: Oysters Rockefeller. After dinner the guests attended the wedding of Eisenhower's personal aide, Sgt. Michael J. "Mickey" McKeogh to a petite, bespectacled lady from the Women's Army Corps, Sgt. Pearlie Hargrave. After the ceremony everyone moved over to Eisenhower's quarters at Saint-Germain for champagne. They were all in high spirits as the evening progressed.[8] The Highland Piper Scotch was out when Eisenhower received an urgent message from an excited courier. *Something* was happening in the Ardennes.

Meanwhile, Adolf Hitler plotted moves from his manorial *Adlerhorst* (Eagle's eyrie) headquarters in West Germany near Bad Nauheim, hoping his Allied enemy would misread the stream of news coming from the Ardennes's Ghost Front. A week before the great offensive was set to begin, Hitler had told his generals his closely guarded secret.[9] There in Ziegenberg Castle, where Goethe once visited, the German leader addressed his assembled generals on December 11 and announced elaborate plans. Col. Wilhelm Viebig, who would command one of the Volksgrenadier divisions in the attack, had seen Hitler earlier during the war, but he was hardly prepared for the 1944 version. "When he came out, I was terribly shocked," Viebig recalled. Hitler teetered as he entered the room, appearing to be supported by SS-Gen. Gottlob Berger and Fldm. Wilhelm Keitel on either side. "He looked old and shrunken with unsightly red blotches on his face . . . worn out . . . but then after he had spoken for an hour life came back. . . . Then his eyes were shining."[10] Rapping his hand on a map, Hitler railed, "This battle will decide the war."

His aging face, marked by deep lines of worry, Fldm. Karl Gerd von Rundstedt, who was in charge of German forces on the Western Front, finally piped up to complain that the plan was too radical: The forces were not great enough; the time was not sufficient. Others nodded. Hitler launched into a tirade, although remaining calm and controlled: Didn't anyone recall the great victories of Frederick the Great? At Rossbach and Leuthen, that Prussian king had defeated enemies twice his strength. How? "A bold attack," he explained. Frederick, doomed to defeat by every European seer, went on to win Germany's greatest victory. "History will repeat itself," Hitler said. "The Ardennes will be my Rossbach and Leuthen. . . . The alliance against the Third Reich will suddenly come apart!"[11]

One SS attaché present for the speech remembered Hitler's closing words: "Gentlemen, if we do not achieve the decisive breakthrough from Liège to Antwerp, we will face a bloody fate in this war. Time is not on our side. This is our last and final chance to alter the fortunes of the war."[12]

"This battle," he emphasized to the assembled generals just before they left, "is to decide whether we live or die. I want all my soldiers to fight hard and without pity. The battle must be fought with brutality and all resistance must be broken in a wave of terror. The enemy must be beaten—now or never. Thus lives our Germany!"[13]

With the loss of control of the war in the air, Hitler knew he must attack with the element of surprise in a lightly held sector where his panzer forces could suddenly cut across Europe. Given the need for "a wave of terror," he entrusted the main effort of his final great offensive to his old SS comrade Gen. Josef "Sepp" Dietrich and Dietrich's Waffen SS–infused 6th Panzer Army. With the shortest distance to the Meuse

River and Antwerp, Dietrich's army would concentrate the best weaponry and resources.

Yet in order to knife through the Belgian countryside suddenly and seize the Meuse bridges before the Americans could react, Hitler called for *special* combat teams accustomed to the 1940 blitzkrieg style of warfare. He needed the same élan now four years later, he told his castle audience. Dietrich heard again that this would be no chivalrous battle: "The Führer said that the impending battle must be won by all means." He went on to explain that Hitler further emphasized "that we would have to act with brutality and show no humane inhibitions. . . . A wave of terror and fright should precede us."[14]

On the early morning of December 14, 1944, a telephone call from divisional headquarters came to the command post of the 1st SS Panzer Regiment at a forester's hut near Blankenheim, Germany. The call requested the senior leaders come at once to a meeting. All was secret; nothing further could be discussed on the phone, but it was clear that the 1st SS Panzer Division had a new mission. That this division wore the name "Adolf Hitler" on their arm cuff bands was not by chance. They were "Hitler's Own," considering themselves an elite within the already elite Waffen SS. The unit had started out as a regimental-sized palace bodyguard more famous for precision goose-stepping than anything military, but over the course of the war its size and armament expanded. By December 1944 it was a full panzer division with the best equipment and resources in the German army. What did Hitler himself think of the unit? "What your fate is, my men of the Leibstandarte, I do not know," he told them at a Christmas celebration, "but I know one thing, that you will be in the front line of every action. . . . As long as I have the honor to stand at the fore of the Reich to lead this struggle, you who bear my name shall consider it an honor to lead every German attack."[15]

As such, although the Leibstandarte had fought in every campaign in the war, its military performance was checkered by an ideological form of conflict that held in total contempt any enemy of National Socialism. In battle such scorn for the enemy translated into war crimes occurring almost everywhere the unit moved: The divisional band leader murdered fifty civilians in Poland in 1939. At Wormhoudt

in France in 1940 Leibstandarte men under the command of SS leader
Wilhelm Mohnke lined up against a barn eighty British prisoners of
the 48th Infantry Division and mowed them down.[16] In Kharkov, on
the Eastern Front, in March 1943 dozens of Soviet wounded had been
shot in their hospital beds and then the hospital was set on fire, sending many more to burn to death.[17] In the wake of Leibstandarte operations in Russia, Italy, and even Normandy, they continued to commit
numerous killings. Yet Hitler did not see this fervor as weakness;
rather, he believed in the SS. And after a cabal of regular army officers
had attempted to assassinate him the previous summer, SS-style obedience and loyalty were all important. Still, militarily, speed would be of
the greatest importance in the upcoming offensive. Hitler knew that
his initial numerical superiority would rapidly fade when Allied reinforcements began to move to the Ardennes:

> In this operation, it will be necessary to pay attention to speed.
> That means, in my opinion, that we should take what can be taken
> quickly, like lightning, without being deflected from our proper
> target.[18]

In the days leading up to December 16, the final attack orders came
from the 1st SS Panzer Corps:

> Carefully selected advance detachments, lead by particularly
> daring commanders will advance rapidly and capture the bridges in
> the Meuse sector before the enemy can destroy them.[19]

"Particularly daring commanders" could only mean SS-Lt.
Col. Jochen Peiper. Peiper was the acknowledged king of the
blitzkrieg advance, the fearsome commander of destructive nighttime, behind-enemy-lines operations, and the derring-do leader of
contemptuous attacks in the face of any enemy. The *Lötlampen
Abteilung*—the Blowtorch Battalion—of Jochen Peiper would lead the
new attack.

Handsome, cultured, and a fanatical Nazi, at twenty-nine, Jochen
Peiper had become the youngest regimental commander in the Waffen SS. Although not particularly tall, he did have the requisite blue

eyes and light hair. After volunteering for the SS in 1934, Peiper entered SS officer's training at the SS leader school at Braunschweig, which produced intensely ideological SS leaders with venomous anti-Semitic roots and loathing for non-Aryans. Even as a youth, Peiper loved speed, starting with avid training on horses in his hometown of Berlin. Despite dropping out of school to join the SS, Peiper had a penchant for reading and literature, and although he was a totally convinced National Socialist, he was hardly the street brawler type. Instead, he fancied himself a "thinking" SS man. Because of his SS–poster boy appearance with social and language skills, in 1938 Peiper was recruited as the personal adjutant for SS Reichsführer Heinrich Himmler—the man who would become the chief architect of the Holocaust.

Peiper served under Himmler until August 1941 and became familiar with the machinery being developed for the murder war against the Jews. In 1939 he witnessed the execution of Polish intellectuals in Himmler's presence near Bromberg; later, in winter 1940, he observed one of the earliest gassing experiments at Posen.[20] Moreover, in his constant relationship with Himmler, he became ever more intimate with the methods that would be used to conduct a mass genocide of sweeping dimension.[21] Indeed, Himmler revered the cold brutality of Genghis Khan and coached his underling, Peiper, accordingly. And Peiper was so impressed that he never forgot a particular key principle of the Mongol lord: Terror could make an enemy flee without even stopping to fight!

National Socialism had at its heart a violence that was not simply tolerated; it was elevated to extreme virtue. Not only were killing and brutality preached as the preferred manner to achieve and maintain power, but they formed the SS man's very vision of the world.[22] "The SS possesses this toughness that will break all weakness," one SS ideological lesson preached. "Let our enemies fear and hate us," Himmler loved to boast.[23]

In August 1941 Peiper left Himmler's company and rejoined his now regimental-sized Leibstandarte Adolf Hitler unit fighting in Russia. Peiper fought with élan, though he also developed a reputation of burning up his troops in battle. Eventually, he was awarded command of the *Schützenpanzerwagen* (halftrack) III Battalion. In Russia Peiper used his halftracks like stallions, conducting warfare more like cavalry than modern armor. He also developed tactics designed to strike fear into any enemy. At Petscheiwka and Stanitschnoje in Russia, his command burned entire villages to the ground.[24] Later, when the Leibstandarte had been in northern Italy, units under his command had set fire to the hamlet of Boves and shot down thirty-four civilians, including the village priest.[25] Many of the SS troopers under his command had matured on the battlefields of Russia, where few surrendered and pity was neither expected nor given.

Peiper's "Blowtorch" battalion had a reputation for burning: The battalion carried modified blowtorches that they had converted into short-distance flamethrowers.[26] One Leibstandarte veteran declared that if you could see smoke and fire on a distant horizon on the steppes in Russia, you would call out "So there is Peiper!"[27] Peiper was brilliantly successful in the recapture of Kharkov in the winter of 1943, and he showed great personal bravery in the failed offensive near Kursk in Russia. In the winter of 1944 he was given command of the Leibstandarte tank regiment at the same time that he received the Oak Leaves to the Knight's Cross, a reward for which he found himself personally received by Hitler himself in February 1944. In the Normandy fighting in early August 1944 Peiper suffered wounds from heavy shelling of his unit's position near Caen and was sent back to Germany for rehabilitation.

Returning to the tank regiment in November 1944, he trained his new recruits as extensively as fuel shortages would allow. After the terrible autumn Allied bombing east of the Hürtgen, Peiper's reconstituted panzer regiment provided humanitarian assistance to bombed-out Düren. "We scraped civilian bodies off the walls," he recalled, "When I saw this, I could easily have castrated the people who did that with a broken bottle."[28]

There were no soldiers in Düren. Only thousands of German refugees. The absolutely unreasonable killing of women and children, the murdering of a city during bright daylight, without any defense, filled our German troops with disgust, indignation and thoughts of revenge.[29]

That autumn, Peiper's training regimen did not let up:

[D]uring training he occasionally intervened with extraordinarily
severe orders. For instance he would ask a company to march all
night from 7 P.M. until 7 A.M. more than 50 kilometers. Afterwards,
he would ask with a smile: "How was the march?"[30]

At the end of November SS-Lt. Kurt Kramm, an SS orderly with the
1st Panzer Battalion, was present during a sand-table exercise at Hof
Buschfeld near Bliesheim. The commander of the 1st Panzer Battalion
immediately under Peiper was SS-Maj. Werner Poetschke, an SS leader
of extraordinary harshness. Later, Kramm would recall Poetschke's dis-
dain for the way the war had been fought in France over the preceding
months. Whereas Peiper used high Prussian language with intention-
cloaked innuendo, Poetschke was rough and to the point: "This humanitarian fussing around is over. . . . Till now we have acceded to certain
rules in the West. All that doesn't exist anymore. This time we are going
to show them what the SS is. . . . We will fight them as the Russians."[31]
In response, Peiper agreed that the next operation would be a "weltan-
schauliche offensive"—an offensive infused with Nazi ideology.

By Thursday, December 14, when the new commander of the
Leibstandarte, SS-Brig. Gen. Wilhelm Mohnke, called a briefing at a
forester's house in the thickly wooded hills around Tondorf, Germany,
Peiper suspected something big. The meeting was scheduled to begin at
11:00 A.M. sharp, but Peiper arrived late, as the roads leading to the
headquarters were jammed with traffic—an annoying portent of things
to come. Already in a foul mood, the divisional chief of staff, SS-Lt. Col.
Dietrich Ziemssen, brought Peiper up to speed on the mission.[32]
SS-Maj. Otto Skorzeny was invited as well, and he brought some of his
officers who were to masquerade as Americans in a military subterfuge
to augment Peiper's forces. Mohnke then launched into a repetitive
monologue, with sentences liberally lifted from Hitler's speech at Bad
Nauheim three days before: "The Führer said that the impending battle
must be won by all means."[33] Mohnke outlined the plan.

The 1st SS Panzer Division would be committed in three strong
battle groups (Kampfgruppen) along assigned panzer rolling roads

(*Rollbahn*). The three northern roads, designated A through C, were assigned to the 12th SS Panzer Division, which would advance on the right flank of the Leibstandarte through the densely wooded hills to Elsenborn, Malmédy, and then move forward to Spa and Theux before reaching the Meuse on both sides of Liège. To the south, roads D and E were assigned to the 1st SS Panzer Division. The main effort would come on Road D. Here, Kampfgruppe Peiper, with most of the division's tanks, would thrust from Blankenheim to Büllingen-Stavelot-Harze, reaching the Meuse at Amay just north of Huy. SS Panzer Grenadier Regiment 2 along with artillery and engineering elements would come behind Peiper, followed by Mohnke and the division staff.

Although planners had Jochen Peiper in mind for the spearhead effort for the 6th Panzer Army, each of the SS panzer divisions would have key SS zealots charged with forging a rapid advance. In particular, the planners pinned great hopes that the advance elements of Kampfgruppe Peiper might reach the Huy bridgehead across the canyon-like Meuse River gorge at the end of the first night of the advance. Mohnke made it clear that Peiper's speed of advance was critical, telling him that the battle "has to be fought with special brutality and without humane inhibitions." Mohnke paused and glared at Peiper: "One should remember the victims of the bombing terror!"[34]

> My division commander again emphasized to me, the prime importance of my task, again telling me of the need for a very rapid breakthrough, the necessity that every man commit himself fanatically.[35]

Fight *fanatically*? Peiper paid scant attention. "I did not read the material given to me at the Division Command Post, because I was in a hurry and I also was in a bad mood. I disagreed with the entire preparation for the undertaking which looked highly defective to me." He went on to explain,

> The very first impression of the terrain I got, with the aid of maps, reassured my opinion that this was a desperate undertaking. I can remember that in this material, among other things, was an order from the *6th Panzer Army*, with the contents that

considering the desperate situation of the German people, a wave
of terror and fright should precede our troops . . . the German
soldier should in this offensive, recall the innumerable German
victims of the bombing terror. . . . Enemy resistance had to be
broken by terror.[36]

SS-Brig. Gen. Fritz Krämer, the Dietrich chief of staff, had a few
more words for Peiper, whom he called to his office. Knowing the
SS colonel was an avid horseman, Krämer encouraged a gallop: "Drive
fast," he told Peiper, and "hold the reins loose."[37] It would be just like in
France, 1940, Krämer said. Don't worry about your flanks, and remember Clausewitz: "The point must form the fist." After long years of
panzer warfare, Peiper hardly needed reminders—he knew to push for
Antwerp. "I don't care how, or what you do," Krämer continued. "Just
make it to the Meuse. Even if you've only one tank left when you get
there." Peiper looked puzzled, so Krämer repeated himself, "The Meuse
with one tank, Peiper. That's all I ask of you."

After that meeting Peiper called an assembly of his own for Thursday evening in order to brief his battalion and company commanders.
They met in a large hall at the Blankenheim forester's house. SS-Capt.
Oskar Klingelhoefer, one of Peiper's subordinates leading the
7th Panzer Company, remembered more strident comments from the
tank regiment commander: "All scruples and humane feelings shall be
thrown overboard." And Klingelhoefer remembered distinctly that
Peiper himself commented, "Situations can arise in which no prisoners
of war will be made."[38] Werner Poetschke was also at Peiper's briefing
and used even stronger language. Both men repeatedly used the word
"terror," with Peiper emphasizing that the enemy should become so
afraid as to run rather than fight.[39]

At the very head of Peiper's battle group would be a particular au-
dacious panzer man—SS-1st Lt. Werner Sternebeck, leading the 6th
Panzer Company. Sternebeck loved fast horses of all types: He led his
Panzer IV Model H like a cavalryman—at least once with a drawn
Cossack saber that he kept in his tank. Totally fixated on medals,
Sternebeck always chose the spearhead in any of Peiper's night-ride op-
erations.[40] In fact, he specialized in that. Some of the enlisted men
thought he was a bit mad but also that he was perfect for Peiper. For

the attack in the Ardennes the spearhead would consist of two Panther tanks in the lead followed by several Mk IV tanks and two further Mk V Panthers, behind those. Several armored halftracks loaded with panzer grenadiers would accompany the tanks.[41]

An enlisted SS man who often served as Sternebeck's orderly was also at the briefing. The young SS-private admitted that, almost as a military medieval page, he attended Sternebeck as if he were a daring Prussian cavalryman. The enlisted man even chose music for the evenings. Now, he and Sternebeck gazed across a table where Peiper prepared to address everyone. Sternebeck's adjutant remembered his words, "Model had commanded that our panzers must roll!" Peiper told them all.[42] The situation for Germany was desperate beyond belief. As the contemporary saying went, it was time to *Alles in die Waagschale Werfen*, "throw everything you have into the pan!" SS-1st Lt. Franz Sievers, the tough commander of a section of Peiper's 3rd Panzer Engineer Company, said there was also a secret order:

> At a later occasion a secret order was shown to me in which it was said, that if the situation requires it that prisoners of war are to be shot. . . . [On two occasions], secret orders were shown to me and I signed something, but I don't know what. I also, on December 15, 1944, took part in a meeting of all Company Commanders of the 1st Battalion. . . . Anyway I also signed something at the hunting lodge [Blankenheim]. I don't know if the order was signed by Lt. Col. Peiper or SS-Capt. Gruhle, but only that it was a secret order. SS-Maj. Poetschke gave all this and more at the meeting on December 15, 1944.[43]

The panzer units would be attacking in wooded terrain, and due to the lack of reconnaissance and the ever-present danger of ambush, the tank commanders were told that they must hold themselves chest high out of the top of each panzer to watch for trouble. "That wasn't too reassuring," one experienced tanker noted. When the meeting let out at 9 P.M., the question of prisoners was even more troubling.[44] SS-Lt. Arndt Fischer would later recall that "at the time Maj. Poetschke said that we should not take any prisoners where the military situation absolutely required it. Poetschke also declared that this was a secret order." Fischer would later vehemently deny his own handwritten statement.[45]

After the war more evidence about what happened at the meeting emerged. SS-2nd Lt. Hans Hennecke stated that "SS Lt. Col. Peiper gave orders before the attack started, to fight a hard, cruel and disregarding fight because this was the last possibility to win." In still another statement Hennecke would claim to recall, word-for-word, what Peiper had told his company commanders:

> In the coming operation, the regiment will have the duty to attack recklessly. No consideration will be paid to man or machine. The coming mission will be the last chance to win the war. Therefore, we will attack like a storm wind [*Sturmwind*]. The enemy must become totally crazed with fear that the SS is coming. That is our obligation.[46]

Was it true when Peiper's panzer regiment was leading a spearhead attack that they would typically shoot them rather than bother with prisoners? "Yes, it is a fact," Hennecke would later agree. "One cannot deny it."[47] SS-Lt. Friedrich Christ, who would lead the 2nd Panzer Company of Panthers in the coming offensive, was heard to leave the matter vague: "We are not placing any value on the taking of prisoners of war!"[48] Yet that edict smacked of Leibstandarte inside language. Why otherwise mention prisoners at all? And what of the men he would lead in the operation? Most had grown up on the steppes of Russia in unending combat. Said Peiper:

> I was their regimental commander. I was their father. They came to me with their troubles. One of my boys told me that your air force had destroyed not only his town, but seventeen of his close relatives . . . they were killed by your American bombs. Now, when these boys came face to face with the Americans who destroyed their families, I could not say it was wrong that they shoot.[49]

"They are the products of total war," Peiper would later write, "grown up on the scattered streets of towns without any education. The only thing [they] knew was to handle weapons for the dream of the

Reich. They were young people with a hot heart and a desire to win or die according to the word: right or wrong my country!"[50]

Tactical considerations were another concern. Looking over his assigned panzer rolling road, Peiper wilted. "We were to advance over roads that were not roads," he later said. The whole offensive plan was just wishful thinking, "trying to repeat the success of 1940, now to be attempted again under completely different weather conditions."[51] Peiper looked with envy at one of the routes assigned to the 12th SS Panzer Division. Although Peiper's Road C traveled over main roads, the reality was that the route was pathetic—thin stretches of tarmac though thickly wooded hills with stretches of unpaved ruddy trails—worse than Russia!

"I immediately pointed out that these roads were not for tanks, but for bicycles." Peiper scowled. Those roads were so narrow in places that a Tiger or even a Panther might not even fit. Moreover, the unpaved sections would likely dissolve into muddy tracks.[52] In the Schnee Eifel, with its thick forest, how would they deploy such armored beasts off the road? His blood pressure rose further when he realized that those at the meeting were ignoring him: "They wouldn't even discuss it. They said it was the Führer's orders."[53] Peiper pulled no punches. "I explained that we had to make an attack in a terrain unsuitable for tanks, that the only chance of success depending upon speed, surprise and relentless commitment of personnel and material."

Looking over the terrain, SS-Brig. Gen. Fritz Krämer, the chief of staff for 6th Panzer Army, was again deeply worried. All the sand-table exercises showed that a rapid penetration was key to any prospects for success. Krämer drove to the bivouac area of the Leibstandarte near Euskirchen to speak with Peiper. Peiper was known throughout the Waffen SS as *the* expert in rapid nighttime armored advance. Could a tank column advance eighty kilometers in a single night in the Eifel, Krämer asked? Peiper was not one to speculate, ordering an experienced tanker, Hans Hennecke, to drive a Panther that distance on the night of December 11.[54] Hennecke made the trek all the way to the town gate at Münstereifel. The next day Peiper wistfully informed Krämer that a single tank could go the distance, but whether an entire column in enemy territory and over glutinous roads could accomplish that was a different question.

During his final briefing Peiper detailed the composition of the lead panzer command, Werner Poetschke's 1st Panzer Battalion, with tanks, SPWs, artillery guns and engineers "composed in such a manner that it should be suitable . . . to solve all coming problems." Peiper added, "This group should advance without regard and not pay attention to unimportant enemy goals nor booty, nor prisoners of war."[55] The last statement would haunt him. His outlook could hardly encourage the old panzer hands at the meeting: "[O]wing to the unfavorable terrain [the first panzer group] would likely be rubbed out . . . the task of this group should be finished if only one Panzer Mk IV were to reach the Meuse." If the first tank group was destroyed—which he fully expected—he planned to move up the heavy Tigers to blast away the enemy. "The *1st Battalion* received a very desperate task, which I very clearly explained to the officers." There was to be no concern for the flanks and no pause in the advance or losses:

> You will go ahead at high speed on the assigned road. Your task will be fulfilled after you have been blown up. The one that will take over after you is the tank right behind you. If shooting has to be done, it will be done while moving. There will be no stopping for anything. No booty is to be taken, no confiscated enemy vehicles are to be examined. . . . It is not the job of the spearhead to worry about prisoners of war. It is the job of the infantry following. . . . Armed civilians will be treated as partisans.[56]

Rather than giving a pep talk, Peiper outlined a bitter mission ahead. Less shooting would be desirable, as the transportation situation and ammunition resupply were tenuous at best. Then, too, he could only promise that they would start with gasoline tanks topped off. Further supply seemed uncertain—a big concern given his fuel-thirsty heavy tanks.[57] They would have to depend on captured fuel, although he gruffly noted that, based on "my experience, that would likely not be possible."

Peiper spent nearly two hours going over details—particularly the composition of his twenty-five-kilometer-long march order. The roads were so narrow that there could be no question of modifying it once battle was joined. The lighter Mk IVs—his quarter horses—would be located in the *Spitze* (spearhead). The heavier Panthers would advance with SS-Capt. Josef Diefenthal's panzer grenadiers just behind. And the big, slow Tigers—the cold bloods—he would locate to the rear. He would command from the forward center of the advance column. SS-Maj. Poetschke, in a Panther, would be just behind the half-dozen other tanks and halftracks leading the point.

As befitted the lead attack element chosen to make good on Hitler's plan to rapidly reach the Meuse River crossings, Peiper's command would be the strongest armored unit in the 6th Panzer Army—even if it were still not up to the established strength: forty-eight hundred men, 72 tanks, eight anti-aircraft Flak panzer, 117 halftracks, and eight hundred additional support troops. For added firepower Peiper could draw on the forty-five King Tiger tanks of SS-Maj. Heinz von Westernhagen's Heavy SS Panzer Battalion 501 as well as an army flak detachment.[58]

Meanwhile, the panzer leaders organized their vehicles and crews for action the next morning. Friday night, just before the attack, experienced panzer hand SS-S/Sgt. Hans Siptrott addressed the third platoon. SS-Pvt. Werner Löhmann, a tank gunner with Panzer Nr. 734, was among those present. Siptrott had been in action since Poland 1939, fighting in all campaigns and often under Peiper. Amassing 680 combat days in the war, he had had eleven tanks shot out from under him and was wounded three times.[59] Peiper nicknamed him "Spitz" because he was always leading his daredevil operations. Siptrott lost two brothers in the war and one sister to what SS men now called "the Allied terror bombing."

"SS-S/Sgt. Siptrott returned from a conference of the platoon leaders and called the third platoon together for a short conference," Löhmann recalled. "He spoke about the support by the Luftwaffe and about the new weapons that were to be used during this offensive." Löhmann was excited to hear that jet aircraft would cover their advance, though that made a lesser impression on Löhmann than did Siptrott's final words at the end of his speech, which he claimed to remember distinctly: "There is a new order, no prisoners of war were to be taken."[60]

In the predawn hours of December 16, a thick curtain of fog hugged the gloomy Ardennes pines. At exactly 5:30 A.M. a pulsing eruption of flame shattered the dark silence and spread across the blank horizon to light up the sky. Mortars coughed, heavy artillery roared, and rockets wailed from their launching platforms. For thirty minutes the drumfire pounded American positions. As soon as the barrage ended, ghostly German forms emerged from the haze and advanced in a slow and ominous walk toward the American foxholes. At headquarters, Fritz Krämer thought the breakthrough would shake loose by 7 A.M. Peiper had been told to allow the infantry to breach the American line, thus forcing him to wait impatiently. His tankers dozed and caught catnaps as they were parked by the frozen road from Schmidtheim near the German border.

In the early morning Peiper arrived at the forward command post of the 12th Volksgrenadier Division that was to spring him loose. Gen. Gerhard Engel's headquarters was a squat concrete bunker in the "Dragon's Teeth" near Hallschlag. Listening to field telephone dispatches with Engel, Peiper awaited word that the foot infantry had broken into the open beyond, at which point he could launch his tanks. However, word never came. Instead, Peiper listened impatiently to static-laden reports on Engel's radio inside the dank pillbox: one more minefield stumbled into, one more road position with stubbornly defending Americans, and, worst, friendly artillery mistakenly bombarding Engel's own men. A disgusted Peiper left around noon, soon reaching his parked line of tanks covered in pine boughs, impatiently awaiting word to advance.

Despite the laggard German infantry, he decided it was time to launch his assault. At 12:30 P.M. Sternebeck's spearhead platoon set off, followed by the rest of the tanks.[61] The long, armored column noisily clattered onto the crowded Blankenheim road and edged forward. With a march speed of twelve miles per hour, they reached Hallschlag by 4 P.M., but there, everything went wrong.[62]

Traffic was not moving on Reichsstrasse 51. Tanks stood about idling, wasting precious fuel. Peiper took off on foot to find out what was going on, dismayed when he came upon the reason. Someone had ordered horse-drawn artillery of the 12th Volksgrenadier Division forward and now the beasts and caissons jammed the road. Peiper ordered his tankers to either push the horses off the road or run them down. Then another frustration, a few kilometers further, near Hüllscheid: Peiper came upon a minefield. Calling up the panzer engineers to

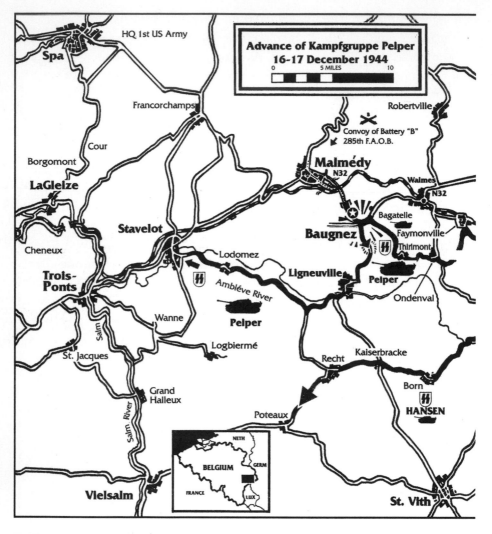

THE ADVANCE OF KAMPFGRUPPE PEIPER

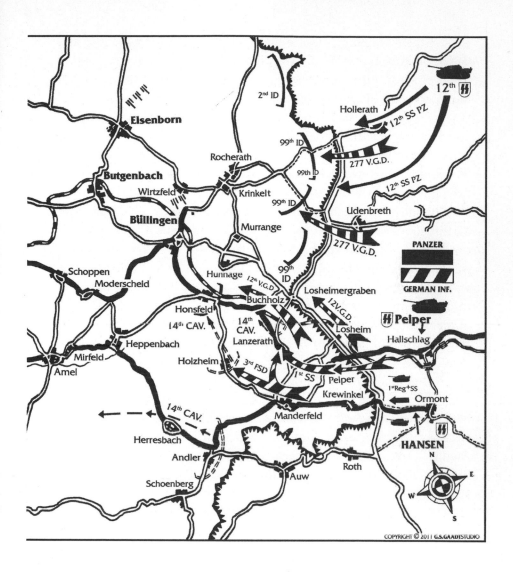

COPYRIGHT © 2011 G.S.GAADTSTUDIO

remove them would only waste precious hours. He ordered tanks and halftracks to run over to blow up the mines until the larger column could proceed. Both of Sternebeck's two lead Panthers were lost, but Kampfgruppe Peiper was moving again.[63]

It was nearly 7 P.M. by the time Peiper's logjam of tanks, vehicles, and men reached the border town of Losheim. There was still another delay. The retreating Germans had blown up a railway overpass earlier that autumn; that oversight would take hours to fix. Instead, Peiper ordered his tanks to sled down the steep sides of the trestle and grind forward on the other side. In total darkness Peiper rode in a halftrack with his infantry leader, Josef "Jupp" Diefenthal. However, after reaching the tiny hamlet of Lanzerath at midnight, Peiper was dismayed to find the war gone to sleep, the 3rd Parachute Division included. Peiper argued with its leader, Col. Helmuth Hoffmann. He told Peiper that the paratroopers suffered severe casualties that afternoon in fighting elements of the 99th Infantry Division on the hill overlooking Lanzerath. Hoffmann warned of heavy American resistance in the band of woods beyond.[64]

Hoffmann's advice did not impress Peiper, who ordered part of a parachute battalion to mount his tanks. Due to losses, he then reorganized Sternebeck's *Spitze* by adding three tanks from the 6th Panzer Company. Now another "hot rod" was with Sternebeck—SS-M/Sgt. August Tonk, who was an older oddball in the panzer regiment. Tonk had his thirty-third birthday on the day the offensive started. He had fought in the German Condor Legion in Spain for Franco and had a mind for adventure. Although Peiper punished him for wearing a turban into battle, Tonk defined any idea one might have of an SS-Moroccan swashbuckler, racing about in a tank.[65]

The *Spitze* rearranged in the darkness and Peiper zoomed down the road—no resistance! At 4 A.M. Peiper reached Buchholz Station, rounding up unsuspecting Americans of the 394th Infantry Regiment, who were shocked to find German tanks in the middle of their bivouac. Just after dawn SS-Lt. Sternebeck's spearhead tanks roared through the tiny village of Honsfeld, and a number of Americans in the town were taken prisoner in their pajamas. However, the Americans resisted once they regained their composure. Many fired on the German column from two-story buildings, picking off grenadiers in the streets below. Unfortunately, the Americans' Alamo-like bravery pre-saged a tragic end when at least half a dozen American soldiers attempting to surrender were shot down.[66]

At 9 A.M. Peiper continued on into the nearby village of Büllingen, where he lost two tanks to antitank shells in an action at its south entrance.[67] Peiper moved on in Panther Nr. 001, driven by SS-S/Sgt. Otto Becker, now heading for Büllingen.[68] But just short of the airfield south of Büllingen, *Kommando Panther Nr. 001* sputtered to a stop with engine troubles.[69] In the bad Ardennes terrain the radio had hardly been working anyway. Wilhelm Nusshag was there serving in the regimental commander's tank as the panzer radioman. Peiper took the cue to move on back to Josef Diefenthal's halftrack. SS-Cpl. Nusshag was not surprised: "Peiper didn't like to ride in tanks," he opined. "He preferred to go in an amphibious car."[70]

From his new mount Peiper located an American fuel depot in the town, where he fueled up his petrol-thirsty tanks. As American artillery blasted the town square, the steel beasts hastily departed. By 9:30 A.M. Peiper had shunted his armor west down the muddy, narrow trails leading to Moderscheid and Schoppen. Suited for bicycles, indeed, huge tanks and halftracks mired in the slush. Peiper decried the additional time lost: "In the course of the breakthroughs, we had nothing really to do with prisoners. . . . We were driving at great speed and firing from all barrels. We penetrated the soft spots of the enemy like an arrow."[71]

With U.S. resistance still befuddled, if Peiper wanted to reach the Meuse River, this would be the day. A mere twenty-four hours later the lines would be hardened and static. Kampfgruppe Peiper had swept everything before it. Not only had Peiper captured four crewed jeeps of the 3rd Armored, but he had also snared Lt. Col. John Ray—a wounded West Point ordnance officer who had served his cadet years with U.S. General Omar Bradley.[72] From Ray, Peiper learned that a full general made headquarters in Ligneuville. Attempting to seize the fleeting opportunity, he ordered his *Panzerspitze* under SS-1st Lt. Sternebeck to push ahead at all possible speed.

A true tank-cavalry type, Sternebeck and his few remaining tanks were waiting for nothing. Sternebeck had lost several Panzer IVs in Büllingen, where a wrong turn took a section of the Spitze into an ambush by an American tank destroyer battalion in Wirtzfeld. He even had to abandon Panzer 614 when it was disabled near the German border and switch to a different vehicle. Yet Sternebeck and SS-M/Sgt. August Tonk were still going along with a Panzer IV each, tailed by a single halftrack of panzer grenadiers. Sternebeck and Tonk lit off in a gallop—at least for a Panzer IVH on the road: twenty miles per hour!

Peiper was about five minutes behind the spearhead in Diefenthal's halftrack, just before the main body of the tank troop. The panzer battalion commander, SS-Maj. Werner Poetschke in Panther Nr. 151 and his adjutant, SS-1st Lt. Arndt Fischer in Nr.152, were just ahead of Peiper, with several armored halftracks supporting the tanks.

From muddy Schoppen Peiper's tanks entered the Belgian village of Thirimont and turned north into a thick section of forest. Riding in the front of Josef Diefenthal's SPW, Peiper entered the woods riding in its metal seat and peering ahead. SS-Cpl. Paul Zwigart was at the wheel of the halftrack.

From there Peiper planned a lightning advance past the major intersection south of Malmédy. Careening beyond that intersection without pause, he would charge through Ligneuville, Stavelot, and Trois-Ponts, whereupon he would flash through Werbomont until he broke into the open green hills before the Meuse River. If he could maintain a fast march, he might reach that prize by daybreak.

He vowed to let nothing hold him up—*nothing.*

CHAPTER 2

Men of the 285th

While SS-Lt. Col. Jochen Peiper thrashed his way through the
Ardennes forest, a virtually anonymous American artillery observation
unit unknowingly prepared to move into his wake. Indeed, the
U.S. Army 285th Field Artillery Observation Battalion (FAOB) seemed
a mirrored opposite to Jochen Peiper's powerful panzer regiment. They
were not an elite combat formation with a storied past. They were
rather a typical U.S. Army Government Issue (GI) unit that specialized
in siting enemy artillery. Nor were they outfitted with tanks, special
guns, or automatic weapons; they were only lightly armed, and given
their mission, were not expected to encounter the enemy in any
ground combat role. Few of its ranks had volunteered for service; most
of the boys were draft conscripts from 1942. And the outfit in danger
of running afoul of Peiper was a single two hundred–man subunit of
the 285th, also known as Battery B.

The U.S. Army declared the 285th FAOB operational at Camp
Gruber, Oklahoma, on January 11, 1943, when members of the 8th
Field Artillery Observation Battalion from Ft. Meade filled their office cadre. The arrival of artillery officers and news of their new des-
ignation ended the speculation for the many bewildered Virginian
and Pennsylvanian boys as to what kind of soldiers they would soon
soon become.

Somehow, when creating the battalion of young men from the United States, the U.S. Army had managed to split the unit into north and south; most of its members were either drawn from the Pennsylvania heartland or the home of the confederacy in Virginia. Those from Virginia and other southern states thought of anyone above the Mason-Dixon line as "damned Yankees," whereas the small-town Pennsylvania Dutch boys were inclined to see their southern neighbors as drawling hillbilly rebels.[1] With long months of training and misadventures, however, they became a cohesive unit, although with a distinctive regional complexion.

Bill Merriken's story was typical of the southern group. Born in Bedford, Virginia, he grew up not far from the foothills of the Peaks of Otter, arguably some of the most beautiful scenery in Virginia. However, Bill's early life was tough; after he lost both parents at the age of eight, his uncle and aunt raised him.

Bill Merriken graduated high school in 1940 and found himself inducted into the U.S. Army at the end of 1942. When first arriving at Camp Gruber, neither Merriken nor any of the others around him knew what kind of unit they would be. There were some other faces from Bedford: Warren Davis lived just on the other side of the mountain— a place locals called Wheedlin Valley. And from the south side of Cumberland Mountain was Richard Walker, a boy who had been popular at Bedford High School. None of the three knew the exact assignment they would have, but they all knew that somehow it involved field artillery. Once he was beyond the bodily insults of basic training, Merriken was surprised to find his life in the battalion something like a Boy's Club obsessed with siting enemy guns.

By the time the 285th shipped off to join the war in 1944, the town of Bedford already had the sad reputation of having suffered more dead per capita than any American community in the war. Many of the "Bedford Boys" ended up in the 29th Infantry Division that was slaughtered on Omaha Beach. Bedford, a town of only thirty-two hundred, saw nineteen of its young men fall on D-Day.[2] When the 285th finally crossed the English Channel on August 31, Bill Merriken was thinking about the bad news from earlier in the summer, but at least the enemy was not shooting at them when they landed on Omaha Beach. Perhaps the Bedford curse was broken.

The 285th had little in the way of fighting implements in their table of organization. By design, they were never supposed to encounter the enemy; instead, they were to observe them. They had no tanks—only trucks—and light machine guns were their heaviest weapons. Carbines were the main firepower. Most of the brief training using these came at Ft. Sill. Theoretically, the lack of heavy weapons was appropriate. Rather than a fighting unit, the 285th was a specialty unit designed to direct American artillery guns and cannons from afar but not fire them themselves.

Personality-wise, their ranks were not filled by fanatics or gung-ho paratroopers, but rather by ordinary American boys sent to win the war against Hitler's Germany. They had no grand designs on Europe or history; they simply wanted to do their job, end the war, and come home.

Twenty-one-year-old George Fox was typical—a farm boy from Warren County, Virginia, who, before being drafted, was most familiar with tilling corn and handling horses and mules. When Shenandoah National Park was formed, his family had to move their farm, leaving a spectacularly handsome section of America where the Blue Ridge Mountains met the Shenandoah River. Moving to Front Royal, his father began a grocery business. George was active in the delivery section of the grocery, using a sturdy red bicycle to ferry goods for customers across Warren County. He was used to riding long distances hauling whatever was needed. Around Christmas of 1942 he got the word from the draft board. Two months later he got off a train at Camp Gruber.[3]

Fox found early training an unsettling experience. As a rural youth familiar with rifles and shotguns, George enjoyed plinking away at the firing range with carbines. And as his basic training continued, George learned that another boy from Front Royal was in his unit: Samuel A. Hallman. But soon, everyone became too busy to look each other up. Camp Gruber was desolate and cold that winter. With twelve guys assigned to shack-like barracks, everyone tried to squeeze around the single potbellied stove.

Some of the boys were from large northern cities. T/5 Theodore J. "Ted" Paluch was known as a Philadelphia streetwise tough guy and a character in the 285th. On Sunday afternoon, December 7, 1941, Ted had been playing pinball when a friend ran in to tell him the Japanese had bombed Pearl Harbor. Two days later he went downtown with his buddy Joe Lenahan to volunteer for the Marines. "Flat feet! They turned me down!" he would always recall in chagrin. Ted continued his job with the Franklin Process Company, but a year later in January 1943, he received his draft notice. He would be in the U.S. Army. "I was really excited," Ted later recalled. "When you're young, you figure you'll do all the shooting." But being an artillery observer was not exactly what he had in mind.

Once in training, Ted was known to have a way with numbers and gambling. Was it skill or good fortune? At poker and craps, he seemed uncanny in his luck. Most weeks that autumn he was reminding Mike Skoda of the money he owed him while the drills continued.

Learning to observe and adjust shot and shell within sight of the grave of Geronimo, the artillery observers of the 285th were ready to ship out to England by May 1944.[4] They departed from Camp Shanks and the Port of New York, aboard Steamship *Mormac Moon* on August 19, 1944. Other than seasickness, the first leg of the ocean travel was uneventful. Many wrote letters home to parents, wives, or girlfriends. As always with such long separations, many romances teetered in the balance. T/5 Thomas Bacon, a youth from New England trained in sound ranging, had planned to get married on a furlough that August, only to have the wedding postponed when they were shipped to France.[5]

Then at the end of August, just a couple of days before they were to reach England, blaring sirens went off on the sea-bound troopship. Everyone had to rush up to the top deck, where they were greeted by a thunderous noise. Out in front of them off the left bow, one of the oil tankers in their multiship convoy exploded, sending boils of orange flame and smoke high into the sky over the gray sea. *Prepare to abandon ship!* the ship squawk box announced. Ted Paluch remembered reaching the topside, where everyone was grumbling and putting on life jackets. "I took one look at that cold water and another at my puny life jacket," he recalled, "and I was scared as hell."[6] A German U-boat that had stalked the convoy not far from Ireland had torpedoed the tanker. Soon the stunned members of the 285th watched barrel-shaped depth charges being flung off from one ship and then another to destroy the intruder. All around, the sea erupted in ugly geysers. Eventually the explosions faded and an "all clear" was announced. There was a lot of talk in the 285th about what the whole thing meant. Even so, more than a few had trouble sleeping that night. "I realized I was really now in the war," Paluch recalled. "I had chills."

On the first day of September 1944 the *Mormac Moon* moored at the port town of Cardiff, Wales. Scores of olive-drab uniformed soldiers marched down the gangplank, grateful to be on solid British soil. For most of the American boys, England was totally foreign land. (Some even claimed the English inhabitants spoke a different language, and many of the British locals were inclined to agree!) Their first bivouac was no tent city but rather Stockton House Manor, in Codford, Wiltshire, which turned out to be an ornate Elizabethan mansion built in AD 1635 and embowered in the English woods. They were there for sixteen days, an exciting time for the young American boys. Al Valenzi had never seen plastered ceilings like that, and he wondered how the Brits trusted them enough to have them stay in such a place. As Valenzi fell asleep, his last thought was, "this beats the hell out of Camp Gruber!"

Al Valenzi had full-day pass in England. Unlike several buddies who would drink their way through a twenty-four-hour leave if they got one, Valenzi had other plans. He arranged for a walking tour of the old English town of Bath. That day was a perfect September afternoon in sunlight. Walking about, he was agog in the ancient Roman resort, with its stunning Georgian architecture—a feast of the senses and another culture away from the States.[7] Speechless after facing the Royal Crescent in Bath, Valenzi returned to the lovely Elizabethan mansion. For him, the day had been like a magic show or a secret swim into another world. Just before sleep, an odd thought occurred to him: Was this the greatest adventure of his life?

On September 16 the battalion moved to an amphibious staging area near Weymouth, England. Two days later they embarked to France "on a beautiful midnight sail across the English Channel."[8] They arrived on Omaha Beach, Normandy—now an infamous place given the terrible casualties suffered there on D-Day. Assembling in the tiny Normandy beachside hamlet of Couville-sur-Mer, by September 19 the 285th prepared to move into action. Its main combat mission would be to help pinpoint the locations of enemy artillery during protracted static combat operations, but that was precisely the problem. The prospect of slow-moving infantry battles in which their services would be needed, vanished with Patton's breakout in August. With the race to Paris and beyond, there was neither combat nor use for artillery observation as the enemy fled back to Germany. Battery B moved from one French town to another during the rapid Allied advance. However, by the time the galloping American advance had finally sputtered to a stop on the German border at the end of September, the prospects suddenly rose to use the 285th with its enhanced artillery observation eyes.

At the Battle of Hürtgen Forest the U.S. First Army's 4th, 9th, and 28th Infantry Divisions took terrible casualties from energy artillery bursts in treetops, raining lethal shrapnel on the American riflemen down below. "I did not see any German soldiers while we were in the Hürtgen Forest," recalled a member of the 4th Infantry's 12th Regiment, "but their artillery fire was unceasing and had a devastating psychological effect on us. It was disheartening, frustrating and fatiguing to be shelled day and night over the course of many days . . . without the opportunity to fight back."[9]

Casualties soared as the Germans used artillery reserves to thwart one Allied attempt after another to seize the heavily wooded Rhineland Hills. Something had to be done about the enemy guns. So on October 15 the 285th reached Zweifall, Germany, motoring across the Zee Creek at Rötgen into a heavily forested belt just south of the industrial city of Stolberg. Deploying their microphones for sound- and flash-ranging section in the dense woods, the 285th sought to find the deadly German guns that made the Hürtgen Forest an exceedingly lethal battlefield: forty-five hundred casualties to advance barely two miles over two weeks.[10] Battery B worked closely with the artillery commanders of the 4th Infantry and 7th Armored Division, who appreciated the quick trigonometric calculations that allowed pinpoint counterbattery to fire onto enemy artillery. The 285th stayed with the burdened infantry divisions in the Hürtgen Forest until December 2, when they moved to Schevenhütte.

At that point they had been in the war for four months, and with nearly two years now together, the cultural adjustments had taken hold. If not always smoothly functioning (nothing in the Army was), the odd mix had evolved into a cohesive whole.

The 440-odd men of the battalion then served as artillery observers for the U.S. 4th Infantry Division in operations against the resistance before Düren. Located on high ground overlooking the Cologne Plain below it, on November 16 members of the battalion watched in astonishment as fleets of silvered U.S. Air Force bombers rained high explosives on the German town and its surroundings. Codenamed Operation Queen, the bombing was intended to choke off German support to the Hürtgen Forest. Düren was totally destroyed—transformed from a factory town into a smoking ruin of civilian death. Of a total population of twenty-two thousand souls, three thousand were killed in the bombing. Those who survived were evacuated to central Germany, as Düren was now little more than a pile of rubble.

Paradoxically, the same carpet-bombing that members of Battery B had watched from the cliff over Düren would soon become a work detail for the Leibstandarte Adolf Hitler opposite them. The Leibstandarte would suspend its training for several days while they assisted police in finding and rescuing desperate souls trapped in the rubble. More often than not, they recovered the pitiful bodies of German civilians crushed or burned from the previous bombing maelstrom. The generals called Operation Queen a qualified success, even if it was a failure.

Regardless of such operations, there were no newspaper heroes or villains being created in the 285th. Artillery observation battalions were the kind of units in the army that the people back home had trouble understanding. They did not operate tanks, fire artillery guns, or participate in ground combat; instead, they were a specialized unit that located enemy artillery batteries so Allied guns and air power could help neutralize the enemy's most deadly combat arm. Typically, the battalion operated behind friendly lines, and because of this, the battalion had only a few casualties despite months of continuous action.

Still, if the mission was mundane by frontline standards, the men were proud of their little battalion. "We find them" was their motto. Even so, there was nothing romantic about their war, as Pvt. William F. Reem wrote home,

> This letter is being written while resting. I have been in a foxhole for sometime and this is the first opportunity to write. It has been raining most of the time. . . . The hole I sit in is to protect from

bombs, shrapnel, etc. . . . As to sleep, well, we get a few winks between quiet, but it's nothing like our beds back home.[11]

Everything was wet, damp, and moldy. Indeed, although Reem was shaving his dirty stubble, he couldn't remember the last bath. His own nose kept reminding him of the state of his body as well.

For forward observers, such as T/5 Albert Valenzi, life was "downright dangerous." On September 30 he had been with the forward guys in rain and overcast when the Germans blasted them with terrifying rockets—the "screaming meemies."

> My first experience with gunfire was in Luxembourg. I was doing plotting at the command post and I had dug a hole—a slit trench and I had my equipment laying in there. We could hear the Germans firing some screaming meemies, the rockets. John Ray got shook up. I was already in the trench. He couldn't stand it. They needed another man so I went out to the OP; Ray took over in my hole. It was very frightening. . . . I had never heard anything like them. When I got out to the outpost, I climbed into a duck blind; it was a dark rainy night and they hit our command post with artillery fire and Ray was killed where I had been. It was our first casualty. I remember we got a hold of another guy near my hole who survived and got him to an ambulance; he had been hit. . . . I got my equipment and it was full of shrapnel.[12]

The German rockets were unnerving; one sergeant in the 285th was eventually evacuated with "battle neurosis." And later on Valenzi was nearby when an artillery barrage in Holland killed Cpl. Allan Conroy. That fall the hits kept getting closer. On November 19 Valenzi and his driver were observing near Walheim, Germany, in support of the 4th Infantry Division. "There were several rounds that we heard going overhead," he recalled, "and then one suddenly landed in the trees above us."[13] His driver was seriously wounded, and Valenzi was bleeding enough to be sent off to the aid station. But after a quick bandage he was back to duty. The unit's next destination was Schevenhütte, Germany—even closer to the Hürtgen Valley. Valenzi's new home was an abandoned concrete German pillbox near the border. Even if cold and damp, he and his buddies nicknamed it "Big One." Thinking back, Al Valenzi reckoned it might as well have been called "Miserable One."

Others drew cozier accommodations. Even if out in the elements during the day, artillery spotter Pvt. James P. Mattera was able to sleep in a German home in Schevenhütte. Yet as an artillery spotter, Mattera needed the highest ground to look for the enemy cloaked in those gloomy, wooded hills. Many days found him climbing stairs to the top floor, seeking bald hillcrests, or even tree climbing. All the while German snipers and opposing artillery declared open season on U.S. Army artillery observers.

Getting close enough to see was an occupational hazard, but the thick forest and need to worm in close made the Hürtgen more dangerous than France. Most of all, Mattera liked to spot from church steeples and bell towers. One of his buddies chided him because of the last two numbers of his U.S. Army serial number, 3349-7213: "Thirteen is unlucky, Mattera," he went on, "with a number like that some Kraut is really going to ring your church bell."[14] Mattera ignored him.

Jim Mattera was not superstitious, but his buddy T/5 Chas Haines was: He carried a good luck charm as well as the New Testament. But even for Mattera in his nice billet, the disconsolate Hürtgen was a woeful place. "The place gave you the creeps," recalled Al Valenzi.

The 285th had been in Schevenhütte since December 2, serving as artillery observers for the U.S. 7th Armored Division in operations against the Germans near Düren. Such a static assignment was unusual for a unit that found itself moving every other day in the campaign of pursuit across France.[15] So when the orders came on December 16 to prepare to move south, no one thought much of it; it was just another move like many before it.[16]

T/5 William B. "Bruce" Summers of Glenville, West Virginia, was pleased to be leaving. "We moved all the time there," Summers remembered. Moving wasn't such a bad thing:

> When we heard we were headed back for Luxembourg, we thought we were going back for a rest. That was the new deal. "Get things packed up," we were told, "you're going back to Luxembourg...."[17]

Not everyone was pleased with the move. T/5 Warren Schmitt was reluctant to leave the big, comfortable foxhole they had built, covered with logs and heated by a woodstove.[18] "We thought we had it pretty good."

Word that their destination—the Ardennes area—was one big rest camp helped to quell doubts. Weren't there lots of USO Camp Shows down there, with doughnut wagons and coffee? There were even hot showers available in a place called Honsfeld. Wasn't Marlene Dietrich supposed to make an appearance too? For Bruce Summers, that had to be better than the artillery duels around Hürtgen, where German snipers were hunting for their hides.

Thank God, they would load up in the morning and head off for greener pastures.[19]

CHAPTER 3

Malmédy

Sunday, December 17, 1944, dawned with hardly a hint that it might shimmer with infamy in the already terrible history of World War II. On that day fate seized the ordinary: artillery-targeting specialists of the U.S. 285th Field Artillery Observation Battalion. For the men in this otherwise forgotten command, the greatest threat eight days before Christmas seemed the weather—gloomy, misty, and cold.

Everyone with access to a wood-burning stove on the Western Front huddled in close to ward off the damp chill. Talk around the stove centered on complaints, particularly, to be in Europe in the misery of a war in December. Now the enemy had launched an attack to the south—or that was the rumor. Yet the big scuttlebutt on armed forces radio was that since the previous day, big band leader Glenn Miller's plane was missing in a flight from England to Paris. And in spite of Bing Crosby's overplayed medley that season, no one expected to be home for Christmas.

Just after dawn Pvt. Bernie Koenig with the 3rd Platoon, 291st Engineer Combat Battalion headed out for his daily patrol from Malmédy to Ligneuville, where he had been for weeks. In contrast to the resort atmosphere that had prevailed all November, the mood in Malmédy that Sunday was weird. Big shells had fallen in the town the day before. After the shelling, the town was largely deserted, as pensive locals stayed close to their cellars. Still, Koenig made his daily patrol—a simple jeep drive that he looked forward to, as he typically waved to friendly Belgian girls along the way. Yet this morning was different. Climbing the hill from town, almost at once he ran into heavy traffic from the 7th Armored Division, and soon he and his buddy gave up trying to get to Ligneuville. "We turned around and headed back to the CP in Malmédy," Koenig would later recall:

> You couldn't really get anywhere because making headway in any direction was impossible. The roads and streets were jammed with vehicles going in all directions. Malmédy was like a giant anthill someone had poked with a stick.[1]

The men of the 285th Field Artillery Observation Battalion knew nothing about the swirl of activity near Malmédy. When reveille woke them at 5 A.M., the telephone section of their little unit was already worrying about numerous reports of German paratroopers dropping in their vicinity. "Received message from the 1st Special Service Company and Lt. Col. White of the 179th Field Artillery Group warning of paratroopers," recorded the S-3, "then the line went dead."[2] Later that morning someone from the 3907 Quartermaster Company recorded shooting one of nine enemy paratroopers who had parachuted during the night into the bivouac of the 5th Armored Division. The operations officer sent the paybook of the dead German paratrooper up to the intelligence people.

Daybreak found the long column of the artillery observation battalion threading its way down from Germany to join the columns of the U.S. 7th Armored Division headed for the Ardennes around St. Vith, Belgium. There, two regiments of the inexperienced 106th Infantry Division looked to be in danger of entrapment. The serpentine route of the trucks took the artillery observers down through the hilly northern Ardennes and then finally toward the riverside town of Malmédy.

Still, at the front line there were no worries. At 6 A.M. the advance party of Battery B—Capt. Scarborough and five enlisted men—departed en route to VIII Corps west of St. Vith near Gruflange, Belgium, where they would receive further information on their final assembly point.[3] Early that morning, Cpl. Ernest W. Bechtel of Battery B ran into his buddy, T/4 Luke B. Swartz. Before the draft Luke had been his neighbor in Reinholds, Pennsylvania—just a field away in the picturesque Amish farming countryside of Lancaster County. Now in Europe in the middle of a dark war and on a gloomy dark day, they were heading south. Bechtel was about to climb onto the GMC two-and-a-half-ton truck when he saw Swartz with his head bowed at the rear of B-25. Bechtel jumped from his truck and went over. Was Swartz crying? Or was it just the depression of being so far from Pennsylvania a week before Christmas? "Why don't you ride with me in B-26?" Bechtel offered.[4]

"No, I'll ride in one of the trucks with a tarp," Swartz said. The gray sky was beginning to spit sleet, and B-26 had no tarp. "Besides," he continued, "this is my last day anyway. Ernie, I'll not be going home." Bechtel raised his head. What was he saying?

"Something terrible is going to happen to us today but you'll be going back." Bechtel started to shake his head, but Swartz didn't pause. "Tell the folks back home that I love them."

"What the hell are you talking about?" Bechtel frowned.

"Most of us will be killed, but you will get through," Swartz muttered. *What?* Bechtel thought. Swartz mumbled the same thing again.

"Don't talk so damned foolish," Bechtel grumbled. "Nothing bad is going to happen." Swartz shrugged. Without a word, he climbed aboard his truck and Bechtel returned to his. Soon the motors coughed to life and they were off. As their trucks geared through the dense woods north of Malmédy, parachutes could be seen in the trees. Paratroopers? Someone said a sniper had fired at them.

They stopped briefly and, almost like an apparition, Swartz suddenly appeared alongside B-26. "So long," Swartz whispered to Bechtel. "And don't forget my message." Was Swartz losing his marbles? Ernie Bechtel didn't know what to say.

Staff Sgt. William H. Merriken was a big personality in Battery B and in charge of their supply.[5] On Saturday afternoon men of the battery were pulled from their forward positions and told to prepare for the move. For that, T/5 Max Schwitzgold and Pvt. Gilbert R. Pittman assisted Merriken. He and his men thought little of the mission—it was just another move. Because they had to be ready to move before light, he and his men worked deep into the night to get things properly loaded into their two-and-a-half-ton truck.

They awoke to find that Captain Scarborough and the other members of the advance party had already left for the VIII Corps sector to arrange things for the arrival of the rest of the battery. Word was that there was trouble brewing to the south. Somebody said the enemy was attacking.

It was "brisk and cold" that Sunday morning of December 17 when they motored off into the fog. The travel route of Battery B threaded south from Eupen into the Ardennes across the *Hautes Fagnes* (High Heaths) and then through the town of Malmédy on the way to St. Vith.[6] Some tried to sleep during the ride; others noticed a rogue enemy plane circling overhead, dropping flares and even a stray bomb. Bill thought it strange to find "Bedcheck Charlie" out here on the road. As they filed down roads lined with dense pines, they did not know that a battalion-sized German parachute commando operation had landed in the area.

T/5 Ted Paluch was in the rear of a three-quarter-ton weapons carrier near the end of the column driven by T/5 Alan Lucas. Normally, Ted operated the switchboard for Battery B, but that morning he was not feeling adventurous, but instead chilled and sleepy in the gloomy light and jouncing ride south. Paluch and T/4 Irwin M. Sheetz and Pvt. Robert L. Smith huddled in the back of their truck, trying to stay warm while chewing the fat. They paid scant attention to the mist-cloaked scenery. "We saw parachutes in the trees and we saw these guys standing around in the woods and we waved at them as we drove by," Paluch remembered. "We had no idea that they may have been German paratroopers."[7]

In the meantime, Baron Friedrich von der Heydte, having gathered only 130 of his 800 *Fallschirmjäger* who had landed the night before, was still waiting by the appointed rendezvous point near the road, when

Suddenly a column of U.S. trucks approaches the crossing. It is too late to hide. We unlock our automatic rifles to be ready to fire. However, nothing like this happens. Passing our position, the Americans on the carriers, sleepily wave their hands comrade-like and we quickly make use of answering the same way! The fellows "on the other side of the ditch" must be fooled by the shape of our paratrooper helmets. Not wanting another experience like this, we withdraw from the crossing into covering terrain after the column leaves.[8]

Thus, undisturbed by the German paratroopers, the artillery observers continued their journey—a fateful result of von der Heydte's earlier decision to wait for more of his lightly armed paratroopers to arrive before challenging any American column.[9] At 11:45 A.M. the battery stopped just north of Malmédy for a forgettable roadside lunch—beef hash, canned peas and pineapple, and bread and butter. For T/5 Thomas Bacon, the coffee was the best, even if thin and tasteless—at least it was hot.[10]

After lunch the twenty-six-vehicle procession continued its move. Just to the front of the convoy was the lead jeep, with Capt. Roger L. Mills and Lt. Virgil P. Lary Jr. They led the column of 140 men in trucks, weapons carriers, and jeeps numbered B-1 to B-26. In the second truck was Merriken, with Pittman at the wheel and Pfc. Aubrey Jeatum Hardiman. "Jeet" Hardiman had been an ace turkey hunter in Buckingham County, Virginia, before coming to Europe and the war. In basic training he showed an aptitude for gunnery and tactics. Now he was one of the only combat-trained men in the 285th, assigned to protect the unit's headquarter section, operating the .50-caliber ring-mount machine gun over the cab, should there be any trouble. Yet Hardiman, soft-spoken and nonchalant, was never called on.[11] There never seemed to be any action. Instead, all three sat in the cab trying to stay warm. Max Schwitzgold, a Jewish boy whom Merriken had somehow taken under his wing, was further back on another truck.

The rest of the two dozen–odd vehicles consisted of a mixture of jeeps, command cars, two-and-a-half-ton trucks, and a few weapons carriers—a fancy name for Dodge GMC trucks with a rear open bed with wooden benches. Because the 285th was primarily a support outfit, it was only sparsely equipped with weapons. Although most men did have a carbine and some had a pistol, many had never fired a gun since basic training. They did have three of the machine guns, but there was only one bazooka for the entirety of Battery B. All of this never bothered anyone before; as the "eyes of the artillery," they were mostly kept out of harm's way.

Other GIs heading the same direction were looking for excitement that morning—or at least a buddy to help stave off boredom. Cpl. Duane Londagin and Lacy Thomasson were from the 552nd Anti-Aircraft Automatic Weapons Battalion attached to the U.S. 78th Infantry Division, stationed in Verviers, Belgium. That morning, Londagin had been ordered to pick up the mail again in St. Vith and was looking for some company. Lacy "Pinhead" Thomasson was around. Would he be up for it? Thomasson had a reputation as a one-off. He had made sergeant only to be busted. "I have my own ass to look after," he shrugged. Lacy was known to go to German houses to ask for booze. "You're crazy, Thomasson," others said. But that day there was nothing to drink and only a humdrum lunch. Lacy had volunteered to go with Londagin. "I thought to myself, that beats sitting here counting buzz bombs."[12] They left about quarter of noon for the two-hour drive back and forth to St. Vith. "I didn't even have a proper overcoat, but got one. I was glad I did—my God it was cold." On the way, they chewed over the typical rumors: The krauts had dropped a few big-caliber shells in Malmédy up ahead. Such senseless and annoying acts by the enemy seemed unending.

Their trip to St. Vith was uneventful, but the cold in the open jeep was punishing. Thomasson was thankful when they stopped at the mail building in St. Vith. Going to the door, there was no postmaster . . . not a soul. Inside, the abandoned place was ramshackle with mail scattered all over—a mess of envelopes and fruitcakes. The scene was weird: Everyone looked to have left in a hurry. Poking around the mess for a few minutes, Londagin concluded they should go back, even without the mail. There were distant sounds of artillery fire, and the atmosphere in St. Vith was creepy. "Okay," Thomasson sighed, "but the boys are going to be awful unhappy." They left in a hurry, their jeep hurtling out of town on the way back.

Meanwhile, just north of the old German town of Malmédy the 285th made another short pit stop so they could empty bladders under the pines after their unsatisfying lunch. However, four vehicles of the Battery B column would make a third unplanned halt in an ironic turn of events. That morning, Sgt. James E. Barrington of Brownsville, Texas, was leading a two-and-a-half-ton truck designated B-26, driven by Cpl. Charles O. Arndt and five others—Cpl. Ernest W. Bechtel was one of these men. As the convoy threaded slowly through the predominantly German-speaking Belgian town of Malmédy, dozens of locals shouted, "*Die Deutschen kommen!*" ("The Germans are coming!"), and a few of the French-speaking civilians ran alongside their vehicles shouting "*Boche! Boche!*" ("Germans! Germans!"). A mass of civilians clogged the roads heading north out of town. Their faces frowned in desperation, many pushed baby carriages and primitive carts filled with bedding and everything else imaginable. "There was great confusion in the town," Bechtel recalled. "People on foot and in vehicles— civilian and military were attempting to flee. It was then that we realized that something had gone wrong."[13]

Without warning, B-26 abruptly squealed to a stop and Sgt. Barrington staggered from the cab vomiting. He was violently ill—food poisoning. Army food! Two other trucks—B-27 and B-28—stopped too, as Lt. Francis Kaizak so ordered. After ten minutes Barrington was taken to a hospital. When that was done, the three waylaid vehicles zoomed to catch up with the convoy further south.

> We had driven less than half a mile when a jeep came roaring toward us out of control, but somehow the driver managed to avoid a collision. The driver of the jeep was incoherent, but several times he clearly mentioned the word "Krauts." An officer riding with him was shot through the neck.

Even though the man was wounded, Lt. Kaizak managed to speak to the officer. That produced no conclusive result, and the little three-vehicle train moved out again. They had gone a short distance when excited men of the 291st Engineer Combat Battalion halted them once more. The combat engineers gesticulated with wide arms before a stand of towering conifers lining the road south of Malmédy. "We're going to blow this row of trees and dump them across the road," the engineer shouted to Kaizak. "Once you're through, you can't return." Kaizak lost his cool, insisting they let him through. The engineers backed off.

The three U.S. Army trucks had driven only a short distance further south up the winding hill when small-arms fire broke out on their left. As they stopped, a much louder volume of machine gunfire erupted in the chaos somewhere further on. "Lt. Kaizak, riding in the cab suddenly went berserk," determined that they reach the rest of the column, which was obviously in trouble. Bechtel entered the cab and restrained him so Arndt could awkwardly turn around to drive and try to find a way back to Malmédy. In the confusion and tangle of traffic, they did not get back until nightfall—checking Kaizak into the same medical aide unit that had admitted Barrington earlier that day.[14] Officially the reason was "battle neurosis," but in the foxhole lexicon, Kaizak had "gone nuts."[15] But what happened to the other twenty-six vehicles of the battery that had already gone ahead?

Bill Merriken was in the second vehicle in the little convoy that didn't stop. As the main Battery B column had approached Malmédy, traffic on the road picked up. Tanks of the 7th Armored now mixed with their little convoy. Just outside of town there were signs on the side of the road: "*Warning: This Road under Enemy Observation.*" That was unusual, Bill Merriken thought, as their little route was supposed to be twenty miles from the front. But the town was heavily congested with American military traffic, some of which seemed to be fleeing. That seemed strange too, but regardless, MPs directed them onto the proper route out of Malmédy. As they left town Bill Merriken saw Belgian women standing along the road; some were crying and waving handkerchiefs. *What was up with that?*

Al Valenzi was in a jeep with Ken Ahrens, Mike Skoda, and Mike Sciranko just behind Merriken's vehicle. Valenzi was a bit worried too, but the sun was peeking out of the clouds. On the way into Malmédy they had seen some German parachutes hanging in the trees and in town, and some 7th Armored guys had handed their crew some captured parachute material. "We cut it up as souvenirs," he recalled, wrapping some of the silk as a scarf around his neck. They stuffed the rest of the material in the back of the jeep. He thought at least they were entering a Belgian town rather than a German one—there might be some goodies! Al already had a prized P-38 pistol, a confiscated enemy belt buckle with "*Gott mit uns,*" but mindful of their poor lunch, his stomach was talking. He was much more excited about the town's culinary offerings—anything other than the indigestible road rations the army doled out.

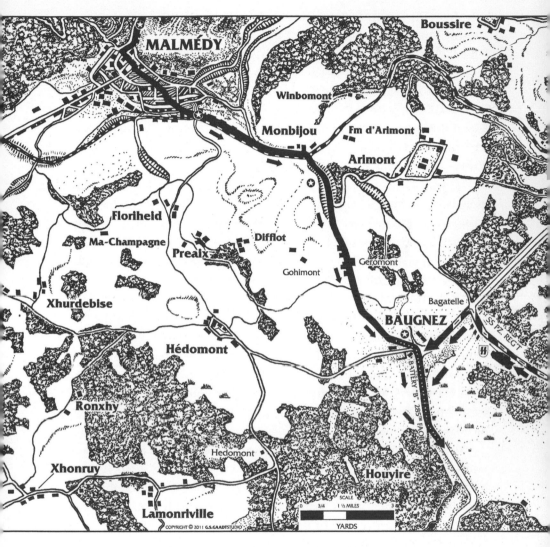

MALMÉDY, BELGIUM

Malmédy was so jammed with traffic that everything came to a standstill as their vehicle crossed the stone bridge over the Warche River. Then a prize: Looking on the right side of the street, Valenzi spied a Belgian patisserie. Knowing the beautiful delicacies in such places, he told his buddies he would be back soon with something better—maybe even wine. As Al approached the *Pont d'Octroi*, he found its doors closed and the sugared pastries behind darkened glass. The owner showed up to shoo him away. As he walked back, refugees streamed across the bridge—a sullen rabble.

He must have looked disappointed, for two young Belgian girls, Yolande and Marie Huby, waved excitedly from beside the bridge. "*Americain! Americain!*"[16] Dressed in their Sunday best, the two girls lived at Beguinage on the south side of Malmédy and were on their way home from Catholic Mass. As Al walked by, ten-year-old Marie smiled broadly and reached back to pull a tricolor Belgian ribbon from her hair. She offered it with an outstretched hand. He took the ribbon and grinned, reaching in his pocket to find a stick of gum to return the favor. He was back on the jeep just as the traffic began to clear. The girls waved but disappeared quickly as the men's jeep sputtered away. Something felt good about that, Valenzi thought—a gift from cute Belgian girls with big smiles. He tied the ribbon around his dog tags and stuffed them in his jacket. "This is luck," he announced to the others as he boarded the jeep.[17]

Just ahead of Valenzi and Merriken's vehicles was the column's lead jeep driven by Cpl. Raymond Lester with Lt. Virgil Lary, who was in provisional command of the battery given Capt. Scarborough's absence. Capt. Roger L. Mills from headquarters was with him. Presently, as the traffic momentarily lifted, the command jeep reached the last houses at Malmédy's southern fringe at a place locals called Mon Bijou.

In Malmédy twenty-five-year-old Lt. Col. David E. Pergrin of the 291st Engineer Combat Battalion had recently arrived at his Company B headquarters on the second floor in one of the last houses on the edge of town. Formerly a tough football player who majored in engineering at Penn State, Pergrin was a determined and resourceful commander when he took his 291st Engineer Combat Battalion from England to Normandy in the summer of 1944. He successfully led his engineers out of the Normandy hedgerows and then took them through the wild advance through France. The autumn in Belgium seemed to settle into a mundane war: quarry, sawmill, and road-fixing operations to support the advance on the Roer Dams. Even so, his group commander, Col. Wallis Anderson, a World War I veteran, knew how thinly defended the German border was in the northern stretches of the Ardennes and had assigned Pergrin's battalion the military mission of screening the approach to Spa, where the U.S. First Army made its headquarters. The 291st Engineer Combat Battalion would trade in their saws and bulldozers for bazookas and rifles if trouble came their way.

Now, on December 17, events took a surprising turn. In the wee hours of the morning, at 3 A.M., Pergrin received a call from VII Corps' Maj. Dick Carville with news that German paratroopers had been dropped somewhere just to the north. Then four big artillery shells—obviously from a very large-caliber German gun—had fallen in the southeastern streets of Malmédy, killing several Belgians, an event that touched off a near panic as locals took to the roads.[18] That alone was plenty weird, but then during the night a trusty phone line between the battalion CP and the engineer group headquarters had mysteriously gone dead. Signal troubleshooters traced down the break to lines neatly severed by wire cutters. Enemy agents?

At noon the following day Pergrin had been speaking to Anderson in Trois-Ponts, who had run into the commander of the 629th Engineer Light Equipment Company coming from Waimes.[19] Things were in a muddle at the front. During the previous night a racket of machine gunfire and growling enemy tanks just to the east had spooked the 629th's forward command post in Bütgenbach.[20] Moreover, Lt. Frank W. Rhea of the 3rd platoon of B Company had been working with the 629th to fill in some cratered roads leading to the ammunition dump in Bütgenbach, watching with curiosity as a bevy of U.S. fighter-bombers strafed something close by. Checking further, Rhea found an MP who told him that enemy tanks swarmed just on the other side of the hill.[21]

Rhea hurriedly returned to Malmédy to warn everybody. Reporting to Anderson, he said a tank destroyer outfit had sent the enemy armor packing, but how the hell did enemy tanks get back this far? Anderson was quickly on the phone to Pergrin. "The Boches are loose east of

Malmédy," he growled to Pergrin. "Take the necessary measures to defend."[22] Because Malmédy straddled the Warche River, it was clear to
him that the Germans would soon attempt to capture the town and its
valuable bridges that provided access out of the heavily forested hills of
the Ardennes. So with two other officers, Pergrin immediately left for
Malmédy to set up a series of strong points and roadblocks with the
241 officers and men he had available. His little company of combat engineers was the only sizable force available. Still, what they lacked in
manpower, Pergrin aimed to make up for with explosives.

He ordered his men to strap quarter-pound blocks of TNT to the
pines lining the roads that led into town on the south and east of
Malmédy in order to blow the trees down across the path if enemy armor approached. On the vulnerable route that led into town from the
south he situated a squad of Company B engineers with orders to lace
the road with mines and cover them with machine guns and bazooka
teams. Although Pergrin was still paper-thin on resources and receiving word of enemy paratroopers floating down south of Eupen, he
knew he had to cover the roads that led into town from the north.[23] To
bolster his defense, he ordered Company C, in reserve at the *Château
Froide-Cour* in La Gleize, to move to Malmédy after dropping off one
squad each to defend the important approaches to Stavelot and Trois-
Ponts, with their namesake three bridges.

Not long after the battalion commander finished airing his concerns to Col. Anderson at 12:15 A.M., a jeep approached with a line of
trucks just behind. It was the lead vehicle of the 285th Field Artillery
Observation Battalion. Pergrin emerged from the house and trotted
into the street, throwing out one hand. Raymond Lester braked to a
stop, but he left the engine running. Pergrin moved into the side of the
jeep and spoke to Capt. Mills, who wanted to know if the 7th Armored
had just come this way. Pergrin replied that they had just cleared the
town half an hour before. That seemed to satisfy Mills, who said he
needed to follow their route, as the division artillery was not far behind. Pergrin told Mills that they had received reports of an enemy
breakthrough near Bütgenbach. It might be prudent, he counseled, if
the battery would swing over to the west and go through Stavelot on
the 7th Armored Division's other march route. The German column
would probably strike Malmédy within the hour.

Mills considered Pergrin's advice but shook his head. They had better stay with the prescribed march route on the N-23 highway. "I can make Five Corners," Mills told him, "and head south to St. Vith, where I am supposed to go by the time they get here."[24] Five Corners was the road intersection nexus at Baugnez just south of Malmédy. Reluctantly, Pergrin waved them on, their thirty-odd vehicles passing with difficulty in the snarled traffic and refugee-choked roads. Several ambulances from the 575th Ambulance Company tagged along on their tail. They slowly sputtered away, climbing the steep incline that led out of Malmédy and the Warche River valley. It was still cold outside, so Pergrin went back to the warmth of his headquarters.

The last vehicles of the column had just disappeared at 12:30 P.M. when two American soldiers burst into Pergrin's command post wild-eyed and out of breath. They had been sent out on a little reconnaissance of the N-32 and had driven their jeep back as fast as it would go. "There's a big Kraut column coming!" one shouted, "Colonel, they've got tanks and halftracks and armored cars—everything, and there's a hell of a lot of 'em! It looks like the whole German army!"

Pergrin tried to calm them down to get a straight story, his worry growing as he learned more. The two men had been just west of Thirimont before almost running headlong into the enemy. Dismounting and observing from an uncomfortably short distance, they had counted sixty-eight enemy vehicles—half of those being tanks.[25] After that, they drove like hell all the way to Pergrin's command post. Pergrin began to realize that something big was happening—and it wasn't good. Turning to Lt. Thomas F. Stack of B Company, he told him he needed fully manned roadblocks east, south, and west of Malmédy. He needed them completed immediately—lots of mines covered by machine guns—everything.[26]

With enemy armor reported just a few miles up the road, he ordered that the barrier just up the way receive special attention. There, charges were to be made ready to blow down a string of towering pines that would stop big German tanks—at least for a time. Then an artillery section of the 7th Armored appeared on the heels of the departed 285th. Although its section commander seemed prepared to heed Pergrin's warning, nothing the bespectacled leader could do would convince its commander to stay with Pergrin in Malmédy. The artillery section's leader had orders to go directly to St. Vith. Pergrin was nearly beside himself.

Then, at 12:45 P.M., a booming echo made everyone in Pergrin's headquarters at Mon Bijou stop midsentence. It was the thunder of shellfire not far away. Then another round and then more. The windows began to rattle, followed by the unmistakable staccato crackle of machine gunfire. There was a momentary hush. Pergrin winced, thinking *That little FAOB outfit has run smack into that Kraut column.*[27]

It was true. At the intersection just ahead—the meeting knot of a quintet of roads GIs called "Five Points"—known as Baugnez to Belgian locals—stood Pfc. Homer D. Ford, a U.S. Army 1944–edition traffic cop: a military policeman with the 518th MP Battalion. There was little glamour in his job, but it was more adventurous than his previous life as a shoe salesman back in the States. At least theoretically, MPs were never on the front lines—no glory, but not too many worries either.

At about 12:45 P.M. Ford was directing the tail of traffic of the 7th Armored Division on its way down the hard-surfaced N-23 to St. Vith. He encouraged them on with whistle and personalized hand signals, but otherwise the job was ordinary. He stood in the middle of the intersection, looking down the road lined with leafless trees.

The Sherman tanks of Combat Command R had just cleared Five Points when a staggered line of American trucks from Company B, the 285th FAOB, appeared, climbing steeply out of Malmédy's deep valley.

As with the tanks, Ford waved the little artillery outfit on—this unit was so inconsequential, altogether so forgettable, that Ford did not even know they were behind the armored combat command. The trucks motored on past him. Then he turned his head, squinting. *What was that?* Strange sounds were just audible from the wooded hills to the east—growling and groaning tank tracks again along the N-32. The Missouri man peered into the gloom. Another lost column of the 7th Armored?

Who were these guys?[28]

CHAPTER 4

"It Don't Look Good Boys"

In Bill Merriken's supply truck the air seemed colder as he shifted down to grind up the hill out of the Amblève River valley. The truck soon reached a crossroads up ahead. "Five Points" was a nondescript place at the top of the crest with a few stone farm buildings—one structure was a café. At that spider-like nexus of roads, the thirty-vehicle column turned south toward Ligneuville. From there they would soon drive to St. Vith and find Scarborough and the 7th Armored Division. Or so they thought.

Past the crossroads the road was straight for a long stretch and lined with stark leafless trees and deep ditches. On either side of the road were knobby mud-laden pastures that sloped downhill before curving with the road into a forest. There were scattered patches of old snow here and there, and the scene was as gray and leaden as the murky Belgian skies.

"Boom!" Everybody jumped. No sooner than the echo began to waver did an even louder sound slap the air. It happened just as the lead vehicles passed beyond the bend in the road—something exploded in the field to the right side of the road. No one needed to tell artillery observers what that was, and from the closely spaced reports, they knew it was from somewhere nearby. Lt. Virgil Lary's vehicle jerked to a halt just in front of them, and he and the others in his vehicle heard intense firing to the rear.[1] It was about 1 P.M.:

We stopped in front of a house on the left side of the road where there was a civilian woman standing in front of the house. This woman just jumped as the shell hit. . . . I jumped into the ditch where the greatest number of men were standing or squatting by this house. Capt. Mills followed me. I stood up and some of the men saw a tank coming down the road. Naturally, small arms was all we had. We threw our arms down.[2]

Before Lary could reach the deep ditch on the west side of the road, he saw an enemy soldier in one of the German halftracks just behind a tank aiming a pistol at him. Instinctively, he ducked behind a GMC truck hood. There he removed his officer's bars and rubbed mud to cover the white markings on his helmet that identified him as an officer. While he attempted personal subterfuge, the German fired at Captain Mills in the ditch.[3] Hearing two shots, Lary called out, "Mills, are you hit?" "No!" he answered.

Not far from Lary, five men managed to escape from the front of the column immediately after being struck by Sternebeck's first volley of shot and shell. Pfc. Donald L. Bower was in the fifth vehicle in the convoy with Cpl. Ted Flechsig and T/4 Wilson M. Jones. As they passed the intersection at Baugnez, Bower noticed a military policeman and a road marker. Then the truck ahead of them stopped and somebody passed back word that there was an air attack.

That seemed enough for Bower and his crew to get out of their vehicle to take cover. "As we stepped off the trucks, machine gunfire was whistling around us. . . . Then mortar shells started dropping." Further back George Graeff and Warren Schmitt were talking casually in their jeep when they were stunned as they watched a mortar shell explode ahead. Next came the ugly clatter of bullets slamming into metal. Warren Schmitt's eyes grew wide watching red tracer bullets darting across the road. They, too, bounded out of their vehicle

Graeff crouched in the culvert beside T/5 Eugene Garrett in the truck right behind them. Both men struggled to load a cantankerous Browning Automatic Rifle—infernally difficult to keep clean. When was it last fired? It wouldn't work, so instead they started to plink away with an M1 carbine. Suddenly, a truck ahead of them momentarily disappeared in an earth-heaving burst—a near miss from an enemy

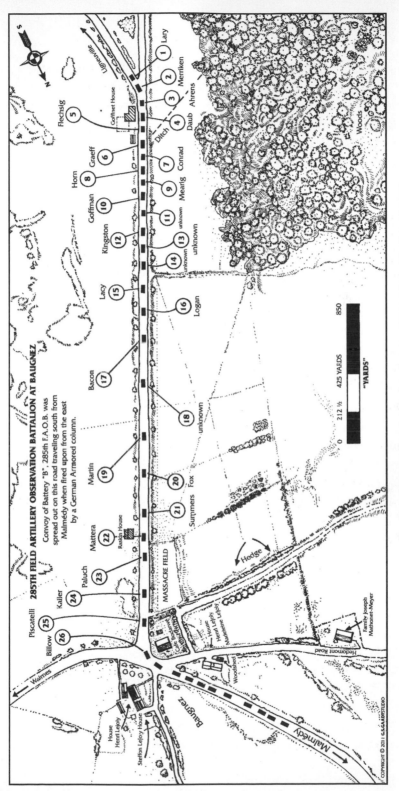

285TH FIELD ARTILLERY OBSERVATION BATTALION AT BAUGNEZ

Convoy of Battery "B", 285th F.A.O.B. was spread out on this road traveling south from Malmédy when fired upon from the east by a German Armored column.

"YARDS"

0   212 ½   425 YARDS   850

285TH FIELD ARTILLERY OBSERVATION BATTALION AT BAUGNEZ

(See Appendix II)

COPYRIGHT © 2021 G&G ARPSTUDIO

mortar round. That shock convinced Garrett, Graeff, and Conrad to move away from the road. Yet as they made a dash for the ditch twenty feet further back, another shell landed, sending deadly shrapnel fragments flying. Conrad slumped to the ground. "Are you hit?" Garrett called. "Yes!" Conrad grimaced.[4] Garrett ran out to drag the wounded man to the shallow ditch.

They had just dropped behind its bank when a German halftrack and tank turned up the road. Looking like prehistoric steel monsters, the armor was soon blasting the GI trucks. "What's happening?" Schmitt called out. "Keep quiet!" Graeff said, hushing him: "We're surrounded."[5] Schmitt had a souvenir German P-38 on him—bad news. He threw it away and fell to the ground. Scared silly, Schmitt crawled on his stomach some fifty feet west from the road to a small ditch filled with water. The first German tank got up to their abandoned jeep, stopped, and began rummaging through it for loot. A second tank rumbled after the first. "I submerged myself in the stream," Schmitt recalled, "and covered myself with grass and mud so that I wasn't captured."[6]

Meanwhile, Ted Flechsig huddled in the ditch, believing they were under attack from German paratroopers. Soon, however, he saw that the shooting was coming from a big tank and a halftrack that were now coming down the road and firing their machine guns to convince the battery to surrender.[7] At first Flechsig thought about taking off across the meadow to the west and dashing for the woods—indeed, Bower and others seemed to try that—but after a burst of machine gunfire, Flechsig saw several fall.[8] Were they dead? There was little time to think, for other buddies in the ditch ahead of him were in trouble. "Several of the boys tried to play dead and the Germans would yell at them and if they didn't get up, they would put a couple of shots into their back and make sure. . . . That caused everyone else playing dead to give themselves up too." Soon they were all marching back toward the crossroads under guard.

Unlike the others in his truck, Bower bounded out of the cab and crawled beyond the ditch by the road to a second ditch about twenty yards to the west where several others plopped down. As he heard other enemy vehicles approach, he decided he would pretend to be dead, leaving himself lying facedown in a ditch half-filled with stagnant water. That the column was actually under ground attack—a big one—was now apparent. Every few minutes Bower would slowly turn his head to peek and see what was happening. His buddies were being marched back to the crossroads, four abreast in the road.

> I saw Pfc. Hardiman and heard Lt. Lary, but I was lying on my face in water acting dead and didn't want to disclose that I was alive. The next thing I saw was the start of the German column. . . . I didn't look up again until the column had ceased. I could hear them stop and looting the trucks, and I heard some of our trucks being driven off. About 15 minutes after the tail of the column passed, I moved to another ditch 15 yards back of the road. I noticed a German machine gun and four Germans in front of the house to my right. . . . About five minutes later I heard brush rustle in a ditch about 15 yards away. Thinking they had sent a man out to get me, I said, 'Kamerad' and came out. I started toward the machine gun, [and] I noticed that in the place where the brush was rustling was an American soldier who I later identified as [T/5 Warren R.] Schmitt. A halftrack went by; a German whistled at me and pointed toward a machine gun nest. I started that way when a soldier in the halftrack took three deliberate shots at me. At the time he shot at me, I had my hands up and was unarmed.[9]

One of the enemy rounds ripped through his jacket but left him unscathed. Bower didn't hesitate, however, and he acted as if he were shot, falling to the ground. After he dropped he noticed that Cpl. Gene Garrett, Cpl. George E. Graeff, Warren Schmitt, and T/5 Robert B. Conrad were in the ditch nearby.[10] Out of the corner of his eyes Garrett saw the Germans fire on four Americans who were attempting to run off from the road toward the woods.[11] "I saw three of them drop and one of them get to the woods," he recalled. Two enemy troopers went out to investigate, and two of the three Americans who had fallen after their fire were apparently uninjured; the Germans made them get up and march back with the others toward the crossroads. The other man was less fortunate. "On the way back, they came upon the American soldier who had dropped first. When they stopped by him, I could see them shoot him with a pistol as he lay on the ground."[12] Garrett, Graeff, and Schmitt decided their best chance was to continue to lie in the ditch and lay low. The men were bunched up together in the ditch, Conrad's head awkwardly lying on Graeff's leg.

Sprawled out on the ground, Garrett and Graeff nervously looked over to the east to see Kenny Kingston and Ted Flechsig walking up the road with their hands up.[13] Near the head of the American column the Germans were already ransacking the captured vehicles. On the main road Gene Garrett saw Lt. Solomon Goffman protesting as young SS men pilfered his pockets. "They shot him in the head," Garrett said.[14]

Lying nearby on the ground, his helmet crouched over his forehead in simulated death, George Graeff had a reasonably clear view of the road out of one eye. After the first two tanks and a halftrack passed, another larger group of lumbering tanks and halftracks moved by. One German on an armored vehicle looked right at him—so much so that he hastily closed his squinted eye and waited nervously as another SS man approached within a few feet to survey the tangle of bodies of himself, Conrad, and Garrett. One fleeting peek revealed a German soldier's boot heel so close to his eye that it was out of focus. Minutes later there was a loud racket of concentrated automatic weapons fire to the north.[15] He didn't dare move.

From his location in the freezing ditch water west of the main road, Warren Schmitt could hear what was happening, the clank and squeal of the tanks. When the SS halftracks stopped, the enemy would get off to gather loot. "The Germans were yelling and acting half drunk," he remembered. "They were laughing and carrying on. . . . When they ransacked the vehicles, they were like a bunch of kids that seemed to be enjoying themselves immensely."[16] Suddenly he heard a loud gunshot and then another, followed by ceaseless automatic fire. "That shooting was very predominant because it was very quiet until that. . . . I heard them firing into the group and the cries of the men, but I didn't actually see it."[17]

The men west of the road in the ditch on the south end of the field lay there for a long time. No one moved; nearly two hours went by as they listened to one German vehicle after another passing on the road to the east. Presently a halftrack came and picked up the SS crew manning the machine gun across from them.[18] As soon as they were gone Garrett asked Graeff if they should hazard to make a run for it now—or wait for dark.

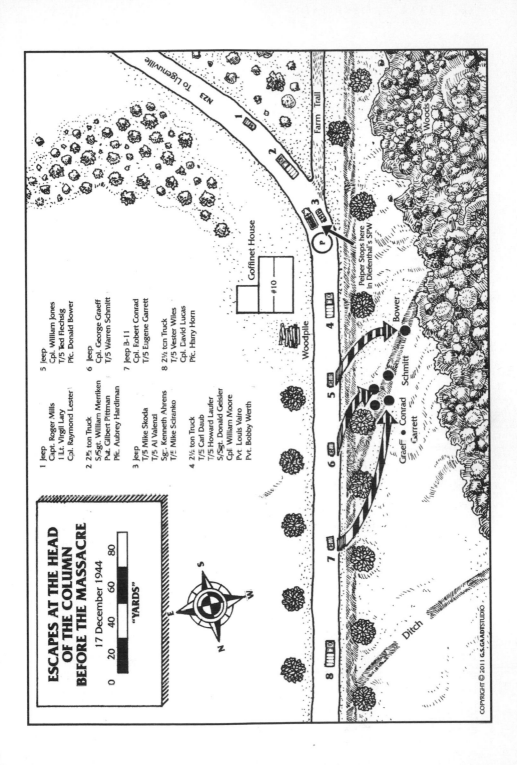

ESCAPES AT THE HEAD
OF THE COLUMN
BEFORE THE MASSACRE

17 December 1944

"YARDS"

0   20   40   60   80

1 Jeep
Capt. Roger Mills
1 Lt. Virgil Lary
Col. Raymond Lester

2 2½ ton Truck
S/Sgt. William Merriken
Pvt. Gilbert Pittman
Pfc. Aubrey Hardiman

3 Jeep
T/5 Mike Skoda
T/5 Al Valenzi
Sgt. Kenneth Ahrens
T/E Mike Sciranko

4 2½ ton Truck
T/5 Carl Daub
T/5 Howard Laufer
S/Sgt. Donald Geisler
Cpl. William Moore
Pvt. Louis Vairo
Pvt. Bobby Werth

5 Jeep
Cpl. William Jones
T/5 Ted Flechsig
Pfc. Donald Bower

6 Jeep
Cpl. George Graeff
T/5 Warren Schmitt

7 Jeep B-11
Cpl. Robert Conrad
T/5 Eugene Garrett

8 2½ tcn Truck
T/5 Vester Wiles
Cpl. David Lucas
Pfc. Harry Horn

N23 To Ligneuville

Farm Trail

Woods

Goffinet House

#10

Woodpile

Peiper Stops here
in Diefenthal's SPW

Bower

Schmitt

Graef • Conrad

Garrett

Ditch

COPYRIGHT © 2011 G.S.GAADTSTUDIO

"Let's go now," Schmitt said. The four men began to crawl off toward a dense stand of trees just to the west. Yet Warren Schmitt was so incapacitated from lying for hours in the ditch that he was unable to keep up with the others; instead, he was only able to edge slowly to the woods.[19] That feeble process took so long that at dusk Schmitt was still only about seventy-five yards south of the café, still creeping toward the woods. From there he could clearly see that building burning. "I saw [German] guards around the house and it burning, but no men coming out. I had a good view of the house burning as I stayed there until after dark. I laid there in the ice water and the mud for two hours before I could move."

After lying in the cold for two hours, the others were not in much better shape. "I was so stiff I couldn't move," Robert Conrad recalled. Previously wounded, he had passed out in the ditch from shock. Garrett shook him to consciousness. Incapable of even crawling, he clumsily rolled out of the ditch.[20] The men had to support Cpl. Conrad, who was "in bad shape due to overexposure and shock." In a roundabout way the group made their way through the dense conifer forests to Malmédy. Although Bower remembered himself "nearly frozen" as they stumbled through to the woods, he heard a long volley of machine gunfire in the distance. He and the others were unable to see what it was all about. While the sky dimmed to dark, he could see the café burning at the crossroads, but the men headed away from the scene. Eventually all reached the outskirts of Malmédy where an old Belgian farmer gave them directions.

Meanwhile, unaware that some of his men were escaping, Lt. Lary, at the head of the endangered column of the 285th, saw about fifteen of his men standing in front of the Goffinet House with their hands up. That was it: Lary told everyone to surrender. "I called for Capt. Mills to come out of the ditch and join the group." They did, as more German vehicles appeared, motioning them to march back to the north.

At about that time some more American vehicles happened on the scene—the ambulances of the 575th Ambulance Company. There was more small-arms fire back up at the intersection as the Germans fired on the ambulances. Lt. Lary incredulously watched, as an American lieutenant colonel was forced to drive an American jeep under German guard.[21]

By that time three or four more tanks came down the road. They told us to take off to the rear of the column, questioning the men about wristwatches and pistols. One said "get someone to drive these vehicles." The men didn't pay any attention to them. They did take three men back with them to drive these captured vehicles.[22]

Those first shots startled Bill Merriken, who was in the vehicle right behind Lary. Lt. Lary's jeep jerked to a halt just ahead of him. More shells and the squeal of brakes—direct fire! In Merriken's truck Pittman swerved to the road's shoulder and skidded to a stop. All three men rolled out the right side of the cab into the ditch on the west side of the road. Suddenly, an improbable sight: a jeep with an officer and a driver approached the head of their column from Ligneuville. They started to stop, but Merriken waved them off and yelled, "We're under fire, go to Malmédy and get help!" The jeep roared off, careening up the road and "going like hell."[23]

Bill ran from the ditch to the east side of the road to see if he could trace the enemy fire. Just in front of him was a house—House #10, the home of Henri Goffinet—with a woodpile by the road—at least it provided some cover.[24] As an enemy machine gun barked to life, several men gathered there with him.[25] He looked to the rear from the ditch and could see that other trucks had pulled off. To the rear of the column was a bend in the road that he could not see beyond. He pulled out his pistol and climbed a slight embankment in front of the woodpile to get a better look.

Listening to the crackle of automatic fire and the loud crump of shells exploding, Merriken felt helpless with his puny handgun. From his vantage point he could see Al Valenzi firing a rifle from the same side of the road. Bill still could not tell where all the firing was coming from, so he crawled down the bank and started toward Valenzi. A shell landed on the third truck behind them, exploding loudly and sending fragments hissing through the air. Merriken fell prone in the ditch. Two more trucks were hit; whoever was shooting had good aim. Al Valenzi crawled to the ditch too:

I could see that the fire was coming from the woods off to our left. They had bracketed us; the front of the column and the rear of the column. . . . As soon as we dove out, our jeep went, boom! It blew apart; it was maybe 30 feet away. I took the pistol out right away and hid it in a log wood pile by an old shed with a big tree in front of it. I grabbed this M-1. I took the safety off and fired one round. I wasn't used to firing it and something went wrong; I couldn't get another shot off. Kenny [Ahrens] said to me, "Keep your head down! Keep your head down!" Just then, a piece of shrapnel hit my arm. I told Kenny, "I'm hit." It wasn't real bad. Ken was just beside me.[26]

Still lying in the ditch, Valenzi heard the distinct clatter of tank tracks on pavement from the rear of the Battery B column. Maybe the jeep had brought back help. "Just then, I heard tanks, and I thought, 'This is our lucky day, our tanks are here to bail us out!'" But one look at the behemoth clanking up the bend in the road two hundred yards away dashed that hope. The iron beast, spitting flashes of machine gun-fire, was flushing his buddies out from cover. They seemed to be only warning shots, but they were still plenty convincing. To Valenzi the enemy tanks looked prehistoric—a mottled paint scheme, its camouflage enhanced by boughs of pine limbs, sprouted an ominously long-barreled gun that looked nothing like a Sherman. To Merriken, too, it seemed gigantic. Having never been in close combat, they had never seen an enemy tank. A stalwart figure stood in its turret—a giant man in a massive steel monster.

Al Valenzi looked to his buddy Sgt. Kenneth Ahrens on his left. "Ken is that one of our tanks?"

Ahrens squinted. "No," he said shaking his head. "It doesn't look like it, does it?'

"Damn!" Valenzi winced. He didn't usually curse, but if anytime was appropriate, this was it. "These guys are firing at us with machine pistols!" They were right on top of the GIs in the ditch just north of them. "*Hände hoch!*" (*Hands up!*) the Germans shouted. Valenzi gawked at the panzer men. They looked young. Some wore camouflage uniforms, but all looked exuberant and confident. "We better stop and put our hands up," Valenzi shrugged. A big tank drew closer. "Good idea," Ahrens agreed, thrusting his arms overhead. Valenzi threw his rifle down to signal that he was unarmed. At this point he noticed he was slightly wounded and bleeding. "Well it looks like it might be over for us," he mumbled.

Bill Merriken looked back to the north. As far as he could see, American soldiers were coming out of the ditch with raised hands. Lt. Lary was right next to him. "It don't look good, boys," he said in an anguished tone. "We might as well surrender. We can't do anything for those people." Disgusted, Merriken slipped his pistol into the woodpile. As the German tank drew closer, he could hear its commander yelling in accented English: "Up! Up!"

Pvt. Jim Mattera saw the tank grinding down the road with its commander standing brazenly in its open hatch. From the ditch he started to shoulder his M-1 carbine. Instinctively, two GIs in the ditch with him, T/4 Oscar Jordan and T/5 James Luers, lurched over to grab the weapon. "Son of a bitch, Mattera!" one hissed. "If you miss him, we are all goners."[27] They quickly pulled down his carbine. Shortly, the tank drew abreast and the driver called for everyone to surrender. The hapless GIs were already reaching overhead. With a hand gesture the black-uniformed commander motioned them back up the road. "I guess I'll be spending Christmas in a prison camp," Merriken thought to himself. He watched as German tanks and vehicles passed by on the road, pushing abandoned American trucks out of the way. The German vehicles were bumper to bumper. Just then a halftrack pulled up with a German officer standing in it.

"It's a long way to Tipperary, boys!" the dark-uniformed man called out in English. There was brief laughter among the Germans standing nearby before the halftrack proceeded on its way south. Merriken wondered why in the hell this Kraut would be calling to them with a refrain from World War I. He didn't know he had just seen the German commander, Jochen Peiper.

Standing in the middle of the perilous crossroads intersection, military policeman Homer Ford had hit the ground after the shooting started. However, after looking up he made a dash behind the café just west of the intersection.[28] Passengers in Al Valenzi's jeep were stupefied, not knowing what they should do in the face of the attack:

We came around this bend. Just before the straightaway, we saw a buzz bomb going overhead. . . . Next thing we knew, we heard gunfire. It was cannon fire. We didn't know where it was coming from, but I saw one of our vehicles get hit. We were still in our jeep, but the next thing you know, hell broke loose. There was gunfire everywhere and machine gunfire. We dove out into a ditch. The first thing that came to my mind was that I had a German pistol. It was a P-38; I had a buckle, belt and stuff. I thought about the parachute too. I was in the ditch. We had good basic training, and went though different courses where you fired weapons, but we really weren't trained to fight. The biggest thing we had was a 50 caliber machine gun.[29]

What now? T/5 Mike Skoda was equally baffled. Where was the fire coming from?

We pulled the convoy off to the right and there was a little ditch we dove into. We pulled out carbines and started firing. . . . Then up this same highway came four or five tanks. . . . We all raised our hands in surrender. Those in the tanks called to us and motioned for us to go down the road 500 yards. We dropped our guns.[30]

T/5 Carl R. Daub of Colebrook, Pennsylvania, was in a two-and-a-half-ton truck, the fourth vehicle in the column. "First thing I noticed were bullets coming through our truck," Daub recalled. The bullets tore through the dark green tarpaulin where he and the others sat riding. Everyone was plenty excited then. Thinking they were being strafed, Daub bolted for the tailgate: "The driver stopped and we jumped out."[31] Yet from the deep ditch, he couldn't locate the source of the gunfire.

T/5 Harold W. Laufer and Pvt. Bobby Werth were with the B Company flash observers in the back of a truck with Carl Daub. "We were laying back there on duffle bags when we came towards the crossroads and they started shooting," Werth remembered. When the bullets ripped through the canvas tarp over their heads, Werth and Daub bounded out. Werth had a German officer's belt and a pistol—big souvenirs—but he got rid of those in a hurry. The two men crouched in the ditch. "But then when the tanks came, well everyone just started walking back."[32]

They were close to a house on the left. Daub, S/Sgt Donald E. Geisler, Pvt. Louis A. Vario, T/5 Charles Haines, T/5 Michael J. Sciranko, and T/5 Harold Laufer ran to the east side of the structure, where a small woodpile stood. The men huddled behind the cordwood as Daub saw Pvt. Al Valenzi fall. "I'm hit!" he called out. Daub yelled from across the street: Did he need help? No, Valenzi replied, he was okay and dragged himself off the middle of road. He could see where the bullets were coming from, he said, taking a few potshots. They were there for about ten minutes when someone called out, "Here comes an American tank." Most of them stood up expectantly. *Damn!* It was a big enemy tank, now firing into the ditch. An enemy figure stood in its turret.

> At first the fellows did not want to put their hands over their heads so [the German] fired a couple of more shots at us. Then, we put our hands over our head. Then I noticed a German point his gun at our Lieutenant Virgil Lary. The Lieutenant was on the other side of the road close by the front of one of the abandoned trucks. The Lieutenant, seeing that he was going to be shot at, jumped behind the truck. When he jumped behind the truck, the German noticed a Captain close by the Lieutenant and when he fired at the Captain, I turned my head and I think I heard him fall in the water.[33]

With that incentive, Daub headed back up the pavement for the crossroads. When he arrived at the intersection he saw two enemy tanks parked there. "In the first tank, I noticed a German with an Iron Cross. He went by me and the second tank searched some of our boys. He leaned out of the tank and took wrist watches and gloves from some of our fellows."[34] Further down the way Daub saw Americans sprawled beside the road. He was unable to tell if they were dead or not. One of them looked to be 2nd Lt. Solomon Goffman, who was lying on top of a Thompson submachine gun.[35]

Then Daub saw one of their own GI trucks being driven off down the road past him to the south and S/Sgt. Eugene Lacey walking the opposite direction under guard. Was Lacy going to drive one of their trucks for the enemy?[36] As the early ones reached the crossroads, one German was asking for volunteers to drive the American trucks off the road. Although many disdainfully ignored the request, Pfc. Harry Horn saw about eight Americans volunteer for the job.[37]

One of these was T/5 Ralph A. Logan, the driver of a two-and-a-half-ton truck who had been midway in the column. After the first German tanks had driven by and signaled everyone to surrender, Logan walked back up to the intersection to find the rest of his buddies standing there with hands held high. "A German came up to the group saying he needed three more drivers to drive our trucks away." Two had already been selected—Sgt. Lacy and Cpl. Bacon. At that point the German asked a man to the right of Logan to drive, but he claimed to be unable. "The German was becoming restless," Logan recalled, so he volunteered.[38] Soon, he and over half a dozen others were moved away from the main group and boarded trucks to drive them south toward Ligneuville. Even while he was at the wheel, a German guard rifled his pockets.

Pandemonium engulfed the long road stretching from the crossroads, with abandoned trucks and over a hundred men cowering in ditches. T/5 Thomas Bacon, Cpl. Carl Stevens, and T/4 John Rupp were in another truck about midway in the column. Their predicament became clear when bullets, like metal hail, began to bang against the steel truck doors. Soon mortar rounds started exploding near the road:

We jumped out of the trucks and into a ditch. They had machine guns shooting at us and I was lying there in a ditch filled with branch water. I fired back with a clip of carbine ammunition until the fellow beside me [Cpl. Carl Stevens] got hit. . . . I started shooting at this machine gun; you could see the tracers coming across. All of a sudden a mortar round fell in front of us and our Sergeant John Rupp yelled, "Bacon, get your head down. You wanna get killed?" A few minutes later the Germans approached from our left: "Drop your guns and surrender." Bruce Summers, George Rosenfeld were there. George kept saying, "Somebody get into my truck and get those rifle grenades out." But nobody was stupid enough to do that. We surrendered. We were walking down the line. I said to a guy who was next to me wounded in the shoulder [Cpl. Carl Stevens], "How is it?" "It hurts like hell," he told me. "We'll get a stretcher out of that truck up ahead." And a German guy came by with his machine gun and he a said, "Chauffeur! Chauffeur!" I told him "Stretcher! Stretcher!" motioning to the first aid truck up ahead. You go on back that away he told me and come with me. He motioned the others back to the crossroads. And when we got to the truck, the German said, "You get in the truck and drive." I realized that we had confused "Stretcher" and "Chauffeur" but I wasn't able to argue—he had a burp gun. He and I went on down the road and we got in line with a couple of tanks. I was going down the road with him.[39]

Tom Bacon, who drove on toward Ligneuville, never knew what happened to the others sent back to the crossroads, but he was plenty worried about his own predicament. Things took a turn for the worse when he and ten other impressed drivers were ordered to stop and line up single-file by the road. They were only assembled for a short time when another Waffen SS trooper appeared, waving a pistol as he paced back and forth. "He stated that he was going to shoot us because our airplanes were bombing his family and his people." He looked even more perturbed when a captain in the American party flatly informed the young German youth that "we were to be treated as prisoners." Then an ominous development: "in the distance I heard the firing of machine guns."[40] *What's going on?*

The agitated SS-man settled down, and Logan found himself, Lacey, and Bacon driven by the Germans on into Ligneuville. There they were locked up inside the Hotel du Moulin with other American captives. The next day he and the others there were marched back toward Germany as prisoners—but only after learning that other Americans had been shot in cold blood in Ligneuville.

What of the others in the convoy, stopped closer to the intersection? About fifty yards south of the Five Points intersection, B-24, the three-quarter-ton weapons carrier driven by T/5 Alan M. Lucas with several riders, including Pvt. Robert Smith and T/5 Ted Paluch, suddenly screeched to a halt. At first no one knew why. Paluch and Smith later remembered that the U.S. trucks seemed to pull off toward the right shoulder of the road.

A German buzz bomb growled overhead, which Smith pointed out to the mess truck just behind them. Then there was gunfire—a lot of it. "As soon as we heard them shoot, we jumped out of the truck." Smith and the others threw themselves into the waist-deep ditch on the west side of the N-23. Paluch was dismayed to find the ditch filled with icy water, but they lay down in the cold muck just the same. *Where was the shooting coming from?* he wondered.[41] "I had never seen so many tracers in my life!"

Two vehicles south of Paluch and Smith, T/5 Charles F. Appman of Verona, Pennsylvania, was driving another three-quarter-ton weapons carrier with no roof—just a windshield—hardly comfortable in the freezing weather.[42] "After my vehicle passed the road junction, the column was fired on by tanks on the road coming in from the east." At first, the artillery surveyor thought the shooting was friendly fire directed at the buzz bomb passing overhead. Like many others in recent days, it toiled noisily overhead from the southeast. Then he saw a surprising sight: "I could see tracer bullets going over the hood of my truck."

> I heard machine gun bullets coming by pretty close and I stopped my vehicle. The boys in the back of my truck hollered for me to stop, which I did. We all dove into the ditch on the right side of the road where we continued to receive machine gun fire and a few mortar shells.[43]

Like Smith and Paluch, Appman and his three other buddies, Pvt. James P. Mattera, T/5 James Luers, and Cpl. Carl Rullman, crouched in the muddy ditch as glowing tracer rounds whizzed overhead. They hastily tore up orders, letters, and personal effects. Elbow deep in the ditch water, they began to try crawling toward the end of the convoy. Maybe, Appman thought, they could escape.[44] Some did—at least temporarily.

At the very rear of the column was T/5 Charles Haines, driving a weapons carrier behind the kitchen truck. Along with him were T/5 Harold Billow, T/5 John A. O'Connell, and T/5 Charles Reding—

a man who had just recently come to the 285th. As the caboose of the convoy, they had the job of removing the route markers as the little company motored along. "I was in the next to the last vehicle in the column," Billow remembered, "when I happened to look ahead and saw everyone leaving their trucks and taking cover to protect themselves from the machine gunfire that the leading German tank was pouring into us."[45] John O'Connell, a twenty-one-year-old from Kansas City, was there too. "After showing approximately fourteen vehicles of my battery the route, I noticed a tank rumbling down the road coming from the left fork. Looking at the tank, I noticed it was German. . . . Simultaneously the tank opened fire with machine guns and other types of weapons. Everyone took cover."[46]

Just behind Appman was Joseph Brozowski, driving himself and Pfc. Paul J. Martin in a three-quarter-ton truck. Surprised by what Martin saw as a German armored ambush, he had no choice but to come out with hands up. Soon they were motioned back to the intersection along with everyone else, where they remained for what he estimated was half an hour. The Waffen SS men then moved them from the intersection into a field just south of the café and assembled them, with their hands up, in lines about twenty-five yards from the road. Most thought they were waiting for enemy trucks to haul them off as prisoners. "While some of the Germans kept us covered by small arms and machine guns on halftracks, other Germans moved among us, taking gloves and watches."[47] Meanwhile, the SS men added more American prisoners to the growing mass—Martin estimated some 160—including medics, MPs, and artillerymen. Then a strange sight:

> While we stood there an American colonel and his driver came along in a jeep. They were captured. The American driver was then put in the back of the jeep and then a German driver drove the jeep carrying the American colonel and the driver down the road towards St. Vith.

Pvt. John Kailer with Pvt. Ralph Law as well as six other men led by Sgt. Alfred Kinsman were midway in the column. At the first sound of shooting, they were in the ditch, too, but hauled out carbines. "We were pinned down there for about fifteen minutes," Kailer remembered. "We

just shoved our rifles up over the hedgerow and fired haphazardly."
They heard a lot of noise coming from the north and east. "Here comes
this column of armor with machine guns, 88s and everything pointed
into the ditch—the Germans shouting for us to come up. With all that
stuff—and us [just] with carbines, we could do nothing but surrender.
We stood up in the ditch with our arms overhead."48 They left their
weapons at their feet as several tanks and halftracks passed by.

Then the Germans approached the gathering American prisoners,
looking for able drivers. "They pulled out their pistols and started
threatening everybody. They finally got enough drivers to drive our vehicles." Kailer saw T/5 David Lucas driving one of the trucks down
south just before the Germans shoved everyone back across a fence until they were south of the café by the intersection. Kailer took close
note of his captors. "The officers and men were exceptionally good
looking," he thought, noting the lightning flashes of the SS on their
shoulders. "It was not a bunch just thrown together. They seemed to
know their business."

A new man to the battery, Charles Reding was aghast at the situation. His truck had stopped right by the intersection. He too had seen
the buzz bomb and thought he heard guns firing at it, but when the enemy robot plane flew away and the firing continued, he knew something was wrong. Peering ahead along the road, he could see the head
of their column being fired on. Reding turned to Harold Billow. "Man,
those are panzer tanks up ahead," he exclaimed. "Let's turn the truck
around and get the hell out of here!"49

Reding watched John O'Connell firing at the tank with a carbine.
What was he thinking? In spite of Reding's suggestion to bug out, Billow
said they would have to go up front to help. A Louisiana southern
boy—strong on "walking sense"—Reding thought that was stupid
("Better a live coward than a dead hero"), but he obeyed.

As they walked up toward the crossroads Reding saw that the enemy
was already there. Approaching, he could hear a German soldier shouting, "Americans surrender! Surrender!" Reding's heart raced, his gut in-
stinct was to flee. "Let's get the hell out of here!" he said. Quickly, he,
Billow, and eight others ran to the back of the café to hide.50 O'Connell
was right behind them. He and T/4 Selmer Leu from the mess truck,
not knowing it was a café, sought in vain to find a cellar in the building.

Instead, they crouched down in the structure's shadow near a hedgerow to its rear, trying to make themselves small. "We lay quietly hoping that the German armor would go past without capturing us."[51]

Just ahead of Haines and the kitchen detail was Pvt. Ralph W. Law, who was driving a two-and-a-half-ton truck under the command of Sgt. Alfred Kinsman. Pvt. John Kailer was in the back of the vehicle along with five others. Kinsman was sitting right across from Law in the cab when direct fire and machine guns engulfed them. "Sgt. Kinsman ordered me to stop the truck and for all to take cover," Law recalled. At first there were no German soldiers by them as the first enemy tanks passed by. "We all ran to a barn on the right side of the road and took cover behind some hay there," Law recounted. That building—more a shed than a barn—behind the Café Bodarwe served as a magnet for Americans looking to evade capture. Eventually it included military policeman Homer Ford, Harold Billow, James O'Connell, Haines, and the six men from the kitchen truck who took refuge inside—at least until they were discovered.[52]

Watching from that place, Ford was surprised at what he saw next: "The woman on the corner must be in good with the Germans," he said of the café owner. "As soon as they came by, she walked out and shook hands with them and gave them something to eat."[53] The woman was Madame Adele Bodarwe. Ted Paluch saw the same thing." She hoisted a basket up to the tank. A guy came down and picked it up."[54]

Rousted from the ditch, Al Valenzi, Ahrens, and the others prepared to walk back up the road from the head of the column with their hands up:

The next thing you know, this German halftrack pulled up beside us as we stood there. There was a German officer in the front and he leaned over and asked me if I could drive. "Can you drive?" he asked me in English. "No, I don't drive." He was a good looking man; clean looking. Then he reached over and pulled off this M-1 ammo bandolier on my shoulder. "You won't be needing this anymore," he told me. His English was clear. I'll never forget that as long as I live. He wasn't wearing a helmet; I had one of these tankers caps on from the recon outfits. There were just two or three of us standing in this small group. . . . I know they took Sgt.

Lacey and another fellow. They left me alone and I crossed the road with Kenny and we could see down the line that they were walking us back towards the intersection. Then they started to search everybody. I worried about that 9mm ammunition I had on me. We were getting closer and closer and closer to them. They came to me and stopped. I was worried. Finally, they started herding us into this field on the left-hand side of the field. I looked around for Mike, but didn't see him. I was still with Kenny and they herded us in there. He was a little behind him in this line up. We were just a big crowd of men standing. I know that a tank started to move up.[55]

In the halftrack that stopped to take Valenzi's ammunition was none other than Jochen Peiper—almost certainly the officer who spoke to him in English.[56] Ken Ahrens saw the same thing.[57]

Charles Appman also emerged from the ditch. Two tanks and a halftrack appeared and then headed down the road to the south. A couple of vehicles behind Appman was Cpl. George Fox's two-and-a-half-ton truck, driven by Pfc. Warren Davis. T/5 Carl Moucheron and two other privates, Robert Cohen and Frederick Clark, rode along in the vehicle's uncovered rear. Like everyone else, Fox and the rest of the crew jumped out of the truck when the Germans fired on them, and they took refuge on the right side of the road. They kept chins down as glowing tracers zipped overhead.[58] "I had my gun, but we couldn't see where the shots were coming from."[59]

Eventually, Fox could see tanks approaching the intersection from the east. At first he thought they were American tanks, but that hope evaporated. Fox didn't know it, but the first vehicle was the Mk IV panzer of Werner Sternebeck.

I saw the lead tank in this column enter the intersection, turn to its left and head for us. I saw that it had wide tracks and was a German tank. . . . When it reached a point about half way between the intersection and where we were, we stood up and raised our arms in surrender. . . . Lt. Lary called out for us to surrender too, but we didn't need him to know that. We had carbines; they had tanks.[60]

The Germans had motioned for them to surrender, so the men threw down their guns. "I am sure that Cohen, Moucheron and Davis, who were walking abreast of me had their hands up."[61] But Fox could not see Clark, who was to his left rear. "Just at this instant a burst of machine gunfire was directed at us from the lead tank," he recalled. "Clark was hit in the chest and fell to the ground. I glanced back and it seemed to me that he had been killed instantly."[62]

Had Clark been trying to get away? Fox would never know. "The heads of a couple of German soldiers were protruding from the turret of this tank and they motioned us to go up the road in the direction of the intersection and the tank continued moving southwardly." After that nearly fatal brush, Fox and those with him toed the line. Hands held high, the men marched obediently back up the road. Near the intersection the Waffen SS men assembled Fox and the others with the larger group, searched them, and ordered them across a fence into a field on the west side of the road.

As they walked along grenadiers in approaching halftracks eagerly pilfered everyone's possessions. They had taken Mike Skoda's wristwatch, paybook, and even his dog tags,[63] but then a German youth reached for his gold wedding ring. "No!" Skoda snapped his fist closed, "*Frau*—my wife!"[64] They let him go, motioning Skoda and others back to the crossroads. Like the others, he was told to cross a three-strand barbed-wire fence into a field south of the café, where others now assembled.

By the side of the road George Fox saw half a dozen German halftracks and tanks lined up. Just behind Fox, in a two-and-a-half-ton truck, the 22nd vehicle in the column, was T/5 William B. "Bruce" Summers, T/5 George Rosenfeld, and Pvt. Samuel Hallman:

We came down through Malmédy and came up to the top of the hill and started back out and I heard some machine gun fire from some place else. I noticed further up the column that people were getting off the truck and I looked and here coming down the road was a tank. They were shooting and some were waving and yelling, 'Don't shoot, it's us!' But I could see the big flash protector on the end of the barrel of the tank and I knew it wasn't one of ours. I then knew we were in bad trouble. We never dreamed that the Germans could be out there. Then everybody started getting off the trucks and getting down into the ditches for protection. . . . But just as soon as we got down in the ditch well, word came from up at the head of the column that we were to surrender.[65]

At the center of the column was Mario "Boots" Butera, who was driving a three-quarter-ton truck with Sgt. Eugene Lacey and 1st. Lt. Perry Reardon. All of the men jumped out of the truck when the shooting started. "Tanks!" someone yelled. They crouched in the road-side culvert. "We might as well give up," Reardon sighed.[66] From his pocket Butera handed Lacey a white handkerchief, which he tied to his carbine to begin to wave the sign of universal military capitulation. The enemy ceased fire and the men watched the advance of two Mk IV tanks.[67] "As they approached us," Butera recalled, "the occupants motioned us to come forward with our arms upraised."

Soon the enemy tanks passed as they continued peeling up Americans from the ditches. Butera saw a single German soldier bearing a rifle and guarding the group of Americans now gathering. Butera did not know it, but the enemy soldier was likely an SS enlisted man named Gerhard Walla.[68] More vehicles continued to arrive. Later a German officer approached to issue orders to the increasing number of infantry guards. Soon Butera and the other GIs were forced to move from the road to a field on the west side of the road after crossing a four-foot barbed-wire fence. "After we were in the pasture, I noticed a civilian come from one of the houses . . . and he walked up to a German soldier and spoke to him. He handed over something to the soldier. I don't know what it was."[69]

Two tanks then came along the road and strafed the ditch with machine gun fire. We raised our hands and we were motioned to get out on the street. . . . As the tanks would come by, they would stop and call to us individually and relieve us of our wrist watches and gloves—the fur ones. . . . I heard one of our soldiers make the remark, "That's the SS men for you."[70]

After that the Germans would "laugh and drive on." Charles Appman reckoned that he was left in the road for about minute or two after the first tanks and the lone halftrack were gone when another group of fifteen tanks and SPWs (he estimated nine tanks and half a dozen half-tracks) arrived, including one bearing "a big fellow with an orange colored or yellow jacket who stood in his vehicle and said something I did not understand. He motioned with his hands and almost immediately we were herded into the field by some German soldiers with rifles."[71] The SS officer (who was almost certainly Josef Diefenthal), turned away from the Americans, gesturing with his left hand toward them while shouting loudly at the guards. The hand motion seemed to be the universal dismissal—*Get lost* or *Get them out of here.*

Whatever he said, the flick of his wrist seemed an immediate cue to get the Americans off the road. The captive GIs moved awkwardly with their aching arms held high or hands clasped on their heads. The half-track bearing the big German in the yellow jacket—and Jochen Peiper too—drove off to the south.

While the Americans climbed over the fence and into the field, Appman noticed that two tanks and several halftracks had moved up across from them. The American prisoners stood there for about five minutes. One German in particular worried Appman. He was carefully loading a machine gun. "I saw soldiers getting a lot of ammunition and putting it near their machine guns. I didn't imagine they would need all of that just to guard us."[72] Appman stared intently at the SS man; he couldn't take his eyes away. He wanted to say something to the GIs standing by him, but the words died on his tongue.

Was this really happening?

CHAPTER 5

"Those Beautiful Trucks . . . "

Square-jawed with a stern face and piercing blue eyes, underscored by a cleft chin, Werner Poetschke was a fearful character. Within the extraordinarily rugged SS officers' corps that made up Jochen Peiper's tank regiment in the fall of 1944, Poetschke was extreme. Even though he had extensive experience in tank leadership with the Leibstandarte Adolf Hitler, Poetschke was a hothead: volatile, unpredictable—a loose cannon. Poetschke demanded absolute dedication in battle from those under him. Punishment could equal death. And for the enemy he expressed only bald contempt. "My backside would shake whenever I was around him," one enlisted man remembered.[1]

Born in Brussels in 1914, he had grown up, like Peiper, in Berlin. At the time of the Ardennes operation, the thirty-year-old's SS-major rank was just under that of Lt. Col. Jochen Peiper. Of course in the Waffen SS, that was *all* the difference. They were both SS officers, but beyond that there was officially no question as to who was in charge. On the surface Peiper and Poetschke got on well enough, but friction brewed just underneath.

Jochen Peiper was the snobbish, well-connected adjutant of Heinrich Himmler. But more than his poster-boy-hero status, there were other matters contemptible to the old tank hands. For one, Peiper was often away from the front—particularly, it seemed, when the going got rough. Why was he always ill—and sent home? Was it just the endless cigarettes, coffee, and insomnia-laced escapades? In truth, Peiper's experience leading the panzer regiment in action had been limited. In January 1944 he had overseen the at-times brilliant but ultimately destructive commitment of his tank regiment in Russia. Later in August in Normandy, after months away, he suffered "a heart attack" just before the suicidal blitz of *Operation Lüttich* toward Avranches.[2] After Peiper was evacuated, Poetschke took over and survived the death ride that followed. Then, too, Peiper continued to ally himself closely with his old half-tracked SPW battalion, now under SS-Capt. Josef "Jupp" Diefenthal. Whispered complaints told of how most of his recommendations for medals went to the SPW people rather than the panzer men now under him. The SPW battalion was his old command—his old allegiance.

Werner Poetschke, however, held the reins fast and knew the tanks; he was the epitome of the tough and fearless nihilistic SS warrior. No one would accuse the SS leader of lacking nerve, but as even his superiors saw it, his bravery fell under that questionable umbrella of a fool's courage. Whereas Peiper seemed properly Prussian and reserved, Poetschke would emote those things that most felt better unspoken.

Certainly, his subordinates greatly feared him. Poetschke tolerated no breach of loyalty or response to orders or even simple omissions of proper dress or salute.[3] Just a minor slip might produce extreme repercussions. And the man was unstable; the smallest thing could set him off. One stumble and an offender might end up on the point of the next bold attack—a misstep that could easily mean death. Yet Poetschke had a Janus-like aspect to his character. At times he was amicable: fighting and training hard but willing to join the other regiment officers in local-tavern drinking binges during the autumn of 1944.

His early career evaluations revealed trepidation from superiors. From 1935 to 1937 he had been with the Leibstandarte, and this is where Peiper knew him. Yet within the troop he was not well liked, as he was known as a loner with a cruel streak that made few friends. Perhaps reflecting his low popularity, Poetschke spent two years as an SS 2nd Lieutenant when promotions should have come sooner. He received the Iron Cross first class in Poland and, in 1940, was cited

for extraordinary bravery during the French campaign, where his reconnaissance troop found an intact bridge across the Meuse-Waal
canal. There, he had boldly charged across the span to the other side
of the river, firing wildly from a motorcycle to bring back a score of
prisoners. The capture of the bridge was decisive, but that was not all.
Soon thereafter he had single-handedly shot down an entire enemy
motorcycle unit and six antitank cannons near the French hamlet of
Dissen. Yet for that feat—one that would generally have earned the
Knight's Cross—Poetschke only was recommended for a long over-
due promotion.[4]

His evaluation later that fall was poor. "He is a very uneven character," wrote his superior. "Again and again he does things his own way
and without authority. While at times he does extraordinary things
with the reconnaissance troops, at other turns, he launches off into
wild escapades with unclear messages and without any result. He has
his own arbitrary rules and makes no friends or comrades. . . . He
misses the necessary experience of how to treat his men." In fact, his
behavior was so extreme that Werner Poetschke was transferred from
the Leibstandarte to another Waffen SS formation: Das Reich.

Later, although the SS leader had earned the German Cross in Gold
for feats of wanton daredevilry in Russia during the summer invasion
of 1941, it became clear that, there too, he was unwanted. In April 1943
he transferred back from Das Reich to the Leibstandarte—a highly unusual move.

Even so, under Peiper's tutelage, Poetschke's evaluations turned
more favorable. Was it because Peiper relished wild ones like Werner
Wolff and Georg Preuss, or was it Poetschke's death-wish bravery?
Even the man's frivolity was unpredictable. "I never knew which Poetschke I would encounter," one said. Indeed, in the winter battles of
early 1944 the new tank leader was wounded three times in fierce fighting. These actions culminated in Peiper's nomination of Poetschke for
a Knight's Cross for the brutal combat fought near Davidkowce on the
first day of April 1944. There—while Peiper was recovering at home—
Poetschke fought off a massive Russian assault with two Panthers and
forty grenadiers followed by a counterattack so reckless and savage that
the surviving enemy fled in panic. No quarter was given; for 156 enemy killed in the action, there were only 2 prisoners. Yet contempt was

not reserved only for the enemy; Poetschke's abuse of those under him was officially underscored in 1944 when a military court investigated him for "unnecessarily severe punishment of his men" in actions at Kharkov.[5]

How did Peiper view him? "He had arguments with Poetschke," subordinate SS-Cpl. Günther Boese told Allied captors, "because he was too strict with his men."[6] Boese was in the staff company of 1st SS Panzer Battalion those weeks before the Ardennes Operation. "An excellent soldier," he said, "but a son of a bitch of the very first order due to his behavior. . . . He knew no consideration of his men and drove them into slaughter." Frequently, according to Boese, Poetschke forced his men ahead at pistol point and often threatened enlisted men for even the smallest infractions; Boese himself was punished for being AWOL from Berlin even though he had a written excuse. No matter, the condemned would spend time with SS-1st Lt. Erich Rumpf's engineer company of the panzer regiment, which "had become a punishment platoon—a *Strafzug*." Now Boese could dig for mines under enemy fire.

Poetschke had even less patience with civilians. According to SS-Cpl. Boese, during the retreat in Russia between Korostenka and Zhitomir in early February 1944, Poetschke ordered two natives he suspected as partisans shot on the spot. And in August 1944, during the retreat from Normandy in the neighborhood of Ranes between Falaise and Argentan, Poetschke executed a Frenchman found carrying a rifle. Poetschke encouraged a ruthless reaction from those under him to any resistance from the local civilian populace. For instance, that August, with the Americans approaching Paris, when SS-Lt. Hans Hennecke was suddenly fired upon from several windows above the street while driving through the city in an SPW, instead of returning the fire, Hennecke supposedly swiveled an MG-42 to shoot down several pedestrians lining the Parisian street. SS-Cpl. Boese, who witnessed this from a following SPW, was present when Hennecke reported to Poetschke, telling him, "I shot a lot of ammunition into the French." Both men laughed.[7]

Now, Werner Poetschke was leading Peiper's 1st SS Panzer Battalion in the Ardennes. On the morning of the second day of the German offensive he possessed orders to stop at nothing to reach the Meuse River.

Indeed, no delay could be tolerated—nothing was to hold them up. Peiper had made that clear with his cavalry-like charge from Büllingen. For Peiper, that roaming style of warfare "was an everyday event"—he was famous for it.[8] Any captured enemy was a liability to such warfare. Peiper said, "In the course of many other breakthroughs we really had nothing to do with prisoners of war. . . . We were driving at great speed and firing from all barrels. We penetrated the soft spots of the enemy like an arrow and the infantry which followed collected the prisoners of war." Peiper described his mission as it pertained to prisoners of war:

> The prisoner of war responsibility was a particularly severe one in the course of this mission. My tasks were of a purely tactical nature and I myself considered it my first duty to be present at the point at all times in order to speed matters up and in order to attempt to achieve some surprises in spite of the great delays of time which occurred at the beginning. . . .
>
>   During the whole mission prisoners did not interest me at any time. In the meeting of my commanders and officers in Blankenheim, I expressly told them that I was not a bit interested in prisoners of war and that the only important matter, as far as we were concerned, was to break through fanatically at maximum speed and that anything which in the course of our breakthrough would remain lying in the ditches, be it prisoners of war or material or tools of war, that they would later be picked up by the infantry following us.[9]

When the Baugnez crossroads was reached at 1 P.M., Peiper said he was between Ondenval and Thirimont on an American jeep seeing what he could learn by interrogating a captured American lieutenant colonel.[10] At the time, Peiper was out of radio contact:

> About this time, I suddenly heard my cannons and machine guns open fire. I therefore realized that the point had hit the main road from Malmédy to Petit Thier and, since at that moment, I was alone with the jeep driver, I drove off to the point in the jeep. The column was behind me since the piece of road between this road fork and Moderscheid was exceptionally difficult. About one kilometer east of the town of Baugnez, I met my armored

spearhead. About five tanks and the same number of halftracks were standing in front of me and they were shooting with all their weapons at their disposal . . . at a range of about 500 meters. . . . At that time myself, I saw an American truck convoy. . . . The column attempted to break down in a southerly direction at great speed.[11]

Peiper transferred to the SPW of Josef Diefenthal. Just minutes before, SS-1st Lt. Werner Sternebeck and M/Sgt. August Tonk in the *Panzerspitze* (tank spearhead) had run into the Americans with two Panzer IVs and a halftrack, shooting up the trucks and dashing past the startled American soldiers.[12] Although the mere threat of dark, hulking tanks with long guns sent American hands reaching in surrender, Sternebeck hardly paused.

Tonk, driving just behind Sternebeck in Panzer Nr. 623, was befuddled. What to do with all these prisoners? As they moved ahead, the American soldiers jumped from the now-stationary trucks into the ditches. The spearhead now had only two tanks. Meantime, Sternebeck did not even stop at the crossroads but rather sped along, painfully aware that he was alone up ahead. The other tanks had not come with him; the SPWs of Rudolf Dörr and Karl Wemmel, originally assigned to the point, were now behind, having been shot up or broken down after leaving Büllingen.[13] Other than Tonk, Sternebeck had only a halftrack load of the 2nd squad of Rumpf's engineers under SS-Cpl. Karl Ohlrogge in his wake.[14]

Right away Sternebeck was on the radio to Tonk. "August, follow up!"[15] Later Sternebeck would claim he had seen a German man at the crossroads guarding the prisoners when he left. That was likely a hapless messenger, SS-Cpl. Gerhard Walla. He also remembered that Tonk, behind him, had turned over the Americans to the advance guard panzer element just behind him. An SS-Sgt. named Manfred Thorn drove the lead tank of the advance guard—the *Vorhut*, or vanguard.[16]

Indeed, the only other element along with Sternebeck's tiny *Spitze* was an ill-fated *Schwimmwagen*—the amphibious jeep—of SS messenger Gerhard Walla. When Walla pulled around the corner at the crossroads, within a few moments, he claimed, he was greeted with a gust of rifle fire from the American column. Totally surprised, his *Schwimmer* lurched into the ditch, with a front tire of his amphibious jeep then

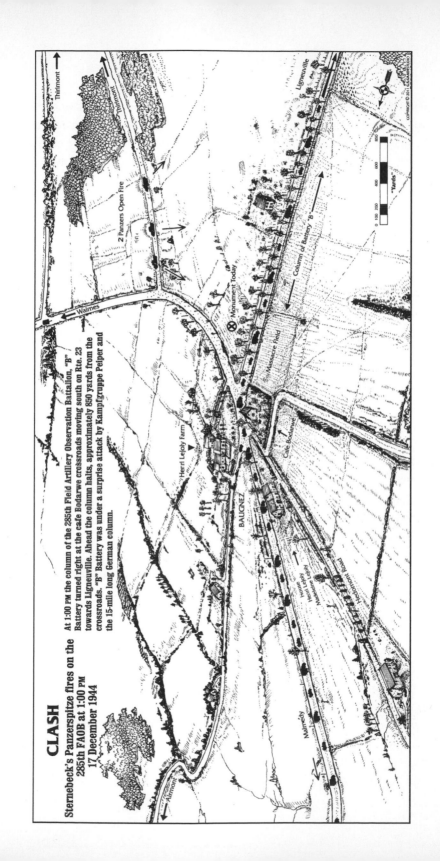

CLASH

Sternebeck's Panzerspitze fires on the 285th FAOB at 1:00 PM
17 December 1944

At 1:00 PM the column of the 285th Field Artillery Observation Battalion, "B" Battery turned right at the cafe Bodarwe crossroads moving south on Rte. 23 towards Ligneuville. Ahead the column halts, approximately 850 yards from the crossroads. "B" Battery was under a surprise attack by Kampfgruppe Peiper and the 15-mile long German column.

Thirimont

Thirimont

2 Panzers Open Fire

Walmes

Monument Today

Ligneuville

Column of Battery "B"

Massacre Field

Cafe Bodarwe

Henri Lejoly Farm

BAUGNEZ

Road

Henri Lejoly
Henri Lejoly
Madame Lejoly

Almont

Malmedy

0 100 200   400   600   800

"Yards"

COPYRIGHT © 2011 E4 CAMPI STUDIO

smashed and twisted. His head whirled. Sternebeck was somewhere ahead. Luckily, the lumbering advance of August Tonk's tank down the road now seemed to quell resistance from the enemy column. Walla crawled out of the ditch only to find that the tanks were gone—now there were just some SPWs passing by. He was all alone with the dozens of Americans now crawling out of their trucks and jeeps.[17] He was outnumbered—and how! They had their hands over their heads but were milling about. Walla felt uneasy, but he sidled up to the café to be greeted by its owner, Adele Bodarwe, who had something for him. It was a welcome bottle of schnapps.[18] "I had no orders to deal with prisoners," Walla recalled. "We left each other alone!" Soon, however, additional German tanks drew near his uneasy outpost.

It was the panzer battalion vanguard—the main body of the tanks. Peiper himself was now very close to the point of Poetschke's tank spearhead not far from the intersection of the road from Thirimont to Waimes. "About five tanks and about the same number of half tracks were standing in front of me and they were shooting with all weapons . . . in a southwesterly direction at a range of about 500 meters. . . . At that time I myself saw the American truck convoy. It might have been 1300 hours."

> I gave an order to cease fire several times, since I was annoyed at having my armored spearhead held up, in view of the fact that we had lost so much time already. Furthermore, I was annoyed at having those beautiful trucks, which we needed so badly, all shot up. It might have taken two more minutes until I was understood everywhere. I, thereupon, loudly ordered them to continue to drive on at great speed.

SS-Sgt. Erich Maute, a medic in the SPW of Rudolf Dörr, was supposed to be right up with Werner Sternebeck and the Spitze, but he had fallen behind amidst the artillery chaos on the streets of Büllingen.[19] Instead, his SPW and one other were now sandwiched between the Spitze—which was only two tanks, a halftrack loaded with pioneers, and an amphibious jeep—and the main body of the tank spearhead. Just ahead was a Wirbelwind flak panzer commanded by SS-Sgt. Paul Schroeder. Behind them were Mk IV tanks—the 7th Panzer Company.

After they stopped, Maute pulled out his rifle and joined in pelting the American trucks with gunfire. As he and the others banged away, Maute noted that some SPWs, including those of SS-Lt. Günther Hering and Erich Rumpf were wriggling by them so as to move ahead on the crowded road. Jochen Peiper was in the backseat of one of the halftracks.

Peiper drove up to the Panther of Werner Poetschke, which was now at the crossroads intersection. Through Poetschke, he could finally communicate by radio.

> I then mounted the vehicle of Major Poetschke and ordered him to send a radio message to the Division, since I did not have any communications of my own. He was to report that the enemy was leaving Malmédy and was retreating to the south and southwest, and that we had reached the main road south of Malmédy . . . I then mounted Diefenthal's vehicle and followed the vehicles we had already proceeded to move to the crossroads. The road [leading south of Malmédy] between the crossroads at the beginning of the forest was pretty well blocked by the American vehicles. And a Panther was right in front of me and it was pushing the shot American vehicles into the ditches by alternately moving to the left and the right. I myself, with the vehicles, followed at a speed no faster than walking. At that time I saw a large number of Americans.[20]

Peiper's memory of his encounter with Poetschke was self-serving and muted. In truth, when he reached the crossroads his temper boiled like fire. By then Poetschke had already reached Baugnez with his own Panther Nr. 151, although evidently he had damaged his tank in some fashion. When his adjutant, Arndt Fischer, in Panzer Nr. 152 arrived just behind him, he saw a Panther already by the café that had tried to take the turn too sharply or some other ill-advised maneuver; it had track damage. Just then Peiper showed up in Diefenthal's SPW, "springing up out of its cab to shout to the commander of the Panther."[21] Only then did Fischer, with a tanker's typical slit-vision myopia, realize that in the Panther was none other than his commander's, Werner Poetschke!

From the appearance of the American column, showing signs of having been pummeled by shot and shell, Werner Sternebeck and

August Tonk had already passed by. Some of the GMC trucks looked like pepper pots. Where was the *Spitze* now? And here again, the tanks of the vanguard 7th Company had been shooting. Peiper screamed. With enough Waffen SS vitriol, the shooting stopped.

Poetschke and Fischer had parked their tanks at the crossroads. The only other German there was SS-Cpl. Gerhard Walla (and likely SS-Lt. Kurt Kramm) in an amphibious *Schwimmwagen*, the sole remaining throwback of the Sternebeck party. Peiper had driven past the six Mk IV tanks of the lead elements of the 7th Panzer Company that had been firing like mad into the American column. The first rounds had been fired from Panzer Nr. 734 at the head column, commanded by SS-Sgt. Horst Pilarzek and driven by SS-Sgt. Manfred Thorn. This was one of the tanks spouting the offending fire that Peiper remanded.[22]

Normally, Panzer Nr. 702 under SS-Sgt. Heinz Schraeder would have been in the lead of the company, with Nr. 701 under SS-Capt. Oskar Klingelhoefer following right behind. Having the company commander to occupy the lead tank was never standard procedure.[23] But the gooey road leading out of Thirimont had slowed Schraeder as well as Siptrott, the 3rd platoon commander. Seeking a shortcut, most of the tanks had tested the muddy rut that led off to Ligneuville directly from Thirimont—all turned back. Now the lead of the entire spearhead fell to Pilarzek's Panzer 734, driven by Thorn.

> [Siptrott's] tank tracks and wheels were so full of mud that he had to unhook it and clean it up. I drove to where Hans Siptrott had stopped in the forest and asked him what the trouble was. Hans told me "You take over the *Spitze*." He was busy with his tank track, which was going to take some time. So in taking over the *Spitze*, I received the order to drive in the direction of Bagatelle. Everything came over the radio from the company chief "Go from Thirimont to Bagatelle." At the point where there are trees on both sides of the road . . . about 500 meters before Bagatelle on the right-hand side of the road. At this point, Pilarzek became nervous.[24]

"There are the Americans, Manfred!" he called down. "What should we do?" If that seemed uncharacteristic for a panzer man,

Pilarzek was short on tanker experience, having just come from another unit. "I don't know much about this," he confided.

"Okay, I'll take over," Thorn agreed, "but you stay where you are
and I'll drive." Pilarzek nodded as Thorn continued. On the road they
were facing just to the west—the main road from Malmédy—Pilarzek
could see a long column of American vehicles approaching. Thorn
barked at the gunner, Werner Löhmann. "Explosive shells at 900 meters. . . . Fire when ready!"[25] The tank shook as each 75mm shell burst
from the muzzle brake.

Thorn could hear Klingelhoefer's tank, Nr. 701, firing too. Driven
by Rolf Ehrhardt, it was just behind him. Even further back in the column, Hans Siptrott in Nr. 731 hustled to catch up and join the firing as
well. "Shortly before coming to the main road, I saw the American vehicles in the distance," he recalled, "and fired two rounds with my cannon on them."[26] In a few short moments they had broadsided both the
first and second American trucks nearly several hundred yards south
of the crossroads. One was burning. The entire American column
halted. "We stopped firing," Thorn added. "I continued my driving
faster than before to get to the intersection as rapidly as possible. When
I came to the main road, I saw five SPWs of our troops coming from
Waimes. They waited for me to pass."[27]

> As I was driving to the crossroads from Bagatelle, I received the
> orders from Peiper over the radio to cease firing at the column for
> the simple reason that this would warn the American officers who
> might be in Engelsdorf [Ligneuville]. Peiper had drawn up close
> behind us. He wanted to get his hands on those trucks as well.
> I headed from Bagatelle in the direction of the Café Bodarwe.
> I drove onto the café at which point the stopped American column
> was about 500 meters long. Many of the Americans were still in
> their vehicles—particularly those in the rear part of the column.
> We had only destroyed the first two trucks. So I stopped in the
> middle of the crossing."[28]

Drawing up beside the café, Thorn saw Americans still sitting in
their trucks with a jeep facing Engelsdorf. He motioned for the men in
the trucks to dismount and surrender. A minute went by. Suddenly a

big Panther tank pulled up alongside, parallel to Thorn's Panzer IV. Dejected American prisoners were dismounting their trucks and lining up in front of the café. Out of the turret popped Werner Poetschke.

"Drive as quickly as you can in the direction of Engelsdorf," he called out to Thorn, "and make contact with Sternebeck."[29] With that, Thorn suddenly realized that he wasn't the first vehicle in the assault. Glancing about, it was obvious that other trucks had been shot up in addition to those he had just fired upon: "There were vehicles everywhere and some of the engines of the American trucks were still running." The missing *Spitze* was *somewhere* ahead.

Thorn obediently drove off to the south, clanking by more Americans treading back toward the crossroads. Some SPWs pulled next to the trucks, and Thorn watched as his comrades eagerly pilfered each. That seemed understandable, as they were all low on food. As his Panzer IV rolled past the long line of American vehicles, Thorn and his crew decided to get theirs too. One American truck seemed to brim with provisions. Manfred slowed down and sent radioman Willi Richter to get what he could—cigarettes, food, and chocolate. Only then did he see that there were American soldiers lying in the ditches.

Just behind Thorn's panzer was Company Chief Oskar Klingelhoefer's tank, driven by Rolf Ehrhardt. The tank company had fired five or six shots at the trucks before Peiper demanded for everyone to stop. As Ehrhardt approached the crossroads behind Pilarzek, he saw Americans standing by the path near the café. "At the crossing before Engelsdorf," Ehrhardt recalled, "I saw a total of 25 to 35 prisoners with raised hands who stood partly by the trees immediately before the right of the field and partly to the left at the first house following the crossing [the café]. A few of our infantrymen were with them." Ehrhardt also pulled up beside the panzer battalion leader's Panther at the crossroads. "Poetschke's car [sic, panzer] stood about 30 to 50 meters from the house [café]. Poetschke himself, pistol in hand, stood at the near side of the car. I remember the pistol so well, as he pointed with it to my car. We stopped short and Poetschke gave us the order to drive on after we received cigarettes from his crew."[30]

Meanwhile Panzer Nr. 702—Heinz Schraeder's—clanked past to follow behind Thorn and Pilarzek as Klingelhoefer briefly dismounted to talk over things with Poetschke.[31] Ehrhardt could not hear what

Poetschke told the panzer leader, but the result sent them packing. Soon Klingelhoefer, too, was on his way, pressing behind the other two company tanks ahead of him.

As they approached the crossroads the strangest element by far in the column of Kampfgruppe Peiper was four U.S. jeeps driven by captured members of the recon company of the U.S. 32nd Armored Regiment. After the Germans seized their weapons and forced them to drive along in the column, Cpl. Edward Bojarski and several other American captives—nine enlisted men and two officers—were now an unwilling element of the German battle group.

Bojarski remembered watching from his vantage point in the middle of the German column as the enemy tanks in front of him began belting with direct fire a U.S. truck column coming from the north. The contest was uneven; the American column looked to be almost unarmed. In any case, the column of green trucks lurched to a stop, and bewildered GIs immediately began piling out. "The Germans were gathering our soldiers at the head of the column," Bojarski recalled. "The column was going slow." *It was a traffic jam*, the Wisconsin man thought. With that, the Germans made Bojarski and the others get out of their jeeps and head to join the other captives being assembled at the crossroads.[32] *What would happen next?* he wondered.

Back at the café, the dense traffic of the Kampfgruppe Peiper slowly snarled toward the crossroads. Shortly after Poetschke stopped, the point SPW of the 11th Panzer Grenadier Company arrived with some infantry. Driver SS-Cpl. Arvid Freimuth, whose SPW was commanded by SS-Sgt. Heinz Hendel in charge of the 2nd Platoon, wheeled up as the point vehicle of Diefenthal's panzer grenadiers. Just to his front, Freimuth spied two Mk V Panther tanks pulled off beside the long column of American olive-drab trucks jumbled on the roadside. Although Freimuth remained at the wheel of his armored troop carrier, Hendel ordered the rest of the infantry out from behind the 14mm steel sides.

Presently, two more SPWs arrived, and their occupants eagerly disarmed the surrendering Americans. They were motioned back toward the crossroads. Freimuth watched as the Americans emerged from the long column of trucks that stretched south toward Ligneuville. American soldiers groggily emerged from the vehicles, hands held high. The German infantry had orders to recruit the American drivers and the assistant drivers. Yet no one could resist the goodies. The Americans had real cigarettes—not that ersatz tobacco that plagued the Reich. Watches, rings, and chocolate too—these were all the spoils of war. Minutes passed.

Just then Josef Diefenthal's radio-command halftrack roared forward. Driver SS-Cpl. Paul Zwigart screeched to a stop, the vehicle's whip antenna waving in response. Inside was Jochen Peiper and Diefenthal was wearing his tan flyer's jacket. Peiper stood up across from two pine bough–covered panzer tanks and several other SPWs, whose commanders emerged and rose up from behind the steel skirts and tank cupolas. Freimuth didn't immediately recognize them, but one of the tankers carried Poetschke, and the other, his adjutant, Arndt Fischer. Diefenthal stood with the tank regimental commander at his side as Peiper raised one hand, looking agitated. "He [Peiper] gave us a bawling out," Freimuth remembered. His SPW was only five meters behind Peiper's vehicle.[33]

Hans Assenmacher, a Rhinelander from Oberhausen, recalled the same scene from inside Peiper's SPW. SS-Cpl. Assenmacher had been sitting beside Diefenthal's driver, Paul Zwigart, as they bumped along on the muddy road from Thirimont. Passing through a belt of heavy pinewoods north of that town, they soon approached the crossroads. Diefenthal and Peiper conferred in the gloomy morning light sitting across from each other on the blanket-covered metal benches behind Zwigart, who was characteristically wearing his good-luck driver's ski cap. Suddenly there was the sound of shooting, so loud that it blared through Assenmacher's headphone-covered ears. Soon the column slowed to a crawl some 150 meters before the Baugnez crossroads, and Assenmacher stood up in the armored halftrack, looking with curiosity. From there he could see that a column of American trucks had run into the first tanks of Kampfgruppe Peiper.

As Assenmacher recalled, there was a lot of firing, most of it German, and some of the American trucks were peppered with bullet holes and clearly ruined. Even though he was distracted by the radio, Assenmacher could tell that Peiper was angry, ordering the firing to cease. Still, even with some tanks taking a shortcut across the meadow for the other side of the crossroads, the column snarled to a stop. Then Diefenthal suddenly rose from his seat beside Peiper, jumped off the

SPW, and trotted off toward the crossroads. Assenmacher paid little attention to the one-sided firefight; instead, at Peiper's behest he had been striving to establish contact with SS-1st Lt. Georg Preuss, the commander of the 10th Panzer Grenadier Company, missing since they had left the Belgian village of Büllingen hours before. Where the hell was Preuss and the panzer grenadiers? And for that matter, where were the lead tanks and Werner Sternebeck? Peiper told Assenmacher to raise Poetschke on the radio.

As they started moving once more, Assenmacher tried again without success to raise them on the powerful 30-watt Friedrich transmitter. Meanwhile, they slushed their way through the muddy ditch alongside the stalled column. Ahead, the sounds of shooting continued. Presently, Peiper's SPW drew near Poetschke's tank near the crossroads, and Peiper started barking out orders even before they stopped. SS-Capt. Diefenthal, who was now back in the saddle, could see that Peiper was displeased. "Stop this firing!" he insisted. "We need these trucks for our supply system."[34] American prisoners were still milling about and being assembled just south of the crossroads—another annoyance. Soon Peiper and the SPW continued on.

Had Peiper told Poetschke anything about the prisoners? Later there was only one brief slip regarding whether they discussed that subject at the crossroads. The indiscretion came from Paul Zwigart speaking with a fellow prisoner later in the summer of 1945.[35] Otherwise none of the witnesses would say more—the Waffen SS code of silence.

Whatever the contents of that fateful conversation, in moments Diefenthal's SPW passed the crossroads and turned off toward Ligneuville, gliding by abandoned U.S. trucks. A sign floated by on their right: Malmédy was only a few kilometers away—and with a much better road to the Meuse than the trail-like *Rollbahn D*. "Let's make an excursion to Malmédy," Diefenthal motioned to Peiper.

"Too bad we can't do that," Peiper responded. "We have orders to the contrary."[36] Even if Herbert Kuhlmann, with the 12th SS Panzer Regiment, was nowhere to be seen, *Rollbahn C*, which passed through Malmédy, was the assigned route for the other SS tank group.[37] Responding to Diefenthal's puzzled look, Peiper moved his hands to the sides of his eyes with the palms facing inward; in boyish mocking contempt for superiors, Peiper simulated the blinders on a horse's bridle. Narrow vision—no matter what, they would stay on the bad roads that went to Ligneuville and then double back north to Stavelot—the long way around. This wasn't like Russia, where such improvisations were made on the fly.

That possibility vetoed, Diefenthal's HQ halftrack had gone only a short distance when Zwigart wheeled behind another SPW that had pulled off to the right side of the road. Still clad in headphones, Assenmacher, who was fiddling with the radio, could hear Peiper bellow something at the German soldiers standing next to the SPW. Peiper waved his hand back in the direction of the crossroads behind them. Assenmacher cocked his head up from the radio set and pulled the headphones from one ear, thinking that Peiper wanted his attention.

"Of which company are you?" Peiper snapped.[38] He was clearly addressing the German soldiers lolling about.

"9th Panzer Engineers," answered one.

"What is the matter with you?" Peiper flared. "Why are you still standing here?"

"We had a link-pin break," was the response.

"Get that fixed," Peiper shot back without hesitation, "and drive on as fast as possible."

They had been at the intersection for scarcely five minutes, but Assenmacher, as he later claimed, was too busy tweaking the radio to notice the American prisoners assembling nearby. Yet as they waited there, Diefenthal had suddenly appeared and jumped on board. "I have appointed SS-Lt. Aschendorf as acting commander," he announced, "as Preuss is lost." Peiper's flash of anger seemed to fade. Because he knew there may be an American general in Ligneuville as well, he expected resistance and wanted thick armor and a big gun ahead of his thin-skinned halftrack. He waved his arm forward, signaling Arndt Fischer's Panther and a couple of other tanks to rumble off south ahead of him. He pulled in behind Fischer, having been at the crossroads for scarcely five minutes. Diefenthal remembered the moment:

I passed the crossroads in my armored car at the head of the column at the time, when there were about 10 to 12 U.S. soldiers. . . . The mass of U.S. soldiers were still standing or lying

near their vehicles, and when we passed them, they were told by
Colonel Peiper to march in the direction of the crossroads.[39]

Another short delay came just down the gently sloping road that
led to Ligneuville. In spite of Peiper's admonitions about time lost to
looting, even he couldn't resist when they came across an abandoned
American jeep; after all, a quick glance revealed that the vehicle was
stuffed with booty. Zwigart screeched the SPW to a stop. Assenmacher poked around the dull-green vehicle, soon emerging with
spoils. Diefenthal reached for a pack of Camel cigarettes, but Peiper
satisfied himself with a fistful of the GI square-shaped K-ration bis-
cuits. As Assenmacher looked over, Peiper was chewing on the bis-
cuits. Then, just at that moment, Assenmacher heard a distant spasm
of machine gunfire. The sound echoed from the direction of the
crossroads—clearly the staccato rip of an MG-42. No one said anything. Peiper raised his arm and motioned everybody forward. As
they roared off, Assenmacher could still hear the sound of firing behind them.[40]

Arvid Freimuth, the SPW driver with the straggling 11th Panzer
Grenadier Company, recalled the encounter, confirming Assenmacher's story:

> It was shortly before [Ligneuville]. . . . Since I was driving at the
> point, we stopped the convoy and took the American drivers and
> assistant drivers prisoner. For that purpose we had to stop and it
> took about twenty minutes. Then, SS-Lt. Col. Peiper came up front.
> He yelled at us and asked why we stopped so long. . . . There were
> two Panther tanks stopped in front of me. . . . Peiper yelled at the
> tank commanders as well as us.[41]

Diefenthal sat in the SPW across from Peiper, Freimuth recalled,
sporting a yellow leather jacket with fur lining and a visored cap.
Peiper was arrayed in a dark submariner's jacket with a front zipper, his
gleaming *Ritterkreuz* (the Knight's Cross) dangling from his collar and
looking like a Hollywood SS panzer man. Their SPW pulled up to the
left behind him as a number of other halftracks queued up by the
crossroads. Freimuth remembered the infantry from the vehicles

searching the prisoners and assembling them in the field. Several other Mark IV tanks arrived, but Peiper was impatient.

Even as Freimuth and his crew hastily departed to follow behind Arndt Fischer's Panther, Peiper was standing in the SPW and still yelling. Freimuth recalled his exact words: "Goddamn it!" Peiper cursed uncharacteristically. "What kind of business is it to stop here for hours?" Peiper turned to the tank commanders scornfully. "The little that is to be done here," he continued, "the men in the rear will do!"[42]

Then the radio crackled. "Fischer proceed!" In response, Arndt Fischer's Panther lurched ahead, with Diefenthal's SPW pulling in just behind. Freimuth fired up his halftrack and followed.

Peering through the steel driver's slit, Paul Zwigart was unhappy to find himself under Josef Diefenthal's thumb. Although Diefenthal thought the tall youth was a good driver, since being buried by Allied bombs in Normandy, Zwigart's nerves were shot. For his part, Zwigart found Diefenthal, who took over III Battalion in August 1944, harsh and unrelenting. Now, as Diefenthal's command vehicle driver, Zwigart seemed to always find himself at the front and in harm's way. Peiper was better, but things always seemed on edge. "He kept coming and going," Zwigart said of Peiper's rides with him in the Ardennes. "He was always in a hurry."[43] The brusque encounter at the crossroads was typical.

But now Zwigart wrenched the big black steering wheel to put their command halftrack back on the road. Clattering ahead, Peiper was soon drafting behind the hulk of Fischer's big Mk V panzer. The prisoners all but forgotten, Peiper roared off toward Ligneuville, relishing thoughts of capturing an American general.[44]

CHAPTER 6

Killing Field

The air was cold as the American prisoners stood on the soggy Baugnez meadow. Why, they wondered, were they still crowded in a large, uneasy group at the crossroads rather than being directed to the enemy rear? Many GIs pondered their fate while continuing to hold their tired hands over their heads. Some clasped their hands behind their necks; others let their exhausted arms float down.

Amid growing apprehension, a large group of American soldiers still hid in the hay and shed behind the Café Bodarwe, hoping to escape notice. It only worked for a time. "We had only been in the barn about ten or fifteen minutes when two Germans approached with burp guns," remembered John O'Connell. "Three Germans spotted us behind the building and commanded us to surrender which we did."[1] Pvt. Ralph Law was there too:

> In broken English, they ordered us to come out with hands up. We went outside the barn where we were searched for weapons. Then, they motioned for us to join the rest of the men, which we did. . . . The rest of the convoy had been rounded up from down the roads. . . . There were a few medics there. I guess there were about 140 there altogether. A German Tiger tank and two tank destroyers

[sic] moved into position and covered us with machine guns. An
open staff car drove up and stopped.[2]

Further behind, in the middle of the column, T/5 Kenneth E.
Kingston drove a jeep. After the shooting began and their predicament
became known, Kingston and Cpl. Flechsig reluctantly surrendered as
a big tank approached. "I threw down my carbine and put my hands
up," Kingston later said. As he walked up the road—midway between
House #10 and the intersection, he listened in surprise as a German officer approached and asked if Kingston could "chauffeur" him. A German tank was moving close by. "I told him 'No.'"[3] Kingston wanted to
say *Go to hell*, but he kept quiet. Still, the SS officer seemed to get the
picture and cursed him. "He kicked me in the ass," Kingston remembered, motioning him and Flechsig to head back down the road.[4] As
they moved along the tarmac, they came upon a German halftrack,
whose occupants motioned to both men: "They called us over to the
vehicle and took the gloves off our hands and went in our pockets and
took our cigarettes."

Kingston had seen Lt. Perry Reardon attempting to hide when he
first hunkered down in the ditch. Now, Reardon was walking to join
them. "I continued up the road," Kingston recalled, "and they searched
us and took our personal belongings. We stood there for about fifteen
minutes." Kingston was situated in the second row of the jumbled prisoners in the field. Eventually, as he remembered it, there were four or
five halftracks situated across from them and a lone tank.

The Americans being assembled at the intersection were not completely orderly, as was evident in Kingston's recollection: "We saw a
couple of fellows get up and take [off] for the woods." He then saw a
German vehicle open fire on those attempting to escape—he believed
they were T/4 Robert Mearig, Sgt. Alphonse Stabulis, Pvt. Charles
Hall, and Pvt. Donald Flack. "We saw these men shot down, but could
do nothing."[5] Meanwhile, the Germans managed to recruit some of
the Americans as drivers; Kingston saw Cpl. David Lucas and Sgt.
Lacy drive away under guard in the two trucks, as German soldiers in
camouflage outfits began to jump down from the halftracks.

"We were standing in the field now and four or five halftracks
pulled up along side the road and we were told to move up against the

fence and then over," Kingston remembered. "Meantime, they were bringing another prisoner down the road. He did not have his hands up high enough, so they shot him three times in the back."[6] Kingston saw other strange happenings. As they stood in the field, an American jeep appeared with an American lieutenant colonel driving, guarded by a German. The American had a bandage on his jaw. Then other U.S. jeeps went by with an SS soldier in each, but Kingston was too wary of their own situation to pay close attention.[7] Soon, enemy tanks joined the halftracks already lining the road.

> There was a tank that pulled onto the road and fired two shots with a pistol and then machine guns. I hit the ground. We lay there for 5 to 6 minutes while they machine-gunned us. Previous to this shooting, I saw no one attempt to run. They then stopped firing and then some of the fellows were moaning. I saw 4 to 5 German soldiers come into the field with small arms, P-38s and shoot these fellows four and five times because they were moaning. I was laying on my stomach pretending to be dead. They came right to us and I was watching the Germans and Pvt. Hallman saw them too—he was lying next to me. . . . One man was shot five times; I heard him moan and then the shots. One fellow took my wristwatch and tried to take my ring. He must have felt a pulse and stepped back a couple of feet and shot me. He shot through my helmet. I pretended to be dead.[8]

Kenny Kingston was amazed to still be alive. "Cpl. Joseph Brozowski— he must have been hit by machine gun fire—I seen him [sic] get up on his knees, moaning and hollering. These fellows came into the field and emptied five rounds [into him]."[10] Kingston had been incredibly lucky, as the bullet only grazed Kingston's scalp. The sweeping hail of automatic-weapons fire went on for what seemed like forever—was it ten minutes? Kingston couldn't tell; his perception of time was completely distorted.

According to Kingston, Cpl. Ralph Indelicato had been treating Carl Stevens for a gunshot wound to the left arm when the shooting began. "He was standing about 15 to 20 feet to the right of us," he said. Charles Appman claimed to have been right next to the medical man when the Germans were sighting guns at them. What did he think the enemy was going to do? "I don't know son," Appman responded, "We'll just have to hope for the best."9 Then, as the enemy pistol shots began, a bullet felled Indelicato, who was in the process of bandaging Stevens. Following that, a second shot and automatic weapons burst out. Appman threw himself to the ground, his steel helmet rolling off, and landing face down in the mud. The man next to Appman was shot in the head, showering Appman's body with blood. A collective wail emerged from the bodies—"soldiers crying and calling out names."

Carl Daub told a similar story. After trudging back up north to the intersection, he found that "[t]here are quite a few fellows in the field already. I was with some of the last fellows who went in the field and one of the Germans was hollering and motioning us to hurry. When they told us to hurry, I went across the fence." Daub thought he stood in the group for fifteen minutes with his hands raised until several enemy armored vehicles stopped and their occupants began to load machine guns.

> I was standing with the boys in the front of the group, close to the center front. It seemed to me like there were 150 American soldiers in the field. In the front of the group Lt. Reardon was telling us to keep quiet and not to move. . . . At that time an armored tank moved up to our right front and tried to point some kind of gun at us. He couldn't turn it towards us, so he left the tank facing sideways. . . . While we were standing there for several minutes . . . a German tank came up the road and a man was standing in the tank. I could see about half of the man. He looked us over and pulled out a gun and took a steady aim and fired and I heard one of the boys close to me fall. He fired a second time and I heard another fellow fall. The third time he fired, I didn't hear anybody fall. He said something and laughed and drove off. Then the machine guns opened up. I remember the machine gun started over towards us to our right hand side. . . . I turned my back to the roads and hit the ground before the bullets went over to the center. It seemed like four guns were firing. . . . While I was lying on the

ground, I heard more tanks move up and they also opened fire. They must have fired for a few minutes and then it grew quiet. Then I heard a German holler. Then they would fire again. They did that several times. When the shooting stopped, I heard the Germans walking around us. I had my face in the mud and I thought they were looking to see if any of us were alive. Every now and then they would say something in German and then they would fire.[11]

When the tank gun pointed into the crowd standing there, Aubrey Hardiman heard one GI gasp. "Here we go!"[12] Ted Paluch remembered,

Before the shooting, they lowered the barrel right at us. I could see the gun, looking right down it. I was in the front left looking at them. . . . I saw some people shaking like a leaf.[13]

George Fox also watched the enemy halftrack train its big gun on the prisoners, noting the heavy German armored traffic and estimating that perhaps twenty enemy vehicles had gone by:

We just stood there in the field, standing up facing the road with our hands clasp [sic] over our heads . . . Other German vehicles continue to go by, headed south. The next thing I remember was a German tank, which pulled off on our side, the west side of the road and head diagonally somewhat southwesterly towards us with its 88mm gun pointed directly at us. It stayed in this position just two or three minutes, as well as I can remember, then backed up and continued on down the roads southwardly. . . . Then a halftrack came along on the road parallel to the fence. It was about in the center of the field, but not quite as far south as the place where I was standing. . . . There was a machine gun pointed at us from this vehicle.[14]

Fox recalled a tank or another armored vehicle drove up behind the halftrack parked across from them. Then a German soldier stood up in the vehicle, took deliberate aim, and shot two or three times.

"I specifically remember the pistol being raised, aimed and fired. . . . Then the machine gun on the halftrack opened up with fire sweeping from the north end of the field to the south end where I was. I immediately fell to the ground, face and stomach down with my head to the south."

T/5 Carl W. Moucheron who had been in the same truck as Fox, distinctly recalled the man firing the pistol shots. He couldn't remember the type of vehicle from which he fired, but he was certain the machine guns, which followed, came from a halftrack. "I hit the dirt as soon as they started shooting."[15] The gun swept through the field several times, but, miraculously, Fox was untouched. Later he heard three distinct German voices coming from the field, where the Germans were shooting any who showed signs of life. "Anyone that moved seemed to get shot," Moucheron recalled, thankful that his only wound was from a bullet that glanced off his helmet.

When the men were first gathered in the field, Pfc. Carl M. Stevens received first aid from Cpl. Ralph J. Indelicato after Lt. Lary obtained permission from the Germans. Shrapnel had hit Stevens's left shoulder, and Indelicato, assisted by Pvt. Elmer Wald, applied a compression bandage to his left arm and shoulder. They were still working on Stevens when fate intervened. "While Indelicato was bandaging the arm of one of our men while we were in the field, they shot him and the man he was helping," Carl Daub remembered. "This was at the beginning of the firing."[16]

Ted Flechsig described a similar scene, but he thought it was a German SS lieutenant who fired the first shots at the north end of the field. Like others, he saw a halftrack try to train a big gun on the prisoners but unable to do so due to a limited traverse:[17]

> One of our men had a wound and one of our medics started to fix him up and the German soldiers allowed him to do it and this German lieutenant—he was looking over the boys and he drew his pistol and shot one boy between the eyes and then he swung around to another boy and shot him . . . that was the signal for the machine gun to open up on us. Then they killed the medic . . . [intending] to kill everyone that was in the field. They continued to spray us back and forth for about five minutes.[18]

"Then the shooting stopped. I heard someone walking around and as these men groaned or cried, he would shoot them with a pistol," Flechsig recalled. "Lt. Reardon acted very bravely," he added. "After they had shot at us the first time, he kept talking to the boys that were groaning and told them to keep quiet, that it was our only chance."[19] Reardon whispered urgently without regard for his personal safety. Then he, too, was shot dead.

Who was the first man hit in the field? Pvt. Donald W. Day, who was in the back row of the prisoners, thought he saw fifteen tanks and halftracks lined up across from them before everything happened. A German officer in an armored car followed these. Day thought it was the officer in the command car who fired first—his victim being a medical corpsman who was helping one of the wounded. "Then the officer motioned towards us and two tanks cut loose with machine guns."[20]

Still another man from the 801st Tank Destroyer Battalion witnessed the shooting at the crossroads. This was Pvt. Clarence M. Musgrove, who had been separated from Company A on the morning of December 17 after their 3–inch-gun positions were overwhelmed south of Honsfeld. Fleeing that debacle, he claimed to have been trapped briefly near a crossroads south of Malmédy where he came upon a German column and hid undetected just off the road:

> I noticed American prisoners being guarded by some German infantry troops. Some German Mk IV tanks and a German command car drew up and stopped near the prisoners. A German officer stood in the command car and fired his pistol, a P-38, at an American medical officer. . . . The armored troops on the tanks immediately began firing light machine guns at the prisoners and this was immediately followed by the firing of burp guns by the armored infantrymen. . . . To my recollection there were six Mark IV tanks, one command car and five halftracks.[21]

Scared witless, Musgrove managed to escape.

From his vantage as a new and very unwilling prisoner, Ted Paluch was more than a little envious when he saw a few men from the head of the column run away to avoid capture.[22] After that, events seemed to take a bad turn. Soon the Germans were taking their cigarettes, watches, and gloves. "When that tank first came around the corner, the lady in the house there ran out to see them. She was pretty happy." The woman from the café hoisted a basket of something up to the tank occupants who looked more than pleased. Soon he was standing in the field next to T/5 Charles Appman, with his hands up near the front of the group on the left side facing the road. Everyone in his little group grew uneasy.

Pvt. Robert L. Smith was close by, having come from the same truck as Paluch. "While they were searching us, I saw about eight tanks coming down from our left rear," Smith later said. "We stood there about five minutes after we were searched. Then a tank came in front of us. The commander of the tank gave an order for us to get back off the road, so we went back across a barbed wire fence into the field."[23]

Ted Paluch witnessed another bewildering sight when an American jeep passed by being driven by an American Lt. Colonel with a bandage over his head. A German was guarding him in the passenger seat:

Then this tank that took up a diagonal position pointed towards us soon came back into the road and moved southwardly. Shortly after this tank had moved down the road, and while all of us were standing in the field with our hands and arms upraised, a German vehicle—something like our jeep—came down the road from the intersection going southwardly and a German soldier in the vehicle took two shots at us with a pistol. These shots hit a fellow on my left and a fellow on my right. Everybody in the field fell flat to the ground at the second shot.[24]

In a separate earlier statement Paluch clarified that the appearance of a German command car at the crossroads seemed to become a dangerous turning point. Was it Josef Diefenthal and Jochen Peiper in their command halftrack? Or was it Max Beutner or Erich Rumpf in their respective SPWs?

Everything was alright until a [German] command car turned the corner. At that time, an officer in the command car fired a shot with his pistol at a medical officer who was one yard away to my left and then he fired another shot. . . . At that time, a tank following the command car opened fire on the 175 men inside the fence. We all fell and lay as still as we could.[25]

Bruce Summers and George Rosenfeld were among the few in Battery B who had any combat experience at all, and they were deeply worried by what they saw as they were ushered off the road and into a field near the intersection. Summers recalled seeing a line of halftracks pull up across from them:[26]

Word came that we were to all go to one end of the field. And we got together there and there was a lot of talking, but I don't remember what it was about. . . . The shooting was over and it was kind of quiet, but everybody was a little confused. We stood there in the field and tried to figure out what was happening. I told George [Rosenfeld] who was standing there next to me. I said George, "I don't see any troops or infantry with these people; they're not going to take prisoners. They're not going to let us loose. Let's you and I try to mosey around and try to get to the back of this bunch of men. Let's get out from the front of this thing." So we started to work our way to the rear of the group. We knew that standing in the front of that group wasn't a good place to be standing. We were off to the left hand side. The tanks were just to the front of us. This was a small tank, or a weapons carrier and it came down and tried to depress its gun on us. There would have been hell to pay if that had happened, but the road was higher there and he couldn't get it far enough down. And he was blocking the other tanks coming down the road, so they pulled him out of the line. And this next tank stopped and this fellow stood up from one of the manholes to the front of the turret and took his pistol. He stood up about from [waist up] and took his pistol out and leveled his pistol and shot two times. . . . [After] those shots there was a lot of firing. I didn't see where it came from; we all fell to the ground.[27]

Cpl. George Fox also claimed the appearance of an enemy command car seemed to initiate the wanton shooting: "A German soldier in an armored car came along the road by the field and fired a pistol through the group. When the pistol started firing, we hit the ground." Fox was beyond shock. "No one tried to break away. . . . We didn't believe they would shoot us."[28]

One man did manage to escape detection: T/5 Charles Reding. "In all the commotion, I made my way unobserved to the building." Unlike the others, Reding moved outside the north side of the café near a hedge and threw himself on the ground. In fact, he saw a GI already lying near the café and fell prone near the man.[29]

Now back in Diefenthal's SPW, Peiper had left Lt. Col. John Ray, who was still in his jeep under guard and woozy from a grazing head wound. Shortly Ray also arrived near the crossroads:

> As the Germans were driving—I don't know how far—maybe a couple of miles—I looked over to the left side of this road. . . .
> I looked across the road and in a big empty field I saw a large number of—I estimate 200 Americans—that were prisoners of war who were herded up like cattle. I could see two or three Red Cross brassards on the arms of these men. They were all herded together. I said to the German enlisted man who was driving the jeep, "Take me over there so that I can get treatment." He told me in English, "You cannot go there, you are injured. We are not going there." We then proceeded on our way and left.[30]

With Peiper no longer in the jeep, the Germans at the wheel drove themselves and the bleeding American officer off to the rear. Now a captive of the Germans a second time in the war—Ray had been captured in 1943 in Tunisia—the lieutenant colonel was too dazed to think straight.

There was still some sporadic gunfire. The lead German vehicles sped on to Ligneuville to the south. As the panzer men approached the crossroads, they could see on the left side of the road, just to the south of the café, a large group of American soldiers assembled in the field with their hands over their heads. Bill Merriken was relieved of his watch, and a frustrated German soldier tried to remove his Bedford High School ring. It was so cold that the ring could not be pried off his swollen finger. Merriken did not protest, but he was nonetheless pleased when the soldier finally gave up and motioned him to join the others in the field.

Ken Ahrens, Valenzi, and Sciranko had been ordered back to the crossroads, and their trek there was a nearly constant procession of German halftracks stopping them for plunder. It took almost twenty minutes to get back to the intersection. Ahrens remembered,

> As I climbed through the fence surrounding the field, I noticed numerous faces that were not attached to my battery. I also noticed some aid men there, one in particular—Cpl. Ralph Indelicato. He was administering aid to one of the men of my battery who had been hit by a piece of shell fragment. The group, as I looked at it, was accumulating on one side into a bunched up group and on the left side it was spread out a little more. I wandered over into the left side of the group facing the road. . . . [The group] was intermingled, approximately six to eight rows deep. I was standing along with Cpl. Skoda at the middle of the left side of the group in approximately the second or third line.[31]

They were collected in a field just south of the café. "We stood there for about five or ten minutes, keeping our hands up all the while," Ahrens recalled. "One German tank was then about fifteen yards from us."[32] John Kailer, standing in the middle of the crowd, estimated that they stood there for nearly ten minutes. Although some vehicles stopped, at least a dozen tanks and halftracks had passed by while the prisoners huddled in the cold.[33]

All the men stood in a group with their hands up. The ranking officer of the group, 1st Lt. Virgil P. Lary Jr., stood up and thrust his hands overhead only to see a German soldier in a halftrack drawing a bead on him with a pistol. He quickly ducked behind one of the vehicles. One German officer began walking down along the group of prisoners, asking if some could drive some of the vehicles they had just abandoned. "We refused to give them any cooperation," Lary recalled.[34]

Behind Warren Schmitt and Gene Garrett was another truck-weapons carrier, driven by Pfc. Charles Hall and nicknamed "Black Jack" because its occupants thought the truck brought good luck. On the seat beside Hall was his commander, Sgt. Alphonse "Stubby" Stabulis, so named for his short physique. In the back of the truck sat Pfc. Donald Flack and T/4 Robert P. "Sketch" Mearig. Being near the head of the 285th column, they saw a German buzz bomb flying overhead. Then, shooting suddenly erupted after they passed the crossroads. They too jumped in the ditch to take cover when shells started falling. "I left my position in the ditch," Mearig recalled, "and ran across the road to a house [Goffinet House] which was just opposite where our vehicle was parked. . . . I entered this house and after I had gotten inside, an old woman with a black shawl came from another house and motioned me to leave."[35] The woman, fearing for her life, was crying.

Not knowing what else to do, Mearig ran back outside and sprinted back to his position by his vehicle on the west side of the road. Hall, who had stayed inside the truck cab until a bullet pierced the windshield, soon joined him. Meanwhile, across from Mearig and Hall on the east side of the road, other soldiers called out that one of the GIs there was wounded and to get help. Mearig was now scared senseless, suggesting to Sgt. Stabulis that "we should make a break and get away." Firmly, the sergeant said no; they would stay with their vehicle. Still, Mearig was determined to get out of there:

> I decided to go without them and crawled over to the fence . . . but they came over and pulled me back to the ditch. It was at this time that we saw vehicles moving northwardly on a road parallel to the road we were on, but some six to 700 yards to the east. . . . The first vehicle that came into the intersection was a German tank. It was well camouflaged and had big wide tracks. . . . After it rounded the corner, it started spraying the ditch on our side with machine gun fire. . . . Before the bursts reached the spot where we were . . . we got out of the ditch and crawled under the fence and into the field and stood up leaning against the fence. This tank continued down the road. . . . The four of us . . . remained in the field behind the fence.[36]

As they drew near the intersection, other soldiers walking on the road were ordered to cross over into the field where Mearig, Stabulis,

Flack, and Hall were already congregated. They were then forced to the back of the mass of soldiers in the field. By this time Mearig noted that more than a half dozen tanks and halftracks had arrived before them, lining the road across from the field. He, Stabulis, Flack, and Hall remained in the back of the group. Then, however, Mearig saw something that frightened him terribly, though he didn't even know why: He saw a German officer in a yellow-tan jacket. Although Mearig didn't know it, he was watching Josef Diefenthal, who was in Peiper's SPW.

> It was about this time that I saw another German vehicle approaching the intersection from the east. . . . What really attracted my attention was a man standing up in it in a rather light yellow jacket. After this vehicle entered the intersection, it turned left and came on down the road southwardly towards the field where we were assembled. . . . I became more frightened than before. I don't know why except that this vehicle seemed to be by itself and I thought perhaps it was a high-ranking officer. I decided to try to get away and walked slowly northwardly, but upon reaching a little dirt road, decided not to go across the lane.

Mearig was using the large group of prisoners to shield his movements from enemy observation. The "dirt road" he mentioned was the farm trail just to the rear of the group of assembled prisoners—a move that would likely leave him, Stabulis, Flack, and Hall naked and exposed before the Germans. They quickly discussed the matter. "Stabulis said we better go back," he remembered. "Sgt. Stabulis, Flack and I were together on this proposition," and they walked slowly back to their positions at the rear of the crowd of POWs. But Hall seemed to have disappeared.[37] When they got back, the German officer in the yellow jacket was out of his vehicle and before the crowd of prisoners shouting something. Mearig could only make out the words "Siegfried Line!" but the officer's displeasure was clear. Something seemed wrong to Mearig. He and his two buddies were still looking to escape.

> The group of soldiers in front of me were standing still and I slowly walked southwardly towards the fence at the south end of the field,

more or less using the men in front as concealment. I know that Sgt. Stabulis and Pfc. Flack were behind me. About two thirds of the way towards the fence there were no more men to provide concealment, so when I reached that point I ran towards the fence as fast as I could. . . . As I came out from behind the crowd and into the clear, two single shots were fired, which were either pistol or rifle in my opinion. . . . [I] turned to my right and headed for the woods west of the field as fast as I could. Machine gun fire was opened up at me, but I was lucky enough to make it to the woods without being hit and was picked up by the 30th Division a couple of days later.[38]

Mearig estimated that he was about a hundred feet away from the mass of prisoners standing in the field when the machine gunfire began. "I fell like I was shot," he recalled. "I laid there and watched and listened. I laid there until just about dark and took off."[39]

Sgt. Stabulis was likely mortally wounded by the machine gunfire. His body was found in April 1945 a kilometer south of the massacre field in the woods to the right of the bend in the road as it descends to Ligneuville.[40] Pfc. Flack had dropped at the sound of the concentrated machine gunfire just to the rear of the larger group of Americans in the field. He would later be shot in the head at close range by pistol fire when the Waffen SS men came into the field to kill anyone still alive. Had "Sketch" Mearig and those running with him unknowingly precipitated the Malmédy massacre?[41]

Because Bill Merriken's group had walked all the way to the crossroads from the column head, they were among the last to reach the rest in the field. He, Pittman, and Hardiman joined the men standing uneasily near the crossroads. They held their hands up with the others. He recognized Max Schwitzgold next to him. Aubrey Hardiman, the trained turkey shooter, worried about the collection of automatic weapons he saw brandished by their guards and considered "spreading out at a time like this." He thought he was lucky to find himself at the extreme north end of the crowd. Minutes passed.[42]

Everyone shivered—it was cold. Bill's arms ached from holding them in the air so long. He looked out across the frost-crusted pastures to the line of pines to the east from where the German vehicles seemed to be emanating from the road. The vehicles turned toward them just after reaching the café at the crossroads. Some halftracks were crossing the field just to the east to avoid the jammed-up traffic.

Other than the shock of now finding himself a prisoner, Bobby Werth, with Carl Daub's little group, thought little of being herded with others into a field near the crossroads. "The Germans were laughing and seemed to be enjoying the whole thing," he remembered.

Bill Merriken's reverie was interrupted when a line of three enemy halftracks pulled up alongside the prisoners in front of the field.[43] The Waffen SS men seemed to be having mechanical problems with one of them. There was lots of yelling and posturing, but Bill could understand none of it. He thought the enemy soldiers were likely waiting for trucks to haul the prisoners back to Germany. In the exposed position in the front ranks, he nervously watched as the arguing enemy soldiers seemed to be trying to depress the big gun of one of the armored vehicles to aim at him and the other standing prisoners.

The knot of men herded in the pasture eyed the development nervously. "They're going to blow us off the field," Merriken thought to himself. Several of the enemy were shouting loudly. Just then, the vehicle with the cannon suddenly pulled back, straightened out, and headed down the road. In the meantime, another tank or halftrack pulled up on the road in its place.

In the cold, Pvt. Jim Mattera stood uneasily beside his buddy, T/5 Charles I. "Chas" Haines, as the Germans adjusted machine guns on the halftracks in front of them. They looked to be sighting them on Battery B. "What the hell is going on?" Mattera muttered.[44] The men strained to continue to hold up their aching arms. A flake or two of snow whirled through the air, and with the pines in the distance, it gave the scene an oddly grim Christmas look. The thermometer hovered just below freezing.

In the foreground Germans in black leather jackets riding in big tanks along with others in camouflage uniforms in halftracks were loading ammunition. Mattera's mind wandered. The day was Sunday. At home, he thought, "most of our families and friends would have dressed to attend church services and to pray for us." He had a sinking feeling. Al Valenzi recalled the same moment:

My arm was bleeding. . . . A tank pulled up and started moving the turret of the gun to lower it, but it wouldn't go low enough. And I thought to myself, "What in the heck are these guys going to do? Fire this gun at us?" The Germans were talking, but I couldn't understand them. They moved the tank up over here and a halftrack moved up. There was someone sitting up in the turret of the gun. There were some other fellows in one of these smaller halftracks.[45]

Al Valenzi suddenly realized that the Germans were planning to execute them all: "I remember looking off to see a row of pine trees in the distance and wondered if that was the last thing I would see. I didn't want to think about it, but I couldn't help it." Time slowed in Valenzi's personal movie—the enemy motioned and shouted, their unintelligible speech adding to the surreal sense. "It was a strange, *strange* feeling," he recalled.

Pvt. Robert L. Smith painted the canvas with only slightly different brushstrokes. One key thing that he saw was a "heavy tank with a very long barrel" that was north of them in the intersection. He recalled that the tank fired two rounds off toward Malmédy—something also seen by Ted Paluch.[46] Then the prisoners were ordered across barbed wire into the field south of the café. Smith recalled they were organized loosely in rows about three men deep.[47] Lt. Reardon was not far from him on the north side of the field:

We milled around in the field for about five or ten minutes, wondering what was going to happen. Finally, they brought a tank down across the field across the road in front of us. They aimed it at us. While we were waiting in the field I saw two medics, Ralph Indelicato, and I don't know the other's name, carrying Stevens. He was bleeding from being shot. They brought him in and started working on him. Just as they started working on him, they started shooting. I didn't see who shot. When I heard the first shot, I fell. I fell face down in the back row facing the road; that would be the left corner of the field. I didn't see anything after that, but I heard tanks coming by on the road and everyone that came by would shoot at us.[48]

Bruce Summers saw the same armored vehicle aiming its gun at the men in the field, but he was certain that it was not a tank but instead some type of weapons carrier with a shorter gun—he thought a 75mm. Now, like many others, he saw it eventually back up and head down the road.[49]

Lt. Virgil P. Lary Jr. was standing in the field with T/5 Michael Skoda at his side. They both held hands high along with everyone else. Both men stared intently as Germans on halftracks forty feet in front of them seemed to be setting up a machine gun. "Look at this," Skoda said under his breath. But Lary shrugged, saying this was only to make sure they didn't try to escape. Skoda could only frown. He then felt paralyzed by a sinking thought that did not even escape his lips: *I think they're going to shoot us.*[50] Lary described what happened next:

> When I got up to the field, they were making a hasty search of the men. . . . My medical corporal requested to give aid to the wounded and was refused and shot. . . . [Then] they pointed a cannon at us— it looked like it was from a halftrack. They were unable to get the cannon pointed just right, so they just moved it down the road. An officer looked at his watch and looked as if he might be getting nervous. They had a machine gun drive [sic] between the two vehicles and an officer in this halftrack shot an individual. He shot into the crowd again. At this time, a machine gun opened up on the crowd again from each side. Those of us who were not wounded hit the ground and laid there motionless while they continued to shoot into the crowd.[51]

Bill Merriken was still standing near the north side of the crowd of Americans in the field. Suddenly he saw a man pop up out of the vehicle on his left—either a tank or a halftrack, he couldn't be sure. Bobby Werth thought it was a halftrack, as did Paul J. Martin, while John O'Connell and Lt. Lary thought it was a command car.[52] Ahrens remembered it as a tank. Bill Merriken focused more on the gun and the man wielding it than he did on the vehicle in which the man stood. To Merriken's horror, the German produced a pistol, took a slow and deliberate aim into the crowd, and fired. A prisoner spun backward from the impact. Cpl. Raymond Lester dropped near Bobby Werth—"He fell right at my feet."[53]

Then another shot. This time, Werth saw that it was a medic, a bullet smashing into his forehead.[54] New Yorker Pete Piscatelli had been standing right next to him.[55] The soldiers jostled about noisily, with the human herd buzzing like bees. "Standfast!" someone cried out.[56] In a split second, another pistol shot rang out, dropping a man off to Merriken's left. Ken Ahrens was standing close by:

> A German who stood on top of this vehicle, pulled out his pistol and, as if having target practice, fired into the group as we stood there, taking deliberate aim. I noticed about ten feet from me in the front row, one of the men of my battery drop to the ground, shot through the head. I heard another shot and saw another fellow from my battery drop.... Immediately after he fired the two shots, the machine guns opened up on us. I spun around and fell face first on the ground. Immediately after I sprawled out on the ground, one of the bullets hit me in the back.[57]

Men on the two armored vehicles were barking excitedly at each other. At that moment, before any of the prisoners could react, a spray of machine gunfire enveloped the crowd. T/5 John O'Connell remembered that they had stood in the crowd for ten minutes before "a pistol shot rang out."

> The crowd, becoming more or less panicky began to stir, but no one ran as an American lieutenant called out for no one to run and keep their hands up. Almost simultaneously one or perhaps two German machine guns opened up on the group of prisoners for no reason I can see. These machine guns were approximately 40 yards in front of us. Most of the fellows were hit by these bursts.[58]

"Lt. Munzinger had just enough time to give the order," he recalled. He was the one who yelled. "Standfast!" while everyone had jostled. "It is my belief that the firing of the pistol was the signal for the machine guns," O'Connell said.[59] With one of the shots, he saw Cpl. Raymond Lester hit in the stomach.[60] The machine guns erupted in an ugly blast.

The hail of lead hit O'Connell in the left shoulder, and as another machine gun began to fire, he spun to the ground.

Images of tragedy, tumbling in slow motion, branded themselves into the memory of Mike Skoda. He would never forget it: "This German officer stood up on this tank, pulled out his revolver and fired it right at us. As soon as he fired it, they opened up with a machine gun to my left and I hit the ground. . . . Everybody was crying and hollering. They kept spraying us with machine gun fire."[61] Bullets slammed into Skoda's buttocks and arm. Virgil Lary, who just moments before had doubted that it would come to this, was standing right next to Skoda. Out of Lary's momentary vision, before he dropped to the ground, he saw one of the first pistol shots hit his driver, Cpl. Raymond Lester.[62] Then a lethal rain of bullets.

Others sensed disaster just before the fatal moment. Charles Appman noticed disquieting body language and shouts from with the Germans guarding them:

> Right before the captured American soldiers were fired on by the man with the pistol, apparently an officer, wearing an officer's cap and a yellow or bright colored jacket, issued some kind of orders before he rode away in his tank. . . . Then about 150 were in this little circle and the Germans that were guarding us told us to get off the road and over in the field, so we had our hands up and crossed the fence, and stood there in the open field and we meddled around [sic] in the circle facing the road. . . . So then, two tanks came up and parked right almost in front of us and they pulled machine guns out and mounted them on the outside of their tank. . . . I asked the Lieutenant who was with me, "What are they going to do?" And the Lieutenant says, "Well, let's hope for the best. . . . " Just about then an order was given to fire. When I heard that, I hit the dust and the machine gun opened up.[63]

Appman had gotten a look at the man who fired the two pistol shots—he wore a steel helmet with a dark uniform. He didn't seem to be an officer, but Appman saw "flashes" on his collar. The German soldier seemed to take deliberate aim with his pistol at a man near

Appman's left and then laughed approvingly after the first shot sent the man sprawling.

Pvt. James Mattera claimed from his hospital bed days later that "a German officer in a command car shot a medical officer and one enlisted man" before all hell—concentrated machine guns—broke loose.[64] In a clarifying statement given to investigators in October 1945, Mattera described how he stood in the middle of the crowd in the field and saw the German soldier fire his pistol, first hitting a medical officer to Mattera's right at the extreme south end of the field and then firing again to hit someone on his other side.[65] He was unsure if the soldier firing was in a tank or halftrack:

> I cannot remember whether this vehicle was a tank, a halftrack or some other type of vehicle. I just saw a man pop up or stand up in this vehicle so I could only see him from the waist up. He yelled or shouted some words in a loud voice, none of which I understood and almost immediately drew a pistol and fired two shots. The first one went to my right and struck a medical officer, who I judge was standing at the spot indicated by No. 19 on the detail [of the map]. . . . I saw his hand go to his chest and he fell to the ground. The second shot was aimed at the group standing more at the north end of the field and I saw a soldier fall. Immediately after those two pistol shots were fired, I estimate three machine guns were opened up on us and all of us fell to the ground.[66]

Sgt. Marvin J. Lewis of the 3rd Armored Division's 32nd Armored Regiment's reconnaissance company had been placed in the crowd in the field after being captured earlier near Waimes and then dumped off with the others at Baugnez. He watched as the Germans left him and his buddies with the assembling crowd in the field, driving their captured jeeps off to the south.

> As soon as all our vehicles had moved out, their column started to come through. The first vehicle in their column was an armored car, and when this first vehicle got up alongside us the officer in charge stood up and took his revolver and shot two men in the front row. Then he moved out and a halftrack pulled in behind him

and two machine guns on the side just sprayed and mowed us down. I got wounded in the leg and we all hit the ground and they kept firing until no one moved. When any of the boys who were wounded started hollering, the Germans dismounted and went amongst us and just hit them in the head with their rifle butts and then shot them. . . . Every time a halftrack would pass they would let a burst of machine gun fire go. We laid there for about two hours until the column passed and then I peeped up and hollered "Anyone able to, let's go."[67]

Cpl. Edward Bojarski was another captive from the recon company. Dropped off at the field south of the café, he joined the rear of the crowd. He remembered the moment when a big gun on a tracked vehicle was turned on the group:

One of the German tank men had turned a tank right at us while in the field. They were just about to shoot an 88. . . . They aimed the barrel right at us and were about to shoot when another officer halted them. . . . On orders from the second officer, they straightened the tank again and were going down the column on the road. . . . The convoy was going slow and the Germans kept getting off and looting our vehicles. . . . Then the column stopped for a few minutes. One of the men got out from a German armored car—with a pistol in his hand. While our American boys were in the field all bunched up, he started shooting. . . . He seemed very young. . . . All the men in the vehicles of the German column seen [sic] this man shooting at us. They started to open up with machine guns.[68]

Cpl. Walter Wendt of Appleton, Wisconsin, was from the same unit. Herded into the field, he found himself huddled beside "Bo" Bojarski as they watched as German halftracks lined up in front of them. "We were standing in a field 15 or 20 feet from the road when a halftrack pulled up even with us, backing across the road so the barrel of the howitzer was aimed directly at us, be he could not lower the gun enough. If he had, we would have been splattered all over the field. After the halftrack left, a command car with two officers pulled up to us."[69] The SS officer in the command vehicle was eagerly puffing on Camel cigarettes. Strange what came to one's mind even on the verge of mayhem: As Wendt's life was hanging by a thread, all he could think of was, *Here are the damned Germans smoking Camels and we are smoking Ramseys—half tobacco and half sawdust!*[70]

> A German command car drove up from the rear of the column. Somebody—it might have been an officer—stood up in the car and started firing a pistol into our men. . . . Then all of a sudden, they opened up on three sides with machine guns and burp guns. I hit the ground and at the same time got a slug in my left elbow. I think there was one tank and a couple of halftracks shooting at us with machine guns; they checkerboarded the area so that they'd cover everything.[71]

"I dropped and made believe I was dead," Wendt recalled. "Then they fired until the moaning stopped. . . . Bullets sang around my ears and mud flew in my face." A machine-gun bullet sliced through the Wisconsin youth's elbow as a bleeding GI tumbled on top. The other soldier was thrashing: "I told him to stay still because moving would draw fire. Finally he did. I don't know whether he was dead or unconscious." Yet listening to the screams and continuous hail of bullets hitting the men in the field, Wendt's mind spun. *I must be the only guy left alive in this whole bunch*, he thought. The steel tracks on the German tanks rattled loudly as Wendt lay there in the field, some of them shooting again into the mass of moaning and groaning men. After some time the clank of the tank tracks and the groans of the dying faded. Then Wendt heard Bojarski's voice first whispering to him. Someone else in the knot of mangled bodies told the men both to hush. A new nightmare emerged: After the tank column passed Wendt observed SS men walk into the field to finish off anyone still alive.

> I was sure they would find me, I was lying face downward and out of the corner of my eye I saw a pair of black shoes right next to me. I held my breath so he wouldn't see any movement, but finally I couldn't hold it any longer and I had to take a deep breath. I was

sure he would see me then and finish me off as his pals were doing to others of our men. But he didn't notice my breath and went away.[72]

Still, Wendt, who, as an armored recon field interpreter, understood German clearly, listened as the SS executioners called out to each other, *"Da atmet noch einer"* (There is one still breathing)[73] Moments later Wendt heard a pistol shot. When the executioners were gone, Wendt was convinced that he owed his life to the dead man splayed on top of him. His own uniform was covered with the man's blood.

Many of the details recalled varied from one witness to the next. Several Americans thought the vehicle, which carried the officer who fired the first shots, was a command car; others thought it was a tank. As for the vehicle at the crossroads that looked like a jeep, could that have been Gerhard Walla's broken down amphibious *Schwimmwagen*? Pvt. William Reem heard a German yell, *"Feuer!"* (Fire!)[74] Jim Mattera also thought he heard a shout to kill.[75]

T/5 Paul Gartska, who was with the rest of the 285th in the field, recalled some tantalizing jigsaw puzzle-like pieces when he spoke to the U.S. First Army the day after the incident. In his mind's eye he clearly recalled seeing the vehicle from which the man had shot the pistol—it had white numerals on its side. The first number he couldn't be sure of, but he was confident that the last two numerals on the tank were "31." The weight of evidence would suggest that Gartska had seen Panzer Nr. 731, commanded by Hans Siptrott—the same vehicle from which Georg Fleps was accused of having first fired into the crowd of prisoners.

For Pfc. Paul Martin, the appearance of a superior German officer on the scene seemed to set the horror in motion. One must ponder whether it was Josef Diefenthal or perhaps Peiper himself?

After we stood in the pasture with our hands up peacefully for about half an hour, a German command car came up. . . . I could not tell the rank of the officer in the car. This officer stood in the command car and gave an order, which I could not understand. Fire was immediately opened on us with a pistol from the command car and then taken up by machine guns on the halftracks and tanks. I stood there until I saw two of our men fall after being shot, and then I fell on my face, laying there expecting to be killed at any moment.[76]

Like most of the prisoners standing in the field, Bill Merriken instantly turned away after the first bullets and fell face-first flat to the earth. On the ground, his head was turned to the left with his left arm covering most of his face. He was unharmed before he dropped, but as he lay there, slashing machine gunfire continued to rake across the prone bodies, hosing them with a deadly shower of lead. Two bullets slammed into his back—one within inches of his spine. There were terrible sounds—the "thunk" of bullets burying themselves in the ground or the dull thud of bullets striking human flesh. Worse were the horrifying screams of the dying. And all the while the loud stammer of the machine guns continued.

Next to Merriken, a machine-gun bullet had struck Pvt. Max Schwitzgold in the chest and he was writhing in agony, his torso draped over Merriken's. Then the machine guns stopped, and several Germans came into the field, giving "mercy shots" to anyone who moved or moaned. Merriken urgently whispered to Schwitzgold to be still, but it was no use. "He was out of his head."[77] There were footsteps, voices, and the loud crack of a gun. Schwitzgold's body lurched as a bullet passed through his body to lodge in Merriken's leg.[78] Even though wounded again, Merriken held his breath, not daring to move. He felt as if he had dropped into a dark well.

This, he thought, *is what it feels like to die.*

CHAPTER 7

"Bump Them Off!"

Just after 1 p.m. Jochen Peiper impatiently left the crowd of American prisoners standing at the Baugnez crossroads. He was enraged by the delay involved. The Panther tank of his immediate subordinate, Werner Poetschke, seemed to have suffered some physical damage. In a brash, ill-advised move, Poetschke had used his vehicle as a battering ram to push some American trucks off the road. It remained just across from the Café Bodarwe, with its muzzle pointing into the field where the American prisoners were gathering. The encounter left Werner Poetschke fuming as well. He dismounted his Panther and walked down among the American prisoners and then skulked back toward the crossroads. "Chauffeur? Chauffeur?" he asked aloud.[1] It was the best English he could muster to recruit American drivers. For the most part the GIs ignored him; some did not even turn their heads.

Meanwhile, SS messenger Gerhard Walla, originally moving with the lead panzer group of Werner Sternebeck, was still trying to extricate his amphibious jeep from the muddy ditch. Sternebeck and Tonk were gone, and for long minutes he had been uncomfortably sitting by the American prisoners at the crossroads. Walla couldn't speak English, but he tried to make it clear to them they should wait for the main part of the battle group to arrive. As much for distraction as anything else, he went to the café for refreshment. Now Walla sat uncomfortably on the hood of his damaged amphibious car, weapon in hand. Presently, two Panther tanks approached. One of the Mk Vs stopped by the café, its steel cupola popping up to reveal Werner Poetschke. Then another big tank, commanded by Arndt Fischer, pulled out into the road to his left and continued on. Walla didn't notice, but just before Fischer's departure, the command halftrack bearing Peiper drove up.

Walla was understandably more focused on Poetschke. Before his punishment assignment with the lead panzer element, the enlisted man had been with the staff company of the I Panzer Battalion. Now Poetschke was speaking to him—an intimidating prospect, as Walla's jeep was stuck in ditch awkwardly. The whole scene had the appearance of incompetence. Other tanks and vehicles passed by. Knowing Poetschke's incendiary temper, Walla quickly explained his situation. Even if his vehicle was hopelessly marooned in mud, at least he was guarding these prisoners and could report that Sternebeck and the leading tanks were ahead. Seemingly satisfied, Poetschke told him "to find SS-Sgt Ochmann further on as we were supposed to requisition some trucks and fuel." Poetschke told Walla to wait around until SS-1st Lt. Rumpf appeared with help to get his vehicle out of the ditch. "What about the prisoners?" Walla asked. "We don't bother with them," Poetschke responded. "The infantry will come."[2] Yet Reinhard Maier, the 1st Panzer Battalion communications operator, heard the same question from Walla but later related that Poetschke gave a very different answer: "Kill them!"[3]

In the jostling panzer column just behind Peiper and Diefenthal were the SPWs from the 9th Panzer Engineer Company and similar vehicles from the 3rd Panzer Engineer Company.[4] The blond-haired leader of the 9th Panzer Engineers was twenty-three-year-old SS-1st Lt. Erich Rumpf. Born to a simple miner's family in Bleicherode am Harz, Rumpf had fought a long time with the Leibstandarte, often in a role that brought him in contact with the prurient unsavory underbelly of the Waffen SS. Even though sympathizers would later claim they were "soldiers like any others," enemies of the Waffen SS claimed that they tested the bottom of any moralistic ethos. At a young age Rumpf had been with the Hitler Youth, and he joined the Waffen SS in September 1939. Graduating as an SS leader, he was assigned to the Leibstandarte on January 30, 1942, and was a convinced SS leader.[5]

"We were adherents to National Socialism," his wife would later write, trying to exonerate her man in prison, "because we did not know anything else . . . but there was war, and war is brutal."[6]

From France to Russia and back again, Rumpf fought with the Leibstandarte on nearly every front, eventually moving to the thankless leadership position of Peiper's disciplinary platoon. That particular group was filled with the worst types in the tank regiment: *Der verlorene Haufen*—the lost bunch.[7] Placing them at the head of an impossible attack was an old European military tradition and a way to get rid of troublemakers. In the fragmented kaleidoscope of the Waffen SS view, such men were typically criminal and expendable anyway. With this in mind, did Rumpf admit that his command took part in the crossroads shooting? Yes, in a way: In a frenzied rash of statements from Schwäbisch Hall, Rumpf crafted alibis and warily described the poor human material with which he was put in charge. For instance, there was the bestial campaign in Russia—a justification that Rumpf was only too willing to invoke.

Yet in Werner Poetschke, Erich Rumpf seemed to meet his match. Poetschke incited the worst type of behavior—or at least some Rumpf sympathetic subordinates said so after the war. Others painted a less charitable picture of Rumpf himself. They said he talked the same game as Poetschke.

Indeed, in a meeting of his unit at the end of November 1944, a radio operator in one of Rumpf's SPWs, SS-Pvt. Walter Fransee, recounted a training speech Rumpf made on the first floor of a school building in Eckdorf, Germany. "The reputation of the SS has to precede by kilometers ahead of us," Rumpf told his audience. "In this connection," Fransee recalled, "he also said that no prisoners were to be taken."[8] Yet for Fransee, such exhortations were hardly new; rather, they fit within other horrific experiences in eastern Europe. He recounted one particular vividly disturbing memory when, at the end of February 1943, on orders, his unit ruthlessly burned to the ground a Russian village near Kharkov—supposedly harboring partisans: "All inhabitants of the village were shot, man, woman or child."[9]

Fransee recalled other horrors in Ziglerowka, Utgatschi, and other scarcely pronounceable villages. Jochen Peiper's command, Fransee said, "burned down an entire village in the East. . . . Ever since his battalion has been called the *Lötlampenabteilung* and has a burning blowtorch as its symbol." The implication was clear: Hardly a smear of shame—that moniker was an SS epithet of honor.[10]

Now in Belgium, the depraved war in eastern Europe came to roost. Even more, in a meeting in mid-December, according to Rumpf, Peiper advised him that in the coming operation "the situation can arise when prisoners of war have to be shot and if necessary the resistance has to be broken by terror." While Rumpf was reading this order, Peiper entered the room where he stood. Peiper glanced at the paper and then, with a slight smile, repeated his sardonic epithet: "Also, a bad reputation has its commitments."[11] It was one of Peiper's long-standing mottos—the suggestive refrain from the Zarah Leander song.[12] Although Peiper later denied owning this catchy phrase, convincing evidence proved otherwise.

Back at the crossroads, Poetschke got his tank operating and then clattered down the road after Fischer and the others in the vanguard. Just before he left, Panzer Nr. 602 under SS-Sgt. Wrabetz came by the crossroads and saw the American prisoners still standing with their hands up. His loader, SS-Cpl. Michael Mundt, recalled seeing some civilians by the café as well as Diefenthal and Peiper in an SPW. They had been parked by a tank across from the assembled Americans. As Mundt proceeded south, he came across SS-Maj. Poetschke on foot, who ordered them to hurry. Mundt was only about a thousand meters from the crossroads (halfway to Ligneuville) when the communications SPW of headquarters company of the 1st Panzer Battalion drove up. SS-Cpl. Reinhard Maier, the halftrack driver, was stunned by the conversation he had overheard:

> After about 20 minutes, a messenger arrived from the rear from the *9th Panzer Engineer Company* that had been detailed to assemble the prisoners and asked Maj. Poetschke what to do with the prisoners. Poetschke in his presence said: "Shoot them."[13]

Thunderstruck, Maier then asked Poetschke if he thought the messenger had received the correct order. Poetschke asked the messenger who was at the crossroads. He replied: "SS-Lt. Rumpf." Poetschke then recalled the messenger and asked him to repeat the orders and the messenger said: "Shoot the prisoners." Poetschke then said "Correct," and dismissed the messenger. Although no record remains, the messenger seems to have returned to deliver the news to Rumpf.[14] Soon, common knowledge in the panzer regiment was that Poetschke ordered the crossroads shootings.[15]

Meanwhile, back at Baugnez, Gerhard Walla watched as Rumpf and his SPWs approached his solitary outpost. Rumpf stopped to talk: "You wait for the last vehicle to come by with SS Lt. Hering and have him take you along." Nearly a dozen cars and SPWs went by, but presently Walla waved down Günther Hering's SPW. After a short discussion Hering hauled Walla's jeep out of the ditch with a tow rope. "I changed my wheel as fast as I could and headed down into Engelsdorf," Walla later recounted.[16] At about that time Rudolf Dörr's and Karl Wemmel's SPWs (1st squad, 1st Platoon, 9 Panzer Engineer Company) arrived at the crossroads. At one point SS-S/Sgt. Dörr bounded from his halftrack to convince an American soldier to surrender. Dörr's radio operator, SS-Pvt. Heinz Kappermann, was there:

> As we turned into the main road, I was able to see out of my radio operator's porthole between 40 to 50 Americans soldiers standing not far from the crossroads. I estimate that they were between 10 and 15 meters off the road. The prisoners were unarmed, had their steel helmets on and were holding their hands folded over their helmets. I remember that 7 or 8 German Mk IV and Mk V tanks were proceeding along the highway. . . . Followed by the second vehicle of the first squad [Cpl. Wemmel] we drove along the highway towards Lignonville [sic] and passed about 14 or 15 American trucks. Almost all of these vehicles still had their drivers in them although they were being guarded by a German soldier. . . . While we were halted on the main highway SS S/Sgt. Dörr appeared at the vehicle, and said as he climbed back in, "I went away from the prisoners because I heard that they are all to be shot, and I do not want to have anything to do with that."[17]

Erich Maute was present as well. A Waffen SS medic from Tübin-
gen, he estimated that when their SPW was only twenty meters from
the crossroads, SS-Lt. Günther Hering approached their halftrack and
ordered Dörr to dismount. Maute thought he observed anti-aircraft
tanks at the crossroads, but he almost certainly saw the three-barreled
flak 1.5-cm "Drilling" SPWs of the 3rd Panzer Engineer Company under Max Beutner. He saw the SPWs of Hering and Rumpf parked on
the opposite side of the crossroads from the café. The SPW driver
stopped for a short time and then rounded the corner by the café.

"While passing the corner," Maute recalled, "I saw SS-S/Sgt. Dörr
talking with 1st Lt. Rumpf." Just off to the side of Rumpf, Maute saw
two officers standing and talking by the small huddle of halftracks
near the crossroad. "One of them was very tall. . . . He wore a brown-
yellow jacket . . . it could have been an Italian flyer's jacket." Next to
the man—almost certainly Diefenthal—was another officer in a two-
part black panzer uniform and looking very upset, as he was yelling.
"He hollered at us that no one should touch those trucks as they were
confiscated for the 1st Battalion," Maute said.[18] Halftracks kept moving past the café.

Maute went on to describe, "On the right side of the road, in a field,
approximately 10 meters or so from the house, I saw American PWs
standing who were unarmed and held their hands over their heads. I
don't remember the number anymore . . . [but] there were very many
of them." Dörr and Wemmel had each picked up one American prisoner and stopped by the field to drop those prisoners off with the others collecting there. As they waited, Maute saw SS-Lt. Hering and Dörr
in the field standing in front of the prisoners. SS-S/Sgt. Dörr seemed
agitated, running back and forth from the prisoners as SS-Pvt. Spaeth
and SS-Lt. Hering stood guard with machine pistols over the prisoners.
Other tanks passed by.

Presently, SS-S/Sgt. Walter Wedeleit's SPW, of Rumpf's penal platoon, pulled up just behind Rumpf's SPW. Also in Wedeleit's SPW were
SS-Pvt. Max Rieder and SS-Sgt. Willi von Chamier.

Rumpf was parked just before the intersection across from the café.
Wedeleit pulled in six meters or so behind Rumpf's halftrack. As they
pulled up, von Chamier observed a woman and man just outside the
café at the crossroads corner. Rumpf waved to Wedeleit's crew to pull

off the road to allow heavy traffic of tanks and SPWs to squeeze by. Ten meters further back was the 1st platoon SPW of SS-Sgt. Günther Her- ing.[19] Von Chamier recalled,

> We stood there awhile when SS-Lt. Rumpf motioned us to come to him. At that time he stood in front of a house [café], which stood directly at the corner of the right-hand side of the street. . . . We had not yet arrived when he shouted to us to get our weapons and follow him right away. He led us—the whole crew of the SPW of SS-S/Sgt. Wedeleit—to a pasture, which was immediately south of the house. We stood on the north side of this pasture next to the street. On this pasture approximately 90 American prisoners were standing with their hands raised. . . . The prisoners had no arms and stood there quietly. . . . Immediately thereafter SS-Lt. Rumpf gave us the following order after we arrived: "Bump the prisoners off." I am not sure if those were his exact words, but the meaning is correct. Thereupon we opened fire on the prisoners of war and at the same time, the machine guns of the tanks and SPWs that also stood on the street at this pasture."[20]

That Willi von Chamier and the others of his SPW had moved be- fore the prisoners on foot, only to find a line of SPWs and tanks al- ready across from the prisoners, is significant. On orders, von Chamier said he personally fired half a dozen shots into the prisoners with a car- bine. He also observed how his cohorts, Rieder, Corenzi, Katscher, and Biotta, joined in:

> We returned to our SPWs and mounted after the prisoners had fallen to the ground. Only Haas remained in the pasture and I saw from our SPW Haas walking once more among the prisoners and shooting the prisoners lying on the ground. One case I remember especially clearly, namely one of those lying on the ground and believed to be dead, raised himself halfway up. He pointed to the rear part of his body, which gave me the impression that he was wounded there. The man was also shot dead by Haas with his machine pistol. After the shooting was over, we received an order from SS-Lt. Rumpf to proceed on our march.[21]

Max Rieder was in the SPW as well:

As we stopped I got off my vehicle to fetch some loot for myself and
the other men of the vehicle, because I saw north of the crossroads
some American trucks standing on the road. . . . When I went to
the American trucks my company commander, SS-Lt. Rumpf stood
just at these crossroads. . . . Adjoining this house on the crossroads
is a field on the right-hand side of the road which leads to
Engelsdorf [Ligneuville]. On this field were already at that time
about 60 to 70 American prisoners of war . . . and had their hands
over their heads. When I returned to my SPW a few minutes later,
loaded with rations from the American trucks, SS-Lt. Rumpf
already stood in front of the house. . . . SS-Lt. Rumpf called to me,
"Rieder, you and all of those in need of it, get your rifle." When I
returned with the rations, the other members of the penal group
were already in front of the prisoners. SS-Sgt. Haas ran about
amongst the prisoners in the field. . . . It was clear to me that the
prisoners were to be shot. I then went back to my own vehicle and
fetched my rifle. . . . At this time SS-Lt. Rumpf stood no longer in
front of the house, but south of the house a little in front of the field
with the prisoners."[22]

Standing by the American prisoners, Rieder saw SS-S/Sgt. Wedeleit
and several members of his SPW get their orders from Erich Rumpf.
Yet even in fixing blame on the shoulders of his superior, Rieder's confession revealed an unfeeling edge:

I stood across the field towards the north end and near the house
and looked at the prisoners who stood with their hands folded
above their heads in the field. A short time after we arrived there,
SS-Lt. Rumpf gave the order to bump off the prisoners. He used the
words, "Bump the prisoners off" or "Shoot into them." I do not
know whether at this time there were any other vehicles standing
near the field. I didn't pay any attention. . . . All the members of the
penal group shot into the prisoners and I also fired five shots. All
my shots were aimed at the same prisoner. This American stood
near the right edge of the field and only about six meters away from

me. He was of medium build and stocky. I aimed all shots at the head of the American and I saw that he collapsed already after the first shot. I then emptied my magazine into other Americans lying on the ground. . . . From the beginning, I saw that I hit him as intended because he fell back in such a way which is common for people who received a shot through the head. The American was undoubtedly dead.[23]

As Rieder banged away, he also saw SS-Lt. Rumpf firing into the prisoners with a pistol. Rieder likewise observed Willi von Chamier and Biotta off to the side, firing their assault rifles. Even SS-Sgt. Helmuth Haas joined in with a machine pistol. Indeed, according to von Chamier, all the members of Wedeleit's SPW had fired into the Americans.[24]

Meanwhile, Rump's SPW was parked just east of the crossroads. Driver Paul Buth of Günther Hering's vehicle remained behind the wheel of the third of Rumpf's SPWs lined up at the crossroads. "I didn't leave my SPW during this time," he was careful to tell interrogators. But he did hear a loud cacophony of machine gunfire just before Rumpf returned and told his driver to resume the march. Shortly afterward Buth saw the results. S/Sgt. Wedeleit's SPW was just ahead of his own with squad leader Haas:

Then when we turned sharply left around the corner I saw lying in the field, bordering the house, about 50 Americans who were unarmed and obviously had been shot shortly before. Just as I was to turn sharply around the corner at the described intersection, I saw SS-Sgt. Haas of the penal platoon, fire with his machine pistol into the Americans who were lying on the ground next to the house. At this place Haas fired two bursts into the Americans, about 15 shots all told. Sgt. Haas rode at that time in the vehicle directly in front of me and I could watch him closely. A short distance beyond the end of the field, I saw in the road ditch on the right hand side of the street an unarmed American kneeling who did not wear a steel helmet. I saw SS-Sgt. Haas fire a burst at this kneeling American. This American held his hands folded in front of his chest praying and the moment I saw him I was under the impression that the American was already wounded immediately before Haas shot at him . . . the distance between Haas and the prisoner was at the most three meters.[25]

Walter Fransee, the radio operator in Hering's SPW, saw Hering join in firing at the kneeling prisoner, describing a disturbing scene similar to Buth's, complete with a detailed sketch. Immediately afterward Fransee saw Hering fire at other American prisoners. This was a small group who came out of the woods with their hands up approaching Hering's SPW to surrender. When he was eight meters away, Hering blasted the first man in the chest with a full magazine of machine pistol rounds. That done, he then casually handed Fransee the empty magazine to reload.[26]

After the short pause in their move south the SPW continued on slowly, with the traffic now collecting ahead of them. About a hundred yards up they pulled off the road, as the traffic had nearly stopped. During the ten-minute stop Maute took the opportunity to dismount and urinate by the roadside. Suddenly, Rudolf Dörr arrived on foot and climbed onto the SPW's metal deck. Maute recounted that he had received the order to bump off the Americans from Rumpf; he was cursing about Rumpf.[27]

Had Rumpf been responsible for the orders to shoot? His underlings, Dörr, Rieder, and von Chamier, said so. Moreover, many saw him at the scene of the massacre.[28] Indeed, two witnesses said Rumpf personally fired his own pistol into the prisoners. And in his own long-winded statement to investigators, Rumpf admitted that he was at the crossroads when the massacre took place, but he lamely claimed the thought of seeing the prisoners shot was mentally too much. In a tortured alibi Rumpf said he hid out in an American truck, stuffing his pockets with American K-rations. He claimed that the orders to shoot prisoners had actually come from SS-1st Lt. Friedrich Christ, who, according to Rumpf, had shown up at the crossroads looking for a posse to help him with the unsavory mission. Unfortunately for Rumpf, other than Heinz Rehagel, no one said that Christ had been present—and both these men needed helpful alibis.[29] Finally, Rumpf composed still another statement in which he claimed to have hidden behind the café at the crossroads rather than see the American prisoners shot.[30]

Rumpf described how his line of SPWs stopped short of the cross-roads, but he observed some other halftracks and an Mk IV tank lined up across from the café. In response to Christ's appeal, Rumpf said that he volunteered Dörr's men only to have them return minutes later. "This man tells me that I should shoot prisoners of war!" Dörr railed. Rumpf said he told Dörr to ignore that command and to be on his way (Dörr's memory of that exchange was *very* different). In any case, his men began returning back from the field just as two Mk V tanks, in-cluding that of Hans Hennecke, drove up to the crossroads and paused in front of the café.[31]

> All of this happened before the shooting started. After I talked to SS-S/Sgt. Dörr, I went to an American truck as I did not want to watch the shooting about to take place. During this time my SPWs totaling four or five stood on the road directly before the crossing. Some other SPWs and panzers drove slowly around the corner. After I stood at the truck for about one or two minutes while the men unloaded "K" rations, the firing at the prisoners of war standing next to the house began, which I could hear but not see. A great number of weapons were fired; machine guns, rifles and pistols. This shooting lasted about one half minute or a little less. Immediately following it, some single shots were fired. After three minutes after the big shooting was over I left the American truck and went to my SPW. I shouted to my men, "Let's go—we move out!" About a minute later we drove off in the direction towards Engelsdorf [Ligneuville].[32]

Peering through the gray mist, not only had Erich Rumpf and his men seen their own SPWs at the north end of crossroads, but they also observed other pine bough–camouflaged German halftracks mixed among the tanks of the 7th Panzer Company. These were the vehicles of SS-Sgt. Max Beutner's second platoon of the 3rd Panzer Engineer Company bearing bridging equipment and arriving early on the scene about the same time that Rumpf stopped just short of the crossroads. Straightaway, Beutner took over guarding the prisoners with one or two halftracks of the 11th Panzer Grenadier Company. Because Peiper had insisted that everyone keep moving, the job of guarding the prisoners was a shifting responsibility—and one that Werner Poetschke looked to end swiftly.

Two of Beutner's Sdkfz. 251/7 SPWs arrived, laden with grenadiers bristling with automatic weapons sticking above their siding of steel bridging equipment. They pulled off to the right side of the road before the assembling prisoners. SS-Pvt. Joachim Hoffmann in Sepp Witkowski's armored halftrack and its crew of twelve had arrived at the Baugnez crossroads after 1 P.M. Just before they reached the intersection they passed three of Erich Rumpf's SPWs parked on the right side of the road. Turning left and continuing on, they found Max Beutner's SPW, with its three-gun 1.5-cm "Drilling" AA guns already trained on a group of about a hundred Americans standing in the field. Ahead, Hoffmann claimed to have seen the assault bridge SPW of Friedel Bode, driven by Herbert Losenski. As Hoffman moved up to pass his platoon leader on the right, Beutner yelled something Hoffmann could not make out. "After I had pulled the SPW to a stop, he told us to get the machine guns ready and that the men should get ready to 'Bump off the prisoners.'"[33]

That deadly preparation took some time; the weapons were not loaded nor sited properly to allow them to fire correctly. Minutes passed as machine guns were moved and belts of ammunition were prepared. Hoffmann dismounted with a machine pistol and posted himself by his halftrack with Gustav Neve, who shouldered an assault rifle. "Bump them off! Bump them off!" Hoffmann later claimed someone was shouting; Gustav Neve remembered that Beutner himself was the one who egged them on, saying, "Bump them off—all of them!"[34] Machine gunner Heinz Stickel in the same SPW recalled seeing sixty-odd Americans standing in the meadow across from him just before receiving direct orders from SPW leader Witkowski to shoot into the crowd.[35]

"As far as I remember," Hoffmann wrote, "the first shots were from Beutner's SPW." After that, everyone joined in the firing. Hoffmann admitted having participated in the shooting. He recalled that there was a line of tanks slowly passing behind them as Beutner stood in the road and ordered everyone to fire. But the scene was too busy for him to take further note: A lot was going on. Like Sprenger, Hoffmann said that he had seen Jupp Diefenthal and Erich Rumpf at the crossroads.

Both were congregated around a Panther some distance north of the prisoners—Werner Poetschke's tank. That all happened just minutes before the shooting took place.[36] After the deadly fusillade ended, Beutner ordered everyone into the field to administer "mercy shots" to the Americans still alive.

Deepening the moral bog of Sievers's command, SS men Gustav Neve, Siegfried Jaekel, and Heinz Stickel gave accounts corroborating Hoffmann. Indeed, they were all in the same SPW directly across from the American prisoners.[37] Based on their multiple accounts, Max Beutner's SPW was the first vehicle on the scene after Sternebeck's tank-spearhead platoon disappeared. As driver Joachim Hoffmann approached, Max Beutner stood in the middle of the road, his hand stretched out, signaling them to halt. The prisoners were to be shot, Beutner informed Witkowski—a conversation a number of this half-track's occupants witnessed. Beutner ordered them to move just a little further on and park across from the prisoners so as not to block his field of fire. Obediently, they geared a few meters ahead.

Soon afterward Beutner was seen conversing with some officers near a Panther located north of the field. Rumpf was among them.[38] Presently, another rogue SPW belonging to SS-Sgt. Gerhard Schumacher of the 11th Panzer Grenadier Company happened on the scene. Without hesitating, Beutner ordered Schumacher to load his short assault cannon and prepare to blow the prisoners off the field. Shumacher turned his SPW to face the assembling group of Americans directly. Even though claiming to be horrified, SS-Grenadier Heinz Friedrich noted, "SS-Sgt. Schumacher seemed delighted at the chance to shoot these prisoners . . . he rubbed his hands together calling out 'Masche, masche!—Goody, goody!'"—the infectious bad-boy expression of SS leader, Georg Preuss. Even so, Schumacher's crew could not depress the short, stubby 7.5-cm cannon from the road to train it on the increasingly uneasy Americans in the field.[39] Frustrated, Beutner waved Schumacher on, Friedrich overhearing him remark that the next tank "would take care of the job." Schumacher's SPW backed up and then waddled off south toward Ligneuville.

Meanwhile, Jaekel and other crew members just south of Beutner's SPW prepared Witkowski's automatic weapons for the execution salvo that was to come.[40] Belts of ammunition were swiftly loaded and machine guns sited so they could fire off the right-hand side of the SPW hulls. At the same time a line of Mk IV tanks from the 7th Panzer Company were making their approach. Just as Beutner had flagged down Dörr's and Schumacher's SPWs moments before, he was now attempting to halt oncoming tanks. Several machines slipped by, but Beutner then signaled Panzer Nr. 731 to stop. The Panzer IV was approaching across the field from the east. On the road behind it paraded a line of additional tanks of the same type. At that same moment more of Beutner's SPWs obediently clanked up. The road was jammed with German armor.

Gustav Sprenger and Hans Oettinger's armored personnel carriers were just arriving when the shooting began, cutting the corner of the traffic-jammed intersection. Marcel Boltz, the Alsatian machine gunner in Sprenger's SPW, claimed to hear a gust of machine gunfire up ahead just before he reached the crossroads. Boltz was also very sure of the 2nd platoon of the 3rd Panzer Engineer Company's order of march—and which vehicles were present. Just ahead was Beutner's SPW, the platoon leader, and just a short way up Friedel Bode and Sepp Witkowski drove their own carriers. If Boltz turned around, he could see the SPW driven by Oettinger.[41] "We will start firing!"[42] Beutner shouted. There was a brief pause. "Shoot!" Grenadier Siegfried Jaekel's yell sounded a split second before the crack of pistol shots shattered the air. Ernst Goldschmidt in Beutner's SPW opened fire. As if on cue, everyone with a weapon immediately fired into the prisoners.

SS-Pvt. Gustav Sprenger was in one of the halftracks commanded by SS-Sgt. Wolfgang Altkrüger. Motoring beyond the muddy roads past the little Belgian village of Thirimont, they heard shooting just before they arrived at Baugnez. There, he spied two SPWs and a lone tank parked near the road intersection. As they turned left toward Ligneuville, Sprenger saw the corner café across from the nexus of roads. Just south of the nondescript building sat an Mk V Panther parked on the right side of the road with its cannon angled down and to the southwest as if it were covering the large throng of American prisoners. Just beyond the cannon in the field was a group of German officers. According to Sprenger, among these were SS-Lt. Rumpf; his platoon leader, Max Beutner; and an officer in a bright yellow jacket who would later be identified as Jupp Diefenthal.[43]

Just as the shooting began, Sprenger stopped his SPW on the road midway across from the prisoners. Immediately across from him, on the left-hand side of the road, was Beutner's SPW. Two other SPWs were parked nearby: SS-Sgt. Sepp Witkowski's SPW, driven by Joachim Hoffmann was just ahead of him to the south, and an SPW driven by SS-Cpl. Oettinger was pulling up behind Hoffmann. Just before Sprenger stopped, he saw the machine guns on Hoffman's SPW suddenly spout a blaze of gunfire that enveloped the Americans standing in the field. In Sprenger's own vehicle, SS man Marcel Boltz fired into the prisoners with an MG 42 while someone in Oettinger's SPW just to the rear began shooting as well.[44] Boltz added to Sprenger's recollection:

> When I stopped in front of the pasture where the American soldiers lay in the field, they were still turning and twisting in their own blood and those in the front of the group nearest the road were moaning and groaning in pain. After the fire from these machine guns ended, I left my SPW and went into the field. . . . SS-Sgt. Beutner came to us from the group that had been standing by the Panther and said "Go shoot those that are still alive."[45]

Although Joachim Hoffmann saw Friedel Bode in charge of the 1st Squad SPW just ahead of Witkowski's SPW, Bode would never speak about his involvement at the crossroads at either the Schwäbisch Hall interrogations or the later trial.[46] However, SS enlisted man Friedel Kies, who had been in the same vehicle, later confessed that all members of his SPW shot on Beutner's orders.[47] Even more importantly, Siegfried Jaekel, just behind Bode's SPW, saw that entire crew—including an unknown paratrooper—preparing to fire moments before the massacre.

Just before Max Beutner and Erich Rumpf tried to locate help to kill the prisoners, the tanks of the 7th Panzer Company began to snake by the halftracks pulled off the road. The grinding traffic was constant. Sternebeck's and Tonk's Panzer IVs and Karl Ohlrogge's SPW with the Spitze were now further ahead. Behind them had been Pilzarek's Nr. 734, driven by Manfred Thorn, with Schraeder's Nr. 702 and then Klingelhoefer's Nr. 701, driven by Rolf Ehrhardt, just behind him. Timing was everything. The crews of these three tanks (734, 702, and 701) continued on to the south while Rumpf and Beutner sized up the assembling prisoners. Unluckily for its crew, the next panzer approaching Beutner's position was Nr. 731 under Peiper's old panzer hand from Russia, *"Spitz"*—SS-S/Sgt. Hans Siptrott.

Both Siptrott and Roman Clotten's panzer behind him, Nr. 723, had gotten mired in the muck near Thirimont. With effort, both Mk IVs were freed to resume their advance. As the two tanks had lost their place in the march formation—Panzer Nr. 734 under Horst Pilarzek was now in the lead—together they took a shortcut just north of Thirimont, cutting across the hedgerow-lined pasture before the Baugnez crossroads. Intending to resume their place in the line, both regained the road just south of the café and across from the assembling American prisoners. Siptrott recalled,

> Approximately 60 American prisoners of war, with hands raised over their heads were standing on the right hand side of the shed in the field. . . . On the right hand side of the road, exactly opposite them were two or three SPWs—I believe there were three. I passed the SPWs at 15–20 km per hour. There I took notice as a commander of one of the SPWs waved at me. . . . I stopped and this commander approached me and said: "Turn your gun around and shoot into them." I answered him, "I don't have enough ammunition for such a thing." . . . I did not know this commander. . . . I believe that the SPW belonged to the 9th *Panzer Engineeer Company* [sic] because the SPW standing nearest to me was equipped with bridging equipment. . . . During the time I was talking to the commander of the SPW, Pvt. Fleps was sitting in the loader's slit. When I turned around, I saw that Fleps, who apparently was eager to shoot, had a pistol in his hand. Because SS-Capt. Klingelhoefer had made a speech to the platoon leaders . . . telling us that we should not take any prisoners, I permitted Fleps to shoot. . . . I said to Fleps "Shoot!" . . . As far as I can remember, he fired two shots, one immediately after the other. Right after that, or almost simultaneously, the SPW standing nearest to me started shooting. . . . Hardly more than a minute after the shooting started, I gave orders to resume march.[48]

The key player in Panzer Nr. 731 was enlisted man Georg Fleps, a Rumanian farm boy who had been with the Leibstandarte since January 1944. Fleps had a reputation as a hothead; he had earlier been involved with the shooting of a Canadian prisoner on August 1, 1944. According to Fleps's later statement,[49]

> Just past the intersection on the right side which leads to Engelsdorf, I saw many Americans standing in the field with their hands up. . . . At this time I was assistant gunner in my tank, which had the number 731. . . . Up ahead of us was a Mk V tank. Behind us drove SS-S/Sgt. Clotten with his tank. . . . On the right side of the street opposite the group of captured Americans stood an SPW with its machine gun pointed at the Americans. . . . As we approached the SPW, the commander gave us a signal with his hand to stop. He said to Siptrott: "We have received orders from up ahead to bump off the Americans. Everything must go quickly. Every vehicle is needed up ahead. Help us with this and make it go fast." Siptrott said at first, "I do not have much ammunition." Then the commander said something else to Siptrott whereupon, Siptrott who saw that I already had my pistol in hand, gave me the order to shoot. I then fired a shot at one of the Americans standing in the front row and I saw him fall over. . . . As far as I know, this shot of mine was the first one shot at the Americans. Immediately afterwards, the SPW behind us (we had driven up a little) began to fire with its machine gun at the prisoners. At that, Siptrott remarked, "These wretched dogs. . . ." When the machine gun on the SPW ceased firing, a single American was still standing up straight. I pointed my pistol at him and fired. Watching my shots I saw him fall. . . . Just as we drove away, the machine guns commenced firing again.[50]

Roman Clotten in Panzer Nr. 723 drove just behind Siptrott. Prior to the events Clotten spied a long line of American trucks that seemed to be guarded by a lone Mk V Panther standing at the crossroads just to his rear. He didn't know whose tank it was, but considering his position near the point, he surmised that it must be the vehicle of Poetschke or Fischer, Poetschke's adjutant, who had been just ahead of them in the line of march. Clotten remembered,[51]

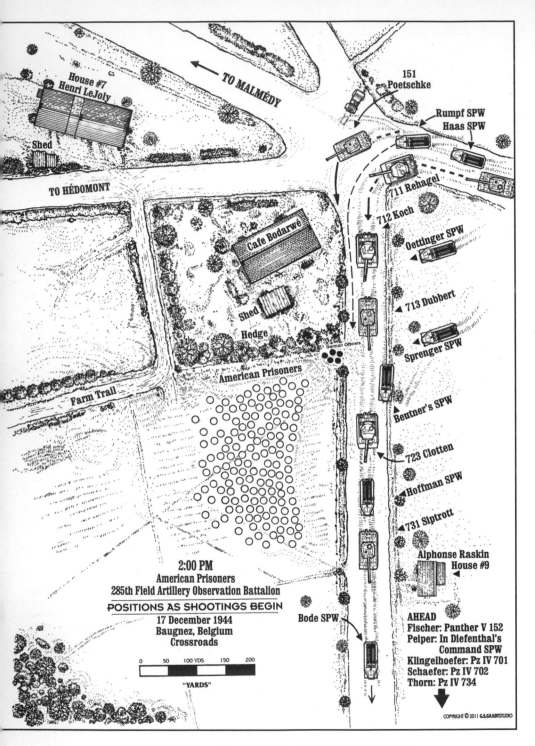

House #7
Henri LeJoly

Shed

TO MALMÉDY

151
Poetschke

Rumpf SPW
Haas SPW

711 Rehagel

TO HÉDOMONT

712 Koch

Oettinger SPW

Cafe Bodarwé

713 Dubbert

Sprenger SPW

Shed

Hedge

German Officers

Beutner's SPW

American Prisoners

Farm Trail

723 Clotten

Hoffman SPW

731 Siptrott

Alphonse Raskin
House #9

2:00 PM
American Prisoners
285th Field Artillery Observation Battalion

POSITIONS AS SHOOTINGS BEGIN

17 December 1944
Baugnez, Belgium
Crossroads

Bode SPW

AHEAD
Fischer: Panther V 152
Peiper: In Diefenthal's
Command SPW
Klingelhoefer: Pz IV 701
Schaefer: Pz IV 702
Thorn: Pz IV 734

0   50   100 YDS   150   200

"YARDS"

COPYRIGHT © 2011 G.S.GAADT STUDIO

POSITIONS AT THE TIME OF THE SHOOTING

We reached the crossing, and without stopping, made a sharp turn to the left. As I was turning the corner where the road makes this left curve, I saw on the right-hand side, in a field next to the road, American PWs standing. . . . They were standing very close together. . . . In front of the PWs, with their backs to the road, stood a few SS men who wore gray uniforms from which I concluded they were not members of the tank crews, but that they belonged to the two SPWs which I saw standing there. The two SPWs were standing in the field in front of the house [café]. I remember that the firing was begun by the SPW people who were guarding the prisoners. This happened just as I was turning slowly with my tank into the road. How many shots were fired, I cannot say any longer. In any case the Americans fell to the ground like lightning. . . . Until the start of the shooting, the Americans stood there with their arms raised and I saw none of them try to escape or showing an aggressive attitude, or else give any cause for being shot at. . . . All guards, about eight in number, who were standing in the field shot into the prisoners. Two or three of them did not return to their SPWs right away, but continued firing at these Americans lying on the ground. . . . There I saw how some of the wounded twitched and still moved.[52]

If self-serving, Clotten claimed not to have shot at the prisoners, but he was unsure about the other tanks. Clotten said he had watched all the machine guns on the SPWs fire as well as three or so soldiers who shot with machine pistols into the mass of Americans. He observed two men—one of whom he recognized as SS-1st Lt. Erich Rumpf—leave his position just south of the prisoners and walk briskly toward Clotten's tank, out of the line of fire. Clotten's vehicle rumbled along slowly at a walking pace as he saw gunfire fell the prisoners. Although claiming to be anxious to get away from the murderous scene, he was forced to halt about twenty meters from the spot where the prisoners were lying. There, SS-S/Sgt. Siptrott in 731 was stopped in front of him, standing tall in his turret. At the moment he halted, his gunner, SS-Pvt. Hermann Bock, grabbed the tank's machine pistol, rose to the deck, and began blasting away. The din was deafening from Bock's weapon, but there was a similar racket to Clotten's rear. Out of the corner of his eye, Clotten saw the tank of SS-S/Sgt. Erich Dubbert behind his own along with two SPWs. Dubbert, too, was firing into the prisoners with a machine pistol.[53] Bock then fired once more. "Stop!" Clotten shouted. "This makes no sense. They are dead anyhow."[54] Besides, he reasoned, there was hardly any more ammunition for their inferior Italian machine pistol.

Siptrott's Mk IV was about twenty meters in front of Clotten's panzer. Further ahead of Siptrott's panzer was another Mk IV—which one he couldn't be sure.[55] Behind Dubbert's tank was one or two SPWs parked across from the prisoners as his tank approached. Behind Clotten stood the tank of SS-S/Sgt. Koch. Later, prior to trial, he produced a sketch that showed that there were two other SPWs parked by the café on the corner as well as a mysterious Mk V Panther near the crossroads. Clotten couldn't be certain, but he thought it was either the tank of the 1st Panzer Battalion's leader, Werner Poetschke, or his adjutant, Arndt Fischer.

So who could have given the orders for the shooting? "The general belief is that it could have been Poetschke," Clotten claimed. "Nobody seems to believe that Peiper gave the order because it is contrary to his nature—everybody believes that is impossible."[56]

Werner Reicke, an enlisted man with the 7th Panzer Company, also witnessed the scene from a different tank. Seated in Panzer Nr. 712 commanded by SS-S/Sgt.Werner Koch, they had been grinding along in the wake of the offensive.[57] After being hauled out of the mud near Thirimont by Erich Dubbert in Panzer Nr. 713, they arrived at the Baugnez crossroads in the early afternoon. Coming around the corner to the intersection, Reicke saw SS-Maj. Poetschke standing by his tank. "He gave the order not to close up too much since there was danger of air attack." Meanwhile, the American prisoners were being assembled and "taken to a field with their hands up." Turning his head to the right as their tank pulled up twenty meters past the intersection, Reicke observed an American medic about to bandage a soldier.[58] For anti-aircraft protection, their Mk IV panzer had a swivel mounted anti-aircraft machine gun on the turret. He recalled,

We reached the crossroads and parked at the right side of the road in the direction towards Engelsdorf. Two halftracks were standing right behind us. . . . My commanding officer, SS-S/Sgt. Koch got out of the vehicle and was standing around outside the vehicle. I was in the rear of the tank about the right side and then I saw American soldiers leaving their vehicles and being taken to the left side of the house in the field. Suddenly, S/Sgt. Koch jumped into the turret of the tank. I too, took my position as assistant gunner. The window for the use of the assistant gunner was wide open so that I was able to see the Americans in the field. Below next to the vehicle some civilians were standing. Suddenly, I was able to see firing to our front. That might have been the two or three vehicles ahead of us. Since my attention was focused only on the American soldiers, I could only see the tracers coming from the two or three vehicles in front of us and from the halftracks behind us, which was directed towards the American soldiers. Shortly, thereafter S/Sgt. Koch also started firing at the American soldiers from the top of the tank. The civilians standing in front of the house put their hands over their eyes and walked back [inside].[59]

"We took off right afterwards," Reicke remembered. "When the firing started, a civilian was standing in front of the house on the corner and she buried her face in her hands and started to cry. . . . How long Maj. Poetschke remained at the road crossing I don't know, but I believe with certainty that he was present when the shooting started as I did not see him leave."[60]

Because he was the tank loader, Koch scolded Reicke for getting his machine gun jammed during the shooting. The shooting mortified Reicke, and even Koch seemed eager to leave the crossroads. They hurriedly left, their tank crunching down toward Ligneuville, but they were by stops and starts in the snarled tank road traffic. As they waited in the logjam, Reicke recalled that Georg Fleps suddenly appeared on foot and asked if Reicke had seen the *Ami* soldiers shot at the crossroads. "I had my fun shooting into them," Fleps boasted."[61]

Panzer Nr. 711 under Heinz Rehagel was nearly the last in the line of 7th Company tanks. SS-Pvt. Hans Joachim Piper (not Peiper) was the gun loader in that tank.[62] He too had seen the prisoners in the field and watched as Koch in Panzer Nr. 712 just ahead of Nr. 711 fired at the prisoners in the field. Rehagel came back to his tank, spoke briefly to an officer from his turret, and then soon joined in the firing on the Americans now lying in the field. Rehagel also later claimed to have seen the prisoners clustered in a field near the crossroads and to have left his tank to discuss things briefly with Oskar Klingelhoefer and Erich Muenkemer, who was in charge of Rehagel's platoon. Upon returning,

> Suddenly it was called from the front: "Panzers are to shoot." . . .
> From that point, there was shooting at the prisoners in the field. . . .
> I looked over to the field and was suddenly loudly yelled at from
> the left. "Now go on and shoot—we have to go on!" It was SS-1st
> Lt. Christ, commanding the *2nd Panzer Company* who, with a
> movement of his arm pointed at me and my vehicle. I was angry at
> the tone of voice which he used and asked in the same manner, "Or
> else what? Who says so?" He replied, "An order from the front."
> Thereupon, I shot with the anti-aircraft MG at the prisoners.[63]

Had SS-1st Lt. Christ really been at the crossroads with Rehagel? This claim was a convenient alibi for an SS officer in trouble, but others have not substantiated this satisfactorily. Indeed, Rehagel's driver, SS-Pvt. Günther Flächsner, recalled seeing American prisoners in the field just south of the café, and although he saw Rehagel speak to a superior officer, he did not recall seeing Christ there:

> Suddenly, two of the tanks ahead of me started firing. The tank
> ahead of me was SS-S/Sgt. Koch's tank. I could not see which tank
> was ahead of him because we as drivers have only a small range of
> vision. . . . I saw the tracer bullet trajectory.[64]

Although Flächsner would later deny it, Rehagel confessed that his tank had joined in the firing on the Americans after he made the turn near the crossroads. Moreover, his loader, Piper, had testified to the same events both in interrogation that fall as well as at the Malmédy trial.[65] Only Rehagel's later repudiation would muddy the water.

Who fired the first shots at Baugnez? In the official U.S. Army account, SS-Pvt. Georg Fleps was the one who fired the first pistol rounds from the south end of the field. However, the recollection of many American survivors claimed the initial gunfire came from one of the halftracks parked closer to the north end of the field. Siegfried Jaekel and Joachim Hoffmann said that the first shots came from Max Beutner's halftrack right across from the prisoners. Indeed, several accounts indicate both Beutner and SS-1st Lt. Erich Rumpf looked to recruit passersby for the execution detail and gave appropriate orders.

Heinz Friedrich, Rudolf Dörr, and Hans Siptrott gave corroborating testimony. Whether or not he fired the first shots, Rumpf did issue orders and join the shooting with his pistol, according to Max Rieder and Willi von Chamier. Although statements saying that Beutner and Rumpf fired were later repudiated, it is significant that neither Hans Siptrott nor even Georg Fleps himself ever denied that Fleps fired shots at the Americans that were followed by a spate of automatic fire.[66] The Carinthian radio operator in Panzer 731, SS-Pvt. Otto Arnold, claimed that after the shooting Hans Siptrott "blamed the riflemen Fleps heavily and abused him in very strong terms and said he would report this incident to his superior officer."[67]

Hans Siptrott gave his own contemporary version, still annoyed with Fleps, fifty years later:

I drove across and I came out in my tank below the crossroads. The Americans were not shooting at us. In the middle of the field the Americans were standing and my loader [Fleps] must have seen them as they tried to escape into the forest. He fired two rounds at them before we continued driving on. I kicked him in the backbone. I told him, "Why are you firing?" I kicked him, because I didn't know why he shot—I was surprised. And we continued driving on. I was sitting on top of the tank looking out and Fleps was the loader and popped out of the loader's hatch. He was out of the hatch to his waist [shows how Fleps stood and how he reached from the commander's hatch with his leg to kick]. I kicked him into the backbone and hit my shin bone and hurt myself.[68]

When asked what came next, Hans Siptrott was decidedly reserved in his choice of words. "Fleps shot at them with a pistol from 300 to 400 meters away," he told the author, who questioned him as follows:

Q: I want to point out in the testimony which you gave soon after the incident you said thirty to forty meters which agrees with what Fleps himself claimed. . . . You don't remember any other shooting that occurred while you were present?

A: Afterwards rounds were fired because they tried to run away.

Q: A lot of firing?

A: Yes. We got out of there.

Q: But you continued on your way down into Engelsdorf [Ligneuville]?

A: Yes.

Q: So rounds were being fired at the Americans as you were leaving?

A: Yes . . .

Q: Do you remember a statement you supposedly made at Schwäbisch Hall on January 7, 1946? It includes a drawing that I think you will remember. [Shows drawing to Siptrott] What can you remember about the statement? You say in the statement that Fleps fired two shots and that you ordered him. The other major difference is the distance. You said he was thirty to forty meters from the Americans. What do you remember about how this statement came to be?

A: I see this drawing. The large diagram [prosecution diagram of the crossroads] is not mine.

Q: I think the small diagram with your signature is your drawing [shows tanks by prisoners]

A: Oh, yes, I made that drawing. It is mine.

In the author's estimation, although it is very possible that Fleps fired the first shot, it is nearly certain that Max Beutner and/or Erich Rumpf, also fired pistol rounds just before all of the SPWs commenced with machine guns. As astutely pointed out by researcher John Bauserman, over half of the U.S. Army survivors' accounts said the first pistol shots came from a halftrack (or command vehicle), whereas the mount from which Fleps fired was Hans Siptrott's Mk IV panzer located just south of the mass of prisoners.[69] Yet this seeming contradiction begs the question: When people are threatened with bullets, will they accurately remember the type of vehicle their assailant occupied?[70] And particularly if all the various vehicles present would fire almost immediately after the first shots? Indeed, the Occam's Razor–like scenario that explains all the events and observations is that Fleps fired the first shots, but Rumpf and perhaps Beutner were pointing pistols at the same time the shots rang out. Their added salvos to the fusillade would make it appear as if the first shots came from the direction one was looking.

And although the official U.S. Army account and Siptrott's Schwäbisch Hall statement would seem to indicate that Fleps fired the first shots, these often-overlooked testimonies differed markedly. The recollection of Werner Löhmann, the gunner in Pilarzek's Panzer Nr. 734, recalled that when he was in Wanne later during the offensive, Fleps told him about his actions at Baugnez during idle conversation. As Fleps had related it, two SPWs with MG 42s had fired on the prisoners on orders. "Upon that I pulled my pistol and fired several shots into them too."[71] But was it true?

At the time the massacre took place, at least two SPWs were in place across from the prisoners: that of Beutner himself, the vehicle of Sepp Witkowski, and, most likely, also Friedel Bode's SPW. Whereas no one in Beutner's SPW would talk at Schwäbisch Hall or later—one suspects they had very good reasons—those in Witkowski's SPW were more forthcoming. Crew members Siegfried Jaekel and Joachim Hoffmann indicated that the first shots came from Beutner's SPW.[72] Finally, Max Rieder, from the 9th Panzer Engineer Company, recalled that after being ordered by SS-1st Lt. Erich Rumpf to shoot the prisoners, he pulled his rifle out of his SPW and then went back to the field where the prisoners were standing with their hands up. There, he found Rumpf already south of the café in front of the prisoners with a pistol in hand. "Our company commander, SS-1st Lt. Rumpf shot into the prisoners with his pistol," Rieder recounted. "I cannot say any longer how many shots he fired."[73]

Regardless of who started it, according to all accounts, when the firing began—just pistol shots—everyone joined in. Thus, for any observers to determine who fired the first shots may have been exceedingly difficult. Everything then happened very quickly. Siegfried Jaekel remembered,

> Then came Beutner's command to fire. My recollection is that the first firing I heard was pistol fire from Beutner's SPW. . . . We fired approximately 75 rounds from the front machine gun. As soon as the first firing began, all the American prisoners who were in the field fell to the ground. Then I went to the rear machine gun, loaded it and starting shooting [again] into the American prisoners. It was during the time that I was firing the rear machine gun on our SPW that Sprenger's SPW pulled up on the right-hand side behind my SPW. I saw SS-Pvt. Boltz firing the machine gun from Sprenger's SPW.[74]

Waffen SS witnesses estimated that the initial burst of automatic fire went on for two to four minutes. Even with that question answered, others remained, such as: Who killed the Americans lying wounded or feigning death in the field? Based on multiple-witness testimony, members of both the 3rd Panzer Engineer Company and the 9th Panzer Engineer Penal Squad moved into the field to finish off anyone still living. When Gustav Sprenger's SPW pulled up, Marcel Boltz fired a volley of machine gunfire into the prisoners sprawled on the ground, but for the most part the heavy volume of fire had ceased. Sprenger claimed to see fifty to eighty Americans at Baugnez, obviously just shot: "When I stopped in front of the pasture where the American soldiers lay in the field, they were still twisting and turning in their own blood and at least those nearest the road were moaning and groaning in pain." Sprenger noticed that a group of officers and men were already in the field applying the *coups de grâce*. Coming from the group who had been standing by the panzer, Max Beutner approached Sprenger with an abrupt order: "Go and shoot those who are still alive."[75]

Sprenger then dismounted his SPW with its commander, Wolfgang Altkrüger, and another grenadier, Willi Biloschetzky. All three used pistols or machine pistols to dispatch any still living; Sprenger himself fired off a 32-round magazine into five Americans who looked to still be living. "I aimed mostly for the chest of those I fired at," he later said. Sprenger claimed he had no doubt that each man he shot was killed.[76]

He deeply regretted what he had done, he later said aloud before his U.S. Army judges, but explained that those were his orders. One must understand that in the Waffen SS an order was *more* than just an order.

Sprenger and his crew were not the only ones who were guilty. In addition to implicating themselves, SS-S/Sgt. Willi Schaefer and SS Strm. Joachim Hoffmann, Gustav Neve, and Siegfried Jaekel with the 3rd Panzer Engineer Company claimed to have seen comrades walking the field, shooting those still alive.[77]

Clearly, some of the 9th Panzer Engineer Company also took part in the morbid duty. At the Malmédy trial both Walter Fransee and Paul Buth testified that Günther Hering and Helmuth Haas, under Rumpf, had administered mercy shots—in one case to kill an American who begged for his life on his knees.[78]

And perhaps worst of all was the lot of Hubert Huber of the 6th Panzer Company, whom numerous witnesses saw stop to get out of his Mk IV tank (Nr. 625) at the crossroad, where he "finished up the Americans which were still showing signs of life."[79] Several described how, while his tank crew looked on, Huber had kicked the prone bodies to find one American soldier still alive at the north end of the field.[80] Huber forced the man to take off his overshoes and hand over his watch. Then, with his pistol, he coldly shot the man in the head at point-blank range.[81]

How did Waffen SS veterans later judge those who shot at the crossroads? One who passed the scene of the massacre was sickened. "Look at this," SS-Pvt. Hans Knospe said to a comrade as his SPW passed the field littered with American dead. "[T]here's been some dirty business here."[82] But the decades-old memory of another anonymous SS veteran tanker was less condemnatory:

> The tension for us never tapered off in the Ardennes attack. With this background I cannot say that the ones who shot the Americans were murderers. You know that in any army there are pigs. There are some who have fast fingers. Luckily, I was not there.[83]

Jochen Peiper admitted that he was at the crossroads just minutes before the event, but his memory after fifteen years was warily focused on irony rather than tragedy:[84]

North of Thirimont, my spearhead (perhaps three tanks and as many halftracks) detected to their left an American convoy heading south on the Malmédy-St. Vith road. When they opened up, I was a few hundred yards further to the rear riding in a U.S. jeep and questioning an American Lt. Colonel who had bumped into us. I learned that Ligneuville accommodated a higher U.S. headquarters and that nobody expected us in that region. I therefore dashed to the leading tanks and had them cease fire and proceed without delay. Perhaps it was still possible to surprise Ligneuville too, despite the battle noise raised at so inconvenient a moment.

When we reached the crossroads and swung south, the passage was partly blocked by crashed and burning trucks. In the road ditch and the adjoining field were quite a number of U.S. soldiers (perhaps sixty, I guess). Apart from those killed and wounded by our heavy fire at so short a distance, were practically three groups to be distinguished: one coming back up to the road with hands clasped behind the helmet and surrendering. We thumbed them back as it was the task of the infantry following later to collect what we had left along the route of advance.

Group two lay close to the road and played dead. I distinctly remember some of our halftrack soldiers making themselves the joke to give them a "warning shot across the bow," whereupon they jumped to their feet and came to the road too, while everybody was roaring with laughter. The third group, last but not least, played dead, too, but was closer to the nearby forest. These soldiers imperceptibly tried to slowly approach the edge of the woods by crawling now and then. Some shots were wasted on them. The spearhead then proceeded towards Ligneuville while the POWs, on their own account and more or less unguarded, assembled near the crossroads and were captured after a short skirmish.[85]

Wistfully, Peiper would later write historian John Toland about the deadly events that came next. "There exist more than one version of what has happened later at the crossroads," he gingerly wrote in 1959, "but nobody really knows, nor do I."[86]

Nobody really knew, or nobody would really say

Members of the 1st SS Panzer Reconnaissance Battalion shown in an amphibious Schwimmwagen at the Kaiserbaracke crossroads between St. Vith and Malmédy. Staged photo taken by SS cameraman early in the battle.

A heavy King Tiger tank at the rear of Kampfgruppe Peiper passes a line of prisoners of the U.S. 99th Division near Lanzerath on the morning of December 17, 1944. Most of these American prisoners were safely conducted to POW camps in Germany.

S/Sgt. Bill Merriken

T/5 Ted Paluch

T/5 Al Valenzi

Cpl. George Fox

Six Malmédy survivors returned to Baugnez on April 9, 1946 to later testify at the Malmédy trial. Left to right: Lt. Virgil Lary, S/Sgt. Kenneth Ahrens, Pfc. Homer Ford, T/5 Carl Daub, T/5 Kenneth Kingston, and T/5 Samuel Dobyns. They posed in front of a temporary wooden-cross moment erected by the Belgian government in the summer of 1945.

T/5 Harold Billow

M/Sgt. Charles Reding

SS-Lt. Col. Jochen Peiper
(*Bayerisches Staats Archiv, Munich*)

SS-Maj. Werner Poetschke

SS-1st Lt. Erich Rumpf

SS-1st Lt. Werner Sternebeck

SS-S/Sgt. Hans Siptrott

SS-Pvt. Georg Fleps

Belgian civilian witness to the
massacre, Henri Lejoly-Quirin
in January 1945.

Mme. Adele Bodarwe, the
proprietor of the café at the
crossroads who disappeared in
the aftermath of the shooting on
December 17, 1944.

Lt. Col. David Pergrin, commander of the 291st Engineer Combat Battalion, who was instrumental in rescuing several Malmédy survivors.

The snow-covered Baugnez field was posted off-limits when the 30th Infantry Division took possession on January 13, 1944. (*Warren Watson*)

While the U.S. First Army graves registration team uncovered the bodies in the field on the morning of January 14, 1944, captured enemy soldiers of the German 3rd Parachute Division were marched by the crossroads and into captivity. (*Corbis/Bettman*)

Robert Pfeiffer, the thirteen-year-
old Belgian boy who witnessed the
massacre, pictured after the war.
(*Henri Rogister*)

Civilian witness Peter Lentz who
barely escaped being shot when
confronted by Kampfgruppe Peiper
on December 17. Lentz as he
appears today. (*Henri Rogister*)

Anna Blaise, who gave refuge to
Bill Merriken and Charles Reding
on the morning of December 18.
Blaise was sixty-two in 1944; photo
taken in 1950.

Marthe Martin, who risked her life
to help escort wounded Virgil Lary
safely to American lines.

Lt. Col. Alvin B. Welsch (standing) in charge of the U.S. First Army Malmédy massacre investigation watches Capt. John A. Synder (physician) examining the body of medic Ralph Indelicato. An unnamed staff sergeant (right) takes notes, January 14 1945. (*Corbis/Bettman*)

Bodies in the massacre field are uncovered and tagged. Scene looking back from the southwest toward the burned-out Café Bodarwe on the upper right.

The corpse of Pvt. Peter R. Phillips was found on the west shoulder of the N-23. Phillips was shot in the back while being marched back to the crossroads for not holding his hands high enough. Photo taken from the south.

A tightly packed group of bodies in the field marked with identification tags and photographed before being removed. The view is looking west toward the home of Léon Mathonet. The number tags identify the bodies of: #5–T/4 Oscar Jordan, #39–Sgt. Walter Franz, #40–T/3 James McGee, #41–Sgt. Benjamin Lindt, #38–1st Lt. Thomas McDermott, #36–Pfc. Thomas Oliver, #37–T/5 Charles Haines, #43–Pvt. William Dunbar, #48–T/5 Dayton Wusterbarth.

A shocked member of the 3060 Graves Registration Company looks upon the snow-covered body of T/Sgt. Paul Davidson, tagged with #53. Given the location at the rear of the massacre field—Davidson was nearly successful in escaping. The home of Léon Mathonet is seen in the background.

Two African American soldiers of the 3200 Quartermaster Company remove a victim from the massacre field on a stretcher.

The frozen body of S/Sgt. Donald Geisler is loaded onto a waiting truck to be taken to Malmédy for autopsy.

The three grim-faced U.S. Army doctors who performed the autopsies in Malmédy: (left to right) Maj. Giacento Morrone, Capt. John A. Synder, and Capt. Joseph A. Kurz.

Massacre survivors Bruce Summers, Ted Paluch, and William Reem pose for a photograph after recounting their story in a U.S. Army historical film taken in Germany in March 1945.

The body of T/5 Robert McKinney is uncovered from the packed snow on the Hédomont road in front of House #7 occupied by Henri Lejoly-Jacob and his family. The frozen path goes back to the crossroads where the Panther tank of Kurt Briesemeister stood when the Americans attempted to escape. The thick hedge through which Bill Merriken and Ted Paluch crossed can be seen behind the standing American soldiers. The roof of the woodshed in which Merriken and Reding hid is just to the rear.

Ted Paluch poses with Mme. Josiane Lejoly-Melchior in 2007. They are standing in front of the hedge through which Paluch escaped on December 17, 1944. Mme. Melchior is the daughter of Madeleine Lejoly who was present in the house when the massacre took place.

Hans Siptrott (Panzer Nr. 731) and Reinhold Kyriss (Panzer Nr. 723 of Roman Clotten) speak with the author privately during an interview in May 1997.

SS-Sgt. Manfred Thorn as he appeared in 1944. Thorn was the driver of Panzer 734.

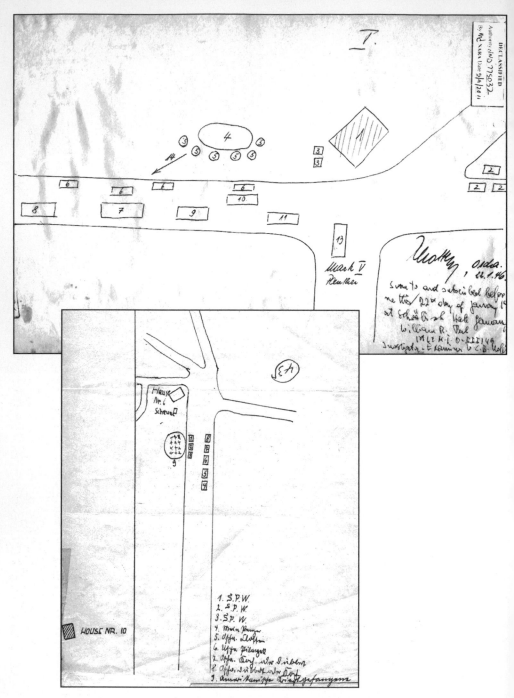

Sketches made by Hans Siptrott and Roman Clotten in early 1946 during the Malmédy investigation showing their detailed recollection of the positions of the American prisoners, SS tanks, and halftracks at the time the shooting took place.

Bill Merriken when interviewed in 1995 at his home in Bedford, Virginia.

Woodshed by House #7 (Henri Lejoly-Jacob) where Bill Merriken and Charles Reding first took refuge after running from the massacre scene at twilight on December 17, 1944.

Bill Merriken and Charles Reding were given sanctuary by Mme. Anna Blaise and concealed in the second floor of her home on the Géromont road. The building is now the Café San Remo.

In 1999, the author and several others went with Merriken back to Baugnez where he returned to the building where he had once taken refuge.

CHAPTER 8

"Let's Go!"

The men in the massacre field lay there a long time. "We were praying and praying and praying," Al Valenzi remembered. Death hung in the cold. "I don't know how long I lay there," Bobby Werth recalled with horror, "but it was a *long, long* time."

> It seemed like we laid there forever and they kept shooting. After awhile I got shot through the leg; the shot ended up in my groin. I could still move my toes. The Germans were looting and were laughing and shooting. They stepped between my legs and I had a ring on and had tried to hide it and then when they came back through and they were shooting anyone alive. I heard the wounded. Some of them were cursing; others were praying. Some were crying and moaning. I was just trying to be quiet. But I was so cold and I was so scared that I know I was shaking. I thought that there is nothing to do here, but run away from here. My mother was a worrier anyway and I was glad she didn't know about this. Strangely, I thought that I had to try to live; if I died it would be very hard on her.[1]

When the pistol and machine-gun shots started, Jim Mattera had only a momentary vision of the gory scene as a hail of metal smashed

[155]

into those standing with him. He dived for the dirt as the crackling sound of machine gunfire continued. As Mattera hugged the ground, he listened to the rapid-fire hammer of the machine guns—a sound he would never forget. Charles Haines was lying next to him. "Mattera," he begged quietly, "I'm hit bad in the back."[2] "Lie still," Mattera whispered. "You'll be all right." There were pitiful moans and cries from the wounded, some calling for their mothers, others for simple mercy. As more died, the terrible chorus began to subside.[3] Amazingly, Mattera was still unharmed. "Was I the only man not hit?" he thought. "Will God let me live?"

"A lot of guys were praying out loud—that's for sure," Ted Paluch remembered. "I could hear them. Maybe I was too."[4] Lt. Virgil Lary also lay in the killing field. "Time stood still," he remembered.

> One German came around my way shooting here and there. A bullet went through the head of the man next to me. I lay tensely expecting the end. Would he see me breathing? Could I take a kick in the face without wincing? I couldn't see him directly. . . . He was standing at my head. What was he doing? Then I heard him reloading his pistol in a deliberate manner. While he was doing this, he was laughing and talking. A few odd steps before the reloading was finished and he was no longer close to my head, then another shot a little further away. He had passed me up."[5]

Bruce Summers was in the middle rear of the group with his buddy George Rosenfeld when the cascade of machine-gun bullets cut down a swath of flesh:

> There was a lot of spraying machine gun fire for two or three minutes—I don't know how long. After that it was kind of quiet, but people were groaning and moaning and dying. George was close to me; I think he was one of the ones groaning that they shot later. Then they walked around through everybody shooting anybody who moved. I had a ring on—a class ring and a guy picked up my hand and tried to pull my ring off and couldn't get it off and I heard him cock his pistol. But just then, someone next to me

groaned and he turned around and shot whoever that was. I have thought to myself that this may have been George who groaned and saved my life.

Bruce Summers nearly gave up the ghost: "There was no question in my mind that I was going to die. This was the end of it. I was really cold," he recalled. "I remember I thought I was going to freeze to death out there and I thought to myself that if I died and ended up in the wrong place, that at least I wouldn't be cold. I didn't move at all. I felt like we lay there a couple of weeks."[6]

Albert Valenzi thought of his father:

Next thing you know, I was hit in the legs; my legs were like a rag doll and were shaking. And I thought, "If I get out of here, then how am I going to run?" I thought, "Don't let me get hit in the belly or then I am done." And I thought, "This is a heck of a Christmas present for Pop." The next thing I know these Germans that were passing by were just firing [at us] indiscriminately, just taking potshots.[7]

As Valenzi lay on the ground, shot in the legs and with burning pain, he heard sounds no one was meant to hear: bullets smashing into flesh followed by shrill screams of men warbling in pain and dying. After a time things became quiet, but then the SS came into the field with pistols. "Germans stayed there and anyone who would move, they would shoot them in the head." Valenzi closed his eyes, straining to hold his breath.

How I did it, I'll never know, because it was so cold. They could see your breath coming out. I opened my eyes a little to see if these guys were going closer; and these guys started to walk in the pile of bodies there. I saw one with his pistol out standing there. "God, if that's the way you're going to go . . . this will be it. . . . You're a soldier."

Out of the corner of one all-but-closed eye, he saw Sgt. Don Geisler suddenly stir and rise to his feet. Valenzi was terrified, thinking, *What*

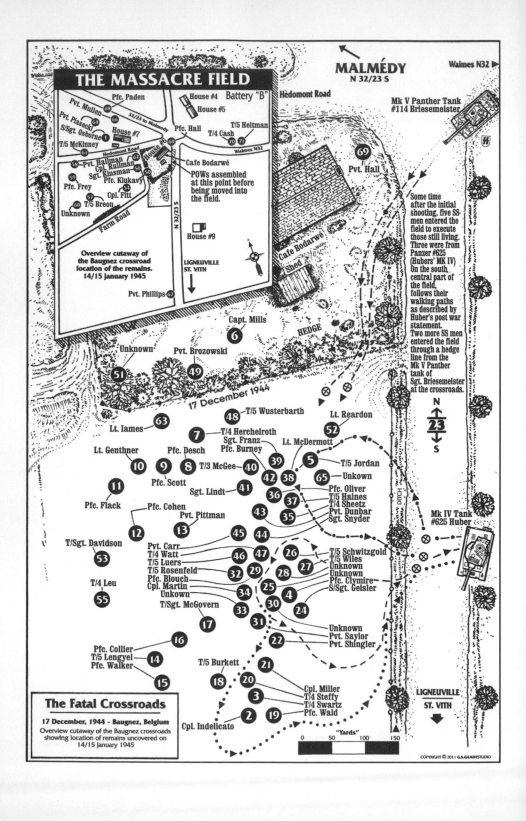

THE MASSACRE FIELD

MALMÉDY
N 32/23 S

Walmes N32 ►

Mk V Panther Tank
#114 Briesemeister

Pfc. Paden
Pvt. Mullen
Pvt. Piasecki
S/Sgt. Osborne
House #7
T/5 McKinney

32/23 to Malmedy
Hedomont Road

House #4
House #5

Battery "B"

Hèdomont Road

Pfc. Hall
T/4 Cash
T/5 Heltman

Walmes N32

Pvt. Hall

69

Pvt. Hallman
Cpl. Rullman
Sgt. Kinsman
Pfc. Frey
Cpl. Fitt
T/5 Breon
Unknown

House #9

Cafe Bodarwé
POWs assembled
at this point before
being moved into
the field.

Pfc. Klukavy

N 32/23 S

Cafe Bodarwé
Shed

Some time
after the initial
shooting, five SS-
men entered the
field to execute
those still living.
Three were from
Panzer #625
(Hubers' MK IV)
On the south
central part of
the field,
follows their
walking paths
as described by
Huber's post war
statement.
Two more SS
men entered the
field through a
hedge
line from the
Mk V Panther
tank of
Sgt. Briesemeister
at the crossroads.

Overview cutaway of
the Baugnez crossroad
location of the remains.
14/15 January 1945

LIGNEUVILLE
ST. VITH

Pvt. Phillips 67

Capt. Milis
6

Unknown
Pvt. Brozowski
51   49

HEDGE

17 December 1944

T/5 Wusterbarth
48
Lt. Reardon

Lt. Iames   63
52
T/4 Herchelroth
7   Sgt. Franz
Pfc. Burney
Lt. McDermott

N
23
S

Lt. Genthner
Pfc. Desch
39
5   T/5 Jordan
10   9   8   T/3 McGee   40   42   38   65   Unkown
Pfc. Scott   36   Pfc. Oliver
T/5 Haines
11   Sgt. Lindt   41   37   T/4 Sheetz
Pfc. Flack   Pfc. Cohen   43   35   Pvt. Dunbar
Pfc. Cohen   Pvt. Pittman   Sgt. Snyder
12   13
45   44
T/Sgt. Davidson
53   Pvt. Carr   47   26   T/5 Schwitzgold
T/4 Watt   46   T/5 Wiles
T/5 Luers   32   29   28   27   Unknown
T/4 Leu   T/5 Rosenfeld   Unknown
55   Pfc. Blouch   25   4   Pfc. Clymire
Cpl. Martin   34   S/Sgt. Geisler
Unkown   30   24
T/Sgt. McGovern   33
17   31   Unknown
Pvt. Saylor
22   Pvt. Shingler

DITCH

Mk IV Tank
#625 Huber

Pfc. Collier   16
T/5 Lengyel   14
Pfc. Walker   15

T/5 Burkett
18   20   21
Cpl. Miller
3   T/4 Steffy
T/4 Swartz
Cpl. Indelicato   2   19   Pfc. Wald

LIGNEUVILLE
ST. VITH

The Fatal Crossroads

17 December, 1944 - Baugnez, Belgium
Overview cutaway of the Baugnez crossroads
showing location of remains uncovered on
14/15 January 1945

"Yards"
0   50   100   150

COPYRIGHT © 2011 G.S.GAADTSTUDIO

are you getting up for? Another pistol shot and Geisler staggered and fell, only moments later to pull himself up again! Geisler stood a third time, now weaving. An ugly clatter of a machine gun, and this time Geisler dropped and did not get up.

Out of the corner of Valenzi's horrified eye, he then saw the same SS men shoot T/5 Charles Haines right beside Jim Mattera. In the cold December air a man's exhaled breath sent off a plume of visible white vapor—a telltale sign of life. All the while both Mattera and Valenzi were consumed with holding their breath. "Don't let them see you. . . . Be dead, be dead," Valenzi said over and over to himself. He held his breath for a long time. The world seemed to disappear inside. Although Valenzi was Catholic, he didn't consider himself that religious—until now. "I prayed and prayed." He repeated one prayer after another— "The Lord's Prayer," "Hail Mary," the "Glory Be." Would he make it to heaven? Killed in his youth, far away from Pennsylvania, dying in a frozen field.

A German boot kicked Jim Mattera to see if he was still alive. He gritted his teeth not to grunt, the SS man somehow getting his foot tangled in Mattera's overcoat belt loop. Mattera prayed too. "Number thirteen be lucky," he said recalling his serial number. "God, please save me."[8] From the other end of the field, Mattera heard an anguished plea in English. The SS man kicking him departed. "Please don't shoot me!" He recognized the voice as Kenny Kingston pleading for his life. He knew the boy from Allentown. They had trained together, soldiered together, drunk together—everything. Real buddies—and now this. Mattera heard pistol shots. *God! Surely Kingston was dead.*

Cpl. Michael Sciranko, the driver in Valenzi's jeep, faced his end like many others:

> I kept my head flattened into the mud and blood as much as I could. . . . As I was lying there, I felt something pierce my butt and from then on I was waiting for the one that would finish me off. Everyone around me was screaming and hollering. I heard someone on my right gasp and say, "I can hardly breathe anymore!" Another on my left got up and tried to run away, but he tripped over my feet and fell next to me. One guy was praying out loud, but a German soon noticed him and gave him the works. All the time,

the bullets were whizzing around and I could hear them hitting steel helmets.[9]

Even though he was in the rear of the group at the crossroad, Pvt. Harry C. Horn had been hit repeatedly in the hail of machine gunfire from German tanks and halftracks. He lay in the field, wounded in the head and shoulder and now bleeding profusely. "One of the Germans armed with a P-38 came within two feet of me and shot one of my buddies through the head. He looked over at me, but the blood from the wound in my head was streaming all over my face and since I froze, he must have assumed I was already dead."[10] Pvt. Jim Mattera heard the Germans canvassing the field call out, "Hey Joe!" in accented English and then shoot anyone who responded. Pvt. William F. Reem couldn't understand the German, "but they laughed and talked and then they shot."[11] Charles Appman remembered,

Now and then I would hear a pistol shot. One soldier gave me a kick in the leg. I didn't move but feared that the frost from my breath would give me away in the cold air. I tried to hold my breath unit it felt I would burst. The most awful sound was the clinking of shells in a German soldier's hand as he loaded a pistol. I lay there thinking of my mother.[12]

Falling to the ground with everyone else, Pfc. Aubrey J. Hardiman was still and quiet. The consummate hunter, he lay there thinking about his chances: "I thought about how when a covey of birds gets up, you usually shoot where the most birds are. I was next to the last man on the end of the line."[13] He lay to the rear of the main group on the north end of the field next to a medical officer. The medic was unknown to him (it was 1st Lt. Carl Genthner of Rochester, New York). Genthner spoke some German, and Hardiman had been whispering to him ever so quietly, as he was wounded. Then a German soldier stepped over them. "He [Genthner] said something in German," Hardiman remembered. The native Virginian couldn't speak German, but the medical officer with the Red Cross armband was addressing the SS man in his native tongue. The result? "He shot him three times. . . . I had been whispering in a low tone to the officer and after that he never answered. He was breathing hard and then he quit."[14] And Hardiman? "I made my mind up to lie still and play dead," he remembered. "I learned how to lie still in a turkey blind."[15] Quiet, still, and silent. "Anyone who moved or made a noise was killed. The German turned me over and took some pictures and papers out of my pockets. After he picked my pockets, he went away."

Mario "Boots" Butera was another GI lying in limbo:

> I lay there until the firing ceased, feigning death. The firing, while it was going on, lasted about five minutes. I was conscious as I lay there and could hear German voices and laughing. Then I heard pistol shots and one of my companions, who was lying beside me moaning and spitting blood, was approached by a German who fired four shots from a pistol into his body.[16]

Harold Billow had been in the front row when the shooting started, but amazingly he was unscathed by the first fusillade of bullets or those that came afterward. Like the rest of the men, he dropped to the ground. With one side of his face down in the dirt, he saw a sight he would never forget. Across the sloping ground by his face, a rivulet of bright red blood streamed by—so close that it blurred out of focus. [17] Meanwhile, the air was filled with groans and gasps. He kept his eyes closed. "While we were lying there," he recounted, "Germans walked up to the ones who moved or were crying in pain and shot them through the head to finish them off." Billow didn't move; he lay still for what seemed like two hours—his flickering eye looking across an expanse of mud-covered blood and all framed against naked trees and a gray sky.

Ken Ahrens was nearby. "Four or five Germans came down through the group," he said, "and when they could see anybody move they would shoot them in head. They would also kick them; anyone who breathed or moved, they would just shoot."[18] Ahrens was badly wounded, with a round burning like a molten coal in his back. "We lay on the ground. The firing lasted for two or three minutes. . . . There was much moaning and groaning. I could hear a stray shot here and there." Ahrens watched as medic Ralph Indelicato gave first aid to a wounded man, only to have the Germans shoot both of them.[19] Pfc. Peter Piscatelli saw the same event.[20]

Pvt. Robert Smith was lying in the back row of the men who had fallen prone at the first shot. He recalled lying there as each German tank that passed by shot into them. But that was not the worst: "Then they came through the field to my right, came around among us and every time anyone would move, they would shoot them. After that, things got quiet."[21] Pvt. William F. Reem was lying in the field next to Smith and could sneak glances to observe the enemy's morbid progress. Periodically, he would whisper back to Smith with a report— not much of it was reassuring. "We lay there in the field, I would say for an hour," he guessed. When could they try to get out of there? As they lay there, the wounded became colder still, some attempting to stifle even their shivering. Under the gray Belgian sky, a few flakes of snow that began to settle on the tangle of men dead and dying in the field.[22] Yet among the bodies many of the corpse-like forms were still alive.

Now the traffic on the road seemed to thin. Someone rose up to look around. "Keep quiet or they will shoot you!" a low voice urged.[23] Even though unwounded and attempting to play dead, James Mattera was now shivering with shock and cold. At this point he really began to tremble, clamping his jaw to prevent his teeth from chattering. They would see him soon—now or never. "Let's make a break for it!" he suddenly shouted. Intending to spring up, Mattera instead staggered and reeled to his feet, his legs nearly without feeling—they seemed detached from his body.

"Let's go!" he yelled. He threw his numb feet forward, almost falling. He stumbled over the bodies around him. He thought twenty or so men scattered in all directions, but the number was, in fact, more than twice that many.[24] The time was around 3:30 P.M. on December 17, 1944.

Fear and adrenaline sent Mattera and the others dashing ahead. The few SS men at the crossroads sprang into action too. A machine gun rattled and pistols banged, splattering an ugly dance on the muddy ground. Bullets chopped down several running soldiers before they reached the path behind the café. Mattera, the Pennsylvania farm boy who hunted rabbits back home, could tell the shooter had the range. Mattera tumbled to the grassy meadow as if he had been hit. When the machine gun shifted to another target, Mattera rose again and sprinted with everything he had. He bolted for some bushes at the edge of the woods. Lt. Lary, among those running, saw one man drop:

> Most of the others ran into the house [café], but I ran behind it and hid in a small shed where I covered myself with straw. The Germans set fire to the house and sprayed our men with machine gun burst as the heat forced them out. I counted, I believe, twelve distinctly different screams of agony.[25]

Perhaps having seen Bobby Werth and some others who first ran to the café at the intersection, Mattera now regained his footing and sprinted toward the woods to the northwest. There, breathing heavily, he met up with medic Roy Anderson, Herman Johnson, and Ted Paluch. Holding up, they would hide until nightfall, looking back on the Café Bodarwe as the Germans set it afire. Mattera believed that a dozen of those who got up from the field ran to the café, only to be forced out and shot down when the Germans set it aflame—a claim a number of others also made.[26]

Several Americans headed for the nearby farm of Henri Lejoly-Jacob. This two-story farmhouse was further west of the café and just south of the N-23, oriented off-angle between the Hédomont and Géromont roads. Lejoly-Jacob's twenty-year-old daughter, Madeleine, had been walking outside her home to watch the American trucks passing by. German tanks suddenly appeared on the road from Waimes and fired on the dark green trucks. Madeleine Lejoly ran as fast as she could. "Bullets were flying everywhere," she remembered. She and her mother, Johanna, ran up to the second floor, watching from a window as the Americans surrendered to the Germans, their hands over their heads. "I remembered seeing the Americans hiding behind the café," Madeleine recalled. During a break in the firing her father ran home, sending his wife and daughter to the basement upon his arrival. That done, he came back upstairs to peer out of an upstairs casement window:

> After I got to my house, I went to an upstairs window and looked out and saw the German soldiers herding the American prisoners into a field west of the road going to St. Vith. The manner in which they were doing that made me suspect that they were going to

shoot the Americans and I did not want to witness that so I went away from the window. I then heard some machine gun firing.[27]

The blaring racket of automatic weapons fire told the outcome. Lejoly ran downstairs to join his wife and daughter hiding in the cellar. Later, there was more gunfire, and coming back upstairs, the Belgian farmer spied American soldiers fleeing from the crossroads: "I went downstairs to the door and I saw some American soldiers running close by my house in a northwesterly direction." By then, his curious young daughter had joined him at the window. "I saw some shot at," she remembered, "and some fell dead."

One of the men running to Lejoly-Jacob's house was William Merriken. He had risen with the rest of the group to attempt an escape, but with the wounds to his right leg, he could only hobble painfully to the north, past the café, as bullets kicked up the dirt. As he approached the house he could see three Americans banging away at the entrance. Someone opened the door and then suddenly slammed it in their face! Still hopping on one leg, Merriken awkwardly made his way to the west side of the farmhouse. Yet his crippled gait so delayed him that an SS trooper confronted him with a pistol—the same man who fired at the others.[28]

In amazing luck the gun misfired, and Merriken threw himself into a hedgerow by the road as the man chased after others. Desperate to escape, Merriken crawled and then hobbled to a ramshackle stable with a woodpile just west of the farmhouse. He took refuge there, hiding in a nest of hay and a woodpile. Later that night T/5 Charles Reding joined him in the shed. Reding had hidden on the north side of the café until forced to leave after the Germans set it on fire. Merriken could hear the loud crackle of the flames, interrupted by buzz bombs that continued to roar overhead. Reding subsequently crawled to the shed, where he found Merriken bleeding badly. Both men planned to leave the dangerous hideout but had to wait for the bright flames to die from the huge conflagration consuming the Café Bodarwe. According to Merriken's telling of the event, Reding knew he was lucky:

He told me that about six [of our] soldiers had been in House No. 6 [Café Bodarwe], which had been set on fire by the Germans and

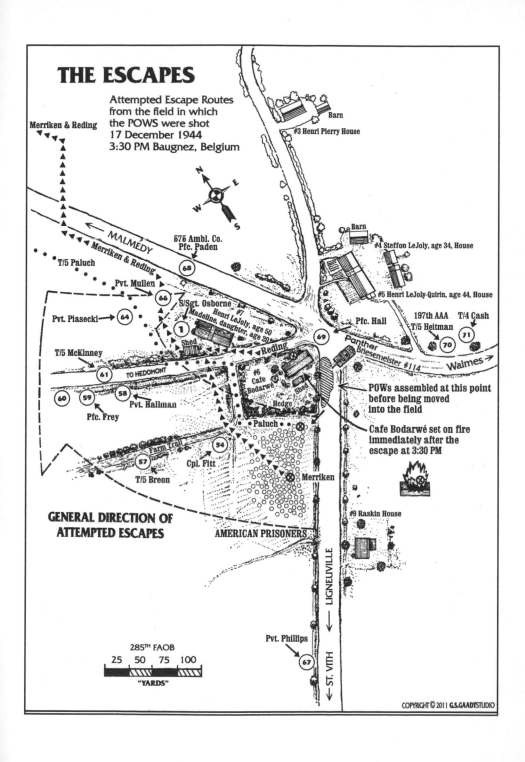

THE ESCAPES

Attempted Escape Routes
from the field in which
the POWS were shot
17 December 1944
3:30 PM Baugnez, Belgium

Merriken & Reding

Barn
#3 Henri Pierry House

Barn

#4 Steffon LeJoly, age 34, House

MALMEDY

Merriken & Reding

575 Ambl. Co.
Pfc. Paden

#5 Henri LeJoly-Quirin, age 44, House

T/5 Paluch

68

197th AAA   T/4 Cash

Pvt. Mullen

S/Sgt. Osborne   Pfc. Hall   T/5 Heitman   71

66

Henri LeJoly, age 50   #7   70

Pvt. Piasecki   64   Madeline, daughter, age 20

1

69

Shed

Panther

Bnesemeister #114   Waimes

T/5 McKinney   Reding

61   TO HEDOMONT   #6   Shed

Cafe
Bodarwé   POWs assembled at this point
before being moved
into the field

60   59   58   Hedge

Pvt. Hallman

Pfc. Frey   Paluch   Cafe Bodarwé set on fire
immediately after the
escape at 3:30 PM

Farm Trail   54

57   Cpl. Fitt

T/5 Breon   Merriken

#9 Raskin House

GENERAL DIRECTION OF
ATTEMPTED ESCAPES

AMERICAN PRISONERS

285TH FAOB
25 50 75 100

"YARDS"

Pvt. Phillips

67

LIGNEUVILLE

ST. VITH

then covered at the front and rear entrances by machine guns; that all had run out of the house because of the fire, and had been mowed down by machine gun fire.[29]

Ken Ahrens also told of his harrowing escape from the field, avoiding the café and running for a patch of woods two hundred yards away: "I jumped up and started running in a westerly direction. In the meantime, I noticed a few other fellows running with me. About that time a machine gun . . . opened up. As we ran, the bullets were flying pretty thick and heavy."[30] With Ahrens was T/5 Paul Gartska, from the 3rd Armored Division, and Cpl. Michael Sciranko.[31] "We were all pretty badly shot up." Al Valenzi was the other man along:

The next thing you know, the shooting stopped. But I thought everybody was dead. It was still and cold, but with some light. All I could see was a heap of bodies. I heard maybe a moan or two. There were no more vehicles going by. I was so frozen and it started to snow lightly. Then I heard somebody on the right side of me say in a loud whisper, "Let's go, let's go, let's go." I was going to go myself. Then I heard Ahrens say, "Come on Al, let's go." I replied, "I can't! my legs!" There were no Germans in the field, maybe there were some out on the road. Ken says, "Let's go this way." I started moving. A few on my right took off to the right and headed for a barn, I think. Kenny and I went through this hedgerow and there was almost a valley and down over a hill. We went up this way and as we took off across this field, they started firing this machine gun at us. I could hardly run. "You can make it." I said, "No, I can't." My legs felt like lead. He grabbed me by the shoulder and half dragged me along. He was shot through the fleshy part of his back. "Come on, you can make it," he told me. We could see the tracers come through. They were still firing at us through this hedgerow until we got on the back side of the hill. . . . It was dusk and now getting dark. We came to a creek and we laid down there for a while. We had no idea which direction to go; we had no idea. We just waited. . . . We saw a jeep coming from the road over there. We could see its cat's eyes—blackout headlights. Snowflakes started to come down. Finally, we recognized that this jeep looked to be American. We took a chance—thank God it was an American captain. We all went there and they loaded us into the jeep.

All of us were talking at once. We were rambling on. We told them our outfit had been shot up. "They killed everybody in the outfit." They saw we were wounded and they drove us down into an aid station in Malmédy. They looked like they were moving. All they did was give me some sulfa and patched us up and evacuated us. They put us in a command car and piled us in there and somebody piled in my legs. My boots were soaked in blood.[32]

When someone called out to go, the size of the group that suddenly rose from the corpse-laden mass surprised Walter Wendt. Many got up and dashed away. Others could run faster than he could, so Wendt took off running north with "Boots" Butera, who had his toes nearly shot off and was hobbling as well. In a rapid limping gait both scudded right by SS tank commander Kurt Briesemeister and the crew of Panther Nr. 114, who seemed preoccupied with their tank treads:

We ran past this building, there was a German tank. I ran about ten feet from the tank crew. They stared in surprise, the gunner got into the tank and started to fire the machine gun and by that time, we jumped into a creek with about three feet of water and ice. . . . We wadded in the creek until we were out of machine gun range.[33]

Mike Skoda lay in the field while a buddy, Pvt. William Reem, whispered to him. Out of a squinted eye he could see what was happening.[34] The Germans were smoking and sitting around talking! "Are you hit?" Reem whispered. "Yes," Skoda murmured back quietly, "but I can't tell where." His whole body was cold and numb. When Mattera made the rallying call for everyone to leave, Mike Skoda wasn't sure he could move. "I'm wounded!" he called out. "Well, we are going!" came the reply. Whole parts of his body had no feeling; the others burned with pain—four bullets had hit him. He thrashed about from under the body of one dead man and awkwardly pushed to his feet. Everyone scattered.

Even though Skoda couldn't feel his legs, he willed them forward. They moved! He joined the other zombie-like forms—a few running, some staggering, and several limping in pain. They crossed the field, running to the northwest and coming alongside a line of hedges that bordered the road west to Hédomont. "We kept along the hedgerow about 500 yards," said Skoda. He ran together with Pvt. Paul Martin, and William Reem, although Martin disappeared in the confusion. When Skoda came to the farmhouse of Joseph Mathonet, his legs were cold and wobbly, his was body shaking, and he was weak from losing blood. "I am going to hide out here!" Skoda stammered. But Reem protested—it was too close to the enemy. "I'm going on," he said and continued on west.

Skoda hobbled around the Mathonet house, but a steel grating covered the windows and he couldn't find a way inside. Then, working his way around the house, he spotted an open door and staggered inside to find it was the farmhouse stable. Inside, he was surprised to find Pfc. Paul Martin. "We were happy to see each other," Skoda remembered—ecstatic even. But their fragile refuge seemed all too obvious—they were just a short distance from the killing field. "I told him I am wounded and losing a lot of blood."[35] Martin told Skoda that he was not hurt badly so he wanted to get away and reach friendly lines. The house wasn't safe, he explained. But Skoda said that he was too weak to do anything else. Scared to the edge of his senses, Martin could only wish him well. He ran off in the gloomy twilight.[36]

Inside, Skoda knew Reem and Martin were right; his was too obvious a hiding place. "I saw a ladder that led to a trap door in the hayloft. I climbed up and covered myself with hay." Reaching that sanctuary, he examined his burning shoulder with his hand: There were holes in the flesh. He wrapped a scarf awkwardly around it and passed out. He did not wake up until the next day.

Thinking the Americans would eventually arrive to free him, Skoda stayed in the stable for four days. They never came. Eventually his wounds became extremely painful and he had to go down from the barn loft to get water. He was so thirsty that he pushed a cow out of the way to get a drink from the watering trough. During one of these trips the farmhouse owner, Joseph Mathonet, spotted him. "I went over to him and tried to tell him what I wanted," Skoda remembered. "He refused to dress my wound. I asked him not to turn me in. He didn't say anything." About two hours later German paratroopers came and took Skoda captive. They took him down out of the barn, but they did bandage his wounds and give him food and water.

To Skoda, the paratroopers of the 3rd Parachute Division looked to be only boys. He was a prisoner again, but at least not of the SS. His new captors even seemed kind. They took him to another barn just to the east. "One of your comrades is lying out there," they told him. He was still alive. Skoda asked them to take him there. "They took me to another barn and there was a fellow from my battery laying there badly wounded. His back was so bad, he couldn't move. His name was Private Thomas."[37] Skoda recognized the boy and told the paratroopers to get his buddy some help, but the language barrier intervened. There was little that could be done. The Germans soon headed east with Skoda—a captive himself. Michael Skoda was the last American to see Pvt. Elwood Thomas alive. He remains missing to this day, his fate a mystery.

When Jim Mattera called, "Let's go!" Bruce Summers leapt to his feet. Whereas some took off for the distant west woods, Summers knew the Americans were at Malmédy, so he intended to get there or die trying. As they ran off, "machine gun bullets were kicking up dirt all around us."

A bunch of them took off towards the trees. . . . I ran straight up the road we came up; I knew it went down towards Malmédy. Talk about running; my legs were so frozen, I could not do much more than walk. And if they were shooting at me, I wasn't aware of it. I came to the road, but I knew I couldn't go down that road, so I went across the road. And as I crossed the road one of the machine guns on one of the tanks opened up and I could see the bullets hit the road up above me and I took one big lunge into the ditch and then into the woods. I ran into two people down there. They were from the same outfit; one was Boots Butera and I said, "We've got to get out of here." And he said, "I can't run." And I asked him why not. He showed me how one of his toes had been shot off. I told him, we were going to have to get out of there anyway.[38]

Summers got to the bottom of the Malmédy road with three others: O'Connell, Werth, and Butera. Then Harold Billow and William Reem appeared as well, and they traveled together until all six came across Lt. Col. David Pergrin's roadblock of the 291st Combat Engineer Battalion. After Pergrin returned the first group of five survivors to Malmédy, he had driven back once more with Lt. Thomas Stack to retrieve another three Americans he found hiding in a ditch.[39] Pergrin then transported the latest group to the hospital. Summers recalled the meeting:

> We went down to the foot of the hill and ran into Lt. Col. Dave Pergrin. He had come out to see what all was going on. He asked me [about what had happened] and we told him. I grabbed his M-1 carbine and said, "Let's go up there and get those bastards!" But he held me back. "No, no, calm down." And they got me and the other two boys and took us down to the hospital in a jeep.

Even upon reaching safety Summers was beside himself. *He was mad.*

> I spent that night in the hospital in Malmédy. I had only been wounded in my hand. But I hadn't even paid much attention to it, although it was bleeding pretty bad. We thought the Germans would be there the next morning. I spent the night with a doctor and another officer drinking a fifth of 3 Feathers whisky to calm our nerves. I ran into Hal Boyle down there and being a blabber mouth, I told him everything and the next day my name was all over the papers.[40]

Bobby Werth also ran with Bruce Summers, chasing Carl Daub and Aubrey Hardiman just ahead:

> When everyone else got up, I decided I would try too. I couldn't do any worse. So I jumped up. There was nothing else to do. I ran and there was a house—a café—and I ran behind it. They shot at us a few times and there was another guy with me and we ran right in front of the tanks across the road and went toward the hill. I guess

we just outran those bullets! They may have only been a couple of halftracks. . . . As we ran off, we ran across a Belgian on a bicycle. When he saw I was shot, he wanted to put me on the bicycle. But there were three of us in the group. One was O'Connell. He was shot through the face and Boots Butera had toes shot off. We just kept running. We were right behind one another. We were headed back towards Malmédy. As we ran further beyond the Belgian on a bicycle, we ran across some American jeeps in the distance. We were scared, wondering if they might be German. We had seen captured American jeeps in this German convoy. We stopped in the road and talked about it. O'Connell said, "I can't last anyway. I am bleeding to death so I am going up there." He went on up there and me and Boots waited by the road. In a few minutes they sent somebody back in a jeep to pick us up and carried us to Malmédy to the hospital.[41]

Daub estimated that they lay in the field for forty-five minutes until things grew quiet. "I decided to run and they fired at us again." Amazingly, he was uninjured, although at first he tripped over one of the bodies in the field. However, he then sprang up forward and ran as fast as he could for the woods. When Daub looked back he could see fifteen men running behind him, but he thought some of them might be German. As he got closer to the woods he heard someone yell "Daub!" He slowed down. It was Hardiman, who was wounded in the foot. "I threw his arm over my shoulder and me and him ran together and escaped." According to Hardiman,

I saw Carl Daub raise up on his arms and look around. I got up and ran to a cedar hedge and Daub came with me. We had gone about 300 yards when they saw us and the tank that surrounded the field opened fire on us. We zigzagged along the hedge while the bullets whistled by. I noticed from the tracers that the shots were high. We came to a gully and followed it into the woods. We went along the edge of the woods for about a mile. We knew the direction to run because the buzz-bombs kept coming over and we knew they were going in the direction to our lines.[42]

As they limped through the woods in the growing darkness, Daub glanced back at the crossroads receding from view to see the café burning brightly. Undeterred, he and Hardiman plodded on through the dense conifers. Eventually they came upon a small Belgian farmhouse where some children were outside playing. Even with the language barrier, they made it known they were hurt and needed to get to the Americans in Malmédy. One of the boys, about ten years old, volunteered to guide them until they got to a hill overlooking the town, its lights now flickering. By then Hardiman was in so much agony that Daub had to help him hobble down the hill. That night they were back in Malmédy and in a doctor's care. The bullet had broken bones in his foot, and running on it had done further damage, but the Virginia boy knew his good fortune. From convalescence at the 28th General Hospital in Liège, he wrote his mother in great relief with a message for his sportsman father and the good ol' boys at the Goodloe Hunt Club. "What I learned in a turkey blind," he wrote home, "helped save my life."

Wounded three times while lying in the field, Ted Flechsig estimated that they had lain in the field for more than half an hour when one of the others whispered that the German tanks had left, saying, "we had better make a break for it."[43] Even though wounded, Flechsig jumped up and ran after Cpl. George Fox, who had been facedown in the field and moved only when he felt someone step on his arm. He rose and chased after three others running west. When the machine guns fired at the escapees, Fox fell to the ground again and crawled along a ditch by a little secondary lane. Later, however, he rose and ran again, not knowing that Flechsig was behind him, but he was relieved to see Flechsig was not German. As they took off to the west toward Hédomont, the men heard the enemy begin to fire machine guns again. After the massacre, Fox was unharmed, but Flechsig was badly wounded. The two moved together "walking real fast" until they came to a wooded crest that overlooked the Hédomont road.[44] Descending down that way, the two came across two Belgian brothers on bicycles:

> When I left the massacre area and started heading west, I heard someone in back of me—I was sure it was a German, but was relieved it was Ted [Flechsig] and he had been wounded. It was getting dark and we continued heading west. We had walked

a long way and when we got to a country road, the Xhurdebise brothers [Franz and Clément] were on the road and offered us their bicycle. We put Ted on the bicycle and started towards Stavelot about eight miles away.[45]

Flechsig was in great pain and hardly able to go on. Doing what he could, Fox held the wounded man up on the bicycle, awkwardly walking alongside. At first the Xhurdebise brothers came with them, but as they neared Stavelot, they turned back: It was too dangerous, so they were going home. Fox continued with Flechsig until they came across another roadblock of the ubiquitous 291st Engineer Combat Battalion near Stavelot. Soon the two were evacuated to the hospital in Liège.

Ken Ahrens described the escape as did the others, but with one pitiable addition. When another called out "Let's go!" and some thirty rose from the field and ran, Ahrens remembered that several were so badly wounded they had only enough strength to draw up briefly before collapsing. "Don't leave me here!" a voice called out—an ignored plea that would haunt his nights for many years.[46]

When Ted Paluch ran, he saw a dozen men veer for the café at the corner, but he headed across the dirt road behind the structure. "While I was running down that road," he recounted, "a guy was shooting at us with a pistol. I got through a break in the hedge and played dead. I laid there in the back of the hedge. He came down the road looking us over."[47] Only grazed by a machine-gun bullet, Paluch fell as if hit by the pistol round, afterward deciding to wait for nightfall on the north side of the hedgerow near the home of Henri Lejoly-Jacob along the road leading to Hédomont. There another American soldier joined him. However, as they waited, they saw two SS men come up to the café barn and set it on fire. As he lay there he watched out of the corner of one eye as one of the German tank crew members operated a hand-cranked well pump. Unmoving, Paluch listened to the loud crackling of fire as flames spread through the Café Bodarwe. Acrid smoke filled the air.

While others got up and ran, risking the gauntlet of German gunfire, he and the other man waited until the German at the well went back into the house. Then they rolled quietly on the ground downhill behind the Lejoly-Jacob house until they were on the other side of a hedgerow that ran north-south behind the café. There, at least, they were not under direct observation. The man was S/Sgt. Herman Johnson from the U.S. 2nd Infantry Division, who, although wounded in the arm, stayed on the ground by Paluch's side waiting until they could escape together.[48] Later that night, when they crawled away to the north, the café was still burning brightly. *Had the men who ran to the café burned to death?* Paluch was horrified by that thought.

One man who had taken refuge in the back of the café was Pfc. Peter C. Piscatelli. Before Mattera called for an escape, the Bronx youth was wounded in six places, including having toes shot off. So handicapped, he was only able to run to a building with other members of the 285th, but then the enemy suddenly approached. "I laid down alongside another of our men and 'played dead.' Two Germans approached us and one of them emptied his pistol into my right arm. . . . They stayed a few minutes and left. I looked up and saw two civilians. . . . A man brought me into their house and a woman started to cry."[49] Would refuge for Piscatelli cost Madame Bodarwe her life?

> The Germans, having seen us, set up a machine gun at the entrance and shot all the men they found. They then set fire to the barn [sic]. At that time, I escaped under cover of the smoke from the fire and made my way back to our lines.[50]

Running on in the night, Paluch and Johnson would eventually meet up with medic Roy Anderson and James Mattera from his own unit and make their way into Malmédy. "The four of us came in together on the railroad tracks," Paluch said. "We came right into the center of Malmédy." Paluch had seen a roadblock ahead on the road to Malmédy and assured the others that after the encounter with the Germans just a mile back, he was not going to risk that. Mattera could go if he wanted, Paluch told him, so Mattera headed for the roadblock. As he drew closer, the alert sentries of the 291st Engineer Combat Battalion, understandably paranoid with the Skorzeny imposters motoring about, challenged him. Mattera cursed the men demanding a password. "Forget the password," he blurted. All those in his outfit were dead. "The Germans are coming!"[51]

Mattera was sent to a nearby aid station. The medics there asked if he was okay. Although the blood covering him was not his own, he was still shaking uncontrollably. "No, I don't think I'm hit," he responded. Removing his uniform, they found holes in the seat of his trousers and gave him a dry uniform. Just then another man, Pvt. John Cobbler from Virginia, staggered in. Even though he was severely wounded, Cobbler had escaped the field too; Sgt. Joe Connors of Company B of the 291st Engineer Combat Battalion brought him to the hospital. Cobbler was bloody and ashen white. "How are you Mattera?" he managed. Mattera said he was okay, but he thought Cobbler looked terrible. How was he? "I'm all shot up," he gasped. Paluch saw him, too, with "blood spurting from his mouth like a spigot." The medics stripped Cobbler and found multiple bullet wounds—some of them in the stomach. He died in the ambulance on the way to the field hospital.

Pvt. John Kailer had jumped up and fled with a group he estimated at over thirty men, but he had glanced back as he ran off toward the northwest. "They still had a tank near the crossroads," he remembered, "and they let loose with the machine guns again." When Kailer took off he ran with Pfc. Carl B. Frey and several others to cross the dirt road that led from Baugnez to the tiny hamlet of Hédomont. There was a hedgerow next to the road.

When this gun started firing, I hit the ground again about two feet from the road and Frey hit it about six feet from the road. They were still firing machine guns and a German soldier came up the road with a pistol and commenced shooting everybody he saw laying there. [He shot them] in the head. I saw him run up the road and saw him shoot at the fellow lying beside me [Pvt. Samuel Hallman] and also saw him shoot at Frey. . . . I was laying partially on my left side with my arm in front of my face and the bullet grazed my right forearm. Then five to ten minutes later, I heard two Germans coming up the road through the field and they were kicking the bodies. I could hear them do this as I could hear the fellows grunt. I heard them speak in German after they kicked a man and they would either shoot him or move on to the next man. Then they came up on the fellow behind me, kicked him three times, he grunted and they seemed to cuss. They shot him and then went across the road, heading north. There were other fellows over there because I saw them stop and I heard shots for quite a while in that direction.[52]

The soldier who fired at Kailer, Hallman, and Frey was the same pistol-wielding SS man who shot at Bill Merriken and Ted Paluch— likely a crew member from Kurt Briesemeister's panzer. Indeed, the tank Kailer had seen at the crossroads was the same Panther Nr. 114. Moreover, Briesemeister was the one who later admitted that he and his men had shot at American prisoners who suddenly leaped up to escape from the field.[53]

Ralph Law lay in the killing field for at least an hour. "No one moved," he remembered.

Then, I saw one of the men raise his head and look around. He jumped up and said, "Let's go!" loud enough so that everyone could hear him. Everyone who could move, at least, tried to get up. It was every man for himself to get out of there. I got up and ran about 50 yards, until the pain in my leg was too much for me. Four or five of us were fairly close together as we crossed the field and started for another road. As I started across the road, a German opened up with a burp gun about 25 yards away at the crossroads. I dropped into the ditch beside the road for cover and because my leg was paining me too much to continue on. . . . The German with the burp gun ran up the road past me, still shooting. After he stopped shooting, he came back down past me. He kicked me in the back, as I was lying on my face, to see if I was dead. Then he continued on back to his post at the crossroads. I turned my head enough to see him there.

They burned down the barn [café] in which we had taken cover. Sparks from the fire fell on me and the light from the fire shone on me so that I had to lay there until the fire died down. I guess it was about 2300 hours when I thought it was dark enough to be safe. By then, my leg was stiff so I could not bend it, but the wound had stopped bleeding. I turned around and crawled down the ditch between the road and the hedgerow, away from the crossroads, for about 50 yards. I went through the hedgerow into the field and crawled about a mile and a half across several fields. As day was breaking, I knew I had to seek cover so the Germans would not find me. There was a farm house near, so I crawled to it.[54]

Letting himself into the ground-floor basement, Law found the house abandoned, but even though he was exhausted and seemingly near his end, he wrapped himself in some quilts and the warmth soon revived him. On the morning of December 18 he saw a bicycle with no one around. Escape! But how would he get on it without a left leg? He hobbled along to prop the cycle against a small tree. Then, by using his arms, he was able to throw his injured leg over the bike. But no pedaling—how would that work? At least the road just in front of him looked downhill. His right foot pushing hard on the pedal and a shove from the tree and he was soon buzzing downhill. After coasting over a mile a nervous American sentry confronted him just before Malmédy. After the sentry pointed guns at Law over failed passwords, there was short conversation, and Law—pale, bleeding, and in shock—was soon on the way back to the 44th Evacuation Hospital in Malmédy.[55]

A number of men who attempted to run from the field were shot down as they ran. One, Pfc. Harry Horn, had lost a lot of blood before everyone scattered. Even so, he got up, weaving and stumbling forward about fifty yards before the Germans opened fire on the running men with machine guns. The tracers danced about his feet. He dropped to the ground once more and lay there feigning death. Rising again after dark, he struggled to his feet and wandered toward American lines, heading off toward the north. However, he was so weak that, after proceeding a mile, he knocked on the door of a local farmhouse. His action was desperate, but he thought he would die otherwise. The Belgian family took Horn in and gave him a jolt of cognac and washed his wounds. The American soldier was fevered and delirious, so the Belgian family kept him until December 22, when the Americans recaptured the tiny hamlet in which he was given refuge.[56]

When the others rose and ran, Pvt. Samuel Dobyns fled in a northwesterly direction, joined by Pvt. Werth and T/5 O'Connell. All three were badly wounded: Dobyns was crippled, Werth had been shot in both thighs, and O'Connell had an ugly wound to his right jaw that was bleeding terribly. Once they came to a road heading for

Malmédy, O'Connell convinced the other two that he had to go on to find help—otherwise he would die from bleeding. If he ran into the Germans, maybe he could get medical help. If he found friendly forces, he would send someone back to get Dobyns and Werth. The plan worked. Although weak and exhausted, O'Connell came across a sixty-five-year-old Belgian who pointed out the proper direction to reach the Americans.[57] Soon, at the roadblock of the 291st Combat Engineer Battalion near Malmédy, a guard challenged him for a password. Someone there sent a jeep back for Dobyns and Werth, and O'Connell was soon in a hospital.

With all the traffic going through the Baugnez intersection, there were several close calls. Duane Londagin and Lacy Thomasson were still speeding north out of St. Vith after their failed mission to get the mail for the 78th Infantry Division. Londagin drove with a lead foot— he was spooked. There was booming artillery in the distance and everyone raced about with wild rumors and wide eyes. Londagin went all the faster as they approached the town of Ligneuville. From there the road snaked up a hill through a dense forest belt. As they neared a sharp curve to the left, the road was so narrow that Londagin, who was driving their three-quarter-ton weapons carrier, had to slow. As they came out from the forest around the bend, they found themselves on high ground looking at the highway that ran north before them. There was an American column not three hundred yards from him. In the distance they saw a tank, then a muzzle flash—it was firing! An enemy tank column was shooting up an American truck convoy that stretched nearly up to their position.[58] "Damn!" Thomasson swore. "Look at this." There was a line of American trucks pulled off to the left side of the road. Londagin slammed on the brakes. "What are we going to do now?" "Get the hell out of here," Thomasson yelled, leaping from his seat.

Londagin thought at first about turning around, but the gun flashes from the approaching enemy tanks convinced him otherwise. Machine-gun rounds started to hit. They both jumped from the vehicle and darted to either side of the road. Moments later their vehicle was smashed by a tank round.[59] "We had no weapons so we high-tailed it away," Londagin recalled. Both men hid underneath the pines on the hill looking down the road. They could see American soldiers being escorted up the road back to the north. German tanks passed their position, ignoring their smashed weapons carrier, but no one seemed to be looking for them. Meanwhile, from the ditch bank, Thomasson and Londagin peeked over the crest of the hill to observe the American soldiers in the convoy being rounded up. "We could see them gathering prisoners all up and down the line and herding them into an open field."[60]

All of a sudden, they started shooting these soldiers in the field. "I'll be damned," I thought, "what the hell are they doing that for?" Then they stopped shooting them and went around kicking them. Any that moved, they shot them. I was about a hundred yards or so away from the scene, straight down into an embankment and across was a valley. German tanks came on past us. I could see a German officer standing up in the tank. . . . I think there were three more tanks behind it.[61]

Londagin was on the opposite side of the road and Thomasson called to him. "They killed a bunch of American soldiers who tried to surrender," I told him. "We got to get the hell out of here!" He ran over to Londagin's side of the road on the west. His pal wanted to get a better look. "I'm not going back over to look again," Londagin said. Just then, some of the Germans spotted them and began shooting. Scared witless, both men fled into the thick forest immediately west of the road, running wildly with all their might. Within minutes they were completely lost.

On the opposite end of the N-23 beyond Baugnez to the north, other troops also ran into the debacle. B Company, 86th (Heavy Pontoon) Engineer Battalion had been in the Malmédy area hauling lumber up to create tent flooring so grateful GIs could avoid sleeping on the cold, miserable ground. It was a mundane job made strange by the artillery shells mysteriously falling in Malmédy the day before. However, that morning, as their three big logging trucks chugged up the hill, they found a bigger surprise. Topping the rise and approaching the crossroads at Five Points, a gust of gunfire swept them. All the trucks stopped behind the last of the ill-fated ambulances along the road.

Scattering after the shooting, several of the GI loggers crawled away to the woods. Even so, Pvt. Vestal McKinney took a bullet in his right leg and crawled into a ditch. Four men of B Company helped him escape with them to safety.[62] One man, Pfc. John J. Clymire, hesitated, staying with his truck.

"We never saw that boy again," McKinney remembered.[63]

CHAPTER 9

Fateful Hours

Battery B of the 285th was not the only group for whom fate skated between life and death at the Baugnez crossroads that Sunday afternoon. Some men's fates were sealed in near anonymity. Two Americans would die in the field with scant explanation of how they got there: Sgt Benjamin Lindt and medic Pfc. Elmer Wald of the 200th Field Artillery Battalion. Similar to the men of the 32nd Armored Regiment Recon Company, Lindt and Wald likely ran into the Kampfgruppe Peiper east of Baugnez, were made captive, and then brought to the crossroads. Neither survived to tell what happened; battalion records merely showed them missing in action on December 18.[1]

Others avoided a deadly fate by the thinnest of margins. On the morning of December 17 T/4 Russell T. Carr of the 18th Infantry Regiment of the U.S. 1st Infantry Division was released from the 77th Evacuation hospital in Verviers after being treated for a skin rash. Seeking his regiment, which he thought was near Waimes, he hitched a ride with a captain and his jeep driver, unknowingly headed straight for a dangerous rendezvous with Peiper's battle group:

> Between the hours of 1300 and 1400 hours, not far from Malmédy, we came around a corner over a small grade and first saw the Germans. However, there appeared to be more U.S. soldiers than

Germans and our first impression was that the Germans were prisoners. As we pulled up near them, a German officer, wearing an SS panzer grenadier uniform jumped in the middle of the road. He had a pistol in his hand. As the jeep started to slow down, I jumped out and hit the dirt. . . . I was about a hundred yards from the German officer and about 300 yards from the others . . . I went down this ditch, and that was the last I saw of the Captain and his driver. I laid in this ditch until I heard shooting which I recognized as enemy fire. I worked my way out of the field and into a patch of woods and eventually back to Spa. There was scattered firing until I worked my way out of hearing distance. I stayed overnight at the MP station in Spa.[2]

In a similar twist, in the early morning of December 17 Staff Sgt. Herman M. Johnson of the U.S. 2nd Division's Company M was riding with his assistant cook, Pvt. Edgar Smith, when artillery fire struck their mess truck near Waimes. Johnson then put Smith, who was wounded, in a jeep driven by Pvt. Wilson with the service company of the regiment. At 8:30 A.M. that morning, as they headed toward the battalion aid station, their jeep literally ran into a German tank shrouded in mist. "We rounded a curve and there it was. . . . They took us prisoner. . . . They asked me what unit we were from, but we didn't tell them anything. At this point they turned the driver loose and kept me prisoner." Wilson had a Red Cross brassard on his sleeve, so they let Smith and Wilson go off to get medical aid. Johnson was not so lucky: "They took me around in an armored car for about three hours." Johnson said the few German tanks and halftracks with him seemed to roam around at will, pausing every so often to cut communications lines when they came across them. But in the early afternoon the German halftrack in which he was riding came to a major intersection. It was Baugnez:

When we arrived at this road junction there were quite a number of German tanks and armored cars on the road leading into the road intersection and the Germans had halted an American convoy of ambulances, two-and-a-half-ton [trucks] and jeeps. . . . They had the drivers and assistant drivers out in an open field. Just as I got out of the armored car, they noticed I had a wrist watch, which was GI issue and they took the watch. . . . Then we came to this field where the other prisoners were and they were all disarmed.

The others were searched for loot as well, and soon thereafter Johnson saw a German soldier draw a pistol and shoot a man not fifteen feet from him. According to his recollection, one German soldier with a light machine gun on an armored car opened fire on the entire group. Johnson was wounded in the side and later in the arm as machine guns swept over him and the other men flew to the ground. And then the worst: "They would come around and if you groaned or moved, they would shoot you again."[3] Johnson lay there with the rest for nearly an hour and half before everyone made a break to escape—running to hide under some old floorboards in the woodshed just to the south of Café Bodarwe. But just before dusk, the Germans set the shed and café on fire, so Johnson wriggled off in the gathering darkness to meet up with Ted Paluch near a hedgerow, after which they ran for the woods.

Meanwhile, Duane Londagin and Lacy Thomasson were lost in the Ardennes. In shock after witnessing the crossroads shootings from the top of the road leading to Ligneuville, the two GIs spent the entire night of December 17 running about in panicked circles deep in the Ardennes Forest. Both men wandered aimlessly in the darkness, somehow making their way to the north and crossing not far from the massacre field to reach the road that led down into Malmédy. As light gathered in the east with both men hiding in bushes, they heard military forces ahead. "We ended up on this hill where we could hear vehicle sounds down below," Londagin recalled. He thought it was a jeep motor, but neither man was sure. Both were still filled with terrible dread from what they had seen the afternoon before.

Then at daylight the two men saw the troops getting coffee, the familiar rumble of a 6 x 6 truck, and cursing and complaining in English. *Cussing!* Londagin knew they were Americans. As if one, both men eagerly bolted down the hill. Soon, however, they had their hands up again, facing two nervous youths manning a machine gun. "Come on down slowly and identify yourselves!" called an edgy voice. Thomasson had no dog tags—he had buried them—and the paranoid soldiers wanted to know why Londagin was away from his unit.

"While we were trying to identify ourselves," he said, "we were inter-rupted by a wild yell off to our right. It was a wounded GI that had just fallen off a bicycle that he coasted on for about half a mile. He had three bullet holes in him. . . . He was part of the patrol that had been lined up and shot."[4]

The GI on the bicycle was Pfc. Ralph Law, who had narrowly es-caped death at the crossroads. His uniform was muddy, torn from crawling for hours, and his left leg was a bloody mess. But as an ambu-lance prepared to load him on board, he called out to everyone there. The Germans were just at the top of the hill, he croaked. They were killing everyone. The little engineer squad into which Londagin and Thomasson had stumbled, now looked at each other. For a time the be-wildered men were given rifles and told to make themselves ready to help defend the roadblock. Still, as an hour passed, no German tanks appeared, and a superior officer arrived, telling Londagin and Thomas-son to make their way back to their unit. Amid all the confusion in Malmédy and Spa, that was no small challenge.[5]

Later that night more cold and bleeding men reached a roadblock of the 291st Combat Engineer Battalion in Malmédy at the intersection of the Géromont-La Vaulx road. Cpl. Bernie Koenig recalled,

Two hysterical G.I.s came down out of the hills, moaning and crying. They told us the Germans had killed everybody down at Five Points. Sgt. Munoz sent them down into town to the aid station with one of his men. This was the way we learned of the famous massacre. It shocked us badly and we vowed that if the Krauts were taking no prisoners, we would take none ourselves.[6]

Pergrin and Crickenberger, too, went out for a second jeep recon-naissance and came within sight of the brilliantly burning café before rescuing another three survivors. And after dark, at 6:30 P.M., Sgt. Charles Dishaw's 291st roadblock nearest the crossroads announced to Pergrin that another five survivors of the shooting had shown up, wild with terror and telling the same story. One of these was T/5 Warren Schmitt, who had been in water for hours before escaping. Covered in cold mud, he looked like a frozen zombie. Soon, all eight would be in Malmédy and the 44th Evacuation Hospital—although that unit was also looking to pull out of the endangered town. Two of the medical drivers for the evacuation from the Malmédy schoolhouse were Pfc. Harry R. Ross and Cpl. Stanley Smith, who had been captured earlier in the day by the SS briefly at the 47th Field Hospital at Waimes. Now, driving back to Malmédy, both men vainly sought their unit before finding out that all medical personnel were leaving. "First we get captured," Ross told an American reporter, "then we lose our hospital!"[7] As the Americans left town, citizens of Malmédy stood in the streets, staring in disbelief as the Americans left. The medical services in the area were in total chaos.

Headquarters of the 546th and 575th Ambulance Companies were located in Waimes, Belgium, and assigned to the 180th Medical Battalion after being assigned to evacuating the casualties of the 99th and 2nd Infantry Divisions. But with the surprise enemy breakthrough on December 17, the fifteen-odd ambulances were assisting the medical evacuation of the threatened 47th Field Hospital at Waimes to the 44th Evacuation Hospital in Malmédy. Nothing went as planned.

After the last of the long convoy of trucks and jeeps of the 285th FAOB ran into the German column and surrendered, luckless ambulances appeared from the 44th Evacuation Hospital in Malmédy. Unaware of the events, they sought to assist with American casualties streaming back from the direction of Waimes.[8] The first of these to run into the enemy carried medics Pvt. Samuel Dobyns and Pfc. Wayne Scott of the 575th Ambulance Company. "They were trying to tear down the hospital," Dobyns recalled. "We were clearing out all the patients."[9] That morning he and Scott evacuated four patients to Malmédy and headed back to get more.

Not knowing German armor was approaching, Dobyns and Scott bounced by the Baugnez crossroads and buzzed east for Waimes. However, they had gone less than half a mile when their Red Cross–emblazoned ambulance was ambushed. "Machine guns from a tank cut loose on us and riddled our ambulance," Dobyns recounted. "The tank was about 25 yards from us. It was the lead tank."[10]

Neither man was injured in the ambush, but they were so stunned to run into the enemy so far behind friendly lines that their ambulance careened off the road, plowing into an adjacent muddy field to the north. Both men dove out of their wrecked vehicle to take refuge in a ditch. Clearly there was no chance to run or escape; a German officer came over to take their surrender and relieve them of personal valuables and cigarettes. At first the German seemed to want to shoot them, but another SS trooper intervened. Dobyns thought he saved their lives. In any case, soon they were on the tank riding the short distance to the crossroads.

Scott was placed on another armored vehicle behind him. Dobyns clasped his hands behind his head while sitting on the tank. Soon he watched the panzer shooting up the rear of an American convoy as it approached the intersection of Highway 32. The Germans searched them both again, and Dobyns was then moved to join the large standing group of prisoners just south of the café at the intersection. "I was nervous," Dobyns remembered with understatement. He recalled that two armored vehicles posted themselves right across from where they were assembled. At that point a tank approached and parked itself between the other two vehicles. "Then one German began to fire into the crowd with a P-38 revolver." As men began to fall and a second pistol shot rang out, Dobyns panicked. "I ran to the rear of the formation and hit the ground," he told Col. Lamar Tooze later on December 17, just after he escaped. "They opened up with machine guns from tanks at about 75 feet."[11] Even though Dobyns had moved from the front of the group to the rear, the machine gunfire still hit him: "It shattered my right foot ankle and my right arm." Although others thought it went on interminably, Dobyns reckoned that the firing lasted for half a minute. After the silence that followed, he hazarded a glance to the east across the field. Over the heaps of GIs before his field of vision, he saw three Germans enter the field. "The ones [Americans] that were moaning or crying for help—they shot them with a pistol."

The other ambulances were equally ill fated. About the time he was taken prisoner in front of the Café Bodarwe, Kenny Kingston spied a series of ambulances approaching from the north. The first in line, under the command of T/5 Dayton Wusterbarth, was a weapons carrier driven by Pvt. Keston Mullen. Directly behind their vehicles was another with Pfc. James "Monk" McKinney and Pfc. Stephen Domitrovich of the 575th Ambulance Company.[12] Next came the ambulance of 1st Lt. Carl R. Genthner and driver, Pfc. Paul "Pappy" Paden. In the last ambulance was Pfc. L. M. Burney and Pvt. Roy Anderson. The medical convoy was headed for the ill-fated 47th Field Hospital in Waimes, but it would never make it. Already a prisoner with his hands up, Kingston cringed as the Red Cross–emblazoned trucks drove up.

A German tank sat at the crossroads and began pelting the ambulances with machine gunfire as they approached. Bouncing along the road that led south from Malmédy, Domitrovich was lackadaisically watching other men of the troop in the back of the weapons carrier ahead of them. "All of a sudden, we saw them pointing and waving."[13] They jumped out of their vehicle, so he and his crewmate did the same. "We were coming up the hill in the traffic and we noticed a lot of shooting," recalled McKinney. "The majority of us thought that it was a plane strafing."[14] He and Domitrovich leapt out of their vehicle to the ground. The vehicles screeched to a stop with their occupants piling out. "We heard gunfire and hit the ditch," Anderson, who had been in another ambulance, recalled.[15] The ditch was filled with cold, dank water.

McKinney and Domitrovich crawled into a barn behind the home of the elder Henri Lejoly-Jacob and his wife, Johanna, just west of the crossroads. They remained there for some time until a German SS trooper rousted them from the shed. Soon their hands were up with everyone else. Domitrovich was dismayed to see some of the Belgian civilians at the crossroads saluting the Germans as they conducted the American prisoners to the frosty meadow south of the café. The men were brought into the field on the northwest side of the group, standing with their hands up. There was increasing worry when they saw the double lightning flash of the SS on the collars of the "young kids" guarding them. All the prisoners had been disarmed and most liberated of watches, money, and cigarettes. McKinney remembered that the enemy ominously lined up three halftracks right across from them:

> I wondered what the Germans were doing, putting us in this open
> field. We were holding our hands over our heads for quite some
> time. While we were doing that there was plenty of German armor
> on the road. When we were out there on the side of the road, they

put three armored half tracks and all of the sudden one of the guys in this car took out his pistol and started picking off the Americans one by one. . . . They doubled up and fell over. . . .[16]

Shortly, Domitrovich spied an enemy soldier coming down the same the ditch they were in. Someone in his vicinity yelled "*Kamerad!*" and they soon stood with raised hands.

He tells us to put our hand on our helmets and asked if we had wrist watches and cigarettes. He takes us up the road to where the other boys are. Every armored car that came by they would get out and search us. . . . We stood there and watched all their stuff. . . . We climbed over a fence and we stood in there for a while and two medics there were fixing a wounded man who was wounded just before we were taken. Two armored cars parked down the road and they decided to use big guns and set up some other guns. I saw somebody stand up in the armored car and shoot at the two who were fixing the wounded man. It must have hit him in the stomach as he doubled up. After that they opened up with fast firing guns. A split second before the first machine gun opened up, I heard a voice next to me say "fall" and I did. I fell, but I was not hit. So I decided to play dead. The firing seemed to last forever and when it finally stopped, blood streaked bodies were piled up around me.[17]

Domitrovich closed his eyes and lay completely still, listening as some of the wounded men pitifully called for help.

The SS men approached and started shooting anyone who moved in the head, all the while laughing and echoing the dying GI's "Mom." It was terrible—terrible. . . . I was thinking of my own mother back in Aliquippa and that Christmas was only a week away. . . . Suddenly a big German boot held still next to me and I felt the cold of a pistol against my forehead and held my breath. The following couple of seconds must have been the longest in my life . . . then for some reason, the SS soldier did not pull the trigger and went on to the next guy.[18]

Eventually Domitrovich would escape—survival that precipitated a personal epiphany: God, he was sure, had protected him. Little else mattered. Could he remember the appearance of the youth who fired? No, Domitrovich told those who interviewed him, "I was too damned scared."

McKinney remembered hearing two shots and then seeing two Americans fall at the front of the crowd just before the machine guns started. The Pennsylvania native recalled that machine guns fired from all three halftracks. "I hit the dirt as if I were dead," he said. For a half an hour after that, "they just kept on waiting for any one of us to move and they would shoot them. . . . They shot a man right near me. They walked up and shot him—I heard the crack of the gun."

> When they started shooting, I just turned around and fell on my stomach on the ground. We lay there for about ten minutes and they were still shooting into the crowd. After I laid there for about twenty minutes, a German came up to one American soldier that was lying close to me. This American was wounded and the German just shot him again. Then he jumped over to me. I had my hands over my head and he took my watch off my arm after we laid there for about an hour.[19]

Kampfgruppe Peiper also pulled unsuspecting conventional U.S. combat forces into its vortex. The fate of the members of the four jeeps of the reconnaissance company of the 32nd Armored Regiment that ran into Peiper's battle group south of Ondenval is a good example. These unfortunate soldiers were brought to the Malmédy crossroads where the other prisoners of the field artillery observation battalion were being assembled. Three of them, Sgt. Vernon Anderson, Pvt. William Barron, and Cpl. John Cummings, were lucky enough to have the Germans convince them to drive the American trucks abandoned along the N-23. The others, however, were deposited with the other members of the 285th FAOB massed at the Baugnez crossroads at around 1:30 P.M. They included 1st Lt. Thomas E. McDermott, 2nd Lt. Lloyd A. Iames, Cpl. Walter J. Wendt, Sgt. Marvin J. Lewis, Cpl. Edward Bojarski, and S/Sgt. Henry Zach. The two lieutenants, McDermott and Iames, would be killed in the Baugnez shooting, but the others would survive in one way or another. Sgt. Lewis remembered how, after capture, they were searched and then put back in their jeeps with a German driving, moving along until they came to the cross-roads at Baugnez:

> When we got there, they already had a supply column [sic, 285th FAOB] and they made us dismount and lined us up with all the personnel of the supply train and put us in a field near the road. Then they started moving out our vehicles.[20]

After bouncing along on German tanks for nearly eight miles and over an hour-long period, S/Sgt. Henry Roy Zach, a native of Burnet County, Wisconsin, found himself approaching an intersection where another task force had more than fifty prisoners already collected. Zach and the others of the little reconnaissance company were then motioned to dismount the tanks, hand over their cigarettes, and go into the field with the other prisoners. Zach did as ordered, placing himself into the swelling group of Americans south of the crossroads behind a fence. Looking out, he was moved into something of a surre-alist reverie. There were cold pines under a gray sky with wisps of mist obscuring the view at any distance. The entire group was understand-ably apprehensive. Some halftracks were pulling up just as they arrived, not seventy yards away:

> There was considerable moving around of the [group] as a whole. I was just brought back with my hands up and they were shifting around and I somehow got to the rear of the bunch and I stayed there . . . they brought up a halftrack that had a howitzer on it and they swung it right across the road. They lowered it and they could not get this gun low enough, or deflected enough to cover us, and they brought up these two halftracks.[21]

Zach recalled that there were two halftracks directly across from the prisoners with another slightly further up.[22] Lt. Iames was stand-ing right next to Zach and could understand German. He heard the Germans talking and suddenly turned to his sergeant, saying, "Zach, they're going to kill us."[23] Zach could only nod as he watched the

Germans train their machine guns on their group. He, Lt. Iames, and Lt. McDermott were standing close together just north of the center of the group in the field. There were four loosely aligned rows, and Zach had managed to get to the rear. "We were not there long," he recalled, "when they started firing." Although the prisoners standing in front of him, with their hands held high, partly obstructed Zach's view, he thought the first shooting came from the "machine guns on the halftracks."

When the firing broke out into the mass of prisoners, Zach threw himself facedown on the ground with his head aligned away from the road. "The Americans in front of me started being blown back towards me," he recounted—human dominoes. "When the machine gun bullets started hitting them, I thought it was a good time to fall and play dead, which I did." While he was on the ground, machine gunfire sprayed the men lying prone in the field. It went on for a long time—he thought for ten minutes. A machine gun round hit Zach in the right hip. "When the machine guns stopped firing off the halftracks," he said, "I heard several large caliber guns go off and it took several shots before one of them hit me." The doctors who later patched up Zach estimated that it had been a 40mm round that nearly tore off his left leg. But the nightmare was not done.

Unlike most in the field, Zach had front combat–line experience with the 3rd Armored Division. After the first shots he knew the Germans were trying to get rid of them all. Many in the group were terribly wounded; even so, he feared for everyone still alive when those artillerymen who had survived began shouting back and forth: "The Germans, armed with pistols then came and killed all the men on the ground who were screaming or moaning in agony."[24] From his position at the rear of the group, Zach could peer to the right and left just enough to observe bullets being fired into the men lying close by. He noticed that the Germans were kicking the Americans in the testicles— if they moved after that, they were shot. Zach had fallen faced down, but he didn't move even a little when he was kicked hard in the rump:

> They stood right next to me and shot my lieutenant. . . . He had
> pretended to be dead, the same as I, but he didn't fool them, I guess
> because I heard them kick him and they made him get to his feet,

but I'll give that lieutenant credit—he was a man. . . . He never begged or whimpered or anything. They just shot him in the head and when he fell backwards he touched my feet.[25]

Some groaned after being shot a final time; others gasped and sighed their final breath. Zach closed his eyes and pretended to be dead, not moving even though wracked with pain. After the executioners left, there were more cries and moans; then the Germans came back a second time.

In the late afternoon when dozens of Americans suddenly jumped up and ran from the tangle of bodies near the road, Zach was too badly wounded to join. He could not use his left leg at all—it was hardly attached, dangling grotesquely by muscle and sinew on each side. And Lt. Iames's execution had shown him what would happen to anyone showing signs of life. Then Zach had also watched some of the Americans run to the shed by the café or into the café itself, only to have the SS men set the building on fire.

The reek of burning wood and sooty smoke permeated the air all afternoon. And still he heard occasional shots. Then his world got cloudy—was he dying? Although he lost consciousness, for a time he was still dimly aware of the burning of the café. "I watched it burn all afternoon." Later, after the Germans left, the sky grew dark, when, "I heard no more moans, groans or movement to indicate that anyone was left alive in the field." He crawled away from the mass of dead toward the café: "I can safely say I was the last person to crawl away from the bodies. I waited until after dark and I went alone."[26]

Zach had crawled only a foot or so when he came upon the lifeless body of Lt. Iames by the hedge that separated the field from the café.[27] By then, the café was quietly burning to ground, but Zach was so badly wounded, wet, and cold that the heat drew him in that direction. He could hardly move anyway. Near the end of his strength, he crawled underneath a sheet of galvanized roofing that lay near the glowing embers of the ruin. "I was getting pretty weak," he said. "I was bleeding quite a bit." Exhausted, he fell unconscious in a deep sleep. Zach awoke near noon the next day. Slowly opening his eyes, he was surprised to find himself even alive. As if in a dream, he heard voices. Realizing he was near death, he called out with all his strength. "I yelled out as loud as I could. . . . I didn't care anymore. I took a chance."

Amazingly, it was an American captain and two enlisted men who chanced driving their jeep to the crossroads. Upon first arriving on the scene, they were shocked to see a pile of dead bodies. Then the Belgian civilians came out, speaking so fast no one could tell what they were saying.[28] Yet the place was hot—the enemy was just around the corner.

Capt. Edward Schenck of the small American party heard Zach's cry. He discovered the severely wounded GI pitifully huddled under a plank of metal roofing and covered by mud and ash. In a near panic to leave, they used the corrugated metal sheet as a stretcher and hurriedly hauled him to the jeep. "Let's get out of here!" Schenck said, throwing the jeep in gear. Seconds later they sped off to the north, leaving the two Belgian men behind them still imploring them with urgent hand gestures.[29]

Although grievously wounded, Henry Roy Zach had survived the Malmédy massacre.

CHAPTER 10

Escape

When "Let's go!" filtered across the crossroads, the rallying cry was not a loud shout but more an urgent whisper. Still, it was loud enough.

With that sudden call, patches of seemingly dead clumps of human beings, lying contorted and frozen in the Baugnez field, suddenly staggered up in confusion. Their motion was halting—wobbling, weaving, stumbling. Once up, they scattered like winged prey, with some running fleet footed and others hobbling in pain. Many ran to the northwest to the passing cover of leafless hedges, Madame Bodarwe's café, or the stone Belgian homes beyond. Some were unable to follow. Several rose and fell back. A few would lie longer, waiting for nightfall, but most left alive in the field sought to escape from the deadly meadow. Many were bleeding; if they waited, they would only expire in the field in agony. Now or never.

S/Sgt. Bill Merriken was one of those. Though desperate to escape, he was badly wounded, with gunshots to the back and knee and soaked in blood. Even if he could lift himself to his feet, he could only stagger helplessly as if an ape—half on his feet, half on his hands. Somehow, amid stabbing pain, he managed to limp and crawl his way to a small ramshackle woodshed. The structure was up the road west of the crossroads on the south side of the farmhouse of Henri and

Johanna Lejoly-Jacob. Faint from loss of blood, he was too weak to continue further. He dropped at its entrance and wriggled inside.

While he lay there in the shack, a dark shape suddenly rose to enter his hiding place.[1] At that moment Merriken summoned all his strength to wield a heavy stick of firewood lying inside. He held it like a baseball bat. If the man approaching was an enemy soldier, Merriken mused, he was going to get a big surprise. "Halt!" Merriken cried in an urgent whisper. "American, American!" the dark shaped insisted. "Come on in," Merriken replied, lowering his voice.

The man quickly pulled himself inside, "I'm Chuck Reding of 285th," the voice said in quiet urgency.[2] The wounded man slumped, dropping the shaft of wood in exhaustion. He knew Charles Reding was that boy from Tennessee who had joined up as a replacement in the Hürtgen Forest. "Are you hurt?" Merriken asked him. "No, sergeant," he replied in a tired, southern tone, "but you look like you are." Reding was right. They agreed that they would have to get out of this shed soon. Although they couldn't see the crossroads directly because of the hedges, they could hear the enemy milling about. And with Waffen SS soldiers all over the place, Merriken and Reding knew the enemy couldn't help but search this place eventually. Besides, it was clear to both that Bill would not last long without medical help.

Together, they proposed to crawl out to the road that led down into Malmédy while it was still dark. They debated the route; after all, the enemy would almost certainly cover the road. "Wait a minute," Merriken said. "Chuck, you had better go on and go it alone, because I don't know if I'm going to make it. You can get help." Reding could see that the man was intent on sacrificing himself. "No, sergeant," Reding said, putting his hand on Merriken's shoulder, "you can make it . . . and we'll make it together." Merriken was not sure he could, but he was too tired to argue. He agreed to try.

Under a jet-black sky they both crawled out of the tiny shack and pulled themselves on their elbows along the back of the farmhouse. Everything about the crossroads was still etched in the eerie light of the burning café. As he crawled downhill, Merriken spied the dark shadow of a body lying at the back of the house. But they kept crawling, snaking along on their stomachs to a fence that ran parallel with the road down into Malmédy. They were careful to inch away from the

burning café, trying to lower themselves into the shadows of the orange glow of the fire. If they moved in its light, both would surely be
seen. They didn't dare cross the road until they had crawled around a
bend where the enemy might no longer be able to see them. In the light
of the burning café Reding could see "Germans all around." Later that
night things became still once more—this was their chance.

By the time they had snaked over to the other side of the road, the
flames had receded. Merriken and Reding flattened themselves on the
cold ground, crawling quietly to the shadow of the ditch on the other
side. From there they made their way on aching elbows along a ditch
by a cattle run, which ran parallel with the main road to Malmédy.
Reding reckoned that the highway was about fifty to a hundred yards
to the northwest. The going was slow, and Merriken kept moving for
fear that he would pass out if he stopped. They crawled for hours in the
icy ditch. At one point both men thought they spied a human shadow
in the darkness up ahead. They waited for what seemed like an eternity
in silence. Finally, Reding threw a stone at the sound, and they waited
for a reaction. They were relieved to find the apparition to be a fence
post. They had no idea where they were or where they would end up.

After hours of edging forward, a dull light began to brighten the
fog. With dawn breaking, both men were still moving on bruised elbows down the cattle path. Yet in full daylight the cold mist lifted to reveal a shocking sight: in the ditch they were fully exposed with a clear
line of sight across an open field to the paved road to their left. Only
the deep draw they were crawling in provided any cover. Still, they
would be quite visible from the N-23 to any German who chanced to
look. Fearful that the enemy would soon see them in the ditch, they
moved up the bank near the path and hid in a thicket of bushes. In the
distance to the west, both men could make out the foggy outlines of a
house.

They were right to hide. Soon the enemy showed up, roaming up
and down the road. Some of them, Reding saw, were driving captured
U.S. equipment. But Merriken was near the end of his resources; he
blacked out, coming to several times during the day. "What's happening?" he would ask. Each time, Reding told him the Germans were all
over. They would have to stay put until nightfall. They could hear the
muffled sound of machine gunfire not too far away; there was no

question that the enemy was still close by. However, Merriken had lost a lot of blood. His back was saturated and he could feel blood trickling down his leg into his right boot. Although Merriken had fashioned a makeshift tourniquet out of his canvas leggings and laces to slow the bleeding from his right knee, he continued to weaken. Lying on his back, he passed out again.

Sometime later that gray Monday afternoon, Reding jostled Merriken awake. "There's a farmer walking across the field toward us," he said, motioning ahead. Reding hesitated. Many of the Belgians in the area seemed to be German sympathizers. Earlier, some of the American prisoners had seen a Belgian woman at the café come out to greet the big German tanks and pass them a basket with food. While Reding and Merriken whispered in the thicket, the farmer approached the top of the fence steps. Merriken thought he motioned them to follow. Reding wasn't sure. Was he about to reveal their whereabouts to the enemy? Merriken was now in severe pain with swollen wounds and was weak from loss of blood. Reding would have to carry him if they were to go any further, and that would be both slow and plainly visible from the nearby Malmédy road. He could not bring himself to chance such a move before it was dark. Yet with the coming of the dreary December Belgian afternoon, Reding saw that he had little choice. His buddy would die here soon: Waking him was becoming difficult, and he was "swollen and feverish." Reding could see the few buildings of the tiny village of Géromont shimmering in the cold air across the field.

Reding lifted the lower wire of the fence. Both men crawled under it and out into the open field. When they were about halfway across, Merriken said he was too weak to go further. Reding helped him to his feet. "Half dragging, hopping and walking," they headed straight west for a clump of stone buildings off in the gloom up ahead. Their steps were slow; the little village was on top of a steep slope, and they had crawled into a deep draw. Merriken somehow balanced on this left leg and Reding placed Merriken's right arm around his neck, dragging the right leg behind him.

They slowly hobbled up the snow-crusted field. Merriken was delirious; he imagined that trees or bushes were men. "I want to surrender," he called out in a loud voice. "Don't shoot me!" But he started cursing, thinking that he could see the enemy ahead. "Come on you bastards and get me!" Reding was horrified. With all this noise, the enemy would find them after all. He grabbed his buddy and shook him firmly. "Stop it," he pleaded, putting his face right up against his. "There ain't anybody here." Merriken fell silent. He had reached the point at which his blood-drained mind didn't give a damn. He was like an angry drunk.

Arm in arm, they approached the stone houses near the road. Reding headed straight for the nearest building he could make out in the gathering darkness. As they crossed the frozen field, Reding heard the sound of a cow being milked into a metal bucket. "A boy from Tennessee can't mistake that sound," he recalled. They then crossed to the west side of the Malmédy road. Suddenly, they were face-to-face with a middle-aged man in coveralls sitting on a stool just under the U-shaped door of a large stone barn. He was calmly milking a cow by the side of a two-story stone house. The man seemed very surprised, rising quickly from his seat and turning. Reding worried that he was German.

The Belgian farmer took one look at Merriken's blood-covered form and understood Reding's clear words, "Help us." "*Vite, vite, vite!*" (Quick, quick, quick!) the Belgian urged them toward the wooden door. Reding was relieved to recognize him as the same man who had approached them earlier. The house was a stout, two-story stone structure with a large wooden door. The man ushered the two Americans inside. They moved into a kitchen with a long bench. Reding dropped to the bench, spreading Merriken out on the wooden table. Both were exhausted and freezing, and the room was warm.

Soon a Belgian woman appeared in the kitchen, lighted by a kerosene lantern. She was older, with fine features and adorned in a simple dress with an apron. Unknown to the men, her name was Anna Blaise, a sixty-two-year-old widow who still tended the farm. Her husband, Joseph Blaise, had died just two years earlier. The man—the two Americans thought he was her husband—was Monsieur Lerho, her hired hand.[3]

The two visitors surprised Anna, and she started speaking rapidly to them in French. Somehow, with Reding's fledgling command of the language (he had married a French woman back in Louisiana), they understood each other a little. Reding, meanwhile, moved over to the window facing the Malmédy road and quickly closed the curtains. "My friend is hurt," he told her in halting French. Soon she came back with a pan of hot water. Where was he hurt, the woman wanted to know. They carefully removed Merriken's muddy field jacket, but when they tried to take off his blood-encrusted shirt, he motioned them to stop. Reding wearily concluded that this was just as well, as removing his clothing might open his wounds. The woman warmed both of the men a cup of potato soup on the woodstove. She seated them at the simple wooden table, where she served the soup and two cups of coffee. She nodded to each, smiling faintly, imploring them to drink. Her kindness touched Bill Merriken. He took one sip and blacked out.

Peering out the white lace curtains, a startled Monsieur Lerho saw something that made him whisper excitedly to Madame Blaise. The old woman hurried over to the window. The Germans were outside, the old woman told Reding; it would be better if they both moved upstairs quickly. Anna, Reding, and the hired hand carried Merriken's limp body up to the loft. The loft was sparsely furnished—a feather bed, a small table, and a chair. They gently lowered Merriken into the bed. The woman whispered French urgently to Reding, but he could not understand; she raised her index figure to her lips: "Be quiet." She closed the door on the two Americans and hurried down the creaking stairs. The woman peeked outside the lace curtains and then moved quickly away from the window. The Germans were walking about on the road—they would surely try to come in. Hopefully, the men would be safe up there. The attic had a small window looking out onto the Malmédy road. Reding could see Germans coming and going. Merriken was lying in the bed. Reding pulled off his buddy's wet boots and then his own. By the time he was done with his friend's shoes, Reding was out cold.

But Reding had a hard time sleeping. At one point there were loud knocks at the door downstairs. The American listened intently, placing his ear to the door. He could hear German voices. They grew louder— now they were inside! How to escape? Reding's heart raced. In the dim light from the window he looked around the upstairs room and spied a trap door in the attic ceiling. What was up there? He considered he might have to crawl up there and leave Merriken for the Germans. From the door, he looked toward the bed. He hated the thought, but what else could he do? Now he could hear Anna was speaking back to them; evidently she spoke German too. Then the sound of the creaking wooden door closing again. The voices receded. Reding was breathing—he looked over at Merriken. The young soldier quietly moaned in his sleep. Was he on his way out? Reding went over and put his ear to Merriken's chest—he was still breathing.

Sometime later that night Merriken awoke to find himself in a room in a soft feather bed. It was an attic room with a single window. He could see Reding standing by the lattice-work glass. "Chuck, what's going on?" he murmured. Reding bent over his bed. "They've been coming up and down in front of the house all night long," he said quietly. "Some stopped one time and banged on the door and quizzed the people here," he sighed, "but we're still alright I guess." Looking at Merriken, saying this with any conviction was difficult. The wounded man's skin was pale, and his sheets were covered in red. Reding tried to keep him from moving. From time to time Merriken would wake, mumble questions, and then black out again, "not remembering what he had told me."

The next morning Reding had planned to set off on foot himself to try to reach friendly lines, but as he prepared to go he saw Germans outside the house again. He would have to wait. Presently, the woman came up to the attic. Merriken was unconscious. "He's bad," Reding told her. He couldn't last much longer.

The two tried to communicate, but the language barrier was challenging. Reding decided to write a note asking for help. He penned two short sentences, but he was worried that he didn't know how to tell his potential rescuers where he was. It read,

> T/5 Charles E. Reding. 34328833, Battery B, 285th Field Artillery Observation Battalion: Holed up in farm house with fellow soldier—wounded—and very ill. Think it safe to send ambulance for us.

He knew he was stretching the situation a lot with the "safe to send ambulance" thing, but he was sure they wouldn't come if he told them the truth. The American handed the note over to Anna. She was careful not to show her confusion—she couldn't read a thing. Looking

Reding in the eyes, she nodded and stuffed the paper down her bosom. Reding went back upstairs. Merriken was still unconscious, but his pulse was steady. It was midmorning as Reding watched her leave the house from the window. His buddy seemed to be in a coma. Charles Reding worried that even if they got the note, the rescue wouldn't come. After all, they were behind enemy lines. Reding was exhausted. He collapsed in a chair and fell asleep.

Anna Blaise was in a dither. What should she do? After leaving her home she hurried next door to consult with the neighbors at the Jamar household. The seven Jamar children sat stone-faced at the table as Anna Blaise blurted out in exasperation about the soldiers in her house. "I cannot do anything more for the wounded man," she explained, "and to them, the best thing would be that they rejoin the other Americans."[4] She was willing to take the note herself the three kilometers into Malmédy, she said, but what would she tell anyone she ran into? Emile Jamar, who sat listening, was just seven days shy of his sixteenth birthday and feeling wiser than his years. "I can go," he said, explaining that because he delivered newspapers all over the area, no one would likely stop him. Besides, he explained, no one knew the back ways of Baugnez, Arimont, and Malmédy like he did. His parents agreed but warned their son not to take risks. Young Emile carefully folded the note and placed it under the sole of one shoe. Who would look there?

Soon Emile was walking—almost running—quickly down the road into Malmédy, only to come upon a number of metallic plates strewn about the big bend in the road at the foot of the hill. Guessing that these were mines, he cautiously tiptoed his way around the objects. His heart pounded in his ears as he got past them to the bottom of the hill leading into Malmédy. Then, just as he was about to cross the railroad tracks at the end of Monbijou Avenue, he came to a roadblock where two American soldiers clamored for him to halt. They had rifles. Soon the GIs were questioning young Jamar, but neither party could understand the other. Emile was exasperated. He dared not produce the message until he found someone who could understand him. The two young Americans could also sense the boy's urgency. They escorted him to the Café Loffet, where a jeep picked him up. Soon someone drove him through Francorchamps all the way to the village of Hockay.

All of this was turning out terribly, Emile thought to himself. Yet as they pulled to a halt in Hockay, his young American jeep driver smiled. *At last, a good omen*, Jamar thought. He was quickly brought to an American officer who understood French.[5] Emile rapidly recited his story as the officer nodded. Finally confident, Emile produced the note from his shoe. "Yes," the man assured him in French, "we will get those unfortunate prisoners at Madame Anna's farm." However, they needed Emile's help to find the way back. Within a few minutes they were back in the jeep, bouncing toward Malmédy.

Threading their way back took nearly an hour of stopping at this and the next checkpoint, each with seemingly more nervous guards than the last. Finally, Emile saw the Chapelle de Géromont rising from behind the road. He waved the driver onto a dirt road that led right up to Anna Blaise's barn. The old woman quickly ran out, greatly relieved.

Three hours after Anna left, Reding heard a vehicle roar up to the house with squealing brakes. That sounded like an American jeep! He quickly rose from his seat and turned to the window, looking down to the street. It was an army-green ambulance with a red cross painted on its door. "Thank God!" He saw the old lady standing by the jeep. She had a big grin on her face.

Reding bounded down the stairs. Two American medics hastily jumped out of the vehicle, hauling a stretcher and running for the door. "Where is he?" they stammered. Reding pointed to the stairs. They rushed up the steps to the loft, and there was Bill Merriken in the blood-soaked bed. Was he still alive? In all the commotion the man came to a little and groaned something unintelligible. The three men picked Merriken up in his bedding, loaded the whole mess on the stretcher, and quickly hauled him down to the waiting ambulance parked by the barn. As they reached the doors of the ambulance, Reding jumped inside the cab. Anna came running out with Monsieur Lerho behind her. The wounded man looked up wearily from the stretcher as the old lady leaned over him. Anna Blaise said a little prayer and gave Bill Merriken a kiss. A tear came to his eye. Emile Jamar had tears too. "*Bon chance*," Emile said.

They could wait no further—the Germans were still about. Of that, Charles Reding needed little reminder. They fired up the engine, and soon the ambulance was barreling down the N-23. "The driver pushed that ambulance as fast as it would go." They careened past the old chapel as they bolted down toward Malmédy, the ambulance driver swerving back and forth so as to present a difficult target for any of the enemy lurking about. They sped up, but there were no shots.

In the rocking ambulance Merriken writhed in pain while Reding looked on. After all of this, would his friend die before he got into the hospital? In minutes they were in Malmédy at a receiving station at the 44th Evacuation Hospital. At the aid station Merriken presented a ghastly sight—a chaplain stood over him, ready with the last rites, as they cut off his bloody clothing. When he saw the chaplain, Charles Reding felt a great anger well up inside. "Not this! Not now!"

Reding entered the aid station, insisting that Merriken receive immediate care. Orderlies came and took the wounded man inside and showed Reding to the door. Only an insistent doctor was able to calm the man. He waited outside. Hours later Bill Merriken emerged from medical attention, again on a stretcher and in a morphine haze. The doctor with him assured Reding that his friend would be okay. Two units of plasma had stabilized him. Medics placed he wounded man on an ambulance that would take him to the 9th Field Hospital in Verviers. As they walked by with Merriken, who was only dimly conscious, Reding didn't know what to say. "How are you?" he managed.

"I'm okay," Merriken murmured weakly. "Good." Reding leaned over the stretcher as it disappeared into the ambulance. "I'll see you later."

"Good-bye, old buddy," Merriken whispered. They closed the door. In quiet reflection, Reding watched the ambulance drive off.

CHAPTER 11

Baugnez

When the 285th Field Artillery Observation Battalion moved south of Malmédy, American soldiers found themselves moving into a foreign region where gauging local sympathies was difficult. There was good reason: The German-speaking section of southeastern Belgium was one of the most culturally confused regions of modern Europe.

Many of the people in southeastern Belgium thought of themselves as German first and foremost—even in the midst of another war. But still others (particularly those in nearby Stavelot) thought of themselves as French and Belgian—an ethnic rivalry that continues today. During the war the Rexist movement, which promoted a Belgian flavor of fascism, elevated the schism. This was epitomized by Leon Degrelle, an Ardennes local from the town of Bouillon. Hitler considered the population of some sixty thousand around Malmédy to be a reclaimed portion of his "greater German Reich," and many of the families in the area had sons fighting for National Socialism. Sadly, by 1944 many Belgian sons fighting for Germany had died in Russia.

When the U.S. First Army liberated Malmédy on September 11, 1944, they found the occupation an uneasy one. Even they conceded that the Belgian resistance had been famously effective in thwarting an easy occupation for Hitler's forces in the Ardennes. Yet the true situation there remained nearly inscrutable[1] As a result, in early December the U.S. First Army eagerly disarmed the remaining Belgian resistance groups in the area. Doing this followed logically, as Gen. Hodges's intelligence officers worried about pro-German groups mixed in the schizoid Belgian culture.[2] The Rexists, now driven underground into Fifth Column status by the American liberation, were nevertheless still active in Ardennes. This reality was evidenced by their pro-Nazi espionage activities and mayhem, such as the brazen political murder of Count Louis d'Oultremont near Charleroi during the liberation at the end of summer.[3] Moreover, even if the war seemed nearly over in December 1944, the local people living around Baugnez still comprised a confusing array of political sympathies.

On the morning of December 17 the situation at Baugnez was calm enough, with only some American ambulances skidding across the crossroads, as they had been for days, to bring casualties to the 44th Evacuation Hospital at the primary school in Malmédy. As it was Sunday, Mme. Marie Mathonet-Maraite, living at a stone home a quarter-mile north of the crossroads, prepared her household to attend the 10 o'clock Mass at the church in Géromont. The mass itself was uneventful, but its aftermath was not. As was always the case, when the locals spilled out of the chapel, it was time to walk back to Baugnez with the others and catch up on gossip.[4] Although the weather was cold and foggy—as it seemed to be of late—that was not the news. Someone excitedly announced that the Germans had launched a big attack to the east that would soon be to Baugnez. Henri Lejoly-Quirin had heard they were already around Büllingen.

Hearing that news, Marie Mathonet fell into a near panic. Her husband, Léon Mathonet, forcibly inducted, was still fighting with the German army. She had three very young children at home—three-year-old twins (Henri and Lucie) and little Annelise, only eleven months old. With war coming again, they would not be safe. Throwing the door open, Marie hastily threw together a few clothes and prepared to flee to Warche-Bellevaux, where her parents could give the family refuge. Wasting no time, she left the house with the three kids in a cart pulled by their farm dog. It was noon. She walked as quickly as she could manage toward Hédomont. Around a half hour later Marie would hear shooting while still on the road. *What was it?*

American soldiers weren't the only victims at the crossroads that Sunday. Even if Baugnez was not a village, a number of Belgian civilians lived nearby. Others were unlucky enough to be near the crossroads on the afternoon of December 17. Fifteen-year-old Peter Lentz from Hepscheid was on his bicycle that day. He and his father were still living there even though his mother and one sister had been evacuated to Malmédy. That Sunday, Peter went to see his mother, using a route that took him from Hepscheid to Schoppen and Ondenval and then to Malmédy. Peter knew nothing of Hitler's last great offensive, but while visiting the family word came that the Germans were in Büllingen. Worried that his sister Maria was alone in Hepscheid, Peter set off hurriedly that morning to bring her back to his mother's location out of harm's way.[5] He pushed his bicycle up the steep road up from Malmédy, hoping to be able to ride again when the grade leveled out. Reaching Baugnez, he saw an American military policeman directing traffic.

Young Peter Lentz wasn't worried because there were many Americans there, so he pushed his bike across the muddy road leading east past a little furniture store on the Route de Waimes. "All of a sudden there was machine gun fire from the direction of Thirimont and I jumped from my bicycle into the water-filled ditch. As I did so a jeep pulled up and as the firing continued, two Americans also jumped into the ditch beside me." The two GIs who jumped in the muddy ditch were T/4 Cecil J. Cash and T/5 Raymond A. Heitmann of Battery C of the 197th Automatic Anti-Aircraft Weapons Battalion, on their way from the massive ammunition supply dump at ASP #126 near Waimes.[6] With word the enemy was approaching, the huge collection of shell and artillery rounds was being prepared for demolition. The two men were on their way by jeep to the 304th Ordnance Company in Malmédy. They left after lunch and were never seen again.[7] Peter Lentz recalled their last moments:

> The jeep came from the direction of Waimes and I threw my bicycle down and jumped into ditch on the north side of the road. I was in the ditch right next to these two Americans. They said nothing to each other and I wanted to crawl away. "No don't do it," the Americans said, "stay here." I was foolhardy at the age of fifteen,

but bullets were still bouncing off the pavement. I wasn't going to look where it was coming from. A few moments later, even without raising my head out of the ditch, I could first hear and later see a big tank drawing close by. Two or three tanks ran by first and we stayed down in the ditch. The second or third German tank stopped and a young German soldier jumped off with a bolt-action rifle. He was right in front of us. I can't say much about his uniform, but he was a very young soldier and less than five feet away. Both of the Americans stood up in the ditch with their hands on their head. The German soldier then shot one of the Americans and then pulled the bolt and shot the other one. They both fell. I could see that one was shot in the chest. He then pulled the bolt to shoot me and I cried out: "*Mein Bruder ist Deutscher soldat und Deutsche wollen mich erschiessen!*"—My brother is a German soldier and you are going to shoot a fellow German![8]

The German lowered the gun and didn't shoot, but there were questions. How old was he? Where were his papers? Lentz explained that he didn't have them—he was just a boy. "Come with me," the SS man ordered. Covered with mud, Lentz got up and started walking. Behind him he heard more shots. They were making sure that the Americans were dead. Peter heard someone speak to the young German soldier shouldering the bolt-action rifle.[9] "This is the way," the voice encouraged, "to fight in the old SS spirit." Petrified with fear, he started toward the crossroads, where he saw Americans surrendering and being moved past the café at the corner.

Meanwhile, Sternebeck's and Tonk's tanks and the lone SPW had moved on down the road toward Ligneuville. When Peter got to the place where a little path led right to Henri Lejoly-Quirin's house, there was more gunfire, and he jumped into the ditch again, this time with a man from Faymonville and his young son. The father and his boy had been on their way to the dentist in Stavelot. The renewed gunfire almost certainly came from the approach of Panzer Nr. 734 leading the 7th Company, which was shooting again at the column and unaware that Sternebeck had just departed not more than two minutes before.[10]

When the firing stopped, the Germans got them all out of the ditch once more. Where was he going? they asked. Lentz said he was evacuated to Malmédy and was trying to get back. "Get to that house," the Germans said, motioning to the home of Henri Lejoly-Quirin, "and we will come there later." On the way to Lejoly's house Lentz again saw the group of about fifty American soldiers with their hands behind their heads standing in the field just south of the café.

Nearly beside himself, he ran into the house of Henri Lejoly-Quirin, who was not there because he was still at Madame Bodarwe's café. Lentz fell to his knees inside the house. "All I wanted to do was pray. I felt silly about it, but I was in a state of panic." Then, a loud peal of automatic weapons fire shook him. Moments later another boy, Robert Pfeiffer, came running inside too. "They are shooting!" he gasped. "They are shooting soldiers in the field!"[11]

Peter Lentz decided he was getting out of there. Half-crazed, he ran out of the house and to the north, relieved to find no shooting outside there—and no Germans. As fast as he could run, he dashed down the dirt trail to Malmédy, which runs parallel to the Géromont road. Presently, he reached an American roadblock, replete with drawn weapons. After convincing American guards to let him through, he eventually reached his family in Malmédy.[12] Still terrified, he told his mother and father of his close brush with death. Later that afternoon in Malmédy there was an ominous thunder- a huge explosion some-where.[13]

Robert Pfeiffer, the other boy who ran yelling into the house of Henri Lejoly-Quirin, was only thirteen. Born in Büllingen on August 9, 1931, he and his mother, uncle, brother, and sister had been evacuated from the area the previous October.[14] Most of his family went to Malmédy, but young Robert went to Baugnez to stay with his uncle Henri Pierry-Pfeiffer at Baugnez (House No. 6 on period maps). How-ever, his uncle did not have sufficient room in his modest farmhouse, so Pfeiffer lodged at the home of Henri Lejoly-Quirin with Lejoly's sis-ter just north of the crossroads (House No. 4), while Robert's mother and sister stayed with forty-seven-year-old Mr. Pierry.

That Sunday, as Robert's uncle was preparing to go to the weekly Mass in Géromont, he and Lejoly noticed a thick stream of traffic coming down from Malmédy toward Ligneuville. Why was that, Pierry wondered? Just then, a local man, Joseph Bodarwe, rode up on his bicycle, puffing and nearly out of breath. "The Germans are back in Büllingen!" he announced. Soon his father spoke excitedly to Henri Lejoly, who took the news stoically. "So the Germans are coming back," Henri said hearing the news. "What can you do?" Henri was a simple farmer. Nonetheless, it was time for the midday meal, so Robert and his family went over to his uncle's house. As they were eating, the table discussion focused on the last two crazy days. So the Germans were in Büllingen? They would not likely get much further—certainly not the twenty kilometers to Baugnez. Henri Lejoly left the farmhouse to go to Madame Bodarwe's café just across the street. It was time for his daily beer.

Robert stayed in the house. "Suddenly there was a lot of firing outside," the boy remembered. No one was looking out the windows, but they knew something was up. For a time, they all ran down into the basement, but when the firing subsided they ventured upstairs. Pfeiffer edged up to the window. Through the panes he saw American prisoners being herded into the field next to Madame Adele Bodarwe's café. "But we were young boys," Pfeiffer remembered, "and we left the house and ran up the rise to the crossroads to see what was there. It was exciting." He ventured out with his older brother Paul, aged fourteen, and his cousin René.

Approaching the crossroads, the boys came upon many stationary vehicles and German soldiers. Because Robert and his brother spoke German, the SS troopers were friendly enough; they gave them some food they captured from the American vehicles. "We are the advance group," one told them. "There is infantry coming behind us to clear up resistance." Robert's cousin shouted that he had found two Americans lying dead in the ditch. His father and uncle pulled their bodies out of the ditch but told the boys to get away from there. Although they were still curious, they skulked back closer to the house while still watching the swirling scene at the intersection:

The Germans were rounding the Americans up and shouting, "*Raus, Raus!*" Soon, there were about 100 soldiers with their hands up next to the café. The Germans had taken their weapons and they were just standing there. I had been there a bit more than an hour and was on the road nearly in the café on the café side of the road. I was standing with my mouth open. My brother Paul had been with me for a while. But my brother became afraid saying, "I'm going back." But I told him that I was staying.

They then starting putting the Americans in the field in ranks and another twenty behind them. . . . The prisoners were standing in the field with their hands over their head. A tank stopped in front of the prisoners. There was a German in the field with them (I think he was an officer) and he left the field and ordered the machine gunner on the tank to open fire on them. "*Feuer!*" he shouted. The man in the turret, he fired a pistol in the air and the machine gunner gunned the men. When the machine gunning started they all fell at once in a pile. The firing started with one vehicle. I was very afraid. I didn't hang around after that.

Terrified, Robert Pfeiffer ran back to his uncle's house, hearing more shots as he fled. Reaching the door, he dashed inside:

When I got back, people in the house said, "You look white as if you have seen a ghost!" I ran inside in a panic, "They've killed soldiers there! They've killed soldiers there!" From the windows of my uncle's house, a quarter of an hour later we saw Americans running who had leapt to their feet. And the Germans were shooting them like rabbits. They were just running in every direction and the Germans were shooting at them.

The shooting subsided. As Robert cowered inside his uncle's home, his curiosity eventually overcame his fear. "Half an hour later, I went outside and there were many American soldiers lying face down in the mud," he recalled, "and German vehicles were going down every once in a while firing into the men lying there."[15]

Later on, when Robert cautiously ventured outside at around 4:00 P.M. to look around, he saw the SS troops set fire to Madame Bodarwe's café because an American rifle had been found in a haystack next to the house.[16] By dark, Pfeiffer recalled it blazing brightly as frightened cows bellowed and German tanks and vehicles rolled on by on the road, illuminated by the fire.

They never found Madame Bodarwe. "I think she died in the flames," Pfeiffer would later say.[17] One American soldier thought he remembered seeing her shot.[18] When Belgians cleared away the debris and rubble of the café later in 1945 they found "a carbonized limb."[19]

And what of Henri Lejoly-Quirin? Henri, the younger cousin of Henri Lejoly-Jacob, was also a witness to the shooting. The forty-five-year-old Lejoly-Quirin lived at a farm just north of the Baugnez crossroads, and although he had a French last name, he looked at himself as more German than Belgian. That afternoon, when the Germans suddenly arrived at the crossroads, most of the locals hid, but Henri Lejoly did not. He emerged from his house to see the Americans with their hands high in the field.

"It was a Sunday afternoon, the day after the German offensive began. I was there at the café by the crossroads, by my house, talking to the lady who owned it." Lejoly recalled.[20] The farmer had gone to the café, which was located on the southwest corner of the crossroads, as he often did at around 1 P.M. in the afternoon to have a beer. As the local man sipped his brew, he was surprised to see a column of ten to twelve olive-green, canvas-covered trucks approach from Malmédy. Frau Bodarwe was with Lejoly in the kitchen looking out the eastward-facing window. The first vehicle stopped just short of the corner of the house, and Lejoly saw three American soldiers get out.[21] They came in. and *bonjours* were exchanged. One American pointed south. "Is this the road to Vielsalm?" he said to Madame Bodarwe. She explained the question to Henri and then nodded. Had they seen the Germans anywhere close by? Lejoly shrugged. He couldn't understand English.

"And just as suddenly as they had come in, they dashed out again and ran round the café. Coming from the opposite direction in the distance we could see a long line of German tanks. The Germans began firing at the Americans. There was a lot of firing. And we hid."[22] "We were looking from the kitchen window and suddenly saw a German tank coming from the direction of Waimes." Frau Bodarwe was short of breath. "Oh, my God, Henri, the Germans are here!" she exclaimed. The big tank drew up close to the open window as the air cracked with gunshots. At least twenty American trucks had passed by them before the big panzer pulled up. "Where should we go? To the basement?" Madame Bodarwe asked. Lejoly shook his head; the café was not safe.

They should seek refuge in the barn. He and Frau Bodarwe ran to the back of the house and slipped out the door along a wall that ran to the stable on the west side. They hid in the stable for five minutes until the firing ended.

About that time several Americans had made their way to the shed behind the Café Bodarwe. Shortly, Henri and Mme. Bodarwe cautiously returned back to the kitchen."The firing stopped and we came out. The Americans had all been captured and were being led into the field beside the café." From the window they saw about thirty Americans assembled in front of the house without weapons and with hands held up. By now, some five or six tanks or halftracks had pulled up, and the Germans were outside searching the Americans. In particular, they seemed to be looking for wristwatches and rings. Lejoly waved to the approaching SS men—not surprising, as he considered himself German. Some said he even pointed out where the Americans were hiding behind the café in the barn.[23] In any case, soon two SS men with submachine guns flushed out Pvt. Ralph W. Law and several others near the café.[24]

In a friendly gesture Lejoly saw Madame Bodarwe open the door to greet the Germans around the big tank parked near her café. To onlooking GIs, she seemed pleased. "I know the woman on the corner must be in good with the Germans," one said. "As soon as they came by she walked out and shook hands with them and gave them something to eat."[25] After all, she had three sons in the German army, and the neighbors remembered that she had greeted the Germans in 1940 with open arms.[26]

Madame Bodarwe offered them a box of cigarettes as well as food and drink before she stepped back to the front door. After that Lejoly saw the Germans order the Americans to march down forty meters or so to the open field just south of the café. The GIs standing in the field looked complacent. "They appeared unconcerned with life," Lejoly remembered. But then "one of the German cars appeared to break down and they appeared upset."[27] After that, one of the tanks came up and stopped in front of the assembled soldiers. "Then it fired on the Americans," Lejoly remembered. The shooting was a salvo of several shots and then machine guns. Lejoly's mouth fell open. "The greater part of the Americans fell to the ground. As I saw most of the Americans falling, I ran away."

There were about 150 prisoners that the SS assembled in the field
by the road. At this moment I went out into the street and watched
as the Germans went through the pockets of the men and it took
about half an hour. A few minutes later a German officer
approached an American medic and pointed a revolver in his
direction. I had just had time to see what was going on when the
shot went off. This was the signal for the killing to commence. The
tanks placed at the corners of the field opened fire mowing down
the prisoners under the gun fire.[28]

Frau Bodarwe was at Henri Lejoly's side when it happened—loud
machine gunfire. "Oh my God!" she exclaimed in French—"*Mon
Dieu!*" Instinctively, her hands rose to her face before she fled back into
the house. Lejoly, too, was stunned. "I did not feel like seeing much of
this," he remembered. Nervously looking from side to side, Lejoly scur-
ried from the backside of Bodarwe's café to the front of his house just
north of the crossroads. Already several Germans in black panzer uniforms were standing at the path to his farmhouse when he came up.
"Why are you shooting the American prisoners?" Lejoly demanded in
German. "I have seen it." An SS man approached. "It's because we have
no time to look after them," he stammered. Lejoly bit his lip. Tanks and
halftracks passed by, bumper to bumper, with German soldiers menacingly staring him down from the tank decks. All seemed to have an automatic rifle.

Lejoly slammed the door behind him. His nerves rattled, he went
inside to have some coffee. His hands shook so badly that even getting
the cup to his lips was difficult. Twenty minutes went by, and the noise
of traffic began to quiet down. Lejoly went out to have a look around,
intending to go back over to the café to see if Madame Bodarwe was
okay. Emerging from the house, he could see that tanks were still passing by, but not as many. Then one of the last vehicles in the line pulled
up in the road across from the path leading to his house. The men in
the tank seemed to have problems with it—its steering mechanism had
gone out again. Suddenly, a young soldier on the tank pointed a gun at
Henri and fired two shots—one that passed close to his right ear! With
that, he ran to his cellar where other locals—Joseph Bodarwe and another refugees—were holed up. Above, he could hear machine gunfire

crashing into his windows. Then a cannon shot exploded at the south end of his home. "Good God!" Lejoly yelled. "They've bombed our house." The dark basement filled with dust. A refugee from Cologne implored Lejoly to stop the crazy German tanker, otherwise they would all die. Climbing the stairs to see his wrecked kitchen, Lejoly grew furious. He stomped outside with his hands held high. He stopped just fifteen meters away from Panther Nr. 114.

"Why are you firing at my house?" Lejoly demanded in German. The troopers were young—half his age. One of the SS "brats" motioned menacingly toward him with an automatic rifle.

"You have spoken to the Americans," one accused. To the SS men, that was betrayal.

"I have two brothers in the German army and I myself was born in Germany. . . . I was German before you were even born!" he yelled. "If you want to see my papers, come into my house." With that, a Waffen SS noncommissioned officer came inside, and Lejoly produced documents in the kitchen. "You've ruined my house," he protested as one SS man reviewed his papers.

The man with a black peaked cap seemed chagrined. His men outside were making a lot of noise; the German officer called to them to quiet down. "They are some really wild individuals," he told Lejoly, giving him a parting salute. "I can't always control them."

The German officer gave Lejoly a promissory note to make a damage claim to Hitler's Reich. It was signed: SS Unteroffizier K. Briesemeister.[29] Although he was originally a baker from Stralsund, by 1944 Briesemeister was a battle-hardened noncommissioned officer who had fought with the Leibstandarte Adolf Hitler since 1940. He had been wounded five times. "I executed the orders of my superiors 100 percent," he would later say. "I was taught to offer my own person to the Fatherland fanatically."[30] Briesemeister said that his Panzer Nr. 114 arrived at Baugnez at about 3:30 P.M. He stopped about ten meters from the crossroads with damage to the tracks of his Panther. While his crew set about repairing the damage, he observed about sixty American soldiers lying dead or wounded in the field south of the café. Were they all dead? Briesemeister told his crew to make sure.

Lejoly did not know that Briesemeister would later admit that he and his men had administered mercy shots to some of the wounded Americans in the field.[31] As the short Belgian man walked outside with him, Briesemeister's tank crew tried to convince their tank commander that Henri Lejoly had helped the Americans. They should get rid of him, they said. "We know how these border people are," Lejoly overheard one say. But Briesemeister prevailed, ordering them to get ready to leave. Meanwhile, Lejoly could see that Madame Bodarwe's barn was on fire near the café, and he boldly asked five or six men to help him put the fire out. "I have no time for that," Briesemeister said. In fact, Briesemeister's crew was the one who had set fire to the barn.[32] And it was his tankmates who had fired at American soldiers as they ran from the flames.

When the big German tank departed, Lejoly went back to his house, not willing to chance any more dangerous encounters with SS men still threading down the road. When he chanced to look out of his house a little later, he saw the entire Café Bodarwe enveloped in flames. The next day Lejoly poked around in the smoldering ashes of the café, expecting to find the remains of the fifty-five-year-old widow. But he found nothing. He never saw Madame Bodarwe again. "I have always thought they shot her," Lejoly said. "If Briesemeister would not have been there, I too would have been shot."[33] That was an understatement, for after Lejoly and Briesemeister emerged from the former's farmhouse, SS-Pvt. Günther Nüchter came up to his tank commander and "told [him] that he had shot a civilian woman in the house next to the field, claiming that 'This woman had a pistol in her hand.'" Nüchter said he had shot Madame Bodarwe, whose body was later incinerated in the burning house.[34]

Thirty-three-year-old Marthe Maria Martin was with her sisters, mother, and father in their farmhouse in the tiny hamlet of Floriheid, which was on a steep hill above Hédomont just southwest of Malmédy. The day had been worrisome. Her family had been delighted with the liberation the previous September, but now rumors said the Germans were back.[35] Some friends had invited the Belgian girl that Sunday to go to Malmédy to visit, and as she was making her way down the steep hill, she came upon the police station on the right. "Don't go any further, Mademoiselle," an officer warned, "The Germans are down there waiting for you." She quickly turned around and went back to her parents atop the steep hill. She told everyone that the rumors were true—the Germans were back. Only the refugees passing through town would believe her, but by now there had been sounds of gunfire. At about 9 P.M. they were all inside saying their prayers. "Someone rapped on my door," she recalled. "We thought it was our turn to die."[36]

Her sister Marie was nearest to the entrance. "I'll go and open it." When she did, the silhouette of a big man stood there in the darkness of the doorway. "He was saying something, but we didn't understand him." Was he German? The girls looked at each other, but their father Louis, said to let him enter. Now, with the stranger inside, the kerosene lamp illuminated the room. They could see that he could hardly walk.

The man looked terrible—muddy and wet, limping on one foot and smudged and rank with cow dung. His boot was oozing red, and blood trailed onto the floor. He kept saying something over and over—"Sick! Sick!"—but no one could understand. There was small relief when they realized he was an American. But the Germans who had shot him must be close by. If they came. . . . The family sat him down near the warmth of the kitchen stove. With a loud groan, they got the bloody boot off. The American had been shot through the ankle. They washed his wounds. As they bandaged him up and put a splint on his ankle, Marie, her father, and her sisters discussed the situation. In the dimly lit farm-house was a refugee boy from Elsenborn who spoke a little English.

Through the youth, the Martin family learned that the man's name was Lt. Virgil Lary from the U.S Army. All his comrades—more than a hundred—had just been shot down south of Malmédy. Marthe gasped at his description. "How did you find the house?" Louis wanted to know. Lary told them that he had crawled there on his hands and knees. He had gone through a little village that they knew must have been Hédomont—and no one wanted to open the doors. Even with drawn curtains, Lary had followed the dim window beacon emanating from the Martins' kerosene lamps. The Belgian family looked at each other: *The Germans would see them too!*

The girls gave the woeful-looking soldier some soup while the family talked. They couldn't hazard keeping the American here; it was way too risky. The Germans would be here soon. Knowing the danger, her father Louis went down to Malmédy with a note composed by Lt. Lary, asking for help. He returned only an hour later. Sure enough, Martin had found the first aid station in Malmédy and tried to get Dr. Paul Kamen, a medic with the 291st Engineer Combat Battalion, to send an ambulance. But Kamen refused, explaining that driving through enemy territory was too dangerous. He did, however, send back some sulfa drugs and bandages. Although those were welcome when Louis returned, Lary was now in increasing pain and insisted on getting to an American hospital. The family was of the same opinion, but for a different reason: If the Germans came, they would all be shot. Still, even with an improvised crutch made from a broom, Lary clearly could not walk himself. But accompanying the American would be suicide if Louis ran into the Germans.

However, knowing the enemy might think differently of women helping a wounded man, Marthe and her neighbor, Marthe Marx, volunteered to escort the American to Malmédy.[37] Doing so was terribly dangerous, but it was the best of a series of poor options. Eventually Louis Martin consented. After midnight they left, with the two young women holding Lary between them, each cradling a shoulder. "We could hear gunfire in the night," she remembered, worrying that they might run into the Germans. If they did, that would be it. She reminded Marthe Marx to speak only German, and if they ran into them, "to shut up and let me do the talking."

Marthe Martin tried not to think about the risk, but she urged her friend to go faster with the limping American. They kept moving—a three-kilometer march down a steep hill carrying an adult man between them. For over an hour Lary groaned in pain as they proceeded, and both girls ached terribly under his weight. Still, they eventually came to the school building in Malmédy used as the 44th Evacuation Hospital. There, a harried member of the Belgian Red Cross offered little help. "Sorry, we can't take him," the woman complained. "The whole unit is evacuating." The Germans were coming. "For the love of God," Marthe Martin said in exasperation. "Take this poor soldier to the Americans." Okay, the woman agreed.

Marthe Martin and Marthe Marx uttered a quick goodbye to Virgil Lary. With that, both women hurried back up the steep hill to their home, expecting to run into the Germans at anytime. Shortly afterward Lt. Lary was taken to the command post of Lt. Col. David Pergrin and then to the 28th General Hospital in Liège.[38] Meanwhile, the two young women arrived back home before daybreak to the great relief of Louis Martin. Taking the American to the hospital had been the right decision: The next day Germans arrived at the little hamlet of Flori-heid.[39] "Whew!" Marthe thought. "Too close!"

The next day, Monday, December 18, Henri Lejoly-Quirin went over to his cousin Henri Lejoly-Jacob's house. In the morning a small party of U.S. Army soldiers arrived, shocked deeply at the mass of dead American bodies. The two Lejoly men helped to show the Americans the location of one GI who was still alive near the café—Henry Zach. Although near death, the American soldiers took him away and he would survive. However, the language barrier was too difficult to bridge, and the Americans were in too much a hurry for the Henris to show them to two other wounded Americans in Henri Lejoly-Jacob's woodshed. One died after two or three days; after a week the other was well enough to leave with the Germans as a prisoner.[40] Or so the Germans said: The American man—likely Pvt. Elwood Thomas—was never seen again.

After the war Henri Lejoly-Quirin was suspected of being a German collaborator and imprisoned. As the major living civilian witness to the massacre, he was forever haunted by the events that day at Baugnez. Over the years his story slowly changed, as such things are wont to do, but Lejoly never denied seeing the massacre. The Kaiser's legions in World War I, he said, would never have done something like what he saw that Sunday. "The Germans shot them down," Lejoly remembered. "I was shocked even though my sympathies were German."[41]

Lejoly's neighbor, Madame Bodarwe, had similar political leanings. The proprietor of the café who had greeted the Kampfgruppe Peiper with liquor when they arrived disappeared. After the war, in 1945, her son Louis Bodarwe came home after fighting in the German Army. He returned to Baugnez to find nothing left of his home. Where it had once stood was only charred remains, with the blackened chimneys emerging from the ashes. His brother Alphonse had died in Russia in 1943, and his other brother, Joseph, had not yet come home. Even after stirring the charred remains of the corner café and following all leads, his mother was never found. What's more, having fought for Hitler, Louis was now a pariah in eastern Belgium.[42]

It was if the entire episode at the crossroads nexus near Baugnez had created an intractable vortex of tragedy. There, at a lonely road intersection, all the suffering of Hitler's last gasp in a terrible war was laid open for the world to abhor—a black hole in the last months of the Second World War.

Indeed, the ghosts who still haunt Baugnez whisper of sadness and secrets not yet healed to this day—or for a long time to come.

CHAPTER 12

Shock

On the damp gray afternoon of December 17, Lt. Col. David Pergrin, the commander of the 291st Engineer Combat Battalion was in his headquarters in a private house along the N-23 highway at the southern edge of Malmédy. At about 2 P.M. he and the others at his command post heard loud and concentrated machine gunfire not far away. *The enemy—this far back?* he wondered.[1] At about 3:15 P.M., after grabbing binoculars and two Thompson submachine guns, Pergrin and Sgt. Bill Crickenberger piled into a jeep and chugged south up the steeply ascending road from Malmédy. Minutes later they passed their own roadblock, where Sgt. Charles Dishaw had recently repelled an enemy scout car with heavy gunfire. They knew it was unsafe ahead.

Gearing down, they went a little further to see if they could locate the source of the shooting. They found it. Not far from the edge of a woods west of Baugnez, they pulled to a stop and crept ahead on foot.[2] Soon after Crickenberger and Pergrin dismounted, three American soldiers "covered in mud" rushed forward from the woods. Two of them were wounded, and all were babbling unintelligibly. "They killed everybody in our outfit!" The man was Al Valenzi.[3] With him was Ken Ahrens, Paul Gartska, and another man from the 3rd Armored Division. "These poor creatures were absolutely incoherent," Pergrin recalled.[4] All were yelling at once.

Without hesitation Pergrin took the men back by jeep into Malmédy, where his medics treated them and gave them dry clothes. The GIs were so unnerved—he said inconsolable—that he spent considerable time trying to get a coherent story out of them. What the GIs told him was sobering: The enemy was not only close by, but they were executing anyone they captured. Meanwhile Lt. Thomas Stack returned from a similar jeep reconnaissance collecting three more hysterical GIs telling of the same experience. At 4:40 P.M. Pergrin called his superior, Col. Wallis Anderson with the 1111 Engineer Combat Group, on the command-post radio set. Over the phone he gave Anderson a brief description of the atrocity and advised that "enemy armor is going along the N32 and the N23" from the crossroads at Five Points.[5] That would put Pergrin's improvised roadblock at Mon Bijou in enemy crosshairs. Racing against time, Pergrin ordered his few reinforcements forward to the series of sparsely defended roadblocks erected along the highway just south of Malmédy. He had only 152 men and few heavy weapons—nothing to stop tanks.

By the time Pergrin got back to check on his roadblocks, more survivors were stumbling into his positions.[6] Over the next twenty-four hours, seventeen escapees from the killing field would arrive at Pergrin's nervous outposts—made all the more jittery by the news that German commandos were masquerading as Americans. Indeed, one German commando squad boldly drove into one of Company C's roadblocks, ignoring orders to halt and the rifle fire that followed, until a minefield blew them to pieces.[7]

Unknown to Pergrin, his message to the U.S. First Army electrified Gen. Courtney Hodges. Not only did news of the atrocity set his headquarters buzzing, but word that Malmédy was in danger also motivated the First Army to dispatch its few reserves to the town. If Peiper seized Malmédy and drove up the Eupen road, most of the U.S. V Corps would be cut off and surrounded. That the Luftwaffe had disgorged paratroopers early that morning south of Eupen seemed to foreshadow enemy intentions in that direction.[8] Their few reserves—sort of a palace guard—comprised the 526th Armored Infantry Battalion and the 99th Infantry Battalion, which was made up of Norwegian Americans, as well as a company of the 825th Tank Destroyer Battalion.

Later, in Malmédy, at 3 A.M. members of the Belgian Red Cross turned over a wounded American, Lt. Virgil Lary, into Pergrin's custody.[9] Speaking with Lt. Lary, Pergrin found the officer's story compelling. He ordered Sgt. Tom Stack to escort Lary and eight others back to U.S. First Army Headquarters immediately so that Hodges and the others could gauge for themselves the gravity of what was happening. Lt. Lary was already anguished by guilt: He had personally decided to take Battery B down the road to Baugnez, against better advice from the 7th Armored. Now it couldn't be undone.

Beyond Lt. Lary, several other survivors arriving at Pergrin's anxious command post were also coherent. In particular, the military policeman of the 518th MP Battalion, Homer Ford, seemed to have a grip. At the chaotic First Army headquarters that Sunday night, U.S. Army Inspector General Col. Rosser L. Hunter approached Lt. Col. Alvin B. Welsch.[10] The Austin, Texas, native was told to investigate the mass killing of prisoners at the crossroad.

Lt. Col. Welsch eagerly spoke to Ford, who was covered with mud, wounded in one arm, and shaking with nerves. Ford described how he had been directing U.S. 7th Armored Division traffic at the crossroads when enemy tanks suddenly appeared. He hid behind a building near the crossroads until the Germans enveloped the scene and discovered him and others. Everyone was disarmed and pushed toward a much larger group—maybe two hundred—out in an open field.

Ford told Welsch that while they were standing there with their hands up, perhaps ten armored vehicles had passed as two of the men guarding them went to a halftrack parked in front of them and consulted a superior.[11] Moments later "They started to spray us with machine gun fire, pistols and everything. Everybody hit the ground."[12] Ford was shot through the arm. Then, as other German vehicles passed the field, they too fired machine guns at the Americans lying in the field. Ford could see nothing with his face to the ground—and he dared not move. Pleased only still to be breathing—and that ever so lightly—he clearly heard the crew of one passing tank shout out in accented English: "So, you dirty bastards will go across the Siegfried line!" Stretched out on the cold ground, Ford could feel the blood oozing from his arm. "I started to shiver," he said, still in shock. "I was afraid they would see me shivering." Then the Germans came into the field. Anyone who moved or made a sound was shot or smashed in the head with a rifle butt.

After more than one hour Ford and several others jumped up and ran off to the west. "Machine gun bullets with tracers came right at us when we were running away," he recalled. Ford later met up with three other men—all of whom were wounded, but all managed to flee two miles to the north without further injury. They eventually coursed back toward the N-32 and a cut onto a road where Ford and others ran, crazed with fear, reaching one of Pergrin's jeep outposts.[13]

By the time Welsch finished speaking to Ford at 8:30 P.M., word came that more men, wounded and worse, were filtering into hospitals, roadblocks, and command posts all around Malmédy. Many were in shock and barely able to speak. Seeing the magnitude of the task, Welsch quickly enlisted help from others in his office—Col. Lamar Tooze and Capt. Oliver Seth. Together, they would cover the hospitals to interview witnesses.

With darkness, some of those wounded, like Pvt. Al Valenzi, faced a night of mental trauma. Having been rescued by Pergrin and his men earlier that evening on the road to Malmédy, Valenzi was badly wounded in both his arms and legs. He was treated briefly at an aid station in Malmédy and then driven off to the 28th General Hospital in Liège. There, even though bathed by morphine, his nerves quaked. He was shaking as orderlies helped him remove his blood-stained uniform. He could give them his possessions for safekeeping, they told him. Reaching though his pockets, he pulled out cigarettes and coins— but then something surprising. It was tri-color Belgian ribbon tied around his dog tags that the young Belgian girl had given him that morning near the bridge in Malmédy. He broke into tears; he couldn't stop crying.[14]

That Sunday night Capt. Leon T. Scarborough, the commander of Battery B, of the 285th Field Artillery Observation Battalion was in Biwer, Luxembourg, looking for his missing unit. It was after 9 P.M. when he got a telephone call from T/5 Eugene Garrett. He told Scarborough that he and three others, Cpls. Conrad, Graeff, and Pfc. Bower, were now with an engineer outfit near Malmédy having narrowly escaped when the Germans captured most of the rest of his command.[15] Garrett explained how the enemy had made them all prisoners and then and shot them down. Scarborough had a difficult time believing Garrett, but the enlisted man was insistent: Their terrible losses had not come from combat but rather a massacre. There were other boys in hospitals nearby, he said, and a few had escaped without major wounds—Garrett knew of Kingston, Paluch, and Mattera. Most of the rest were dead or maimed. Nobody else was left. Scarborough was stunned.[16]

Meantime, Cpl. Ernest Bechtel and the men in trucks B-26 to B-28, delayed by Sgt. Barringon's food poisoning in Malmédy, now arrived late on December 18 in Biwer, Luxembourg. They had several close calls. The Germans were still attacking with reckless abandon, not ten miles away near Echternach. After dropping off the crazed Lt. Kaizak in Malmédy the night of December 17, Bechtel and his driver, Charles Arndt, thanked their lucky stars. *Whew!* they thought. Both men were Pennsylvania Dutch: "*Ich bin froh os sel vorbei iss*" (I'm glad that's over with) Arndt blurted. Bechtel responded in kind, "*Jar, ich aa*" (Yes, me too).[17] But two officers from a tank unit were in earshot and confronted both of men with cocked pistols. *So, these were the English-speaking kraut commandos everyone was talking about?* "Do you know what we do with spies?" a scrawny lieutenant snarled while waving a .45-caliber Remington pistol. He trained the muzzle on Bechtel's forehead. Just then artillery rounds fell. In the resulting confusion, Arndt and Bechtel got away.

Now in Luxembourg, the three remaining trucks and twenty-eight men of Battery B reached safe haven. Until his arrival, an officer who had been the battery commander back in the States, Maj. Floyd B. Kelsey, approached Bechtel and eagerly shook his hand. "I am happy to see that you got through," Kelsey said, immediately following with a question: "What had happened to the rest?" Bechtel told Kelsey he had escaped before reaching the Five Points crossroads and did not know who had escaped the ordeal.

Days later Bechtel learned that his Lancaster County neighbor and close friend, Luke Swartz—who had somehow foreseen his death that day—was among those who did not make it back. The curtain fell like an emotional thunderclap. "I sat down and wept in sorrow and anger," Bechtel remembered.[18]

On the evening of December 17, Col. Lamar Tooze traveled from the U.S. First Army to the 77th Evacuation Hospital in Verviers, Belgium. There he talked with the few survivors from the crossroads who were in a condition to speak—many were mute behind a drug-induced haze. At U.S. First Army headquarters the situation was plenty tense— word had it that the same SS men who had killed GIs near Malmédy were now headed toward Gen. Hodges and his headquarters at Spa. Yet word of the shootings galvanized everyone. Tooze had been sent the short distance to Verviers to get firsthand reports. There, he spoke to Pvts. Samuel Dobyns, Robert L. Smith, and Donald Day, who all described a terrifying experience. Dobyns admitted that he had fled at the first sound of the pistol shots—any sensible human being would want to run after that.

An Irish American boy, T/5 John Anthony O'Connell from Kansas City, was also there in the hospital. Although badly wounded in the jaw, back, and hand, the youth was eager to talk. Seized with the epiphany of a man who had just slipped past the clutches of death, O'Connell described the shooting. The initial burst of a machine gun hit him in the shoulder. Later, he told Tooze, he lay in the field while machine guns raked the group. He was severely wounded in the jaw and began to bleed profusely. Like others, he told how he feigned death in the field while one after another of his comrades were shot. "We laid there for quite some time," he told the colonel, propped up in his bed. Maybe it had been only fifteen minutes—he wasn't sure. "During that time the Germans would come up and if they heard anyone moaning in pain they would shoot them with a pistol." O'Connell had been praying quietly with another Catholic boy, Cpl. David O'Grady, lying next to him. Suddenly a shot rang out and a bullet sliced through O'Connell's hand before hitting O'Grady in the stomach. "Hold on," O'Connell whispered to him.

"Did you see any person shot?" Tooze asked.[19] No, O'Connell said. His face had been buried in the mud as he feigned death, hoping his act would not come true. Still, a disturbing memory emerged from those minutes: "I heard a fellow soldier begging for a medic," he told

Tooze, "and a shot rang out and he no longer spoke." The voice sounded like Cpl. Brozowksi.

> I lay there thinking I was bleeding to death and not knowing what to do. Many thoughts ran through my mind. I knew if we got up to run we would be shot down. I also knew that if I stayed there, it would be just a matter of time until we died.

O'Connell described how one of his buddies, not so badly wounded, bravely stuck his head up to observe the German guards without being noticed. Their patient wait went on for a time, but finally O'Connell whispered urgently, "Now, is our chance to get away!" For O'Connell, that moment, when two dozen left-for-dead men arose, was as if Lazarus himself had come to the killing field. He kicked O'Grady at his feet and urged him up—no response. O'Connell knew he couldn't wait, so he leapt over the bodies. The Germans fixing their tank at the intersection seemed to have been taken by surprise; he and the others sprinted nearly thirty yards before the panzer and machine gun by the intersection coughed to life.

As he ran, O'Connell heard a voice call for help. Coming upon a pathetic sight—a man straining to stand up—O'Connell stopped to haul the man to his feet. He could keep him up, but neither were going anywhere, "and the Germans were closing in." The man had been shot at least two or three times and seemed to fade in his arms. It was a heartrending moment. O'Connell let him drop out of his arms and ran. He stumbled ahead, weak from loss of blood, as gunfire danced around his legs. He ran with everything he had. His head was spinning, with his throat and chest covered with blood dribbling grotesquely from his jaw. As he sprinted, O'Connell saw T/5 Charles R. Breon running alongside get chopped down by the machine gunfire.[20] Another fell too. "I was fortunate in not being hit and kept going across the field."

By the time he reached the woods, O'Connell was nearly delirious from loss of blood. Among the pines he came across a frightened breathless kid from Texas—Bobby Werth. He was badly hurt too. Both groaned quietly, bleeding and loping through the gloomy woods, pushed only by adrenaline to thread their way through the forest along the main road. Some forty-five minutes later, in the gathering darkness, they came across some engineers laying mines. Both babbled at once: They were terribly wounded, and their ghastly appearance shocked the engineers. Soon, however, O'Connell and Werth were under a medic's care, but everyone in Malmédy was abuzz, dashing around. Within an hour he and Werth were moved from the 44th Evacuation Hospital in Malmédy.

Now, in Verviers, some seven miles up the road, O'Connell lay exhausted in his hospital bed, but his lucid memory inspired Col. Tooze to stay at his side. An attendant propped him up on the bed. Could the Midwestern youth help identify the man who had fired the pistol? O'Connell shook his head—impossible.

That was enough. Tooze changed the subject. Where was he from? Tooze wanted to know. Kansas City, the youth responded. In patriotic fervor the young man told the colonel how he had quit junior college to join the army in 1943. Now here he was—far away from the wheat fields and Mom and Dad. Was there anything else? the colonel asked, leaning over his bed.

O'Connell took a long breath and sighed deeply. "I can truthfully state," he whispered from behind a bandaged jaw, "except by the grace of God, we are alive."

Epilogue

On the very last day of 1944 the U.S. 30th Infantry Division looked to attack and recapture the crossroads south of Malmédy at Five Points. It was, after all, where the infamous massacre had reportedly taken place two weeks before. Deep snows now starkly outlined the Ardennes terrain. Pvt. Francis Edwards thought the snow-encrusted trees "made for a beautiful Christmas like sight," but he toiled with everyone else to fashion outfits out of bed sheets, drapes, and anything else to help camouflage with the icy white. Otherwise the dull-green uniforms stood out conspicuously, helping enemy gunners.[1] Approaching enemy lines under cover of darkness would be less suicidal.

A squad-level patrol on the night of December 30 from the 120th Regiment first reported the crossroads free of the enemy, although a larger follow-up reconnaissance ran into a German outpost. They recoiled after a great deal of shooting.[2] The following night, three hours into the New Year, two platoons of B Company set out across the snow to size up the enemy defenses near Baugnez, now in possession of the German 3rd Parachute Division. After trudging through deep snow, the main body of the ten-man raiding party reached the crossroads and came under fire from an enemy strongpoint to the south. In minutes Capt. Murray Pulver, in charge of Company B, found the entire night operation in danger of disaster.

A sparkle blinked in darkness and quickly turned into a fan of German automatic-weapons fire coming from the woods and a nearby house. The surprised patrol was caught in an exposed enfilade. Rifle grenades commenced to drop out of the black sky, exploding willy-nilly. The patrol leader and another GI were killed, with several others wounded. As this took place a platoon sent to flank the enemy on the right stumbled on uneven humps in the snow. In the bright moonlight a few of the "uneven humps" were uncovered. They had come upon snow-covered bodies in the massacre field, twisted and frozen, lying on top of each other. But there was little time for curiosity or investigation. At about the same time, in the woods near the house, the patrol captured a single German paratrooper and then pulled back, still under fire. Pulver could only report that the Germans were still plenty strong in the area around Baugnez-Thirimont.[3]

The attempt had been costly; so a stronger effort would have to wait for over a week due to the fearful weather—windblown snow and subzero temperatures. The opportunity finally came on January 12, 1945, when the 30th Division battled once more for the crossroads—now covered with two to four feet of drifted snow and pockmarked with craters churned up from artillery fire. That night infantrymen of the 119th Regiment of the 30th Division dug foxholes around the foggy crossroads, only to find upon waking that they shared the snowy field with victims of a mass killing. At one spot lay a grotesque rigid posture with his outstretched arms nearly reaching the foxhole recently dug by Pvt. Herschel Nolen of Durant, Oklahoma. "There are others around here still lying under the snow," he said, waving his hand. "If that's the way they want to fight—then that's alright with us," Nolen said. "But let us fight that way too." Pvt. Glenn L. Hubbard in a nearby foxhole agreed. "If the people back home could see this, maybe they would stop their bickering."[4] By the morning of January 13, the 120th Infantry Regiment had largely retaken and consolidated the area.[5]

The folks back home could not see the scarred and blackened crossroads with the gutted and burned-out café. Along the road leading to the burned-out structure just to the north was a dozen or so wrecked American trucks and jeeps, abandoned and now partly covered in white. Bare birch trees stood out starkly against the bright-white snowfield, with dark splotches of shellfire having pitted the ground. The gray bark of the trees bordering the field was split and gleaming yellow from exploding shrapnel. Only two dozen yards from the charred ruins of the café were the partially exposed bodies of the young men killed at the crossroads.

Even though most of the corpses were hidden in the deep snow, here and there icy winds exposed the frozen forms. The contorted soldiers in death edging out of the drifts gave a starkly macabre appearance. Several lay face up with their hands held over their heads and their mouths half open as if totally surprised by death.[6] One snow-dusted face looked straight ahead as if lost in eternity, staring up at the dark blue sky now crisscrossed by bomber contrails. Another dead man was frozen in painful grimace. Several fell huddled together, looking as if they sought warmth from the cold. One soldier clutched his stomach in a death spasm while a medic with a bullet hole through his Red Cross emblem stared straight ahead in a fixed gaze. Birds or small animals had eaten the eyes of some victims.

Lt. Col. Alvin B. Welsch of the Army Inspector General's office, who had been placed in charge of the U.S. First Army investigation into the atrocity, closely followed the progress to retake the Baugnez fields and clear the enemy from the crime scene. On January 13, 1945, Welsch traveled to have a personal look, intending to uncover the massacre victims buried in knee deep snow. By day's end, enemy shellfire drove him away.[7]

A battalion of infantry was attacking on each side of the crossroad and at 1100 hours I proceeded from Malmédy with a small reconnaissance party to the Géromont crossroad. At that time, there was about two feet of virgin snow throughout the area and the road was impassable to a quarter ton truck, necessitating that I walk to the crossroad for about a mile and a half through the snow. On the way up there my party encountered enemy sniper and machine gun fire as well as artillery and mortar fire. After I arrived at the crossroad at approximately 1300 hours, I noticed from the condition of the snow, that none of the attacking infantry soldiers had gone south of the crossroad. . . . [The field] was still under direct observation and small arms and artillery fire from the enemy. I managed to crawl to the edge of the field with a Signal Corps photographer [Pfc. John Boretsky] and took some pictures. At that time, the entire field was still covered with virgin snow and no bodies could be seen. Later that evening, contact was made with the infantry battalion commander and he was requested to see to it that the field would not be disturbed by his troops during the night.[8]

Early the next morning Welsch returned with D-Day combat photographer, T/3 Richard Taylor, and medical officer, Capt. John A. Snyder, and the men of the 3060 Graves Registration Company, who would gingerly shovel and sweep to uncover the dozens of bodies under his direction. After being located and tagged, the solidly frozen corpses were transported on stretchers to waiting trucks of the 3200 Quartermaster Company.[9] The weather was very cold—well below freezing—but the sky was clear with a weak sun. Indications that the enemy was still close by was ever-so apparent as the graves registration people nervously gabbed with members of the 30th Infantry Division, who were holding weapons at the ready in deep foxholes along the road.

That Peiper's underlings had perpetrated a major war crime at the crossroads seemed certain to Snyder and the other medical examiners. The day after the corpses were uncovered, on January 14, 1945, Lt. Col. Welsch and his team began the gruesome task of recovery. The 2nd squad of C Company of the 291st Combat Engineer Battalion under Sgt. Albert Melton used mine detectors to help locate remains buried in the snow and assuage worries that the bodies might be booby-trapped. Brooms swept away the frozen white.

Although the crossroads victims had been dead for over almost a month, the seventy-two bodies recovered in the field were maintained in an icy Ardennes deep freeze.[10] "When they were found," Welsch remembered, "the bodies were frozen hard." But the worst were the wounds: Many appeared to have been inflicted by small arms fired at such close range that those uncovering them observed powder burns in the temples and foreheads of the victims. Welsch saw one man "stretched out on the ground and lying on his stomach with the back of the head completely bashed in."[11]

They used dog tags for identification and organized personal effects with the bodies so they could return the items to the families. Francis Miner, who was with the graves registration crew, grimly noted that many of the men had head wounds and were grouped in such a way to suggest that they had been mowed down. "All of us felt varying degrees of anger, hatred and loathing for the Nazi murderers," he re-called.[12] For the African American soldiers of the assisting quarter-master company, the process was deeply disheartening. Many of the gray corpses were icily twisted in a fetal position or with their hands thrown over their head in surrender. Some were frozen to the ground.

Capt. John A. Snyder examined the dead men as they were uncov-ered. After being photographed, the icy bodies were hauled awkwardly onto litters, their fatigues dusted in snow and soaked in solid blood. The litter bearers then carefully loaded the grotesquely frozen victims from stretchers into the back of four-ton trucks and moved them off to Malmédy.

Over two depressing days they moved the frozen bodies to a bombed-out railway station in Malmédy for autopsies. The improvised morgue reflected horror. "At times the floor resembled a skating rink with the melting snow and the blood which continued to seep onto it from the bodies. The bodies of the Malmédy victims were warmed to the point that clothing could be removed. Personnel from the 44th Evacuation Hospital then carefully performed the autopsies.[13] Photo-graphs were taken to document the process. Snyder, Capt. Joseph A. Kurz, and Maj. Giacento C. Morrone examined each body in detail to determine wounds and cause of death before turning the remains over to a graves registration detail that then buried the men at Henri-Chapelle cemetery some forty kilometers to the north.[14]

What Capt. Snyder saw those three days crystallized infamy: This was no ordinary combat action. Although his trenchant notes recorded most bodies with multiple gunshot wounds, a total of twenty of the seventy-one dead appeared to have been shot in the head at distances close enough to produce powder burns.[15] More-over, three had evidently died from severe blows to the head, and a number had been crushed by vehicles after they fell in the road. As many of the deceased still carried money and jewelry, simple greed or robbery could scarcely have been a motive. Nevertheless, it did not escape the doctors' attention that nearly a dozen—like T/5 Luke B. Swartz and Pfc. Elmer W. Wald—were killed instantly, felled with their hands reaching over their heads.[16] Perhaps most pitiful of all was Cpl. Carl H. Rullman, who was frozen in death with his hands clenched over his face, as if in a futile attempt to protect himself as his executioner prepared to shoot him in the head.

And what of Kampfgruppe Peiper, which had been heading for the Meuse River and glory? They never made it. Later on December 17 the long tank column pushed through Ligneuville, blasting across a contested bridge at Stavelot the next morning, but it was turned back by another blown span in Trois-Ponts. Undaunted, Peiper continued his blitz by rushing through La Gleize and driving across the Amblève at Cheneux to attempt to reach Werbomont. Beyond that point the terrain smoothed out for a final dash to the Meuse. However, this final effort also failed, as the ubiquitous American engineers turned him back with a blown bridge over tiny Lienne Creek. In La Gleize that afternoon, Peiper met SS-Maj. Gustav Knittel, in charge of the 1st SS Panzer Reconnaissance Battalion, who had come from Stavelot. "They've bumped off quite a few at the crossroads," he told Peiper.[17] The leader of his Tiger tank battalion, Heinz von Westernhagen, told his superior the same, but the commander of Kampfgruppe Peiper was still focused on reaching the Meuse River.

By the morning of December 19 Peiper was able to double back to La Gleize and launch a brash assault to take him west of the village of Stoumont. However, Peiper's big Panther tanks were ambushed not far beyond and destroyed. By then, the American 30th Infantry Division and parts of the 3rd Armored had hemmed in his incursion, and over the following days Peiper was forced to relinquish Stoumont and pull back to circle his tanks in La Gleize. In dire danger of capture or total annihilation, fewer than a thousand of Peiper's spent battle group walked out from encirclement in the middle of the night on December 24 to reach friendly lines at Wanne the next day.

"We left with 3,000 men from Germany and now we have 717," he announced hoarsely to his operations officer. "You can find the others the whole way along our path."[18] Peiper's exhausted announcement evidenced little emotion for his losses. Of course, nothing at all was said of civilians, for clear evidence showed that his and Knittel's men had butchered dozens of innocent civilians in and around Stavelot, Trois-Ponts, and Wanne itself.

More surrendered American soldiers were shot in Ligneuville, at La Vaulx Richard near Stavelot, Stoumont, and at Petit Thier. In the closing days of December the remnants of Peiper's armor and other units of the 1st SS Panzer Division moved to the area around Bastogne in obedience to Hitler's orders to capture that key crossroads city that had hobbled the advance of his great offensive in the south.

Although Jochen Peiper, the head of the infamous battle group, did not know it, word of the Malmédy incident spread like wildfire through the Allied press. A day after it happened, the *Washington Post* headline jolted American readers: NAZIS MASSACRE CAPTIVE YANKS IN BELGIUM, SURVIVORS REPORT.[19] As early as January 1945, American reporters were calling it murder.[20] When famous American wartime correspondent Hal Boyle first reported on Malmédy on December 18, emotions boiled:

> Weeping with rage a handful of dough-boy survivors described today how a German tank force ruthlessly poured machine gun fire into a group of about 150 Americans who had been disarmed and herded into a field in the opening hours of the present Nazi counteroffensive.

To get the story, Boyle rode in a jeep with Jack Belden of *Time* magazine to the medical clearing station at Malmédy. The sky was overcast as they bounced along, aware that an enemy offensive was swirling in the gloom. "The Germans are coming!" warned jumpy Belgian locals. Nor did the wide-eyed look on the faces of U.S. reinforcements moving up to the line inspire confidence. With full approval from the U.S. First Army, Hal Boyle had been led to a small room in Malmédy where some of the twenty-odd crossroads survivors were located. Boyle interviewed T/5 Sgt. William B. "Bruce" Summers, who had been with the 285th Field Artillery Observation battalion. Summers spoke with tears in his eyes. Other survivors could hardly contain sobs long enough to speak:

> They opened up on us from their armored cars with machine guns. We hadn't tried to run away or anything. We were just standing

there with our hands up and they tried to murder us all. . . . There was nothing to do, but just flop and play dead. . . . We had to lie there and listen to German noncoms kill with pistols every one of our wounded men who groaned or tried to move.[21]

Would the American front break? Everyone had the jitters in Paris as Belgian civilians hid in their cellars, only peeking out of their windows, which were now denuded of the American flags that had once graced many homes.[22] Some locals even ridiculed the Americans as they pulled back. One Reuters correspondent ventured that the real objective of the shooting near Malmédy was terror—to break the American will to fight.[23] That tactic seemed to backfire, however. Emboldened from a brush with death at the crossroads, survivor Bruce Summers was stirred to anger when he spoke to Associated Press reporter Hal Boyle. "Those dirty bastards! Damn them." he raged. "Give me a rifle and put me in with infantry. I want to go back and kill every one of them."[24]

The Waffen SS men on whom Summers vowed vengeance were only fourteen kilometers away. Among them was the SS colonel-in-charge. According to Heinz von Westernhagen, on December 18 in La Gleize, when Peiper learned of the massacre, he called it "a mix-up"—a muddle, a confusion—a "*Durcheinander.*" [25] He thought the incident was just another blot within the expected brutality of modern war. It was regrettable, even if the very tenets of National Socialism endorsed such violence.

On December 22, 1944, five days after the Malmédy massacre, SS-Brig. Gen. Wilhelm Mohnke's headquarters of the 1st SS Panzer Division moved to the château in Wanne, Belgium. The village was on a steep wooded hill just eight straight-line kilometers to the southeast of Peiper, but it was separated by the confluence of the Amblève and Salm Rivers. There in the village, where the communications vehicle set up at the divisional headquarters, the field Teletype clicked off a priority message signed by Hitler himself. The Führer's message, relayed by Gen. Alfred Jodl, inquired into who had committed the atrocity the Americans now reported:

When I heard of the shooting of 120 American prisoners near Malmédy, I immediately, on my own initiative, had an investigation started through the Commander West so as to report the result to the Führer.[26]

A man from the 1st Company of the Panzer Signal Battalion in a special communications car received the message around December 25, 1944. He heard a short conversation between his commanding officer SS-1st Lt. Helmut Liebrich, and an SS master sergeant of the 2nd Company, in which Liebrich discussed the matter with the operations officer, SS-Maj. Ralf Tiemann. They made an investigation, Tiemann claimed, but they had no results. The witness, radio operator SS-Cpl. Gerhard Ellhof, seemed unaware that the scene of the crime was hardly any distance away.[27] Nor was there any mention that 1st SS men had shot several civilians in Wanne itself. Further, dozens of Belgians had been brutally murdered at Stavelot and the surrounding hamlets.

If Hitler truly had been concerned about the atrocity at Baugnez, this clearly did not carry over to the Waffen SS and the Leibstandarte Adolf Hitler. Peiper would not only survive the Ardennes, but he would be rewarded for his action at Malmédy.

If Peiper wasn't aware of the questionable nature of what transpired at the crossroads, how could one explain Wilhelm Mohnke's glowing official record of the incident as he recorded it on December 26 after Peiper had first come to his command post? His divisional commander enthusiastically recommended the SS lieutenant colonel for the Swords to the Knight's Cross. In most cases such endorsements would be made based on the unit commander's own after-action report. Mohnke's composition at his division headquarters the day after Christmas spoke in admiring tones of Peiper's actions on December 17:

> Without regard for threats from the flanks, and only inspired by the thought of a deep breakthrough the Kampfgruppe proceeded via Möderscheid-Schoppen-Faymonville to Engelsdorf and destroyed at Baugnez an enemy supply column and after annihilation of the units blocking their advance, succeeded in causing the staff of the 49th Anti-Aircraft Brigade to flee.[28]

As Baugnez was specifically named, there could be little doubt that the incident referred to in the three-page report is what would become known as the Malmédy massacre. And by his own admission, Peiper had learned of the incident a day after it occurred and a week before Mohnke formulated his description. Why would such an incident—a blot—be singled out for a decoration? Translation of the ambiguous German term used for annihilation—*Vernichtung*—is one issue. Conventional interpretation would see it as simply describing the battlefield destruction of the enemy. However, within the National Socialist lexicon—*Vernichtung* could also mean the elimination of an enemy. After all, the concentration camps at which Jews were being liquidated were referred to as *Vernichtungslager*—elimination camps.

The likelihood remains that after years of savage war on the Eastern Front, men of the Waffen SS had come to admire such harshness. Certainly, that is the way Heinrich Himmler (for whom Peiper was a dedicated adjutant from 1938 to 1941), would have seen it. The correct interpretation will probably never be known, but it cannot be discounted that Peiper and Mohnke may have understood Vernichtung to embrace the killing of prisoners of war. Rather than a blemish on one's record, such an event was an accolade. On Thursday, January 11, 1945, a Teletype message addressed to Jochen Peiper flashed from Berlin to the headquarters of the 6th Panzer Army: "In consideration of your continuous display of heroism, I award you the Swords to the Oak Leaves of the Knight's Cross." Adolf Hitler himself signed it.[29]

On the other side of the Atlantic, Hitler's opposite, U.S. President Franklin Delano Roosevelt, contemplated the latest dire news from the fighting in Belgium. The last day of the year in Washington, DC, was gloomy—drenched by cold rain. The American president pondered prospects against a suddenly rampaging German enemy. At noon the wheelchair-bound president received Secretary of War Henry L. Stimson in his White House bedroom for a briefing. Was it possible the desperate enemy was doing anything to buy time to develop atomic weapons? Perhaps his intelligence was wrong, the president worried. As rain splattered on the White House windows, Stimson told the president that an SS column had killed more than a score of American prisoners near Malmédy the previous week. There was no doubt about the cold-blooded killing. "Well, it will only serve to make our troops feel about the Germans as they already feel about the Japs," Roosevelt commented dryly.[30] Perhaps, he hoped, it would increase American resolve on the ground.

Meanwhile, with his commendation in hand, Peiper left the Ardennes in early January 1945 to fight again as a battle group leader in Hungary. There, Kampfgruppe Peiper would continue to fight in futile combat through February and March and, then, in the closing weeks of the war, in Austria. After the conflict was over Peiper was located in a Nuremberg POW camp in August 1945 and immediately detained for lengthy interrogation along with other suspects from his battle group.

In June and July of 1946 Peiper and the other eighty members of his command in the Ardennes were tried for war crimes in the Malmédy massacre trial held in Dachau, Germany.[31] Unbowed and unapologetic, Peiper testified at length in the trial. At its end he was found guilty and sentenced to death by hanging, as were many of his men. Mike Skoda, who had survived the shooting at the crossroads, had no sympathy for Peiper and the others. "The SS bunch have at least been tried," he commented dryly. "We were given no trial, just shot down."[32] The sentenced SS men were imprisoned at Landsberg, where Hitler himself had been incarcerated in 1924 before coming to power.

In its eagerness to establish Peiper's guilt as well as that of those under his command, the U.S. Army used questionable methods during the pretrial investigations. As became evident in the author's research, many of those who were guilty were not apprehended, and some, accused of war crimes that never happened, were still sentenced with the rest.[33] At Schwäbisch Hall, where the pretrial interrogations were held, mock trials, threats against families, and other questionable means coerced some of the confessions. Later, pro-SS propaganda often inflated pretrial irregularities to include widespread allegations of physical mistreatment of prisoners at Schwäbisch Hall. This led to a U.S. Senate investigation amid the Cold War, which, at the time, was altering the politics of postwar Germany. As a result, the sentences of many of the Malmédy defendants were later commuted to life and, then, to time served. On December 22, 1956, Peiper was released after spending eleven years in Landsberg Prison.

On parole Peiper lived quietly in Stuttgart, working for Porsche and later for Volkswagen, although Peiper's involvement in war crimes his battalion committed in Italy continued to haunt his life in Germany.[34]

Eventually, Peiper retired to the remote French village of Traves in the Haute-Saône. There he supported himself as a translator, maintaining a lively correspondence with old SS comrades. Although shunning public attention and portraying himself as an apolitical unlucky soldier and an intellectual, in private Peiper was defiantly unreconstructed. After receiving several death threats in May 1976, Peiper was murdered in a fire attack on his house on the eve of Bastille Day, July 13, of that same summer. His attackers were never identified.

SS-Maj. Werner Poetschke, the tough SS man most likely to have given the order to have the Americans shot at the crossroads, was later killed in the fighting in Hungary on March 24, 1945.

Peiper's infantry-leading protégé at the crossroads, Josef Diefenthal, retired to Eüskirchen after the war, refusing all attempts at contact. With a silence seldom broken, he died in April 2001.

Paul Zwigart, Peiper's driver at the crossroads, was still living in 1997 and interviewed by the author, but he resolutely refused to talk about the crossroads. SS-Sgt. Max Beutner, who seems likely to have directed the shooting at the crossroads following Poetschke's orders, was later killed in the Ardennes fighting near Stoumont on December 21, 1944. SS-1st. Lt. Erich Rumpf, who was also implicated as having directed Poetschke's orders to fire on the prisoners at Baugnez, survived the war. After release from prison he worked as an electrician in Hannover, happy to escape attention. His SPW driver, Karl Veil, however, is still living but remains silent.

Former SS-S/Sgt. Hans Siptrott, the commander of the infamous Panzer 731, is still living in Germany, never having contradicted that Fleps fired shots at the crossroads nor denying that a mass shooting took place afterward. He did, however, deny giving Fleps orders to shoot and blames the massacre on Americans attempting to flee.[35] Despite being a controversial figure, Siptrott remains proud of his military record and was forthright in an interview. Manfred Thorn, who was driving Panzer 734 ahead of Siptrott, still lives in Nuremberg, having spent much energy questioning the Malmédy investigation, particularly how things were handled at Schwäbisch Hall.

The man accused of having fired the first shot from Siptrott's Panzer IV, SS Romanian Georg Fleps, was paroled in 1953 and went on to work as a fabric dyer in Ludwigsburg. He eventually settled in the Stuttgart area, lamenting that what transpired at the crossroads ruined his life. "I have a permanent feeling of regret since December 17, 1944," he wrote in 1986. "No priest in the world can forgive me for that."[36]

Werner Sternebeck, the dashing panzer leader who first came across the Americans at Baugnez, was released from prison in 1948 and reentered the service after the war. There, in the Bundeswehr, he rose to the rank of lieutenant colonel. However, his daughter, Sigrid, was so shocked to learn of his SS past that she joined the leftist Red Army Faction. Rumors still swirl that Sternebeck killed himself in 1990 after his daughter was arrested in East Germany following Marxist bombing attacks.

August Tonk, who commanded the speeding Panzer IV following Sternebeck at Baugnez, drove trucks in Hamburg after the war and faded from view. Arndt Fischer, whose Panther tank led Peiper away from the crossroads just before the shooting, became the SS-lieutenant colonel's dentist after the war.

Others successfully forgot the past. Roman Clotten, the leader of the tank behind Siptrott who saw everything (and whose crew participated as well), became a successful doctor in Freiburg after the war. Disappearing was easier for enlisted men like Gustav Neve and Ernst Goldschmidt, both released from prison in 1954. They had been shooters on the halftracks that sprayed the Americans with bullets at the crossroads. After release from prison they lived undisturbed, successfully melting into postwar obscurity in Germany. The author knows of only one other alleged shooter still living who still claims to the author that he and the others in the SPW of Max Beutner did not fire at the crossroads.[37] Yet, if they did not shoot, then who, other than possibly the SPWs with Rumpf could have loosed concentrated machine gunfire on the GIs in the first place? Somehow nearly a hundred American soldiers at Baugnez were killed or wounded—a fact that remains beyond all denial.

Many if not most of the American Malmédy survivors manifested mental torment associated with the events of December 17, 1944. Terrible nightmares haunted Bill Merriken for years, leaving his family estranged and confused. Bobby Werth could scarcely contain himself while talking about the events with the author. T/4 Robert Mearig, who returned from the war to become a postman in Litiz, Pennsylvania, was forced to retire after suffering a nervous breakdown in 1975. "I'd go to bed and cry like a baby," he said. "I'd get up and sit in the living room and still cry." He wrote the author, "It took me forever to get over it. In fact, I don't believe I did to this day. So much happened. Every now and then I get flashbacks. . . . No one will ever know how we feel about it."[38] Mearig died in 2007.

Psychologically damaged by the experience at Baugnez, Harold Billow recovered at the 185th General Hospital in England. As he improved, he ventured into Manchester for better times. Soon he was courting an English girl, Bera Waller. In a strange coincidence, the two married on December 17, 1945, exactly one year after the massacre. Returning to Pennsylvania in 1946, he sought to forget the war and the terrible episode still haunting him. Even as the author composed the final draft of this book, Harold Billow could hardly bring himself to talk about the event. "I remember crawling through the barbed wire to get into the field and all of us standing with our hands up."

> I still think about it a lot. I see things in my head. Every once in a while I still get nightmares. They are so bad, I have to come downstairs and have something to eat. Then I go back upstairs to sleep. . . . My memory is still there, but I don't like to think about it. It gets to me pretty good.[39]

Even if still tortured, Harold Billow has not forgotten. Four times a year, in honor of those lost, Billow stakes out one hundred American flags in his front yard in Mount Joy in a precisely spaced arrangement. "When I put out the flags, it reminds me of that day. I feel happy that somehow some of us got out of there alive."

Stephen Domitrovich, today living in Beaver, Pennsylvania, often still thinks of December 17, 1944, even if he would rather not.

> They came up to me and I saw a German's boot right by me and started praying. My buddy next to me was shot. You can't know what it was like. *God save me. . . . God save me.* I prayed, *God, if I get out of here alive, I'll never miss mass. . . .* I lay there for hours. Then

some of us got up and ran and we ran up to a hill and there was a farmhouse overlooking Malmédy and ran into a Belgian fellow. He wanted to have nothing to with us. "*Boche! Boche!*" Somehow he let us know that the Americans were on the other side. We went over there and found some Americans with a truck. I was really out of my head, but not wounded. I knew I was safe then. I felt deeply grateful to God for having saved my life. . . . I ended up in the Liège hospital—I was out of my head. I was sedated. I didn't know what I ate or what I did.[40]

After about a month he was sent back to the front with the 575th Ambulance Company, but he was still unsteady. "The captain kept me in his quarters because I was still having problems," he remembers. "He would not let anybody talk to me."

In May 1945 the 575th Ambulance Company moved to Rheims, France, for Victory Day, although for a while it looked like they might get sent to Japan. Thankfully, the threat of a bloody invasion of Japan ended too. Domitrovich returned home to Pennsylvania, where he opened up a deli selling sandwiches, coffee, and groceries. There he met his charming Greek wife, Helen. Although Domitrovich has been back to Europe twice, he has never been back to Malmédy. "I wouldn't want to," he said. "Too many bad memories."

When survivor George Fox returned to Front Royal, Virginia, in 1945, the war was not his focus. "I really tried to forget all that." Still, even after resuming the grocery business, he could never quite see life the same way. Fortunately, normal life in America returned. In November 1947 he met his future wife, Marjorie, on a blind date. Happily lost in raising a family, he worked for American Viscose Company. In 1981 Belgian researcher Gerd Cuppens, who was investigating Malmédy, contacted him. "He visited us, and we visited him in Europe. He was alright at first." Cuppens introduced Fox to Rolf Ehrhardt, who had been at the crossroads in Oskar Klingelhoefer's Panzer 701. They got on well, but Fox didn't know that Ehrhardt's tank had been at Baugnez just moments before the shooting. "Eventually, Cuppens wrote that the massacre didn't even happen," Fox added with dismay.[41] Feeling betrayed, Fox didn't speak to anyone about Malmédy for years. "I was disgusted." However, he did reestablish contact with Ted Flechsig, who had also survived the shooting. In 1990 Fox and Flechsig returned to Belgium to a warm reunion with Clément Xhurdebise, who, for forty-five years, had saved the bicycle that the two men had used to escape.[42]

Today George Fox, the Virginia farm boy, still likes to grow vegetables. Bicycles still figure large in his life—he and Marge both ride. After a cup of black coffee with sugar, he was thoughtful as he looked out from his retirement porch in Florida. "I wonder why I survived there sometimes," he relates. "Maybe somebody saved me—all those people were shot. I think some must have been dead in front of me. I think back on when Vernon Manuel had me baptized when I was seventeen." At the end of a pleasant winter afternoon chat, George Fox tells me he has the most important thing of the interview to relate. "But you don't need to write it down." Something secret? I drop my pen. He gazes at me with sparkling blue eyes, "I am glad to still be alive."

Kenneth Ahrens, who was still living while this book was being written, had consigned the entire sad event to the past. After a single short interview he said he would never talk about Malmédy again. In explaining his silence to the author, Ahrens revealed that he no longer wanted to revisit the episode—even in thought. Reminders were unwelcome. Exiting a life laced with tragedy, Ken Ahrens died in 2004.

1st Lt. Virgil P. Lary, the highest-ranking officer who survived, could never rid himself of the guilt he felt because he led his men into the massacre after ignoring David Pergrin's warning in Malmédy. But neither could Lary leave the subject—he was obsessed with the tragedy. After his involvement in the trial and later in the Senate hearings associated with the Senate Malmédy investigation, he retired to Ft. Lauderdale, where he succumbed to depression and alcoholism.

Lary reached out to other survivors. Kenneth Ahrens was one of them: "Lary had started calling me in 1945; we spoke pretty often by phone. . . . It bothered him a lot. Probably that led to his drinking problem. He felt responsibility since he was leading the battery. Lary was more or less responsible for us until we were to get up with Capt Scarborough around St. Vith."[43]

Years after the war Lary contacted Ralph Indelicato's sister Catherine Lyon and spoke to her just before Christmas, saying that her brother should have gotten the Congressional Medal of Honor for tending to the wounded just before he was shot. But to Lyon, he seemed terribly disturbed. "I was the commander," he told her, "and I took these young men to their death."[44] Lary died of cancer in 1981, but in one of his last letters to a friend, he claimed to have really died in December 1944 at the crossroads.[45]

Most tragic of all was the story of Carl R. Daub—a survivor who was called as a witness at the Dachau trial in 1946. After the war he worked in the roofing business with fellow survivor Ken Ahrens. Their relationship went on for many years until he started his own business. Over time Daub exhibited increasingly erratic behavior. While working in roofing during the day in Colebrook, Pennsylvania, he lived in an old army tent at night, increasingly estranged from his family and the outside world.

Then, in 1988, something snapped. On May 31 Daub killed his wife with a claw hammer and assailed his thirty-two-year-old son at home before racing off to escape. His wrecked automobile was found later that same night near Bangor Mountain in the Poconos. An expansive manhunt with a heavily armed police team and tracking dogs failed to locate Daub, who appeared on *America's Most Wanted* in 1990. The mystery of his whereabouts was solved in November 2003 when a hiker came upon his remains deep in a Pennsylvania forest, not far from where his car had been found near Route 191. Had Daub died from wounds from the wreck or suicide? The postmortem examination of the remains found on Kittatinny Mountain could not settle the question.[46]

Surgeons removed the bullets in William Merriken's back and knee at the 9th Field Hospital in Verviers, Belgium. The doctors decided to treat the open wounds with penicillin and bandages and hold off closing them until they could tame the infections. In the hospital in Verviers, converted from a big auditorium, Merriken was heavily sedated. Sometime on Wednesday, December 20, he awoke from his drug-induced sleep to the sound of screams and a large explosion outside. Glass was scattered all across the floor of the ward. He looked around in a momentary panic. He settled back in his bed—he was not at the crossroads but in a big hospital. The next morning a nurse explained that enemy shelling had hit the hospital.

Still heavily sedated, Bill was shipped via train to Paris, then Cherbourg, and finally on to a hospital ship across the Channel. In England he became a patient at the 123rd General Hospital in the peaceful western English coast near Hereford, Wales. The town was so quiet that "you would not have even known a war was going on." There, they finally sewed up the wounds in his back and he regained his strength. Even so, his mental wounds did not heal.

Often during that January and February of 1945 he would awake from terrible nightmares. Always it was the same: A man in a dark uniform standing in a halftrack. He points a pistol, then gunfire . . . screams. "Nurse, nurse!" he would call. "It's just a dream," they would tell him, bringing him back to his bed. After the sting of a hypodermic, his form would fade from the field, lost in a fog.

Daytime was better. He made friends at the hospital, and trips to the pleasant town of Hereford made things almost normal again. Strangely, Bill Merriken was seized with the desire to go back to his Army unit. He recovered, staying at the hospital until April 13, 1945. The war was over when Merriken returned to the 285th Field Artillery Observation Battalion in June 1945. By then, he was a different person. He was drinking and seemed distant to those who had known him before. Eventually his discharge papers arrived, and in December 1945, a year after his encounter with fate, Bill Merriken was on his way back across the Atlantic.

In 1946 he returned home to the green pine hills of Bedford, Virginia. On the surface things were okay. He went back to college and got a degree in business administration. He was offered a good job with Standard Oil Company, and in 1956 he married his pretty wife, Betty. Together they raised a family. Yet how long does it take to heal wounds so deep? Bill suffered bouts of depression that he could not explain. Something he could not bring himself to share—not even to an understanding wife and a concerned family—haunted him. It was his dark secret.

The hidden demons came out at night to find him. He dreaded sleep. And during the day there was the ever-present threat of a visit from the relatives of Warren Davis and Richard Walker, hometown boys from Bedford who had died in the field at Malmédy. Sisters, brothers, and mothers came by with questions for which there were no satisfactory answers. As best he could, he told them what he knew. Keeping it together was difficult. Recounting the sadness of losing young sons and brothers was terrible enough, but he was thankful that at the time he did not know how they died.[47]

Over the years Merriken was able to regain control slowly. "They're not as frequent now," Bill said of the nightmares, but the ghosts still returned on occasion. His demons were memories from a cold December day in a Belgian field near a crossroads. Christmas time was the most difficult. He was never completely free of it. "I think about it every day." said Merriken quietly. "I left part of myself out in that field." A pause and he looks away—a shaken faith. That part of himself was still missing fifty years later. Bill Merriken died in October 2006.

The man who had saved Bill Merriken's life, Charles Reding, wrote to his mother from England after the ordeal.

> When I got back behind our lines everybody seemed to think I needed a rest after what I had been through so I am in England in a hospital taking a rest. There's nothing wrong with me except I am a little nervous sometimes. . . . Two colonels and several other officers have told me I would receive some kind of award like a silver star for bringing this wounded buddy back with me. If I do get something I will send it to you and you can show it to everybody and brag on your baby boy![48]

In Reding's mind the December days of 1944 didn't bother him. Yet something invisible had taken root. Although married in 1952 and later fathering five children, "his continuing nervous condition" brought on an instability that consumed his family. The promised commendation never came. Yet Reding stoically accepted the lack of official recognition. "I was pleased with being able to save my life and helping Bill." That, he said, was reward enough."[49]

On January 10, 1945, Al Valenzi's father, at 323 Logan Street in Sewickley, Pennsylvania, received the dreaded Western Union telegram:

> The Secretary of War desires me to express his deep regret that your son Technician Grade Five, Albert M. Valenzi has been reported missing in action since December 17 in Belgium.

By then the newspapers were filled with dreary stories of the Battle of the Bulge and the terrible losses in Europe. Understandably, Al's father was beside himself. Then, after ten tortured days, another telegram arrived. John Valenzi dreaded to open the hastily delivered message:

> Reference my telegram of 10 January and subsequent letter, report now received states that your son . . . was slightly wounded in action on December 17, 1944, in Belgium and is not missing in action as previously reported. Mail address follows direct from hospital with details.

Saints be praised! His son was alive after having been shot twice in the leg. Only later would they learn about his close brush with death. Valenzi himself was nearly overcome by his experience:

> It was dark when they got us to the aid station. We were on a weapons carrier when we evacuated. Ken [Ahrens] and I were taken to Liège later that night. We wanted to stay together. They took us to the same hospital, but they put him in a different ward. I was in shock. They fixed us up and put us in beds. The next morning, there was an officer who came in from the Inspector General's office who spoke to us. I told them what I could remember, but I was in shock. . . . I was wounded in my left arm and legs. There were other people, but from different outfits. This was the first time I really became aware of what was going on, I was shook up pretty bad, because of what happened.
>
> I was still a little bewildered about what had happened. I wrote my father a letter. . . . I was relieved and happy that I was not hurt so bad. I had a nice bed, hot meals and nice nurses. I think about it every Christmas. . . . Sometimes, I would have nightmares and the nurse would come in and give me a hot cup of cocoa. My nightmares were gun flashes. This has never left my mind in fifty years.[50]

Meanwhile, the local papers declared him something of a hero. What had it been like in the massacre field at Malmédy? they wanted to know.[51] "The thoughts which ran through my mind as I lay there and prayed and prayed and prayed, you can't imagine," he told the local reporter. "I saw newsreels the other day of what happened to my outfit, but I couldn't bear to look at them."[52]

In December 1945 Al came back with the 285th and was discharged at Indiantowngap Military Reservation. Al Valenzi went back to his home in Corapolis, Pennsylvania, where he had graduated high school in 1940. There he tried to resume a civilian life. After they were married he and his wife, Virginia, settled into a comfortable life, raising their son, John, while Al worked for the postal service. Although always aware of his unique part in the history of World War II as part of the "greatest generation" and a Malmédy survivor, Valenzi never harbored ill feelings toward the enemy. "There is some good in everybody," he confidently told the author.[53] A kind and gentle man, Al Valenzi passed away in April of 2009.

Ted Paluch survived the massacre and went on to serve with the 285th Field Artillery Observation Battalion for the remainder of the war. In October 1945, still with the 285th in Europe, Paluch and several others survivors were called to Wiesbaden to look at SS men in a lineup to see if any could recognize Peiper as having been at the massacre scene. "They had them in a lineup," Paluch remembered, "but we couldn't honestly place him as having been there—or any of the others for that matter. . . . These guys looked so clean and scrubbed compared with the Germans we saw at Malmédy. But Peiper looked like a real soldier. When he was requested to turn, he would click his heels and turn precisely."[54]

After discharge from the service in December 1945, Paluch returned to Westfield, Pennsylvania. Until retirement Ted served as a Philadelphia traffic manager. Over time he eventually renewed his contacts with veterans from the 285th, first returning to Baugnez in the summer of 1976.

Ted remained single all his life and believes a light mind is one of his keys to "being one of the lucky ones." Today, he expresses his long interest in numbers by deftly playing the horse races. Beyond that, Ted appreciates a good steak, doting over dozens of nieces and nephews, and pondering the latest news on the Phillies or the Eagles.

Although he has become accustomed to being something of a historical celebrity, Paluch does not dwell on Malmédy. "I am not a vengeful person," he said. "The Germans were probably following orders."

Many years later Ted Paluch returned to the crossroads. With the author, he located the place in the hedge by the road where he squirmed to safety in the gathering gloom on December 17, 1944.

On December 17, 2007, sixty-three years later, Ted Paluch stood shivering on the north end of the massacre field at Baugnez, surrounded by a curious crowd of onlookers. He walked carefully, looking about as if searching to match a vision in his head of a terrible time many years before to what he was seeing in front of him. The ditch was no longer deep like it had been, he said. Sixty years before only his head and shoulder poked out as a big German panzer approached. He motioned to the ground—this is where he had stood. This was his place in history on that fateful Sunday long ago, as dozens of others were cut down beside him.

Ted looked out toward the road. "The tanks were there," he said with his quiet Jersey accent. Now, in the icy weather—ten degrees—his eyes grew misty. "A lot of good friends are gone now," he nodded to a gathering crowd as he placed a wreath with gloved hands. Large plumes of vapor rose from his breath in the frozen stillness at the crossroads. This day was even colder than December 17, 1944. There were speeches from elegantly dressed Belgian dignitaries as everyone patiently shivered. A review from the honor guard, then an awkward silence. Someone from the press spoke up. Did Mr. Paluch have anything to add? The reporter was hoping for something profound, poignant. "Yes," he said, as if waiting to be asked.

"Let's go inside and get the hell out of the cold."

APPENDICES

APPENDIX I

SURVIVORS AND VICTIMS

TABLE A.1
U.S. Army victims at the
Baugnez crossroads, December 17, 1944

No.	Tag	Rank	Last Name	First Name	Cause of Death[a]	Unit
1	None[b]	Pvt.	Bloom	David L.	shot in the head	B Battery 285th FAOB
2	29	Tec 5	Blouch	Carl H.	died from bleeding	"
3	57	Tec 5	Breon	Charles R.	died from blow to the head	"
4	49	Cpl.	Brozowski	Joseph A.	shot in the head	"
5	18	Tec 5	Burkett	Samuel P.	shot in the head	"
6	45	Tec 5	Carr	Paul R.	died from bleeding	"
7	None	Pfc.	Carson	Homer S.	shot in the head	"
8	RL[c]	Pfc.	Clark	Frederick	concussion	"
9	C	Pvt.	Coates	James H.	MG or small arms fire	"
10	Died[d]	Pvt.	Cobbler	John H.	MG or small arms fire	"
11	12	Tec 5	Cohen	Robert	shot in the head	"
12	16	Tec 5	Collier	John D.	shot in the head	"
13	RL	Pfc.	Davis	Warren	shrapnel	"
14	53	T/Sgt.	Davidson	Paul G.	shot in the head	"
15	8	Pfc.	Desch	Howard C.	shot in the head	"
16	43	Pvt.	Dunbar	William J.	shot in the head	"
17	54	Cpl.	Fitt	Carl B.	shot in the head	"
18	11	Pfc.	Flack	Donald P.	shot in the head	"
19	39	Sgt.	Franz	Walter A.	MG or Small Arms Fire	"
20	59	Pfc.	Frey	Carl B.	shot in the Head	"
21	24	S/Sgt.	Geisler	Donald E.	shot in the Head	"
22	RL	2nd Lt.	Goffman	Solomon S.	MG or small arms fire	"

(continues)

TABLE A.1 (*continued*)

No.	Tag	Rank	Last Name	First Name	Cause of Death	Unit
23	37	Tec 5	Haines	Charles F.	high explosive shells	"
24	69	Pfc.	Hall	Charles E.	unknown, crushed	"
25	58	Pvt.	Hallman	Samuel A.	MG or small arms fire	"
26	7	Tec 4	Herchelroth	Sylvester	shot in the head	"
27	RL	Tec 4	Jones	Wilson M.	MG or small arms fire	"
28	5	Tec 4	Jordan	Oscar	MG or small arms fire	"
29	56	Sgt.	Kinsman	Alfred W.	unknown	"
30	None	Tec 5	Laufer	Harold W.	died from blow to the head	"
31	14	Tec 5	Lengyel, Jr.	Alexander	MG or small arms fire	"
32	RL	Cpl.	Lester	Raymond E.	shot in the head	"
33	55	Tec 4	Leu	Selmer H.	shot in the head	"
34	RL	Tec 4	Lucas	Alan M.	crushed	"
35	46	Tec 5	Luers	James E.	shot in the head	"
36	34	Cpl.	Martin	Lawrence	shot in the head	"
37	61	Tec 5	McKinney	Robert	crushed	"
38	21	Sgt.	Miller	Halsey J.	shot in the head	"
39	RL	Cpl.	Moore	William H.	crushed	"
40	A	1st Lt.	Munzinger	John S.	shot in the head	"
41	RL	Pfc.	Murray	David M.	unknown	"
42	None	Cpl.	O'Grady	David T.	MG or small arms fire	"
43	36	Pfc.	Oliver	Thomas W.	shot in the head	"
44	1	S/Sgt.	Osborne	John D.	died from blow to the head	"
45	RL	Pvt.	Perkowski	Walter J.	shrapnel	"
46	67	Pvt.	Phillips	Peter R.	shot in the head	"
47	64	Pvt.	Piasecki	Stanley F.	shot in the head	"
48	13	Pvt.	Pittman	Gilbert R.	MG or small arms fire	"
49	52	1st Lt.	Reardon	Perry L.	MG or small arms fire	"
50	32	Tec 5	Rosenfeld	George R.	high explosive shells	"
51	62	Cpl.	Rullman	Carl H.	shot in the head	"
52	RL	Tec 4	Rupp	John M.	shrapnel	"

No.	Tag	Rank	Last Name	First Name	Cause of Death	Unit
53	31	Pvt.	Saylor	Oscar	MG or small arms fire	"
54	26	Tec 5	Schwitzgold	Max	shot in the head	"
55	35	Tec 4	Sheetz	Irwin M.	shot in the head	"
56	22	Tec 5	Shingler	John H.	shot in the head	"
57	44	Sgt.	Snyder	Robert J.	MG or small arms fire	"
58	RL	Sgt.	Stabulis	Alphonse J.	MG or small arms fire	"
59	20	Tec 4	Steffy	George H.	MG or small arms fire	"
60	44-B	Pfc.	Stevens	Carl M.	shot in the head	"
61	3	Tec 5	Swartz	Luke B.	shot in the head	"
62	15	Pfc.	Walker	Richard B.	died from bleeding	"
63	47	Tec 4	Watt	Thomas F.	MG or small arms fire	"
64	27	Tec 5	Wiles	Vester H.	MG or small arms fire	"
65	2	Cpl.	Indelicato	Ralph J.	shot in the head	HQ Battery 285th FAOB
66	6	Capt.	Mills	Roger L.	shot in the head	"
67	17	T/Sgt.	McGovern	William T.	MG or small arms fire	"
68	41	Sgt.	Lindt	Benjamin	shot in the head	200th FAB
69	19	Pfc.	Wald	Elmer W.	shot in the head	"
70	63	2nd Lt.	James	Lloyd A.	shot in the head	Rec.Co. 32nd Arm'd Rgt.
71	50	Pfc.	Klukavy	John	died from bleeding	"
72	38	1st Lt.	McDermott	Thomas E.	shot in the head	"
73	40	Tec 3	McGee	James G.	MG or small arms fire	"
74	42	Pfc.	Burney	L. M.	shot in the head	"
75	10	1st Lt.	Genthner	Carl R.	shot in the head	"
76	68	Pfc.	Paden	Paul L.	shot in the head	"
77	9	Pvt.	Scott	Wayne L.	shot in the head	"
78	66	Pvt.	Mullen	Keston E.	shot in the head	546th Amb. Co.
79	48	Tec 5	Wusterbarth	Dayton E.	shot in the head	"
80	4,23	Pfc.	Clymire	John J.	high explosive shells	86th Eng. Bn.

(continues)

TABLE A.1 (continued)
Killed 200m east of the massacre field
prior to main shooting, December 17, 1944

No.	Tag	Rank	Last Name	First Name	Cause of Death	Unit
81	70	Tec 5	Heitmann	Raymond A.	MG or small arms fire	197 AAA AW Bn
82	71	Tec 4	Cash	Cecil J.	shot in the head	197 AAA AW Bn

Members B Battery, 285th FAOB
by December 17, 1944, with unknown fate

No.	Tag	Rank	Last Name	First Name	Cause of Death
83		Pvt.	Thomas	Elwood E.	body never found; officially declared dead
84		Pvt.	Vario	Louis A.	body found at Neuhof, Germany, 11 miles east of Malmédy

SOURCE: Autopsy reports of Capt. John N. Snyder, Capt. Joseph A. Kurz, and Maj. Giancento C. Morrone, Medical Corps, 44th Evacuation Hospital, Malmédy, Belgium, January 14–16, 1945; also Lt. Col. Alvin B. Welsch, "Information to Establish Prima Facie Case Required by SHAEF Court of Inquiry," HQ U.S. First Army, January 27, 1945; NA, RG-549, War Crimes Cases Tried, Case 6–24, Box 23.

[a]The indicated cause of death often does not describe all wounds. Many were wounded first and then had a shot to the head (i.e., Schwitzgold). See the original autopsy reports for details.

[b]Those indicated *None* for tag number indicates that the body was brought in for autopsy without a tag although these were among the missing tags (25, 28, 30, 33, 51, 60, and 65). Among those autopsied who were missing tags were two soldiers who were killed during the recapture of the massacre field: Pvt. Delbert J. Johnson (likely Tag #60) was listed as MIA in a failed attack to recapture the field on January 3, 1945. The body of 2nd Lt. Charles E. Sweeney (120 Inf. Rgt.), killed in the recapture of the area, was also recovered from the field and among those missing a tag.

[c]RL= Recovered later than the tagged bodies. A number of victims of the massacre were recovered after the snows receded in February to April 1945; forensic examination of the bodies before being interred determined cause of death.

[d]Pvt. John H. Cobbler died at an aid station in Malmédy the day after sustaining wounds.

TABLE A.2
Americans surviving the encounter
with Kampfgruppe Peiper, Baugnez crossroads,
December 17, 1944

				UNIT B BATTERY, 285TH FAOB	
No.	Rank	Last Name	First Name	Wounds	Notes
1	Sgt.	Ahrens	Kenneth F.	back	Witness for the prosecution Malmédy trial; ran with Sciranko, Valenzi, and Gartska
2	T/5	Appman	Charles F.	unharmed	Escaped with two others; to 291 Eng C. Bn
3	T/5	Billow	Harod W.	unharmed	Ran into café; left west on Hédomont road
4	Pfc.	Butera	Mario	foot	Escaped with Moucheron and Summers
5	T/5	Daub	Carl R.	unharmed	Witness for the prosecution Malmédy trial; escaped with Hardiman
6	Pvt.	Day	Donald W.	leg	Escaped with Robert Smith
7	Cpl.	Flechsig	Theodore G.	shoulder/ leg/ hand	Escaped with Fox
8	Cpl.	Fox	George L.	unharmed	Escaped with Flechsig
9	T/5	Garstka	Paul J.	unharmed	Escaped with Ahrens, Valenzi, and Sciranko
10	Pfc.	Hardiman	Aubrey J.	foot	Escaped with Daub
11	Pfc.	Horn	Harry C.	arms/stomach	Escaped after dark, refuge by Belgian family
12	Pvt.	Kailer	John R.	chest/arm	Ran with Hallman and Frey who were shot
13	T/5	Kingston	Kenneth E.	leg	Witness for the prosecution Malmédy trial; escaped with Reem, Profanchick, and Smith
14	Pfc.	Law	Ralph W.	leg	Crawled to safety after dark
15	1 Lt.	Lary	Virgil P.	leg/foot	Witness for the prosecution Malmédy trial; ran alone to Martin sisters near Malmédy
16	Pfc.	Martin	Paul J.	foot	Escaped with Skoda
17	Pvt.	Mattera	James P.	unharmed	Met up with Paluch and group near Malmédy

(continues)

TABLE A.2 (continued)

No.	Rank	Last Name	First Name	Wounds	Notes
			UNIT B BATTERY, 285TH FAOB		
18	S/Sgt.	Merriken	William H.	back	Escaped to hide with Reding
19	T/5	Moucheron	Carl W.	head	Escaped with Summers and Butera
20	T/5	O'Connell	John A.	jaw/shoulder	Escaped with Butera and Werth
21	T/5	Paluch	Theodore J.	grazing hand wound	Joined up with Johnson and Anderson and after dark
22	Pfc.	Piscatelli	Peter C.	arm	
23	Pvt.	Profanchick	Andrew	unharmed	Escaped with Kingston, Reem, and Smith
24	Pvt.	Reem	William F.	unharmed	Escaped with Kingston, Profanchick, and Smith
25	Cpl.	Sciranko	Michael T.	leg	Escaped with Ahrens, Valenzi, and Gartska
26	T/5	Skoda	Michael J.	shoulder	Escaped with Martin
27	Sgt.	Smith	Charles E.	unharmed	Escaped with Kingston, Reem, and Profanchick
28	Pvt.	Smith	Robert L.	unharmed	Escaped with Donald Day
29	T/5	Summers	William B.	unharmed	Escaped with Moucheron and Butera
30	T/5	Valenzi	Albert M.	legs	Escaped with Ahrens, Gartska, and Sciranko
31	Pvt.	Werth	Bobby	legs	Escaped with O'Connell and Butera
			UNIT 575 AMBULANCE COMPANY		
32	Pvt.	Anderson	Roy B.	foot	Ran with Paluch and Johnson
33	Pvt.	Dobyns	Samuel	arm/ankle	Witness for the prosecution Malmédy trial; escaped with O'Connell and Werth
34	Pfc.	Domitrovich	Stephen J.	unharmed	Ran with large group with Bojarski
35	Pfc.	McKinney	James M.	unharmed	

No.	Rank	Last Name	First Name	Wounds	Notes
32ND RECON. COMPANY, 32ND ARM. RGT.					
36	Cpl.	Bojarski	Edward J.	unharmed	Had been captured before between Ondenval and Thirimont; ran with five other men
37	Sgt.	Lewis	Marvin J.	leg	Had been captured before between Ondenval and Thirimont
38	Cpl.	Wendt	Walter J.	arm	Had been captured before between Ondenval and Thirimont
39	S/Sgt.	Zach	Henry R.	badly wounded; leg/hip	Had been captured before between Ondenval and Thirimont; hid after dark
40	S/Sgt.	Johnson	Herman	arm	Had been captured east of Waimes; joined up with Paluch after dark
518TH MILITARY POLICE BATTALION					
41	Pfc.	Ford	Homer D.	wounded	Witness for the prosecution Malmédy trial; ran alone to Malmédy
UNIT B BATTERY, 285th FAOB					
42	Pvt.	Bower	Donald L.	unharmed	Escaped from front of convoy before the surrender
43	T/5	Conrad	Robert B.	unharmed	Escaped from front of convoy before the surrender
44	Cpl.	Garrett	Eugene	unharmed	Escaped from front of convoy before the surrender
45	Cpl.	Graeff	George E.	unharmed	Escaped from front of convoy before the surrender
46	T/4	Mearig	Robert P.	unharmed	Escaped after first shots fired; wandered for days before being found
47	M/Sgt.	Reding	Charles E.	unharmed	Managed to hide and later escape
48	T/5	Schmitt	Warren R.	unharmed	Escaped from front of convoy before the surrender
49	Pvt.	McKinney	Vestal	wounded	Escaped before massacre
50	Pvt.	Cobbler	John H.	badly wounded	Escaped, died later at Malmédy

TABLE A.3
U.S. POWs who drove vehicles away by
German orders on December 17, 1944,
before the massacre and survived in German captivity

No.	Rank	Last Name	First Name	UNIT
1	T/5	Bacon	Thomas J.	B Bat., 285th FAOB
2	Sgt.	Lacey	Eugene L.	B Bat., 285th FAOB
3	T/5	Logan	Ralph A.	B Bat., 285th FAOB
4	T/5	Lucas	David L.	B Bat., 285th FAOB; died 1945 in German captivity
5	Sgt.	Anderson	Vernon	Rec.Co. 32nd Arm'd Rgt
6	Pvt.	Barron	William E.	Rec.Co. 32nd Arm'd Rgt
7	Cpl.	Cummings	John I.	Rec.Co. 32nd Arm'd Rgt

APPENDIX II

ORDER OF MARCH: 285TH FIELD ARTILLERY OBSERVATION BATTALION AND OTHER ASSOCIATED UNITS*

Vehicle No., December 17, 1944, Baugnez Crossroads

1. Jeep: Cpl. Raymond Lester (driver), Lt. Virgil P. Lary Jr., Capt. Roger Mills
2. Two-and-a-half-ton truck: Sgt. William Merriken, Pvt. Gilbert Pittman (driver), Pfc. Aubrey Hardiman
3. Jeep: Sgt. Kenneth F. Ahrens, T/5 Albert Valenzi, T/5 Michael Skoka, Cpl. Michael Sciranko
4. Two-and-a-half-ton truck: T/5 Carl Daub, T/5 Harold Laufer, Pvt. Bobby Werth, S/Sgt. Donald E. Geisler, Cpl. William H. Moore, Pvt. Louis A. Vario
5. Jeep: Pfc. Donald Bower, Cpl. Theodore Flechsig, T/5 Wilson M. Jones
6. Jeep (B-11): Cpl. Robert B. Conrad, T/5 Eugene H. Garrett
7. Jeep: T/5 Warren R. Schmitt (driver), Cpl. George E. Graeff
8. Two-and-a-half-ton truck: T/5 Vester Wiles, Cpl. David Lucas, Pfc. Harry Horn
9. Two-and-a-half-ton truck: T/4 Robert Mearig, Sgt. Alphonse Stabulis, Pfc. Donald Flack, Pvt. Charles Hall
10. Jeep: 2nd Lt. Solomon Goffman
11. Unknown
12. Jeep: T/5 Kenneth Kingston (driver)
13. Unknown

(continues)

---

*Note that this listing is necessarily incomplete, both with incomplete rosters for many vehicles and others completely unidentified because many occupants did not survive. See map on page 63.

14. Unknown
15. Weapons carrier: M/Sgt. Eugene Lacey, 2nd Lt. Perry Reardon,
    Pvt. Mario Butera (driver)
16. Weapons carrier: T/5 Ralph Logan, Pfc. David Murray
17. Two-and-a-half-ton truck: T/5 Thomas Bacon, Cpl. Carl Stevens,
    T/4 John Rupp
18. Unknown
19. Weapons carrier: Cpl. Joseph Brozowski (driver), Pfc. Paul J. Martin
20. Weapons carrier: Cpl. George Fox, Pfc. Robert Cohen,
    T/5 Carl Moucheron, Pfc. Warren Davis, Pfc. Frederick Davis (driver)
21. Two-and-a-half-ton truck: T/5 William Summers,
    Pvt. Samuel Hallman, T/5 George R. Rosenfeld
22. Weapons carrier: T/5 Charles Appman, Pvt. James Mattera,
    T/5 James Luers, Cpl. Carl Rullman
23. Two-and-a-half-ton truck: Sgt. Alfred Kinsman,
    (B-23) Pfc. Robert Law, Pvt. John R. Kailer
24. Weapons carrier: Pvt. Robert L. Smith, (B-24) T/4 Irwin Sheetz,
    T/4 Thomas F. Watt, T/4 Alan M. Lucas (driver),
    T/5 Theodore J. Paluch
25. Mess: Pfc. Howard Desch; Truck: Pvt. Andrew S. Profanchick,
    T/4 Selmer Leu, S/Sgt. John Osborne, T/5 Charles Breon,
    Pfc. Peter Piscatelli
26. Weapons carrier: Cpl. Harold Billow, T/5 Charles Reding,
    T/5 Charles Haines (driver), T/5 Luke B. Swartz,
    T/5 John A. O'Connell

APPENDIX III

ORDER OF MARCH: KAMPFGRUPPE PEIPER AT THE BAUGNEZ CROSSROADS, DECEMBER 17, 1944[1]

Initial Contact with 285th Field Artillery Observation Battalion

PANZERSPITZE: 6TH PANZER COMPANY

Panzer 611: 1st Lt. Werner Sternebeck*; Cpl. Otto Fischer (radio); Pfc. Michael Mundt (loader); (driver and gunner unknown)

Panzer 623: S/Sgt. August Tonk*; (rest of crew unknown)

9TH PANZER ENGINEER COMPANY

1st Squad—2nd SPW: Cpl. Karl Ohlrogge (squad leader; KIA, Ligneuville); Pfc. Herman Buttner (driver); Pfc. Ferdinand Schimpel (driver); Pfc. Manfred Lussen (medic); Pfc. Heinz Kappermann (radio operator); Pfc. (FNU) Gramlich (rifleman); Pfc. (FNU) Steckner (rifleman); Pfc. (FNU) Steiger (machine gunner)

1ST PLATOON

SPW: Lt. Günther Hering (platoon leader); Pvt. Paul Buth (driver)[†]; Pfc. Fritz Pupkulies (machine gunner); Pfc. (FNU) Späh (messenger); Pfc. Walter Fransee (radio)[†]

(continues)

---

* Sentenced at Malmédy trial

† Testified at the Malmédy trial

[1] This accounting is necessarily approximate based on best available sources. Included here are only vehicles bearing on the central event and not all those passing by before or after the shootings began.

1ST PLATOON (*continued*)

Wirbelwind Flak Panzer IV: M/Sgt. Heinz (Paul) Schröder (KIA, Stoumont, December 21); S/Sgt. (FNU) Hahn (KIA, Stoumont, December 21); Pfc. Adolf Macht (KIA, Stoumont, December 21); Pfc. Heinz Scholz (KIA, Stoumont, December 21)

Platoon leader SPW: S/Sgt. Rudolf Dörr (group leader); Sgt. (FNU) Held (SPW commander); Cpl. (FNU) Höppner (driver); Sgt. Erich Maute (medic)*; Pfc. Rudi Hoppe (gunner)†; Pfc. (FNU) Franke (gunner)

2 SPW: Cpl. Karl Wemmel; Cpl. Hans Elsinger (driver); Pfc. (FNU) Zimmermann; Pfc. (FNU) Radanke; Pfc. Gerhard Süss

Schwimmwagen

Staff Company 1st SS Battalion: Lt. Kurt Kramm†; Pfc. Gerhard Walla†, and S/Sgt. Paul Ochmann*

Between Panzerspitze and Vanguard

9TH PANZER ENGINEER COMPANY, PENAL DISCIPLINARY PLATOON

1st Squad SPW: S/Sgt. Walter Wedeleit (platoon leader); Sgt. Helmuth Haas (squad leader); Sgt. (FNU) Biotta (SPW leader); Pfc. Max Rieder (rifleman)*; Pfc. (FNU) Corzieni (rifleman); Sgt. Willi Chamier (machine gunner)*; Cpl. (FNU) Katscher; Pfc. Arthur Barth

Headquarters Company SPW: 1st Lt. Erich Rumpf (company commander)*; Sgt. Karl Heinz Hagestedt (radio operator); Cpl. Richard Weck (messenger); Sgt. Walter Korf (company troop leader); Cpl. Karl Veil (driver); Cpl. Heinz Heirens (driver); Pfc. (FNU) Frank

---

* Sentenced at Malmédy trial

† Testified at the Malmédy trial

1ST PANZER BATTALION HEADQUARTERS COMPANY

Panther 151: Maj. Werner Poetschke; Cpl. Alexander Kanger (gunner); Paul Müller (driver); (rest of crew unknown)

Panther 152*: Lt. Arndt Fischer*; Pfc. Wolfgang Simon (driver, KIA, Ligneuville); Cpl. Josef Duda (gunner); Pfc. Günter Weseman (loader); Pfc. Günter Ikrat (radio)

1st Panzer Battalion Radio Command SPW: 1st Lt. Rolf Buchheim†; Cpl. Reinhard Maier (driver); S/Sgt. (FNU) Narowtski; (rest of crew unknown)

3RD PANZER ENGINEER COMPANY

Headquarters SPW: 1st Lt. Franz Sievers*; S/Sgt. Willi Schäfer (group leader)*; Cpl. (FNU) Gottschlich (driver); Cpl. (FNU) Schwald (messenger); Cpl. (FNU) Schleipmann (messenger); Cpl. (FNU) Kohlenberger (radio troop leader); Pfc. (FNU) Eberding (radio operator); Sgt. Paul Bär (driver)

2ND PLATOON

Platoon Leader's SPW: Sgt. Max Beutner (platoon leader); Cpl. Ernst Goldschmidt (driver)*; Sgt. Edgar Dickmann (assistant squad leader); Cpl. George Deibert (driver); Cpl. Max Hammerer (messenger)*; Pfc. Gerhardt Schlingmann (messenger); Pfc. Willi Hanke (machine gunner)

1st Squad SPW: Sgt. Friedel Bode (troop leader)*; Cpl. Peppi Meier (driver); Pfc. Josef Aistleitner (machine gunner); Pfc. Friedel Kies (machine gunner)*; Pfc. Ernst Schäffler (assistant driver); Pfc. Herbert Losenski (troop leader); Pfc. Johann Wasenburger (rifleman)*; Pfc. Bertel Schulte (driver)

2nd Squad SPW: Sgt. Sepp Witkowski (group leader); Cpl. (FNU) Gailshofer (driver); Pfc. Hans Toedter (troop leader); Pfc. Heinz Stickel (machine gunner)*; Pfc. Siegfried Jaekel (rifleman)*; Pfc. Harry Ende (rifleman); Pfc. Gerhard Walkowiak (rifleman); Pfc. Emil Hergeth (rifleman); Pfc. Hubert Storch; Pfc. Joachim Hoffmann (driver)*; Pfc. Gustav Neve (assistant driver)*

(continues))

3rd Squad SPW-1: Sgt. Wolfgang Altkrüger (troop leader); Pfc. Gustav
Sprenger (driver)*; Pfc. Günther Mans (assistant driver); Pfc. Marcel
Boltz (machine gunner)*; Pfc. Franz Kissewitz (machine gunner);
Pfc. Manfred Müller (machine gunner); Cpl. Alfred Gerharz (rifleman);
Sgt. Karl Heinz Rose (medic)

3rd Squad SPW-2: Cpl. Willi Biloschetzky (group leader); Cpl. Johannes
Oettinger (driver); Sgt. Hannes Martens (motor sergeant); Cpl. Hans
Schneider (machine gunner); Pfc. Sigmund Köhler (gunner)

Vanguard

7TH PANZER COMPANY

Panzer 734: Sgt. Horst Pilarzek; Sgt. Manfred Thorn (driver);
Pfc. Werner Löhmann (gunner)[†]; Pfc. Heinz Karas (loader);
Pfc. Willi Richter (radio)

Panzer 702: Sgt. Heinz Schrader; (rest of crew unknown)

Panzer 701: Capt. Oskar Klingelhoefer (company commander)*;
Pfc. Engelbert Bock (gunner); Pfc. Peter Mühlbach (loader);
Pfc. Helmut Rentsch (radio); Cpl. Rolf Ehrhardt (driver)[†]

ELEMENTS OF 11TH PANZER GRENADIER COMPANY

SPW—2nd Platoon Leader: M/Sgt. Heinz Hendel (2nd Platoon leader) *;
Cpl. Arvid Freimuth (driver); S/Sgt. Oswald Siegmund (motor
sergeant)*; Cpl. Günther Heinrichs (medic); Pfc. (FNU) Lassen (gunner)

SPW—2nd Platoon: Sgt. Paul Kannen; Pfc. Herbert Stock*;
Pvt. (FNU) Haehnel; Pfc. (FNU) Kumpf; Pfc. (FNU) Sonneborn;
Pvt. (FNU) Schumann

III Battalion and Kampfgruppe Command

III Battalion Command SPW: Capt. Josef Diefenthal*;
Lt. Col. Jochen Peiper*; Cpl. Paul Zwigart (driver)*;
Cpl. Hans Assenmacher (radio)[†]; Cpl. Paul Fackelmayer
(assistant radioman)

---

*Sentenced at Malmédy trial

[†]Testified at the Malmédy trial

SPW of 4th Platoon 11. Panzer Grenadier Company:
Sgt. Gerhard Schumacher (group leader); Cpl. Edmund Tomczak
(assistant group leader)*; SS-Cpl. Heinz Friedrichs (driver)*;
Pfc. Willi Braun (gunner); Pfc. (FNU) Weiss (gunner);
Pvt. (FNU) Konior; Pfc. (FNU) Lidge

7th Panzer Company

Panzer 731: S/Sgt. Hans Siptrott*; Cpl. Oswald Wettengel
(gunner; wounded December 30); Pfc. Georg Fleps (loader)*;
Cpl. Gerhard Schäfer (driver); Pfc. Otto Arnold (radio)
Panzer 723: S/Sgt. Roman Clotten*; Pfc. Hermann Bock (gunner,
wounded December 31, 1944); Pfc. Reinhold Kyriss (loader);
Pfc. (FNU) Kammler (radio); Cpl. Ernst Köwitz (driver)
Panzer 713: Sgt. Erich Dubbert; Pfc. Johannes (Hans) Mulling (gunner);
Pfc. (FNU) Menzel (loader); Pfc. Anton Stephan (radio);
Pfc. Alfons Ziesemann (driver)
Panzer 712: S/Sgt. Werner Koch; Pfc. Heinz Partenheimer (gunner);
Pfc. Werner Reicke (loader)[†]; Pfc. Edward Ahrends (radio);
Cpl. Josepf Ölgötz (driver)
Panzer 711: Lt. Heinz Rehagel (platoon leader)*;
Pfc. Willy Brandt (gunner); Pfc. Hans Joachim Piper (loader)[†];
Pfc. (FNU) Künzel (radio); Pfc. Hans Flächsner (driver)

1ST PANZER COMPANY[2]
Panzer 111: Lt. Hans Hennecke*; Cpl. Kurt Plohmann (gunner)[†];
Cpl. Ernst Köhler (loader)[†]; Pfc. Jakob (Ernst) Rock (radio);
Cpl. Willi Bahnes (driver)

(continues)

---

[2]Panthers of the 1st Company passed the men lying in the field after the
main shooting, but they did not stop: Pz 131 (Thomas), Pz 101 (Kremser),
Pz 102 (Pidun), Pz 121 (Strelow), Pz 124 (Mayer), and Pz 125 (Drechsler).
Pz 115 (Richartz) arrived with Hennecke in Pz 111, although Hennecke
stopped only because of running into one of Rumpf's SPWs. According to a
witness in Pz 125, his crew and that of Pz 125 shot into the Americans lying
in the field while they passed by. (Statement of Josef Zitzeslberger, February
7, 1946, NA, RG-549, Box 34.)

Panzer 114: Sgt. Kurt Briesemeister*; SS-Pvt. Günther Nüchter (loader; wounded La Gleize, December 23); Pfc. Hans Tielicke (gunner); Cpl. Joseph Heß (radio); Sgt. Rudi Storm (driver)

6TH PANZER COMPANY

Panzer 625: S/Sgt. Hubert Huber (wounded December 20, Stoumont)*; Pfc. Martin Krikschas (gunner); Pfc. Karl-Heinz Schröder (loader); Pvt. (FNU) Schreier (radio); Pfc. Josef Rauch (driver)

Panzer 602: Sgt. Walter Wrabetz (wounded December 20); Pfc. Kurt Dethelfs (driver)[†]; (rest of crew unknown)

SS Panzer Regiment 1, Headquarters Staff Company

SIGNALS SECTION[3]

SPW-1: Sgt. Hans Hillig*; Lt. Horst Krause; Cpl. Walter Lehn; Pfc. Kurt Schneider; Pfc. Franz Gässl; Cpl. Horst Kiefer[†]

SPW-2: M/Sgt. Robert Hartmann; Cpl. Günther Zander; Cpl. Walter Landfried[†]; Cpl. Karl-Heinz Eberhard; Pfc. Adolf Weiss[†]

SPW-3: S/Sgt. Heinz Diner; Cpl. Otto Ries (driver); Pfc. (FNU) Panneck; Pfc. Adolf Hoch; Pfc. Hugo Fandrich; Pfc. Rudolf Zimmermann[†]

---

* Sentenced at Malmédy trial

[†] Testified at the Malmédy trial

[3] Members of the three radio SPWs witnessed the shooting of American prisoners in the field by Hubert Huber. See statements of Hillig, Weiss, and Zimmermann in Case 6-24, Box 34 and testimony of Walter Landfried, *U.S. v. Bersin*, op. cit., 808–853, 1363–1366.

APPENDIX IV

MALMÉDY: IN SEARCH OF THE TRUTH

"The past is not dead. It's is not even past . . . "[1]

On July 24, 1945, the government of Belgium erected a simple timbered cross draped with American flags at the site of the Malmédy massacre. That summer day the children of Malmédy, adorned in gaudy red, white, and blue costumes designed to look like the American flag, made a mass pilgrimage through the still-ruined streets of the Belgian town to climb the steep road up to the Baugnez crossroads. In addition to members of the U.S. Army, a fleet of dignitaries were present at the solemn ceremony: the Belgian King and Queen, the mayor, the local gentry, and the press. Nine months later, on April 9, 1946, while the Malmédy trial was still in preparation, six American survivors of the event that had taken place six months before gathered uneasily before the temporary monument: Virgil P. Lary, Kenneth Ahrens, Homer D. Ford, Carl R. Daub, Kenneth E. Kingston, and Samuel Dobyns. In particular, Lary, Ahrens, and Ford grimaced at the camera as if still in pain.

Today, in honor of the victims, at the Baugnez crossroads immediately across from where the Café Bodarwe once existed (and is now rebuilt) stands a permanent monument erected in July 1950. Although the killing field was actually on the other side of the road, the monument itself is a fitting memorial. On the left section of the memorial, appointed with flags flying both the Belgian and U.S. colors, is a small, roofed chapel. To the right of this place is a long, mortared stone wall engraved with the names of eighty-four Americans who died there with another man—the eighty-fifth listed as missing. There is no mention of Madame Adele Bodarwe, who disappeared that day from the café next to the field and whose ultimate fate still remains a mystery.[2]

What really happened at that forlorn crossroads nearly seventy years ago on that Sunday afternoon? After the controversies of the Dachau trial, the Senate investigation, and decades of SS contention and revisionism, can we separate fact from fallacy? And what can be said of the mass of written matter already purporting to give the final word on Malmédy?

In questioning the official U.S. Army accounting engraved in stone, in the 1980s Belgian writer Gerd Cuppens attempted to dissect and discredit the commonly accepted picture.[3] Relative to the physical evidence, Cuppens agreed with the official early U.S. investigation conducted in January 1945: that seventy-one American bodies were discovered within 250 meters of the Café Bodarwe.[4] However, he disagreed that all these men had been killed in the field during the massacre event—or at least with contention that all had been prisoners at the time they were shot.

Indeed, it is true that the name of Pvt. Delbert J. Johnson was on the monument for a time in error. A member of the 526th Armored Infantry Battalion, Johnson was killed later in January during the recapture of the field. The wall also includes a dozen other names who were mortally wounded in the field at Baugnez on December 17, but whose bodies were not recovered with the main group.[5] Some managed to flee after being wounded, only to expire, whereas others were later shot on the run. Beyond that, however, for a time the wall did not include the name of Pfc. John H. Cobbler, who died in a Malmédy aid station the same afternoon he was mortally wounded at Baugnez. Both of these errors have since been corrected.

Although the author agrees that the specific numbers on the wall are not entirely accurate, it is easier to show that Cuppens's subjective opinion is specious. He writes, "84 names have been engraved on the Baugnez memorial. . . . It is sure that many among them have fallen during the battle against the Germans and the bombardment by the tanks."[6] In fact, as disclosed by the numerous American witnesses, only a few Americans were wounded in the approach fire by Kampfgruppe Peiper—T/5 Al Valenzi and Pfc. Carl Stevens were both wounded by shrapnel. None were killed.[7]

Moreover, Cuppens charged that Raymond Heitmann and Cecil Cash of the 197th AAA AW Battalion were killed on December 19, and

Sgt. Benjamin Lindt and Pfc. Elmer Wald of the 200th FA Battalion were killed on December 16. In fact, solid evidence shows that Heitmann and Cash were executed in the ditch near the Bagatelle intersection during the approach of Kampfgruppe Peiper (as witnessed by Peter Lentz) and that the German advance caught Wald and Lindt and shot both in the field where their bodies were recovered (Tags #19 and #41, respectively). As if to underscore this fact, Elmer Wald's hands were frozen over his head in death when photographed in the field before being removed for autopsy.

Many of those who died in the field had multiple wounds, but the cause of death for forty-one victims was a close-range shot to the head, and six died from a severe blow to the skull.[8]

How many men survived the massacre? The author must first point out that seven prisoners escaped the violence at Baugnez by volunteering to drive trucks for the Germans.[9] Beyond these, exactly 49 men managed to escape the clash with the Kampfgruppe Peiper and survived.[10] Of these, six men managed to dash away from the road as Sternebeck's spearhead approached: Bower, Conrad, Garrett, Graeff, Schmitt, and Vestal McKinney. Each one of the remaining 43 men who escaped from the massacre field proper were subjected to massed gunfire, and all but sixteen were wounded. The bodies of others who were not so lucky shielded most of the unharmed. A careful count reveals that a total of 127 men were present in the massacre field before the shooting took place. The total number involved in the overall event numbered 140. The sources for these numbers and the individual dispositions is given in detailed tables in the appendices.

In terms of the scenarios as to what happened at Baugnez that fateful day of December 17, 1944, I briefly summarize the various theories earlier authors have enunciated, emphasizing those that appear to have most credence.

In 1971 British author Charles Whiting composed *Massacre at Malmédy: The Story of Jochen Peiper's Battle Group, Ardennes, December, 1944*, an early account, albeit with a cavalier treatment of sources.[11] Although the popular book captured the emotional atmosphere of the controversial event, it made no attempt at serious scholarship. Indeed, so fascinated was Whiting by his access to Jochen Peiper in 1969 that the author was biased by selective information

that his subject provided. Whiting uncritically repeated several apoc-
ryphal stories that remain part of the legend of Jochen Peiper. That
said, it is clear that Whiting discerned that a mass shooting had indeed taken place at Baugnez. When the author spoke with Whiting in
2001, he related how his earlier discussion with Georg Fleps left him
with the impression that he had indeed fired at Baugnez and was still
mired in guilt from the event.

The earliest explanation of what happened at Baugnez from the
Waffen SS perspective came from SS-Gen. Paul Hausser while Peiper
still moldered in prison. A terse comment in his book, *Waffen SS im
Einsatz*, adroitly avoided the tangle of troubling details and simply
termed Malmédy a confusing episode—an artifact of the speed and ferocity of the modern battlefield:

> This incident took at most 12 minutes. Just the speed of the events
> during high tension on both sides explains the difficulty to clearly
> reconstruct the sequence of events and, beyond that, to explain any
> question of guilt.[12]

Yet confusion was not the only explanation. At about the same
time semi-official Waffen SS "theories" emerged for the sordid events.
Dietrich Ziemssen first espoused these scenarios in a work designed
to disparage the Malmédy trial so as to save Peiper and others condemned to death from being hanged as well as to aid the release of
those otherwise still held at Landsberg Prison.[13] In that slim volume
an early hypothesis was put forward: that Poetschke's vanguard mistook the American prisoners standing at the crossroads for combatants and shot them down.

> It has been established that between the lead panzer element,
> which consisted of only two panzers, and the panzers of the
> advance guard, there was a large interval, and that this distance
> could result in the lead vehicles in the advance guard, which were
> advancing in battle readiness, mistaking these American soldiers at
> the road intersection as being another enemy column, causing the
> lead panzers of the advance guard to open fire at a distance,
> resulting in new losses.[14]

The same hypothesis was subsequently incorporated into the divisional history for the Leibstandarte Adolf Hitler. Later still, these suppositions were repackaged with additional pseudo-exculpatory material assembled by the chronicler for the SS panzer division.[15] Yet in reviewing this theory, one must realize that in composing it, none of the firsthand American testimony from survivors was reviewed. That would quickly reveal that almost all survivors described the fatal hail of machine gunfire as having come from *stationary* armored vehicles at a distance of twenty to thirty yards fired at the Americans standing in the field. Nor are the carefully composed period maps of the massacre scene consistent with fire taking place from a distance. They revealed instead a mass of tightly grouped bodies deliberately shot down.

Arguably, the most evenhanded detailed study of the Malmédy massacre has come from the scholarly investigation by Dr. James Weingartner, a history professor at Southern Illinois University. Persuasively, Weingartner also recounted the often-invoked alibi that "shifting and jostling" American prisoners or even an American officer's command to "Standfast!" "caused a nervous young SS trooper to fire with his pistol resulting in panic among the American ranks and the opening of massed automatic weapons fire by the Germans."

> But this scenario is difficult to reconcile with certain facts. Several armored vehicles had been assembled along the road with their guns trained on the prisoners. It seems unlikely that potential magnitude of firepower would have been gathered unless it had been decided to shoot the Americans. But the most telling circumstance mitigating against the escape hypothesis is that none of the defendants or the defense witnesses attempted to argue that the prisoners had been shot while they were attempting to escape.[16]

And what of Ziemssen's Waffen SS scenario—composed in the early 1950s—that the Americans assembled at the crossroads were mistaken for combatants and were shot down "by succeeding elements of Kampfgruppe Peiper roaring down the road?"

> This is even less likely than the escape scenario. . . . The American survivors testified unequivocally that the German fire had come

from armored vehicles *parked* along the road, not traveling upon it; and it is clear, further, that at no time were the prisoners unguarded. The range at which the shooting had taken place, moreover was short—so short that the prisoners could not have been mistaken for combatants.

To Weingartner, that there had been a war crime at Baugnez was beyond question:

Neither allegation of attempted escape or mix-up, even if true, could excuse the fact that subsequent to the mowing down of the prisoners, groups of SS troopers walked through the field shooting those Americans showing signs of life.

The larger question for Weingartner was not whether there had been an affront to the laws of war at Malmédy, but rather how the war crime came to pass. Had there been superior orders to take no prisoners? That was not completely clear: If such orders existed, they were likely not written down. But relative to personal responsibility for the shooting, Weingartner came to the same conclusion as did the author: Werner Poetshcke had them killed as a matter of expediency.[17]

Indeed, the head of the 2nd Panzer Company, SS-1st Lt. Friedrich Christ, lent credence to this scenario in an early interrogation by Dwight Fanton, well before accusations of irregularities at Schwäbisch Hall. He admitted that murder may have occurred at Baugnez:

FANTON: "What would you think of soldiers and commanders who perpetrated such atrocities?"

CHRIST: "I served for six years at the front. I was in so many situations, in Poland and Russia that it would be quite easily possible that an individual, whether be an enlisted man, NCO or officer could be led to do something like this if a very important goal depended on this factor [surprise and speed]. . . ."

FANTON: "In other words you are telling me that if you were to preserve the element of surprise, that if you had to use all your personnel to sustain the advance, murder of prisoners would be justified?"

CHRIST: "It is quite possible."[18]

One would think that with such levelheaded analysis that the picture would be complete. Yet the old Waffen SS alibis for what happened at Malmédy have stubbornly resisted rectification. Indeed, so ensconced are these legends that even the most thorough research seems unlikely to still the apologist machinery. A quasi-historical evaluation of the event in Germany's official publication of the Order of the Knight's Cross, the OdR, is a recent example.[19]

Gerd Cuppens's book, Massacre a Malmédy? is another clear illustration. Whereas claiming newfound objectivity in the 1980s, Cuppens—a Belgian—instead regurgitated the retold story of SS sympathizers: The Americans were fired upon three separate times in the meeting engagements with the lagging elements of Kampfgruppe Peiper, leading to a large number of unfortunate casualties made worse by the American movements while they were captive.[20] Yet Cuppens failed to notice that the extensive testimony uniformly recorded only two Americans wounded in the short meeting engagement: Carl Stevens and Albert Valenzi. There were no other casualties until three others (Solomon Goffmann, Frederick Clark, and Peter Phillips) were shot on the walk back to the crossroads for failing to hold their hands up high enough after surrender, or protesting the seizure of personal property.

Cuppens also failed to acknowledge the testimony of Belgian witness Peter Lentz, who saw Heitmann and Cash gunned down in cold blood on the road between Baugnez and the Bagatelle before the main shooting. Moreover, Lt. Lary and Capt. Mills were also shot at during this time when the prisoners were being rounded up, but avoided being hit. Still, other than the wounding of Stevens and Valenzi in the first meeting engagement, these later killings hardly fit into the fanciful Waffen SS revisionist picture of multiple combats, with the Americans suffering many casualties. And there are the other eighty-odd dead Americans who must be somehow explained away who were found shot in a tangle of bodies in the field south of the Baugnez café.

Cuppens made much out of the fact that many details within the American testimony revealed differences, which, to him, called into question the veracity of all eyewitness accounts. One point of disagreement, for instance, was the type of vehicle from which the first shots were fired. Yet any serious inquiry into eyewitness reliability in crime-scene events will reveal that most often potential victims focus on a crime weapon, thus naturally superseding attention to other details of the shooter.[21] Consequently, it is not at all surprising that although the witnesses could not always agree on the vehicle from which the firing was made, they almost always agreed on the weapon initially used: a pistol firing two or more shots. They also are unanimous in what happened next: a machine gun or machine guns, mostly unobserved, as the witnesses instinctively threw themselves onto the ground to avoid the lethal spray of bullets.

In the author's evaluation of the Malmédy shooting, greater weight was given to facts supported by multiple witnesses—a method borne out by forensic crime scene eyewitness research.[22] Generally, one witness alerts one to possibility, two unrelated witnesses provides substantiation, and three or more witnesses makes the case persuasive. This method, applied both to the mass of American testimony and the less reliable confessions of SS men from Schwäbisch Hall, paints a compelling picture of what really happened that December day in 1944.

Patrick Agte, in his hagiography of Jochen Peiper, skirted the thorny issue of what transpired at the crossroads in convenient ways. His scenario incorporated the time-tested alibis used by Ziemssen, Tiemann, and Cuppens before him. Yet he went even further: Within his account, the American prisoners (whose testimony was hardly considered) were to blame for what befell them after Sternebeck's *Spitze* passed by. "The prisoners moved south of the Café Bodarwe in an undisciplined manner," he wrote. "As a result, they were not clearly identified by the following tanks and SPWs as unmistakable POWs."[23]

Although American discipline may have not been entirely ruly, the SS guards of the convoy are the ones who directed the mass of Americans into the field after Peiper and Diefenthal arrived with the armored vanguard. Indeed, Peiper and Diefenthal passed by with Fischer and his Panther in the lead as well as several tanks of the 7th Panzer Company just behind that. Even described by Peiper, none of these events had killed Americans when he arrived on the scene, although many pretended to be dead by the roadside, seeking the possibility to escape.

Clearly, the Americans who were killed at the crossroads were not shot by a second meeting engagement with the armored vanguard but rather by the guards in the halted halftracks of the 3rd and 9th Panzer Engineer Companies that remained behind. Hans Siptrott merely happened into the melee while the SS engineers were preparing the execution detail. Even Agte admits that Georg Fleps fired two shots into the American prisoners, as Hans Siptrott, who was in charge of the tank, related this to him (and the author). "The two pistol shots which Georg Fleps fired from the tank were a reaction to an attempt by a group of Americans to escape to a nearby woods."[24] To Agte, any who ran made the shooting of the American prisoners justifiable, legal, and not a war crime.

Relative to modern accounts, John Bauserman's work *The Malmédy Massacre* and also Michael Reynolds's chapter on the Malmédy massacre in *The Devil's Adjutant* remain the most objective and unbiased assessments.[25] Bauserman's book, using both German and American sources in an innovative investigative method, emphasizes the same facts presented here. There was indeed a shooting and a war crime, and it was neither a meeting engagement nor a "mix up." Moreover, Bauserman was the first author to fathom the approximate sequence of events—both American and German—that led to the shooting. Although Baugnez was resolved as a battlefield incident and does not appear to have been planned, once the prisoners were assembled, the massacre seems to have become a deliberate shooting likely brought on by battlefield expediency within the fast-moving German battle group.

Michael Reynolds's dissection of Peiper's combat operations in the Ardennes covers essentially the same theories and reaches similar conclusions.[26] Reynolds debunks the old "two engagement" hypothesis that Peiper's adjutant, Hans Gruhle, advanced in the Leibstandarte divisional history.[27] This story can be dismissed by the overwhelming mass of American testimony, which showed the firing came not from tanks and halftracks barreling ahead toward the crossroads, but rather from a series of halftracks and tanks parked across from the U.S. Army GIs standing in the field. Then, too, Reynolds exposes the preposterous embellishment of the story, as Dr. Franz Uhle-Wettler purported and author Trevor Dupuy later adopted, that the Americans, having been left behind by Sternebeck, recovered their arms to fire on the German halftracks and tanks that followed.[28] "Beyond belief," Reynolds rightly concludes.

Finally, Reynolds noted, as did this author, that the attempt at escape by Robert Mearig, two comrades, and Samuel Dobyns just as shots were fired may have helped to precipitate the massacre—or at least the ill-advised pistol shots admitted by Georg Fleps that preceded massed machine gunfire. The other possibility, for Reynolds—and the most likely for this author—is that a deliberate battlefield decision was made to execute the prisoners. This likely resulted from Peiper's orders for maximum speed combined with the difficulty of evacuating the large number of GIs without a loss to the striking power of the spearhead.

What can be added to the above? As has been shown in the author's own research, it is quite true that a small group of three to four Americans attempted to flee the scene just as the first shots were fired. However much this behavior might complicate matters, the fact remains that the SS men on the halftracks in front of the Americans were siting machine guns and preparing ammunition for the anticipated shooting to come. The execution detail was in its final stages—made crystal clear by the earlier failed attempt to train a halftrack-mounted 7.5-cm howitzer on the Americans to aid in their liquidation.[29] Over a dozen American witnesses remembered how the enemy had strenuously endeavored to train the big gun on the men standing in the field. Others watched as machine guns were mounted on the side of the SPWs so their muzzles could be trained on the increasingly nervous crowd. Although charges of "poor military discipline" might be leveled, those few who ran were perceptive enough to recognize a fatal threat.[30] Two survived.

Two additional facts obliterate justification for Peiper's men's behavior at the Baugnez crossroads. First there is the fact that eighty men were shot down in addition to those few who tried to escape. Moreover, the bodies of some of these men were found frozen a month later, many with their hands still raised over their heads in the universal posture of surrender. The mass of Americans were brutally shot down by automatic weapons fire while massed in the field. Except for a few at the rear of the group, none of the others were moving or attempting to escape. Surely a single accidental trigger-happy pistol and machine gun would not fell eighty men and leave none wounded to be taken prisoner. And if the mass of Americans had all attempted to run, more than half the bodies would not have been found in a dense tangle of bunched-up corpses twenty yards from the road and compressed in an ellipse of death barely forty yards wide.

Although a number of men were found away from the main mass of the bodies, by far the most frequent cause of death—as determined by autopsy—was from a point-blank shot to the head. These were largely men who lay in the field for an hour after the shooting before the attempt to escape after one survivor yelled, "Let's go!" German machine guns from Kurt Briesemeister's Panther Nr. 114 fired once more upon those who ran at that time. That tank had remained behind at the crossroads to repair track damage. It also appears that several others ran from the Café Bodarwe after it was set aflame and were among those found shot down west of that building.

Three U.S. Army surgeons performed detailed autopsies on the dead men in the field in January 1945, revealing that many had been executed by shots to the head or neck—shots so close that the autopsies revealed powder burns. To shoot a mass of unarmed prisoners must generally be considered a war crime. However, to shoot down a mass of prisoners and then move through the field to execute any surviving the first onslaught—and not take these prisoners—must be considered a war crime under every rational classification.

As to the genesis of the SS decision to execute the prisoners, the most likely explanation is one of battlefield expediency. Then, too, there is the moribund ethos in Kampfgruppe Peiper. In Russia these men had long practiced a way of battle that had little value for enemy life. As all accounts agree, Peiper arrived on the scene with the prisoners being collected, but he was in a terrible hurry to attempt to capture the American headquarters just ahead in Ligneuville. To test Peiper's patience, there were also lollygagging SS troopers looting the American convoy and several broken down German armored vehicles. Peiper's armor had little infantry to spare to guard prisoners, and he made sure all under him knew that no delay would be tolerated. Peiper met Werner Poetschke at the crossroads and conferred in a heated encounter.

Their auspicious meeting took place moments before Peiper roared off behind the Mk V Panther of Arndt Fischer. In his wake he left the mass of American prisoners standing with raised hands. Minutes later they were shot.[31] Thus, Poetschke, on his own initiative, may have been the one who ordered the prisoners liquidated. There was also further aggravation for him—namely, the frustrating refusal from the Americans to drive the abandoned GMC trucks for the German column. The orders to shoot the Americans then moved from Poetschke to Max Beutner and Erich Rumpf, who were assigned to the 3rd and 9th Panzer Engineer Companies, respectively, and commanded the gun crews who were present on the armored halftracks there.

However, the possibility cannot be ruled out that Peiper himself ordered Poetschke to have the Americans shot before he departed the crossroads. Whereas many SS accounts lay the blame on ordering the shooting at the feet of Werner Poetschke—conveniently deceased in Hungary in 1945—it remains significant that *before* being brought to Schwäbisch Hall, Paul Zwigart, the driver in Diefenthal and Peiper's command halftrack, had something more to add.

In a POW camp in Ebensee, Austria, in summer 1945 Zwigart confided to a doctor with the 7th Panzer Company that the orders for the shooting had come from Peiper himself.[32] The truth will likely never be known. The author made several attempts to speak with Hans Assenmacher and examine the correspondence of Paul Fackelmeyer, who were also in the same vehicle. Not surprisingly, neither endeavor was successful. Similarly, although the author spoke to Paul Zwigart, a condition placed on the interview was that nothing about the crossroads nor the "jeep incident" would be discussed. Zwigart has never talked about the crossroads. The secret remains—but so does the curiosity from the outside world. "I will take Malmédy to my grave," lamented Manfred Thorn, the young SS tank driver just ahead of Hans Siptrott, "and it still won't have died."[33]

In several helpful interviews with the author spanning a decade, Thorn, the driver in Panzer Nr. 734, maintained that although he passed the surrendered Americans at the crossroads at about 1 P.M., he was just far enough ahead not to see the shooting, but he soon learned of it:

I drove to the intersection. I pulled in approximately along side the café and beyond, Americans were just sitting on their vehicles on the road to Hédomont. I noticed that six or more meters from me, a jeep was standing facing the road to Engelsdorf [Ligneuville]. Three or four Americans were on the jeep. We ordered the Americans on the trucks to surrender and dismount their trucks. Suddenly Poetschke arrived in a Panther. He came up just behind my tank. He stopped just on my right. We were all facing the café at the intersection. I could see jeeps and trucks coming and going in both directions. Poetschke pushed between with his Panther. A minute or two before Poetschke arrived, the American prisoners dismounted their trucks and were lined up alongside the café. The Americans assembled just to the south of the café. I stuck my head out of the driver's hatch. Poetschke addressed me from his tank. "Drive at once to Engelsdorf [Ligneuville] and make contact with the Spitze of Sternebeck. . . . " We rode along towards Engelsdorf. Some the American vehicles still had their engines running. SPWs passed by me. Vehicles were everywhere. . . . At the stone quarry, I had track trouble and then a Panther came by me. Must have been Fischer. I heard Siptrott coming up behind me. He told me about Fleps shooting at the crossroads. Why had he fired? He said, "Now, we've got these guys shot!"[34]

As inappropriate as SS apologists' dismissive attitude toward the Baugnez atrocity might be, the scenario the U.S. Army prosecutors painted at Dachau was not so much in error as misguided. Looking to heap more scorn on the Kampfgruppe Peiper, they entertained far-fetched scenarios beyond Baugnez—conjuring up a mass killing at La Gleize that never happened. Furthermore, all that made less of the legitimate criminal acts against Belgian civilians at places such as Stavelot, Parfondruy, and Wanne as well as of smaller-scale killings of American soldiers at Wereth, Honsfeld, Ligneuville, Stoumont, and Petit Thier.

Perhaps the greatest failing of the Malmédy investigation and trial was that of the prosecution, in using questionable methods and over-reaching its claims of war crimes, instead damaged its own credibility not only during the closing stages of the trial but, more importantly, within the judgment of history. The legacy of that failing, instead, was they obfuscated the Waffen SS forces' legitimate guilt for war crimes at Baugnez on December 17, 1944. Unfortunately, that miscarriage of the truth today still haunts both the memory of those who lived and died there as well as the historical record itself.

Certainly there can be no humane wars—Peiper himself reminded his judges that none "are fought with kid gloves."[35]

> Would you see a moral difference between setting house on fire with a flame thrower from a distance of 50 meters . . . or massacring civilians with submachine guns from a distance of 50 meters or from a height of 50 meters from a helicopter? It is really nothing but hypocrisy to bless war and condemn its methods.[*36]

Peiper's lament notwithstanding, the horror of deliberate and callous war crimes, whether they be Baugnez or My Lai, remain highly disturbing episodes in the already-sad human experience of modern war. Indeed, in the aftermath of the Malmédy massacre a written order from the headquarters of the 26th Division's 328th Infantry Regiment on December 21, 1944, advised, "No SS troops or paratroopers will be taken prisoner but will be shot on sight." Compliance with the order is unknown, but it necessarily made for greater danger for surrendering SS men after December 17, 1944. Indeed, green soldiers of the 11th Armored Division seem to have shot some sixty surrendered German soldiers in Chenogne, Belgium, on New Year's Day 1945. The guilty were never punished, although witnesses have come forth since the war. At the time the U.S. Army looked to sweep all incidents under the rug. As Gen. George Patton wrote on January 4, 1945, "The 11th Armored is really green. . . . There are also some unfortunate incidents in the shooting of prisoners. I hope we can conceal this."[37]

As vilified as the Nazis have been over the last century, it is important to understand that such incidents are not confined to any one culture, people, or government. The key difference for the Waffen SS in World War II was that whereas other armies saw such atrocities as an unfortunate result of the madness of war, the most fanatic of the SS—as epitomized by some within Peiper's command—earnestly invoked the nihilist spirit of Genghis Khan. They saw ruthlessness and terror as a dark strength to be embraced and exploited. Still, the raw reality remains. "The ways of today's warfare are so monstrous," wrote Pierre Boissier, "that the soldier is put into a world which does not have a common standard with any other world."[38]

NOTES

Prologue

1. In the year 648 Saint Remacle had founded two abbeys in the Ardennes, one in nearby Stavelot and the other at Malmédy's city center. Later, in the eighteenth century, two towering gothic cathedrals were constructed, and Malmédy became a magnet for economic trade. In 1815, after Wellington's victory on the plains of Waterloo, in deference to the Prussian aid in evicting Napoleon, the town was given over to Germany. However, Germany's loss in World War I saw the region returned to Belgium. Even today, the prevalent cultural confusion of the region and its people is both characteristic and part of its charm.

2. "Subject: Hitler Youth, 15 December 1944," First Army Interrogation Center Bulletin #1, National Archives (NA), Record Group (RG)-407, 101.2.13, U.S. First Army G-2 Records, Box 1497.

3. Author's interview with Armand Reutsch, Malmédy, Belgium, October 23, 1995.

4. Author's interviews with William Merriken, July 4 and September 22, 1995. Also, statement of William H. Merriken, February 1, 1945, NA, RG-549, Entry 143, Case 6–24, Box 42. These extensive records at the National Archives from the Malmédy investigation and trial ("War Crimes Cases Tried," Malmédy, *United States vs. Valentin Bersin, et al.*, Case 6–24) are henceforth referred to as *U.S. vs. Bersin*, RG-549, Case 6–24. Also, "My Personal Story, by Bill Merriken," Charles B. MacDonald Papers, U.S. Army Military History Institute (USa.m.HI), Box 7.

5. For "almost like a lowing . . ." and "I'm from Lancaster County . . ." (below), C. M. Stephan interview with James P. Mattera, "Murder at Malmédy," *Army*, December 1981, 34.

6. For "will cross the Siegfried line . . . ," see Testimony of Homer D. Ford, taken at Hq First U.S. Army, December 17, 1930, by Lt. Col. Alvin B. Welsch, National Archives, RG-153, Entry 56, Case 6–24, Box 77. Corroboration of the German rebuke to those in the field is also given in testimony of Robert J. Mearig, October 10, 1945, RG-549, Box 30, and interview of Gene Garrett, 285th FAOB, November 1987, courtesy of William Cavanagh.

7. Account of Walter Wendt, 3rd Armored Division from letter to author, December 4, 1998. Also letter to John Bauserman, dated March 8, 1988. Wendt was lying among the survivors on the ground while the mercy shots were administered. The native of Wisconsin was of German descent and could understand the language.

8. Max Schwitzgold was a young Jewish soldier whom Merriken knew from the supply section. Interview with Merriken, July 4, 1995.

9. The unsurfaced road at which Merriken encountered the German soldier led to the tiny hamlet of Hédomont two kilometers to the northwest. The house just west of the café where he saw Americans beating on the door was that of Henri Lejoly (Nr. 7). To see the detailed map from the trial proceedings, "Exhibit A, Testimony of Kenneth E. Kingston, October 8, 1945, WCB File 6–24, NA, RG-549, Case 6–24, Box 30.

10. Gustav Berle, "Notes from Gommorrah," unpublished manuscript provided to author. Interview with Joe Thiele (205th CIC), February 9, 1997, and letter of March 4, 1997.

11. "Report of the Supreme Headquarters Allied Expeditionary Force Court of Inquiry re Shooting of Allied Prisoners of War near Malmédy, Belgium," NA, RG-331, SHAEF Records, Entry 56, Box 127.

Chapter 1

1. The Ardennes forest was named after a pagan goddess Arduinna. Others claimed the "Forest of Arden" as the identified location of Shakespeare's *As You Like It*, act V, scene 1.

2. Charles B. MacDonald, "The Neglected Ardennes," *Military Review* 43, no. 4 (April 1963): 74–89; "In the Ardennes Country: A Military Survey of the Battleground," Incl. 2 to VII Corps G-2 Periodic Report 8, Eisenhower Library, *Bitter Woods Papers*, Abilene, KS, Box 17.

3. Hitler's fateful decision was recorded in the personal notes taken by German air force general, Werner Kreipe: "Persönliches Kriegstagebuch des General der Flieger Kreipe," NA, RG-238, Foreign Military Studies, MS# P-069.

4. "Hitler couldn't understand why the west didn't take the chance to fight against the East," recalled Hitler's adjutant, Otto Günsche, "He knew the East was the most dangerous military enemy. . . . He could have won against the Russians if the West held off attacking into Germany. . . . Hitler couldn't understand why the West helped Jewish communism. Guderian saw the realism of the front, but Hitler saw beyond." Interview with Otto Günsche, October 16, 1963, John Toland Papers, "The Last Hundred Days," Library of Congress (LOC), Box 16.

5. For the day-to-day experiences of American infantry deployed in the Ardennes in autumn 1944, see Charles B. MacDonald, *Company Commander*, Infantry Journal Press, 1947.

6. Tabulation from original records: NA, RG-338, T-311, Roll 18, Frames 210020–210025; field tank strengths taken from "Schw. Waffen Pz. Division,

10.12.1944" as supplemented by OB West maps for the period: BA-MA, Freiburg, Bundesarchiv. RH 2 W/608 for December 17, 1944.

7. David Eisenhower, *Eisenhower at War, 1943–1945* (New York: Vintage Books, 1987), 556.

8. John S. D. Eisenhower, *The Bitter Woods: The Battle of the Bulge* (New York: DaCapo Press, 1969), 213–214.

9. The conversion of Ziegenberg Castle and the surrounding zone into Hitler's *Adlerhorst* command center was fantastically resource intensive: thirty-eight thousand cubic meters of concrete. For camouflage workers planted two thousand trees and thirty-three thousand shrubs, and they seeded hundreds of acres of lawns, with farmhouses displayed for aerial eyes. When the command center was first built in 1939, Hitler scoffed at its extravagance, saying it made him look like a *"pferdeliebenden Adeligen"*—a horse-loving nobleman. Franz W. Seidler and Dieter Zeigert, *Hitler's Secret Headquarters: The Fuhrer's Wartime Bases from the Invasion of France to the Berlin Bunker* (London: Greenhill Books, 2004), 46–57.

10. "Wilhelm Viebig," NA, RG-338, Records of the MIS 6824 Detailed Interrogation Center, Boxes 88–92, MIS/Y X/156, March 20, 1945. Viebig was not inspired by the infantry assigned to him. Jokes were making the officers' rounds that the Volksgrenadier might as well be called the *"Metalsturm*: lead bones, gold teeth and silver hair."

11. For a recollection of Hitler's concluding remarks: Heinrich Springer interview, May 19, 1997. Springer was the Waffen SS adjutant in Fldm. Walther Model's Army Group B during the Ardennes operation.

12. Ibid.

13. "When I was received on 14 December 1944 by Division Commander, SS-Brig. Gen. Mohnke, he told me that he was present at the meeting with the Führer and that on his orders, it had to be fought with special brutality. . . . 'It has to be fought without humane inhibitions and one should remember the victims of the bombing terror.'" Statement of Jochen Peiper, March 21, 1946, NA, RG-549, Case 6–24, Box 6.

14. The statement of Josef "Sepp" Dietrich, March 22, 1946, NA, RG-549, Box 33.

15. "As long as I have the honor of leading the struggle at the head of the Reich," Hitler told SS men in a holiday festival in Metz, "it is also an honor for you, who bear my name, to be at the forefront of the struggle!" Max Domarus, *Hitler Speeches and Proclamations*, vol. 3 (Bolchazy: Carducci Publications), 2173.

16. Ian Sayer and Douglas Botting, *Hitler's Last General: The Case Against Wilhelm Mohnke* (London: Transworld Publishers, 1989), 32–112.

17. Ernst Klee and Willi Dreßen, *Gott mit uns: Der deutsche Vernichtungskrieg im Osten 1939–1945* (Berlin: Frankfurt am Main, S. Fischer Verlag, 1989), 155–157.

18. "Sometimes you cannot catch up in weeks with what you failed to do, or missed doing, in three or four hours. A reconnaissance unit, or a small motorized unit, or an assault gun brigade, or a panzer battalion is sometimes able to cover in three or four hours 20 to 40 decisive kilometers which afterwards could not be gained in six weeks of battle." Hitler's speech to his generals on December 28, 1944, D. S. Parker, ed., *The Battle of the Bulge: The German View: Perspectives from Hitler's High Command* (London: Greenhill Books, 1999), 213–227.

19. Percy E. Schramm, "The Attack Orders of the Three Armies Taking Part in the Ardennes Offensive," Appendix 2; "Preparations for the German Ardennes Offensive," NA, RG-338, FMS, MS # A-862.

20. Volker Riess, *Die Anfänge der Vernichtung 'lebensunwerten Lebens' in den Reichsgauen Danzig-Westpreussen und Wartheland 1939/40* (Berlin: Frankfurt am Main, Peter Lang, 1995,) 304–308. Mass carbon monoxide gassing of patients from the Tiegenhof asylum had begun three weeks earlier in December 1939 in a sealed bunker known as Fortress VII. These were among the earliest experiments within the Nazi regime using poison gas technology. Peiper's admission of his presence at this infamous event was first elicited in the Malmédy trial: "Cross examination of Joachim Peiper," June 22, 1946, *United States vs. Valentine Bersin et al.*, Dachau, 1946 (hereafter *U.S. v. Bersin*), NA, RG-153, Roll 3, Frames 189–190. For the executions near Bromberg in 1939: "Vernehmung von Col. Joachim Peiper," Landsberg/Lech, April 17, 1947, NA, RG-238, M-1019, Roll 52, Frames 185–189. After witnessing the executions, Himmler told those present he "regrets it, but it must be done."

21. For an in-depth discussion of this topic, see Jens Westemeier, *Joachim Peiper, Biography of Himmler's SS Commander* (Atlgen, PA: Schiffer Books, 2007).

22. Hitler was a devoted apostle of Friedrich Wilhelm Nietzsche (1844–1900).

23. For "Hard as steel . . ." and "We have a right to be harsh . . . ," see "*Unsere Härte*," *SS Leithefte* 9, 1943, pp. 1–3, NA, RG-242, T-611, Non-Biographic Material Microfilmed at the Berlin Document Center (BDC) by the University of Nebraska, Roll 44.

24. International Military Tribunal, "Trial of Major War Criminals: Testimony of Paul Hausser," Nuremberg, August 5–6, 1946, vol. 20, p. 432. After the war it came to the attention of the Nuremberg International Military Tri-

bunal that the Russian villages of Staroverovka, Stanitschnoje, and Jefremovka were burned to the ground and all inhabitants were shot. Although the testimony could not be emphatically linked to the Leibstandarte, the circumstantial evidence was plenty incriminating. Peiper had been in Stanitschnoje and Jefremovka, and he received a battlefield commendation for his actions there.

25. Westemeier, op. cit., 137-146.

26. Oswald Siegmund, *Meine Ehre heisst Treue: Von der Leibstandarte ins Landsberger Kriegsverbrechergefängnis* (Essen, 1992), 54.

27. In a taped interview on December 27, 2004, Waffen SS veteran Fritz Kosmehl related that even before Peiper joined the tank regiment, he and the SPW battalion were widely known to burn villages. Therein their moniker: the *Lötlampen Abteilung*—the "Blowtorch Battalion."

28. Jochen Peiper to Charles Whiting in 1969, related to author in interview in August 2001.

29. Jochen Peiper, "Kommentar zum Buch 'Massacre at Malmédy von Charles Whiting," September 1971. Provided to author by James Weingartner.

30. Extended handwritten statement of Erich Rumpf, no date, NA, RG-549, Case 6-24, Box 32.

31. Statement of Kurt Kramm, March 16, 1946, NA, RG-549, Case 6-24, Box 32

32. Peiper's testimony at Dachau, June 21, 1946, *U.S. vs. Bersin*, RG-153, Case 6-24, 1903.

33. Statement of Sepp Dietrich, March 22, 1946, NA, RG-549, Case 6-24, Box 33.

34. Statement of Jochen Peiper, March 21, 1946. NA, RG-549, Case 6-24, Box 6.

35. *U.S. vs. Bersin*, 1903-1904. In response to the question, "Did he explain to you what he meant by fighting fanatically?" Peiper responded, "He did not especially explain that, but what the expression meant was no concern for one's person and material."

36. Statement of Jochen Peiper, March 21, 1946, op. cit.

37. "Hold the reins loose," Fritz Krämer implored. "The main point was to reach the Meuse irrespective of flanks; this was the same principle we employed in the French campaign in 1940." Robert E. Merriam, *Dark December* (Chicago: Ziff-Davis, 1947), 105.

38. Affidavit of Oskar Klingelhoefer, March 18, 1946, NA, RG-549, Case 6-24, Box 6.

39. Statement of Friedrich Christ, December 17, 1945, NA, RG-549, Case 6-24, Box 6.

40. Interview with Werner Ackermann, March 13, 2010. Also a follow-up interview by Ann Shields on August 8, 2010.

41. Composition of Sternebeck's lead tank platoon, or *Spitze*, at Blankenheim consisted of two Panthers and three Panzer Mk IVs. Two Panthers and a Mk IV were lost during the night of December 16 after hitting mines outside of Hüllscheid. Sternebeck's personal tank, 614, was lost to a mine near Merlscheid, after which point he transferred to Panzer 611 under SS 2nd Lt. Karl Heinz Asmussen. Due to losses, the *Spitze* reorganized on Peiper's direction in Lanzerath at midnight by adding three tanks from the 6th Panzer Company and two SPWs from 9th Panzer Engineers under SS-S/Sgt. Rudolf Dörr. However, three more Mk IVs were knocked out just outside of Büllingen after a wrong turn at 7:30 A.M. After that point Sternebeck's *Spitze* consisted only of two tanks (611 and 623) and a single halftrack.

42. Interview with Reinhold Kyriss, May 20, 1997.

43. Statement of Franz Sievers, February 27, 1946. *U.S. v. Bersin*, 386–391. Sievers prepared a detailed sketch of the room layout of his meeting with the panzer leaders on the evening of December 15, 1944 where he signed secret orders, which is still with his statement at the National Archives. Sievers would later repudiate his damaging statement at Landsberg. Still, it is noteworthy that Siever's recall of Peiper's watchword—"A bad reputation has its commitments" (*Aber auch ein schlechter Ruf verpflichtet*)—is borne out by Peiper's wartime handwritten letter to Hedwig Potthast, Himmler's mistress, in March 1943. Wrote Peiper: "We have become known beyond the borders of our division because of our successes and because of our persistence and enduring matter-of-factness. But even a bad reputation has its obligations— (I freely quote Zarah Leander). Our reputation precedes us as a wave of terror and is one of our best weapons. Even old Genghis Khan would gladly have hired us as assistants." Letter from Jochen Peiper to Hedwig Potthast, March 24, 1943, *NSDAP Hauptarchiv*, Himmler Collection, Microfilm Roll #99, Hoover Institution, Stanford University. This letter is extremely significant to an understanding of Peiper's view of fighting, in which he reveals his wartime motto was taken from Nazi wartime cinematic diva, Zarah Leander in the film *Zu neuen Ufern*.

44. In the Schwäbisch Hall statement of Arndt Fischer, dated March 31, 1946, he wrote that during the evening briefing of the company commanders at Blankenheim on December 15, "at the time SS-Maj. Poetschke spoke about that we should not take any prisoners where the military situation absolutely required it. Poetschke also declared that this was a secret order." At his trial Peiper denied that any such discussion ever took place, nor that there was a separate regimental order. *U.S. v. Bersin*, 1913–1915. Fischer would later

denounce his Schwäbisch Hall statement, both at Landsberg and personally to the author in an interview on May 15, 1997. However, Fischer's liaison officer, SS-Lt. Kurt Kramm, was at the same meeting and contradicted Fischer's later denials in several statements. It is significant that after the war other old SS veterans considered Kramm a turncoat, rebuffing his postwar attempts at contact. In particular, Rolf Reiser, who worked diligently for decades to exonerate the Leibstandarte, made early denials as to the existence of such orders. "That a verbal or written order concerning the shooting of American POWs during the offensive in December 1944, through officers of the Panzer Regiment or 1st Panzer Division has been ordered, it is not known to me at all." Statement of Rolf Reiser, January 3, 1946, NA, RG-549, Case 6–24, Box 37.

45. Fischer's original handwritten statement is in NA, RG-549, Case 6–24, Box 9. For testimony agreeing with Fischer's original mention of the "secret" order that prisoners be shot when conditions warranted, see statements of Kurt Kramm, Friedrich Christ, Oskar Klingelhoefer, Benoni Junker, and SS 2nd Lt. Hans Buchheim. In particular, Kramm's courtroom statements to that effect at the trial were never repudiated. "We will fight in the same manner as we did in Russia in the action that will follow," he recalled Peiper saying. "The certain rules that have applied in the West until now will be omitted." Kramm's testimony is *U.S. v. Bersin*, 186–222.

46. Peiper's original words, in German, are: *"Der kommende Einsatz wäre le letzo Chance den Krieg zu gewinnen. Wie ein Sturmwind müssten wir angriefen. Der Feind muesse eine wahnsinnige Angst vor der SS bekommen. Dies sei unsere Verpflichtung."* Handwritten statement of Hans Hennecke, March 13, 1946, NA, RG-549, Case 6–24, Box 36.

47. Testimony of Hans Hennecke on December 11, 1945, NA, RG-549, Case 6–24, Box 23.

48. Georg Bunda was the gunner with Panther 231 in Christ's company. "Interrogation Notes #1," interrogations of defendants or other SS men held at Dachau by the defense team in April and May 1946, Willis Everett Archives, courtesy of James Weingartner. In screening results prior to Schwäbisch Hall, SS-Pvt. Hans Hübler and Karl Daub, in Pz. 225, claimed that "Christ told his men to fight a ruthless fight and conduct themselves in such a way as to spread terror among the American troops and made it clear that prisoners of war would not be taken." Screening Results, December 10–19, 1945, IC#78, Ellis Papers.

49. Perry's recollection of his conversation with Peiper in Landsberg, February 1947, MMIH, 935–937. Perry wondered aloud to Peiper about the German Luftwaffe bombing of civilian targets in England. "Peiper," he began, "what about Coventry?" "The destruction of Coventry is an infamous British

lie," Peiper said looking straight at him. "Nothing like that ever happened." Perry looked to drop the subject, but Peiper didn't let go; he wanted to talk about Düren: "When my boys who have lost their families are confronted with your American killers, if it is violation they shoot them down, then you can say we violated international law. But had circumstances been otherwise, there would have been no violation."

50. "My boys may charge me with all they want. The main thing is that it helps them. They are not evil and no criminals." Jochen Peiper to Willis Everett, July 4, 1946, Everett Papers.

51. Regarding the differences from 1940: "And there was the third dimension—the enemy air force." Peiper interview from 1971 from Hans Kettgen to Harvey T. Rowe and then to author.

52. *Rollbahn*, or Route, D, assigned to Peiper by Fritz Krämer, was unpaved for a stretch west of Honsfeld to Schoppen and also between Pont (two kilometers southwest of Ligneuville) and Logbierme. The road was exceedingly narrow for a number of stretches, and any sections that the Americans had used for supply that fall would be only useful for one-way traffic. Route D passed over 113 kilometers on roads to go from Hallschlag, Germany, to Amay on the Meuse River.

53. "An Interview with Obst. Joachim Peiper," September 7, 1945, NA, RG-338, Foreign Military Studies, ETHINT-10, 7.

54. Although Peiper implied that he personally drove the Panther (e.g., in ETHINT-10), this was not the case. Instead, Hans Hennecke drove the Mk V, and he reported back to Peiper the following day. Interview with Arndt Fischer and Rolf Reiser, May 15, 1997.

55. Peiper statement at the Malmédy trial, *U.S. v. Bersin*, Case 6–24, 1905.

56. *U.S. v. Bersin*, 1906–1908.

57. A captured German document revealed the magnitude of the gasoline problem. Kampfgruppe Peiper required at least two hundred thousand liters to move the battle group one hundred kilometers forward. NA, RG-407, G-2 Periodic Report No. 196, VIII Corps, December 30, 1944, 208-2.1, Box 3965.

58. NA, RG-338, T-311, Roll 18, Frames 210020–210025, Field tank strengths taken from "Schw. Waffen Pz. Division, 10.12.1944." Supplemented by study prepared by Timm Haasler for the author.

59. Plea for mitigation of sentence, Hans Siptrott, July 12, 1946, *U.S. v. Bersin*, 3238.

60. Werner Löhmann testimony at the Malmédy trial, *U.S. vs. Bersin*, 318–325. It must be added that Siptrott emphatically denied passing on such an order in the author's interview with him on May 17, 1997. Although Siptrott also

denied the orders in an affidavit from Landsberg on January 21, 1948 (citing physical abuse at Schwäbisch Hall), note that *all* of the Malmédy defendants submitted similar statements in an effort to gain freedom from prison. In any case, Werner Löhmann never recanted his testimony made at Dachau on May 20, 1946.

61. Initial composition of the tanks in the *Spitze* and their march order from Blankenheim:

Pz. 122—SS-Sgt. Valentin Bersin (Panther)

Pz. 113—SS-2nd Lt. Bahrendt (Panther)

Pz. 614—SS-1st Lt. Sternebeck

Pz. 611—SS-2nd Lt. Karl-Heinz Asmussen

Pz. 725—SS-S/Sgt. Horst Rempel

62. Testimony of Roland F. Messner, August 22, 1947, NA, RG-549 War Crimes Case Tried, *U.S. v. Otto Skozeny et al.*, Case 6-100, Box 77, 351–354. Messner was in Sternebeck's Panzer Nr. 614 and closely described their movements on December 16, 1944.

63. Asmussen was an old drinking buddy of Sternebeck and other party kings in the 6th Panzer Company. *Tagebuch von Benoni Junker*, 1944, Courtesy of Timm Haasler.

64. For the action at Lanzerath, see Alex Kershaw, *The Longest Winter* (Cambridge: DaCapo Press, 2004). Also note author's daylong interview with Lyle Bouck on February 9, 1996. Belgian farmer Adolf Schür told the author in an interview in Lanzerath on October 18, 1995, that he saw twenty-seven dead of the German paratroopers buried in the temporary grave across from the Café Palm in Lanzerath. Other villagers put the number of German dead at around thirty or forty. Fritz Roppelt, *Der Vergangenheit auf der Spur: 3. Fallsch. Jg. Division* (Hössbach b. Aschaffenburg, 1993), 427.

65. For the colorful stories on August Tonk, interviews with Ackermann March 13, 2010, op. cit., and Reinhold Kyriss May 20, 1997.

66. In the official U.S. Army history, Hugh Cole (*The Ardennes: Battle of the Bulge*, OCMH, 1965) claimed, "Irrefutable evidence shows that nineteen unarmed Americans were shot down in Honsfeld and fifty at Büllingen." The author's own detailed investigation of the action showed that although Cole's figure is inflated, surrendered American soldiers *were* murdered in Honsfeld. Although isolated soldiers may have been shot in Büllingen, there was nothing close to the number Cole mentioned. A total of twenty-two soldiers of the 612th TD Battalion died in Honsfeld on December 17. At least seven of these, according to accounts of witnesses interviewed by the author, had not surrendered but were killed in combat. However, two of the three medics of

the battalion carried off by Kampfgruppe Peiper on that day have never been found and must be assumed to have perished. All told, we can establish that at least six American soldiers were shot down in cold blood after surrendering in Honsfeld on December 17, 1944, not including the three medics who were kidnapped into medical service of the Leibstandarte and never seen again: T/5 Michael Kardos, Pfc. Robert Farley, and Pfc. James J. McGinity. Members of the 612 TD Battalion certain to have been shot while attempting to surrender on December17: Pvt. William Bradley, Pvt. James Milliner, T/5 Edward Stegall, Pvt. James Crowell, T/5 Robert Thomas, and Pvt. Cecil Mann. Others exhumed from the mass grave in Honsfeld on February 5, 1945, who may have also been executed: Pvt. Homer K. Reedy, Sgt. Darwin R. Wortman, Pvt. Everett Locke, T/5 William J. Laukkonen, and Pvt. Leo J. Kroll. Sworn statement of Maj. Jack B. Day, V Corps, U.S. Army, February 22, 1945, NA, RG-549, Case 6–24, Box 33.

67. The Dachau Court asked, "Have you heard the witness statements in this case—Wilson, Morris and White, who testified that prisoners of war were killed in Honsfeld?" "Yes," Peiper said. He recalled it. "And is that true?" the Court asked. "I can't state anything about this, because I wasn't present." Peiper testimony, *U.S. v. Bersin*, 1921–1922.

68. Peiper's crew in command tank 001 on December 16 included veteran driver SS-S/Sgt. Otto Becker, Morse code radio operator SS-Cpl. Wilhelm Nusshag, and radioman SS-Cpl. Paul Schierig. The gunner is unknown. Interview with Wilhelm Nusshag, Rgt. Stab Kp., May 10, 1999.

69. Evidence that Peiper switched to Diefenthal's SPW at this point becomes an important facet. Testimony of Josef Diefenthal to Dwight Fanton, Wiesbaden, November 14, 1945, NA, RG-549, Case 6–24, Box 33. Note that this testimony was before any of the alleged abuse at Schwäbisch Hall. Question: "Was Peiper riding in your vehicle when you left Büllingen?" Answer: "Yes." Q: "How long had he been riding in your vehicle at that time?" A: "Col. Peiper mounted my vehicle before the airfield at Büllingen." Diefenthal said of Zwigart: "a good natured fellow and an excellent driver."

70. Interview with Wilhelm Nusshag, op. cit., "On 16–17th December [1944] it was still dark when everything started moving. Then it happened that our tank was disabled near Büllingen. There was an engine failure and the driver and I stayed with the tank. We tried to get it fixed and somebody came from ordnance and got the tank moving. We drove ahead, but we couldn't catch up with the battle group. They had gone to La Gleize."

71. Peiper testimony at the Malmédy trial: *U.S. v. Berzin*, 2045.

72. Interview with Col. John Ray, Natick, MA, May 15 and 18, 1998.

Chapter 2

1. Perspectives from members of the battalion were related to the author at a reunion of the 285th FAOB in September 1995. The author also conducted extended interviews with William Merriken and Ted Paluch spanning a decade. On December 15–19, 2007, the author accompanied Ted Paluch back to Baugnez in an emotional journey with a series of lengthy discussions that took place over those days. The term Pennsylvania Dutch is actually a misnomer—a linguistic adaptation for Pennsylvania *Deutsch* for the German immigrants who settled this bucolic region of northeastern Pennsylvania in the eighteenth and nineteenth centuries. "Several of those guys almost spoke English," joked veteran Ted Paluch sixty-three years after serving with Battery B.

2. Alex Kershaw, *The Bedford Boys: One American Town's Ultimate D-Day Sacrifice* (Cambridge: DaCapo Press, 2003).

3. Interview with George Fox, January 18, 2010.

4. For the history of the 285th FAOB, I consulted the official U.S. Army records at the National Archives: RG-407, FAOB-285-285-0.3 Organizational history as well as the monthly After Action Reports. The battalion informal history maintained by Charles Hammer after the war supplemented this research and was made available by Ted Paluch.

5. Interview with Thomas Bacon, September 21, 1995.

6. Author's follow-up interview with Ted Paluch, February 8, 2010.

7. Interview with Albert Valenzi, September 26, 1995.

8. · Bacon interview, September 21, 1995.

9. Jack E. Oliver, "As I Remember: A World War II Journal," Boone County Historical Society, Columbia, Missouri.

10. Charles B. MacDonald, *The Siegfried Line Campaign* (Washington, DC: OCMH, 1984).

11. William Reem to his parents, October 4, 1944. Provided to the author by Reem's daughter.

12. Valenzi interview, September 26, 1995. As recorded in the 285th AAR: "Pvt. John Ray was killed and two others wounded when the forward observation post was hit."

13. Follow-up interview with Albert Valenzi, January 13, 2008.

14. James P. Mattera, as told to C. M. Stephan Jr., "Murder at Malmédy," *Army*, December 1981.

15. From the Battalion AAR for September 1944: The routes taken from September 19–21: Couville-sur-Mer, France, 22; Corrouges, 23; Dampierre, 24; Vervins, 24–27; Klimmen, Holland, 28–30; Voerendaal, Holland.

16. Capt. Leon T. Scarborough was not with his battery on December 17 but instead had gone down to the U.S. VIII Corps in Luxembourg on the evening of December 16. There he clarified their mission, which would take them down to Luxembourg to support the U.S. 4th Infantry Division that was under strong attack by the German Seventh Army. Scarborough arrived at the 16th Field Artillery Observation Battalion in Luxembourg about noon. He waited for nearly three hours without the appearance of his command, only to learn from Capt. Floyd Kelsey, the battery's route marking officer, that his battery had been attacked near Malmédy. He would not know what had happened to his command until December 18. Testimony of Capt. Leon T. Scarborough to Capt. Oliver Seth, December 28, 1944.

17. Author interview with William B. Summers, September 21, 1995. The other "outposters" with Summers in Battery B were T/5 George Rosenfeld, Cpl. David O'Grady, and T/5 John M. "Johnny" Shingler. All would be killed on December 17, 1944.

18. Interview with Warren Schmitt, November 12, 2007.

19. U.S. First Army G-3 records show that the 285th FAOB Battalion was detached from VII Corps and attached to the VIII Corps effective December 17 at 6 A.M. "U.S. First Army to VII and VIII Corps," U.S. First Army G-3 Files, NA, RG-407, 101.3.3, Box 1529.

Chapter 3

1. Cpl. Bernard Koenig, "Account of Malmédy," 3rd Platoon, 291st Engineers, Janice Holt Giles Papers, *The Damned Engineers*, Western Kentucky University (hereafter Giles Papers).

2. "285th FA Obsn Bn S-3 Journal from 151510A to 170655A," NA, RG-407, FAOB-285-0.3.

3. "Account of Destruction of Battery B Column on 17 December 1944," Appendix I to AAR 285th FAOB for December 1944, NA, RG-407, FAOB-285-0.3.

4. Ernest W. Bechtel, "The Untold Story of Battery B," 1982, USa.m.HI, Charles B. MacDonald Papers, Box 7. Also Ernest W. Bechtel, "Into the Mists of Malmédy," papers of Charles Hammer, 285th FAOB, WWII-5959, USa.m.HI, Box Battery Rosters etc.

5. Author interviews with William Merriken, July 4 and September 22, 1995. "Statement of William H. Merriken, 1 February 1945," NA, RG-549, Case 6–24, Box 42. Also "My Personal Story, by Bill Merriken," Charles B. MacDonald Papers, U.S. Army Military History Institute, Box 7.

6. The specific route of Battery B from the Battalion AAR: Schevenhütte to Zweifall to Rott to Eynatten-Eupen-Malmédy en route to Gruflange, Belgium.

7. Author interviews with Theodore Paluch, September 17, 1997 and December 2007. Paluch was in the twenty-fourth vehicle in the overall column.

8. Willi Volberg, "My experiences with the Operation Stösser, Hohes Venn, December, 1944," Eschweiler, 1983, U.S. Army Military History Institute, Carlisle, PA, MacDonald Papers, Box German Accounts.

9. Had not the German paratroopers been widely scattered, the 285th would have been stopped by the armed roadblock that von der Heydte planned to erect at the Baraque Michel crossroads. Had the 285th been forced to detour west, the little unit would likely never have run across the Kampfgruppe Peiper.

10. Author interview with Tom Bacon, September 21, 1995.

11. Ralph S. Rainey, "The Boy Played Possum at Malmédy," no date or edition, Charles Hammer Papers, 285th FAOB, USa.m.HI, Box Battery Rosters, etc.

12. Author interview with Lacy Thomasson, August 26, 1995, the 552nd AAA AW Battalion. Trained as a 40mm gun crew chief on the heavily armed anti-aircraft halftracks, Thomasson became a member of the battalion medical detachment in Verviers that autumn.

13. This and all quotes associated from the story of convoy vehicles B-26, B-27, and B-28: Bechtel, "The Untold Story of Battery B."

14. It would be December 18th before the three delayed trucks of the Battery reached their parent unit in Luxembourg—and then with fateful news.

15. For "Battle Neurosis," see 285th FAOB AAR for December 29, 1944.

16. Author interviews with Al Valenzi, September 26, 1995, and December 13, 2007. In 2006, through research by Henri Rogister, Al learned that the girls who had given him the ribbon at the Pont d' L'Octroi were Yolande and Maria Huby. "*Les recherches du GI américain aboutissent?*" *L'Organe de Malmédy*, January 18, 2006.

17. "This is luck": from 1995 oral history by Al Valenzi as recorded by George Gaadt ("Angel at the Crossroads," January 2010).

18. The big shells had come from one of the 70-foot long, 28-cm K25 rail guns of Railroad Artillery Battalion 725 that was firing from a railway line just east of Monschau.

19. Story of Pergrin and the 291st Combat Engineer Battalion: author interview with David Pergrin, September 23, 1995. Also see Janice Holt Giles, *The Damned Engineers* (New York: Houghton Mifflin, 1970), 90–94.

20. 629th Engineer Light Equipment Company, Summary of Combat Operations, December 1944, January 13, 1945, NA, RG-407, ENCO-629-0.3.

21. Letter from Frank Rhea to author, no date, but 1996. Also, letter from Frank Rhea to Janice Holt Giles, December 2, 1968, Giles Papers.

22. Janice Holt Giles to Frank Rhea, July 16, 1968, Giles Papers.

23. Pergrin also ordered his Company A back from the exposed village of Amblève that same morning, where they barely missed being ambushed by the German columns surging forward.

24. Author interview with David Pergrin, March 20, 1965, Giles Papers, Box 30.

25. 291st Engineer Combat Battalion, Action against Enemy, After Action Reports, December 1944, January 1, 1945, NA, RG-407, ENBN-291-0.3.

26. Letter from Thomas Stack to author, June 21, 1996.

27. Author interview with David Pergrin, September 23, 1995.

28. Statement of Homer D. Ford to Alvin D. Welsch, December 17 1944, NA, RG-153, Case 6-24, Box 76. The statement was taken at 7:30 P.M. Also, Ford testimony from *U.S. v. Bersin*, Dachau, May 22, 1946, 524–539.

Chapter 4

1. Atrocity Report, Kenneth F. Ahrens, Sgt, E&E Report 2907, December 18, 1944, NA, RG-549, Case 6–24, Box 22.

2. Albert Valenzi interview, September 26, 1995.

3. "As one of the tanks approached near, one of the officers stuck his pistol out and apparently was going to shoot at me, but he changed his mind and shot at Capt. Mills instead." Interview with 1st Lt. Virgil Lary, December 21, 1944, by CIC Agent Philip Poirier, CIC Detachment. 419, CIC Field Office, Paris, NA, RG-549, Case 6–24, Box 42. Also statement of Virgil P. Lary to Capt. J. M. Gauthier, G-1 Division, SHAEF, 203rd General Hospital, December 22, 1944, NA, RG-549, Case 6–24, Box 42. In his early interviews Lary claimed that the pistol shots had come from a German standing in a halftrack that came up later. After the original shooting, Lary estimated that he lay in the field for an hour and a half. When the Germans appeared to lose interest, Lary made a dash with others (Sgt. Ahrens and Cpl. Moucheron) toward the woods. However, his foot was badly wounded, and rather than try to keep up with the others, he hid in a manure pile in the woodshed of one of the Belgian homes, waiting until dark to crawl away.

4. Testimony of George E. Graeff to Dwight Fanton, October 9, 1945, Wiesbaden, NA, RG-549, Case 6–24, Box 30. Graeff included a detailed sketch of his movements and those of Garrett and Conrad in the testimony. As the road was elevated from the ditch where the three hid, he and the others were largely unobserved as the German column proceeded south.

5. Testimony of Cpl. George E. Graeff to Oliver Seth, December 29, 1944, NA, RG-153, Case 6–24, Box 76. "We laid there and waited and when they came down to my jeep they stopped a tank, got out, and started looting

it. Corporal Schmitt had a box of D-ration bars in the jeep and one Jerry came up, picked them up and hollered: "*Alles, Alles!*" and started distributing them. . . . We couldn't see much after that, they had us down with machine guns."

6. Sworn statement of T/5 Warren R. Schmitt to CIC Agent Richard G. Zimmerman, December 20, 1944, NA, RG-549, Case 6–24, Box 23.

7. Testimony of Cpl. Theodore C. Flechsig to Maj. Woodward C. Gardiner, 28th General Hospital, December 20, 1944, NA, RG-153, Case 6–24, Box 76.

8. Eugene Garrett saw the same four Americans attempt to escape and then be fired upon. Thus, there were a number of witnesses, including Kenny Kingston, who saw the same event.

9. Testimony of Pfc. Donald L. Bower to Capt. Oliver Seth, U.S. First Army, December 29, 1944, NA, RG-153, Case 6–24, Box 76.

10. Cpl. Robert Conrad was the driver of jeep number B-11 with T/5 Eugene Garrett. They were the sixth or seventh vehicle in the column of 285th FAOB vehicles.

11. Those Garrett saw running likely included Pfc. Donald Bower, Cpl. Theodore Flechsig, and T/5 Wilson M. Jones.

12. The man Garrett saw executed by pistol shot may have been T/5 Wilson M. Jones, whose body was not recovered by graves registration until April 1945. After seeing a second GMC truck in the column struck by mortar fire, T/5 Eugene Garrett and Robert Conrad decided that they best move away from the road. "We moved back to a little ditch that ran at an angle from a cow trail" several yards west of the main road. Garrett heard someone yell "*Kamerad*," calling to Bower, who was shot at and then fell down as if dead next to Garrett and Conrad in the ditch. "They got Bower," Graeff heard Garrett say. Yet all three men decided their best chance was to act as if they were dead and lay where they were. Even so, Garrett was able to peek up once to see a large group of guarded American prisoners marching back toward the crossroads with Lt. Lary heading group. Garrett estimated that they lay in the ditch for some two hours as enemy tanks passed by. Testimony of T/5 Eugene H. Garrett, December 29, 1944, NA, RG-153, Case 6–24, Box 76.

13. Testimony of George E. Graeff to Dwight Fanton, October 9, 1945, Wiesbaden, NA, RG-549, Case 6–24, Box 30. "Then we couldn't see anything further until it seemed like an hour later, a German soldier came over and tread on a rifle that was lying between Cpl. Garrett and myself. He looked at us and turned around and walked away. We couldn't see anything else. We were too scared to raise our heads." Graeff also saw the man executed by a burst of machine gunfire, who was identified as either Clark or Phillips. Graeff also mentioned that other SS troopers who came by the soldier's body

pumped in additional pistol rounds. Clark's corpse was not discovered until the spring of 1945, and an autopsy could not satisfactorily reveal the cause of death. However, it is noteworthy that in the autopsy of Pvt. Peter R. Phillips (Tag #67), who was also found along the road on the way back to the intersection, Capt. Joseph Kurcz concluded that Phillips had been killed by multiple shots to the back and head.

14. For the execution of 2nd Lt. Solomon Goffman: Taped interview of Gene Garrett, November 1987. Goffman's body was found in February 1945 some distance from the Baugnez crossroads on the road to Ligneuville. The author found several survivors repeating, secondhand, that Lt. Lary saw Goffman was shot when he protested the seizure of his possessions.

15. Graeff testimony, December 29, 1944, op. cit.

16. Testimony of Warren R. Schmitt to Lt. Col. Alvin B. Welsch, HQ First U.S. Army, December 25, 1944, NA, RG-153, Case 6-24, Box 77.

17. "After I raised up out of the ditch later on, I saw the men lying there, but I didn't actually see them shot." Ibid.

18. This SS machine gun crew was likely posted by House #10 (Henri Goffinet). In a deposition given on March 6, 1946 (NA, RG-549, Case 6-24, Box 6), SS-Pvt. Gustav Neve described how a group of SS men of the 9th Panzer Engineer Company were located in this position near the curve in the road to Ligneuville. Neve told how the SS men fired on half a dozen U.S. Army soldiers south of the main field but that he did not actually see the Americans killed. A similar statement given by Gustav Sprenger on February 27, 1946 (Box 7) echoed the general outline of the event.

19. "I lay in the stream for approximately two hours and after that time was so numb that I could not move the lower half of my body, but by crawling and dragging myself, I made it to some woods. I rubbed my legs to get back circulation and then by means of my compass found my way back to the road. I went down the road until halted by a friendly guard and was then taken to an aid station. That was about 2030 when I arrived there." Statement of Warren Schmitt, December 20, 1944, op. cit.

20. Testimony of Cpl. Robert B. Conrad to Capt. Oliver Seth, U.S. First Army, December 29, 1944, NA, RG-153, Case 6-24, Box 76. See also Graeff, December 29, 1944, op. cit.

21. Many others saw the bandaged American Lt. Col. pass by, including T/5 William Summers, T/5 Ted Paluch, Pfc. Paul Martin, Lt. Virgil Lary, and Pfc. Jim Mattera: Testimony of Pfc. James P. Mattera to Maj. Gardiner, December 25, 1944, U.S. First Army, NA, RG-153, Case 6-24, Box 76. The man who had been captured near Waimes was Lt. Col. John Ray.

22. Lary was wounded twice in the foot while lying in the field. Testimony of 1st Lt. Virgil P. Lary to Capt. Oliver Seth, 28th General Hospital, Liège, December 18, 1944, NA, RG-153, Case 6–24, Box 76. Unable to run with the others, Lary crawled away from the field after it became dark.

23. Ted Paluch saw this same jeep roaring up the road from Ligneuville toward Malmédy while they were crouched in the ditch near their truck. See his testimony of October 10, 1945. Paluch visited the crossroads with the author in 2007 and made a point of noting that the ditch in the winter of 1944 on the west side of the road was much deeper than anything seen there today. The jeep was with the 165th Signal Photo Company, attached to U.S. First Army. The jeep's occupants, Cpl. Ernest B. Braun and driver Pvt. Ivan "The Terrible" Babcock, were on their way to Verviers to headquarters after coming from St. Vith, where they had collected film from S/Sgt. George Douglas. They came up the road south from Ligneuville just as the 285th first came under fire. "What are those funny fire flies in front of the windshield?" Braun said to Babcock as they approached Baugnez. By the time they realized what they were seeing—tracer bullets—there was nothing left to do but drive fast and weave around the trucks stopped on the road. They eventually reached Verviers. S. C. "Buddy" Lovette to the author, April 6, 2011.

24. This farmhouse immediately before the curve in the road to Ligneuville had a woodpile just to its north that was the focal point for the Americans seeking cover at the head of the 285th column after the first shooting by the Kampfgruppe Peiper. Two families, those of Henri Goffinet-Curz and Léonard Muller, occupied the farmhouse in December 1944.

25. Testimony of T Sgt. William H. Merriken to Ralph Shumacker, October 9, 1945, Wiesbaden, Germany, NA, RG-549, Case 6-24, Box 30. As Merriken remembered, those with him by the woodpile were T/5 Max Schwitzgold, Pvt. Aubrey Hardiman, T/5 Harold Laufer, Sgt. Walter Franz, S/Sgt. Donald Geisler, Sgt. Kenneth Ahrens, T/5 Albert Valenzi, T/5 Carl Daub, Cpl. Ralph Indelicato, and Pvt. Gilbert Pittman.

26. Valenzi interview, September 26, 1995, op. cit.

27. James P. Mattera, as told to C. M. Stephan Jr., "Murder at Malmédy," *Army*, December 1981.

28. "I heard a blast and looked around to my back, which was to the northeast. I saw German tanks coming up and I also saw an ambulance which was leaving on the right hand side of the road headed toward Malmédy.... As the Germans sprayed the intersection I was on, myself and about 15 other soldiers that were in the convoy took cover behind the house on the southwest side of the road.... I could see the German tanks go on up the road, and later

some of the tanks stopped in front of the house and on the intersection where I was." Testimony of Homer D. Ford, taken at Hq First U.S. Army, December 17, 1930, by Lt. Col. Alvin B. Welsch, NA, RG-153, Case 6-24, Box 77.

29. Valenzi interview, September 26, 1995, op. cit.

30. Testimony of T/5 Michael J. Skoda to 1st Lt. Vincent P. Clarke, Ra.m.P Camp No. 1, Lucky Strike Area, Normandy Base Section, France, May 28, 1945. NA, RG-549, Case 6-24 (specific box unknown: copy courtesy John Bauserman).

31. Testimony of T/5 Carl R. Daub to Oliver Seth, December 18, 1944, 28th General Hospital, NA, RG-153, Case 6-24, Box 76. Also see twelve-page testimony of Carl R. Daub to Dwight Fanton, October 10, 1945, Wiesbaden, NA, RG-549, Case 6-24, Box 30. The house by the woodpile that Daub described was House #10 on the crossroads maps where a number of Americans took refuge from the halted front of the Company B column.

32. Interview with Bobby Werth, 285th FAOB, September 21, 1995. All statements of Werth come from this interview unless otherwise noted.

33. Testimony of Daub, October 10, 1945, op. cit.

34. Daub's testimony regarding the German with the Iron Cross (Knight's Cross) is curious, as the only members of Kampfgruppe Peiper with this insignia at the crossroads that day were Werner Poetschke and Jochen Peiper himself. However, the testimony of Lary and Kingston clarifies that the officer wearing the Knight's Cross around his neck whom Daub referred to was also asking for volunteers to drive the trucks—almost certainly Werner Poetschke.

35. 2nd Lt. Goffman's body was not found with the other bodies in the massacre field. His remains were recovered in February 1945, with the listed cause of death as gunshot wounds. Lt. Lary said he had seen Goffman shot for protesting the loss of his valuables during the initial search.

36. Indeed, Sgt. Eugene Lacey was one of the members of the 285th who was forced to drive trucks for the Germans and survived the war as a prisoner. John Bauserman spoke to him in Oklahoma in 1988, but Lacey was unwilling to say anything about his experience at the crossroads or afterward. Bauserman, personal communication with the author, August 26, 2007.

37. Official statement of Harry C. Horn, April 10, 1945, NA, RG-549, Case 6-24, Box 22. The fortunate men who volunteered to drive the American trucks away were T/5 Thomas Bacon, Sgt. Eugene I. Lacey, T/5 Ralph A. Logan, T/5 David I. Lucas of the 285th FAOB, as well as Sgt. Vernon Anderson, Pvt. William L. Barron, and Cpl. John I. Cummings of the reconnaissance company of the 32nd Armored Regiment of the 3rd Armored Division.

38. Account of Ralph A. Logan, Charles B. MacDonald Papers, USa.m.HI, Box 7. Logan would spend the rest of the war as a prisoner of Stalag IVB and, later, Work Camp #17 in Zittau, Germany.

39. Author interview with Thomas Bacon, September 21, 1995.

40. Logan to Gerd Cuppens, January 27, 1982, Gerd J. Gust Cuppens, *Massacre a Malmédy?* (Bayeux, France: Editions Heimdal, 1989), 95. Logan was a prisoner after December 17, 1944. Relative to the machine gunfire he heard while threatened on the Ligneuville road, "It is only at war's end, that I hear for the first time about the massacre at Baugnez."

41. Author interviews with Ted Paluch, 1997, 2007, and 2011. Also testimony of Pvt. Robert L. Smith, December 17, 1944 at 77th Evacuation Hospital. NA, RG-153, Case 6–24, Box 77, and interview at Wiesbaden on October 11, 1945, RG-549, Case 6–24, Box 30.

42. Letter of Charles Appman and account prepared for the author, "The Malmédy Massacre as Remembered by Charles F. Appman," March 30, 1996.

43. Testimony of T/5 Charles F. Appman, 285 FAOB, to Alvin B. Welsch, HQ U.S. First Army, December 18, 1944, NA, RG-549, Case 6–24, Box 23. Also see interview of Charles Appman by Capt. Roland Young, U.S. First Army HQ, December 18, 1944, Box 42: "They lined up the whole B Battery in a circle and then told us to go over the fence into the field southwest of the house. They had us there in a circle for ten or fifteen minutes. One fellow pulled out a pistol and shot point blank into the crowd and one fellow to the west of me dropped. He fired again and someone to the back of me dropped. Then almost immediately they opened with machine gun fire. I hit the ground with the rest and made believe I was dead. I laid there while they searched the bodies and I could hear the German laughter with immediate fire at the moaning ones. I stayed laying there about an hour. Then we decided we would make a break for it." In his second interview with Roland Young on December 18, Appman was fairly certain that there were just two German tanks that fired on them in the beginning—later followed by more tanks and halftracks: "So finally, there came two tanks that came up the road towards us . . . and they strafed the ditch." Also sixteen-page testimony of Charles Appman to Dwight Fanton on October 9, 1945, at Wiesbaden, RG-549, Case 6–24, Box 30.

44. Charles Appman and Jim Mattera would survive December 17, 1944, although Luers and Rullman would not.

45. Statement of Harold Billow, 185th U.S. General Hospital, undated but early 1945. NA, RG-549, Case 6–24, Box 41. Also see statement of Harold Billow to George E. Flaccus, undated but early 1946, while Billow was with the 1041st Air Engineering Squadron.

46. Testimony of T/5 John A. O'Connell to Col. Lamar Tooze, 77th Evacuation Hospital, December 17, 1944, NA, RG-153, Case 6–24, Box 77.

47. Testimony of Paul J. Martin, Private 1st Class to 1st Lt. Eugene H. Burris, JAG Department, Fort Oglethorpe, Georgia, August 24, 1945, NA, RG-153, Case 6–24, Box 76.

48. Pvt. John R. Kailer to Capt. Oliver Seth, 28th General Hospital, Liège, December 22, 1944, NA, RG-153, Case 6–24, Box 76.

49. Account prepared for author by Charles Reding, Houma, LA, March 28, 1996.

50. Pvt. Peter Piscatelli was in the group seeking refuge in the café. The following men were with him: S/Sgt. John Osborne, T/5 Charles R. Breon, Pvt. Andrew Profanchick, Sgt. Alfred W. Kinsman, Pfc. Howard E. Desch, and T/5 John O'Connell. Testimony of Pvt. Peter C. Piscatelli to Oliver Seth, 47th Field Hospital, December 18, 1944, NA, RG-153, Case 6–24, Box 77.

51. Testimony of John O'Connell, December 17, 1944, op. cit.

52. In the kitchen truck were: Pfc. Harold Desch, Pvt. Andrew Profanchick, T/4 Selmer Leu, S/Sgt. John Osborne, T/5 Charles Breon, and Pfc. Pete Piscatelli. Only Profanchick and Piscatelli would survive the day. Homer Ford's description of his hasty departure from directing traffic: "We took cover as best we could behind a brick building [the café]. . . . I would say six other fellows hid in the barn. . . . We went around the house and got in the barn in some hay and tried to hide. They came around and pointed at me, so we all went outside and give in [up]. . . . The fellow who was guarding us had a submachine gun. . . . They searched us and took our firearms and everything. Then they marched us over with the rest of them, with our hands up. Then we were all lined up." Ford testimony, December 17, 1944, op. cit.

53. "She is an old-like woman—I would say 50 years old." Ford had identified Adele Bodarwe, whose sons were in the German army.

54. Author interview with Ted Paluch, September 17, 1997.

55. Valenzi interview, September 26, 1995, op. cit.

56. "I have often wondered, if the officer I saw in the halftrack was Peiper," Al Valenzi said in 1995. Through detective work, the author was able to ascertain that Peiper's halftrack crew indeed looted the jeep of Albert Valenzi, who remembered a halftrack approaching their vehicle as they hid in the ditch after the first German tanks passed by. After shots, they got up, and one of the halftrack crew took Valenzi's ammunition belt. Valenzi remembered an English-speaking, clean-shaven German officer in the halftrack who wore a soft panzer cap and asked Valenzi if he could drive; this would have been Peiper himself. Valenzi interview, September 26, 1995, op. cit. Peiper, in his own testimony (*U.S. v. Bersin*, 1930–1931) mentioned that he stopped just

where the road from Baugnez entered the woods about five hundred meters beyond the crossroads, which was precisely where Valenzi's jeep was abandoned. Also in their vehicle was T/5 Mike Skoda, Sgt. Kenneth Ahrens, and T/5 Michael Sciranko.

57. "There was a Cpl. Valenzi with me who had a bandolier around his neck. On our way up the road, a German staff car stopped us and called him over to the side of the car. Then the officers took the bandolier off his neck." Kenneth F. Ahrens to Capt. Clyde L. Walker, March 11, 1945, in Paris, National Archives.

58. Moucheron estimated that he and the others in his truck were in the ditch for about fifteen minutes before their surrender. Testimony of T/5 Carl W. Moucheron to Maj. Woodward C. Gardiner, 28th General Hospital, Liège, December 18, 1944, NA, RG-153, Case 6–24, Box 77.

59. Author interview with George Fox, January 18, 2010.

60. Ibid.

61. Testimony of Pvt. George L. Fox to Ralph Schumacher, October 11, 1945, Wiesbaden, NA, RG-549, Case 6–24, Box 30.

62. Ibid. Also see author's follow-up interview with George Fox on January 18, 2010, when Fox emphasized that Clark was only about ten feet behind him. The shots that killed Clark had come from a German shooting from a vehicle only fifteen to twenty feet in front of them. "They motioned for us to move up to the crossroad and after that everyone kept their hands high and moved along." The body of Frederick Clark was not tagged, his corpse only being discovered in February 1945, at which time it was interred into Henri Chapelle Cemetery in Belgium. See John Bauserman, *The Malmédy Massacre* (Shippensburg, PA: White Mane, 1995), 89 and 110. The listed cause of death was concussion, but the lack of a proper autopsy and the numerous witnesses makes gunfire the likely source. Clark's remains were later returned stateside; he rests in Gettysburg National Cemetery. Twenty-two massacre victims remain buried at Henri Chapelle: Joseph Brozowski, Paul Carr, John Clymire, John Cobbler, Warren Davis, Carl Genthner, Lloyd Iames, Alfred Kinsman, John Klukavy, Alexander Lengyel, Raymond Lester, Alan Lucas, James Luers, James McGee, Halsey Miller, Stanley Piasecki, Gilbert Pittman, George Rosenfeld, Wayne Scott, George Steffy, Carl Stevens, and Luke Swartz.

63. Valenzi, interview on February 10, 2008.

64. Skoda testimony, May 28, 1945, op. cit.

65. Author interview with William B. Summers, September 21, 1995.

66. Statement of Pfc. Mario Butera, 91st General Hospital, March 16, 1945, NA, RG-549, Case 6–24, Box 22. Butera had been treated at the hospital since December 27, 1944.

67. The Mk IV tanks were those of SS-1st Lt. Werner Sternebeck and SS-M/Sgt. August Tonk.

68. See Walla's story in chapter 5.

69. Butera statement, March 16, 1945, op. cit. "The group which I was part, stood in the pasture for 10-15 minutes wondering what the next move on the part of the Germans would be. As we stood there, I noticed a German tank emerge from the woods on our left and approach within 20 yards of us. A German soldier was standing in the turret. . . . I heard a pistol shot and after two more shots, one of my fellow men fell to the ground. The other group joined us and Lt. Reardon asked permission of our guard to administer first aid to the wounded soldier. A first aid man from my organization went to the wounded soldier and carried him within 10 feet of where I was standing. As he was administering first aid, I heard more shooting and saw the medical man and his patient sprawl on the ground dead. The man sitting in the tank armed with the machine gun, commenced a raking fire across our group and by the time the fire reached us, I had fallen on the ground. The third and fourth toes of my left foot were shot off." When someone shouted encouragement to run, Butera took off to the north, eventually being met by Dave Pergrin just before Malmédy.

70. Appman testimonies, op. cit. In Appman's testimony of October 9, 1945, he was emphatic that with the first tank was a single halftrack. "This vehicle [too] turned left and continued down the road." Appman's recollection squares exactly with the composition of Sternebeck's tiny Spitze: his tank, the other Mk IV of August Tonk, and the SPW of SS-Cpl. Karl Ohlrogge.

71. Appman testimony, October 9, 1945, op. cit. The officer in the yellow jacket was undoubtedly Josef Diefenthal. Appman recalled he was a "big fellow with a light complexion" who wore a visored officer's hat. In his statement Harold Billow (op. cit.) recalled a similar scene: "Right away everyone started to surrender and give up and they marched everyone into the field at the side of the road. After they had everyone in this field, there was a German on one of the tanks who set up a machine gun alongside the tank and then there was some German officer who pulled up in a command car." Like Law, Billow claimed that the man who shot two men with a pistol was one of the officers.

72. Account prepared for author by Charles Appman, op. cit.

Chapter 5

1. Author interview with Reinhold Kyriss, May 20, 1997. "He was totally unpredictable."

2. Rolf Reiser remembered that Peiper was ill when he left the tank regiment in the summer of 1944—a fact that most who knew him recalled. Ger-

hard Walla, with the tank regiment, thought in December 1944 that Peiper was a nervous wreck. To him, Peiper was more of a figurehead leader, whereas Poetschke was the true champion of the tanks. Did Peiper have a nervous breakdown after Normandy? Sigurd Peiper's letters to Hedwig Potthast in autumn 1944 reinforce that view.

3. Kyriss interview, May 20, 1997, op. cit.

4. "Beförderung des SS Ustuf. Poetschke,1./SS-A.A.," May 16, 1940, and "Beurteilung des SS Obersturmführer Poetschke," September 19, 1940, BDC File for Werner Poetschke, NA, RG-242 BDC A3343-SSO-386A.

5. "Vorschlaglist Nr. 3173 für die Verleihung des Ritterkreuzes des Eisernen Kreuzes," signed by Peiper on April 24, 1944. For the disciplinary action, see "Feldgericht der Leibstandarte SS Adolf Hitler: Mißbrauch der Disziplinarstrafbefugnis: SS Haupsturmführer Werner Poetschke," May 18, 1944, BDC File for Poetschke, op. cit. The action was over harsh treatment of a motorcycle platoon during the actions at Kharkov in January 1943.

6. There is corroboration for Peiper's uneasy relationship with Poetschke. In a 1985 interview with Gerd Cuppens, Hans Hennecke in Lübecke mentioned that "Poetschke and Peiper were not at all friends," he confided, "and sometimes they would argue." Gerd Cuppens, *Massacre a Malmédy* (Bayeux, France: Editions Heimdal, 1989), 60.

7. "Interrogation Report: Rottenführer Gunther Boese," February 23, 1945, NA, RG-549, Case 6–24, Box 22.

8. Author interview with Otto Dinse, May 21, 1996. "Every night we were on wild rides deep inside Russian lines. We didn't even know where the front line was. . . . Peiper always took advantage of things. He always had a tank platoon with his battalion. He attacked one night and broke through, penetrating sixty kilometers north, that completely took the Russians by surprise. One cannot imagine; the enemy was standing on the dark street and we just marched right through. I had the tank of the adjutant and we didn't even have communications with the division headquarters. . . . It goes like this in Russia: at 4 or 5 in the morning the sun rises and then the Russian artillery begins, and then at 8 A.M. in the morning the tank battle starts along with other fighting. But we took off at 12:01 A.M. and drove around. We did this with tank attacks also. We did it time after time. We nicknamed the halftracks 'open coffins.' . . . The *Schützenpanzerwagen* were only strong enough to stop rifle rounds; if an anti-tank gun fired on it, it was gone. Accordingly, Peiper always got tanks to go along and he attacked with tanks intermingled with SPWs. He would lead with an SPW out front with a tank behind a few more SPWs with another tank. That's how we rode all our attacks."

9. Peiper testimony, *U.S. v. Bersin*, 2031–2032.

10. Asked when he first saw the American trucks south of Malmédy being fired upon, Peiper ventured that it was sometime between "1300 and 1330 hours." Ibid., 1929.

11. Peiper's testimony at the Dachau trial (1927–1928) is at odds with accounts of those in Diefenthal's halftrack, who do not recall Peiper having left the vehicle. In a Schwäbisch Hall statement, Hans Assenmacher, Diefenthal's radio operator, clearly placed Peiper in the SPW beside Diefenthal as they approached the crossroads. Moreover, even in his later statements from Landsberg that were intended to exonerate his colleagues, such as that of November 5, 1947 (RG-153, Box 81), Assenmacher maintained that Peiper was with them when the first sounds of gunfire were heard, emphasizing that Peiper himself ordered the firing from their SPW to stop.

12. Sternebeck as related to Rolf Reiser at Ebensee, Austria in summer 1945, statement of Rolf Reiser, January 3, 1946, NA, RG-549, Case 6–24, Box 37. "I remember how Sternebeck once told me that he had met a troop of American POWs, led by a Captain. They were passing by his panzer. He waved his hand for them to go back further. He also spoke about a shooting behind him and that American soldiers were running away, or trying to run away and that he had shot with his pistol a few times."

13. SS-S/Sgt. Rudolf Dörr claimed that his SPW in the *Panzerspitze* first had the assignment to pick up mines for the attack group but "became stuck in the woods after Büllingen and we had to be left behind. We were later pulled out by a tank and rejoined our outfit at Stavelot." Dörr had been captured at La Gleize and was interrogated on January 16, 1945, by Maj. Oliver Seth at the 168th General Hospital, Testimony of S/Sgt. Rudolf Dörr, NA, RG-153, Case 6-24, Box 70.

14. Thanks to Timm Haasler for preparing the research document, "Summary 9.(Pi.)/SS-Pz.Rgt.1" for the author.

15. Statement of Rolf Reiser, January 3, 1946, NA, RG-549, Case 6–24, Box 37, 6. At Ebensee POW Enclosure Nr. 2 in Barracks Nr. 20, SS-Lt. Helmut Pönisch was located in the same room with Reiser (in 1943 he had attended the 1st SS Panzer Officer Candidate class in Putlos with Reiser). While rooming with Reiser, Sternebeck had brought in an issue of *Yank* magazine, which showed shot Americans at Malmédy. Sternebeck remarked to those present, saying "that he will probably be held responsible for that because he led the point of the offensive, despite the fact that he did not have anything to do with all that." Helmut Pönisch fought with the staff of 1st SS Panzer Regiment in Normandy.

16. For Tonk handing the prisoners over to a tank driven by Manfred Thorn: Screening results from SS Rttf. Alfred Krafft, IC #78, Screening results from November 15–24, 1945, Ellis Papers, in author's possession. Although

Thorn told the author in several interviews that he encountered Werner Poetschke guarding the prisoners, he does not recall seeing Tonk at the crossroads.
Reserve Bundeswehr panzer officer, Wolf Mauder, has studied the movements
of Kampfgruppe Peiper in detail and estimates that the distance from
Sternebeck's point tank to the vanguard following up as approximately two
kilometers, with a time interval of about ten minutes. The author believes this
could have been as short as two minutes but certainly not more than ten. Author interview with Wolf Mauder, May 19, 1997, Heppenheim.

17. In his statement SS-Lt. Kurt Kramm, the SS orderly for the 1st SS
Panzer Battalion, indicated that he rode in the amphibious jeep with SS-Cpl.
Gerhard Walla, SS-S/Sgt. Paul Ochmann, and SS-Sgt Narowtski until they
reached Ligneuville. This is at odds with Walla's story. Statement of Kurt
Kramm, March 16, 1946, NA, RG-549, Case 6–24, Box 32. In his statement
Kramm indicated that by the time they reached Baugnez, the Americans were
already dead in the field.

18. Author interview with Gerhard Walla, May 10, 1999.

19. Also in the SPW of Dörr (Platoon commander) with Maute was SS-
Sgt. Held (SPW commander), Cpl. Hoeppner (driver), Pvt. Hoppe (MG#1),
Pvt. Franke (MG#2), Pvt. Heinz Kappermann (radio operator), and Pvt.
Gramlich. Statement of Heinz Kappermann, December 23, 1944, NA, RG-549,
Case 6–24, Box 41, and statement of Erich Maute, January 22, 1946, Box 32.

20. Peiper's testimony, *U.S. v. Bersin*, 1929–1930.

21. Interview of Arndt Fischer by Timm Haasler, January 12, 2006, courtesy of Timm Haasler.

22. Author interview with Manfred Thorn, March 23, 1996, Bütgenbach,
Belgium; Statement of Maute, op. cit. Maute had been a medic in the LSSAH
since 1942.

23. It was standard procedure in the Leibstandarte (and the entire German
army in general) that the platoon leader or company commander tried to be
as near to the point as possible but never led the attack because if the commander were killed or wounded, that loss could easily cause the entire assault
to break down.

24. Thorn interview, March 23, 1996, op. cit.

25. Follow-up interview with Manfred Thorn, May 11, 1999.

26. Author interview with Hans Siptrott, May 17, 1997, Esslingen.

27. This was likely the SPWs of Dörr, Wemmel, and those with Rumpf and
the rest of 9th Panzer Engineer Company.

28. Thorn interview, March 23, 1996, op. cit.

29. Engelsdorf is the German name for the village of Ligneuville. In the
author's follow-up interview with Thorn on May 11, 1999, Thorn vividly

recalled the words from Poetschke before the café: "*Fahren sie auf nach Engels-dorf und nehmen die Verbindung auf zur Spitze Sternebeck.*"

30. Testimony of Rolf Ehrhardt, October 30, 1946, NA, RG-549, "English Summaries and Translations of German Documents Related to War Crimes," 290/59/18/2-5, Box 13. After leaving the crossroads Ehrhardt related that "About 600 meters further on we overtook car [Panzer] 734 of Pilaypik [sic, Pi-larzek] which had stopped because of some defect. I cannot give the exact or-der of the motor vehicles of my company. SS. Sgt. Schraeder and 734 were ahead of me (out of sight). As I overtook 734, I arrived in Engelsdorf before him. . . . I cannot give the exact time when I arrived in Engelsdorf. It must have been a short time after 2nd Lt. Fischer's Panther had been hit as I still [now] saw Fischer wounded." In Ehrhardt's detailed recollections in 1981 of the Ar-dennes events, he told of having trouble descending down to Ligneuville: "The road required some attention because the technology of the Mk IV was not de-signed for going down curves downhill. Arriving in Engelsdorf, we first saw [Panzer] Nr. 702 unharmed [Schraeder's tank] and also the burning Panther of Fischer, Peiper—and likely Diefenthal too—as well as a number of SPWs." Re-port from Rolf Ehrhardt, 7th Company, 1st Panzer Regiment, LSSAH, no date but 1981, eighteen-page report provided to author by Wolf Mauder.

31. "As commandant of the spearhead tank of the 7th Company, I was not an eye witness to the events at the crossroads." Statement of Heinz Schraeder, September 22, 1947, NA, RG-549, Case 6–24, Box 15. Note that after Thiri-mont, Panzer Nr. 734, driven by Manfred Thorn, was actually ahead of Schraeder.

32. Testimony of Edward Bojarski to Lamar Tooze, U.S. First Army Head-quarters, December 19, 1944, NA, RG-153, Case 6–24, Box 76.

33. This revealing testimony of Arvid Freimuth was taken at Dachau on October 30, 1945, well before the investigation at Schwäbisch Hall. NA, RG-549, Case 6–24, Box 31. However, during the investigation, Freimuth commit-ted suicide, claiming that he had perjured himself—which is possible, as his only confession at Schwäbisch Hall concerned a fictional alleged shootings at La Gleize. The author used the October 30, 1945, statement, as its contents contained nothing controversial but did shed light on Peiper's actions at the crossroads on December 17, 1944. The crew of Freimuth's SPW included SS-Lt. Heinz Hendel, Cpl. Kurt Wittwer, Pvt. Olaf Jassen, Pvt. Herbert Stock, and Cpl. Günther Heinrichs.

34. Testimony of Josef Diefenthal to Dwight Fanton, November 14, 1945, in Wiesbaden. NA, RG-549, Case 6–24, Box 33. This thirty-two-page interview with Diefenthal remains one of the centerpieces of the early investigation.

35. Although Poetschke almost certainly ordered subordinates to shoot American prisoners, the possibility that Peiper told Poetschke to do away with the captives cannot be excluded. Indeed, Paul Zwigart, who was driving Diefenthal's SPW at the crossroads, told SS NCO medic Josef Frank that while both were held captive in the fall of 1945. "Zwigart driver of the vehicle in which Peiper and Diefenthal were driving at the time of the shooting at the crossroad, told Frank, Schlachter, Moosbrugge and others that Peiper gave the order at the crossroads," Dwight Fanton's Personality Card Index File, NA, RG-549, Case 6–24, Index to Defendants in the Malmédy Case, Card for SS-Sgt. Josef Frank, 7th Panzer Company. Although most rumors prior to Schwäbisch Hall charged Poetschke with originating the orders to shoot the prisoners, hearsay continued to attribute the original source to Peiper. For instance, SS-Sgt. Emmerich Bukor, in the headquarters battery of the artillery regiment, recounted to American interrogators in the fall of 1945 that "he had heard about the murder in Hungary in February 1945 from Richard Huber of the *II Battalion*, that Peiper had given the order to other officers to shoot the Americans." Interrogation of Emmerich Bukor, IC #73, "Screening Results 15–24 November 1945," Ellis Papers.

36. Testimony of Josef Diefenthal, December 12, 1945, NA, RG-549, Case 6–24, Box 33.

37. At that hour Kuhlmann, in charge of the 12th SS Panzer Regiment, was involved in a ferocious battle with the U.S. 2nd Infantry Division for possession of the twin villages of Rocherath-Krinkelt, not far from their starting point. They would never advance closer to Malmédy than Bütgenbach.

38. This conversation and all the particulars from the statement of Hans Assenmacher, February 6 and 11, 1946 at Schwäbisch Hall, NA, RG-549, Case 6–24, Case 6–24, Box 36.

39. Statement of Josef Diefenthal, April 20, 1948, Landsberg Lech, NA, RG-549, Box 15.

40. Although Hans Assenmacher produced statements in 1948 alleging mistreatment at Schwäbisch Hall and errors in his account of the "Jeep incident" incriminating Paul Zwigart, he never recanted his version of the events with Peiper at the crossroads on December 17, 1944. See Affidavits, June 17 and November 19, 1948, NA, RG-549, Case 6–24, Box 70.

41. Freimuth Screening Interview, no date but fall of 1945, NA, RG-549, Case 6–24, Box 31. Also statement of Arvid Freimuth, "Interrogation of Freimuth (Shumacker)," NA, RG-549, Case 6–24, Index to Defendants in Malmédy, Supplemental Card file. Josef Diefenthal said he had also heard Peiper's complaints to Poetschke, but he claimed to not recall the conversation.

42. Freimuth statement, ibid., 9. Paul Fröhlich had also been in Peiper's SPW since Büllingen: "Peiper was very concerned with time. Peiper reached the crossroads and yelled out some orders to get moving." Interview with Karl Paul Fröhlich May 19, 1997.

43. Interview with Paul Zwigart, May 20, 1997, Aspach. "I liked Maj. Peiper, but I cannot talk about Diefenthal. We cannot speak about him." The author's interview with Zwigart was exceedingly tense, with comrade Dr. Franz Neundorff, former SS-Lt., standing by to ensure no slipups. The jeep incident at Cheneux as well as Malmédy was placed off limits before the meeting.

44. In fact, Gen. Edward Timberlake in Ligneuville had fled by the time Peiper arrived. Kampfgruppe Peiper captured dozens of soldiers with the 9th Armored Division, eight of whom where executed after being taking prisoner, an event that took place by the road near the entrance to the town. Later, Peiper would interrogate Captain Seymour Green, then a prisoner at the Hotel du Moulin.

Chapter 6

1. Testimony of T/5 John A. O'Connell to Col. Lamar Tooze, 77th Evacuation Hospital, December 17, 1944, NA, RG-153, Case 6–24, Box 77. "After searching us, they escorted us to a nearby field approximately 40 yards away, where quite a number of American soldiers were gathered together as prisoners."

2. Testimony of Pfc. Ralph W. Law, February 19, 1945, 52nd U.S. General Hospital, NA, RG-549, Case 6–24, Box 22. Law's "Tiger tank and two tank destroyers" were likely Poetschke's Panther #151 and SPWs under Beutner's command. "A German officer stood up, took aim and fired two pistol shots at the prisoners. I heard a man yell in pain. The German officer gave a command in German. The machine gun on the tank and two men, standing beside the tank, with burp guns opened fire. I hit the ground as soon as I realized they were firing on us. . . . I was hit in the left leg while I was lying on the ground. My leg pained me at first, but after a couple of minutes it became numb. I lay there not daring to move. . . . I was conscious of someone walking among the men on the ground with a pistol. One man close to me was hollering with pain. I heard a shot close by—then he was very quiet."

3. Testimony of T/5 Kenneth E. Kingston to Capt. Oliver Seth, 77th Evacuation Hospital, Verviers, Belgium, December 23, 1944. Also see Kingston to Lt. Col. Alvin B. Welsch, December 25, 1944, HQ First U.S. Army, NA, RG-153, Case 6–24, Box 76. Later, statement to Oliver Seth on December 29, 1944, NA, RG-549, Box 23. Also statement of Kingston to Dwight Fanton on October 8,

1945, in Wiesbaden, Germany (RG-549, Box 30) and the map of the crossroads with the location of the tagged bodies along with a numbered key.

4. Given the balance of the evidence, it seems most likely that the English-speaking Werner Poetschke was the man who asked for drivers. Kingston to Dwight Fanton on October 8, 1945, op. cit.

5. In all likelihood the men Kingston saw were actually Bower, Graeff, Conrad, and Garrett five vehicles up the column. It is clear that Mearig, Stabulis, and Hall accompanied the other prisoners back to the crossroads and did not attempt to escape until just before the main shooting. See detailed testimony of T/4 Robert Mearig, October 10, 1945. Sgt. Alphonse Stabulis's body was recovered one kilometer distant from the massacre field toward the south woods in April 1945. The body of Pfc. Flack was found immediately behind the mass of dead soldiers from the main massacre and thus was possibly one of those Kingston saw. However, Hall's body was found just in front of the café (and had been crushed by a tank), which would indicate that Hall did not follow the route taken by Mearig, Stabulis, and Flack. Mearig escaped, wandering in the Ardennes Forest for days, hiding from the Germans and cold and hungry until picked up by the U.S. 30th Infantry Division with frozen feet. He was the last survivor of the shooting to be found—and, coincidentally, rescued by a tank driven by Ralph "Mont" Pfautz, an old friend of his from their hometown of Lititz, Pennsylvania.

6. This was could have been Pfc. Frederick Clark or Peter Phillips, whom others saw shot as they were marched back up the road. See testimonies of Fox and Graeff. "He was just walking along and he didn't have his hands high enough. The Germans said something to him and then shot him."

7. The officer Kingston saw was Lt. Col. John Ray, whom Peiper had captured near Waimes earlier that day. Interview with Col. John Ray, Natick, MA, May 15 and 18, 1998.

8. Kingston feigned death for a long time with the others: "[Pvt. William F.] Reem was laying there behind me. He said he couldn't stand it so he was going to get up and run. Some of the fellows told him to stay down or we would all get killed. . . . I saw Pvt. Reem get up and start running and then Appman and Pvt. Profanchick. They started under a barbed wire fence and I took off and ran after them. We ran across the open field and they fired at us with machine guns while we were running. Some of the fellows went around the house while three or four of us went around the back of it. . . . We ran two and a half miles across country into Malmédy." In the hospital Kingston would get a shot of morphine and would later meet up with Charles Appman, Harold Billow, and Bruce Summers, who was already speaking with a war correspondent. "Just then, they

brought in Butera and laid him alongside me on the next cot," said Summers. Suffering from shock and trauma, Harold Billows was beside himself and had to be sedated. In his memory (statement of William F. Reem to Lt. Col. Alvin B. Welsch, December 18, 1944, NA, RG-549, Case 6–24, Box 23) Reem heard Kingston say "No! No!" when the Germans attempted to remove his wrist watch. Reem then heard Kingston shot, but then asked him after the Germans left "if he was hit." Kingston had been shot twice in the leg but thought he could still run.

9. "The Malmédy Massacre as remembered by Charles Appman," prepared for author, March 30, 1996.

10. In his autopsy at the 44th Evacuation Hospital, Maj. Giacento Morrone found that Cpl. Joseph Brozowski had been wounded repeatedly—in the leg, right arm (which may have been used to shield the head), and to the face. His body (Tag #49) was found on the extreme north end of the field on the left-hand side of the hedgerow that bisected its periphery. Autopsy report of Maj. Giacento C. Morrone, Medical Corps, 44th Evacuation Hospital, January 22, 1945, NA, RG-549, Case 6–24, Box 23.

11. Later in the testimony on October 10, 1945, Daub clarified that he was not sure if the vehicle that attempted to train a large gun on the prisoners in the field was a tank or halftrack. It was "a short gun with a large muzzle"—a good description of the *Sd Kfz 251/9 Ausf D* SPW with a 7.5-cm short cannon with a limited traverse. German halftrack crews often referred to this infantry support vehicle as the "*Stummel*" (Stump). The halftrack was likely the mount of SS-Sgt. Gerhard Schumacher of the 11th Panzer Grenadier Company. Later in the testimony on October 10, 1945, on p. 9, Daub clarified that after the man in the tank fired pistol shots into the group, the tank began to drive off, at which point machine guns started to fire immediately. This squares exactly with Hans Siptrott's description to the author.

12. Testimony of Pfc. Aubrey J. Hardiman to Maj. Woodward C. Gardiner, December 18, 1944, 28th General Hospital, NA, RG-153, Case 6–24, Box 76.

13. Author interview with Ted Paluch, September 17, 1997.

14. Testimony of Pvt. George L. Fox, October 11, 1945, Wiesbaden, NA, RG-549, Case 6–24, Box 30. Fox said that he had been standing at the south end of the field near tags 30, 33, and 37. In the author's interview with Fox on January 18, 2010, he indicated he was in about the second or third row of those standing in the field. He also claimed both pistol shots came from the north end of the field and struck Americans standing on that side of the assembly.

15. Testimony of T/5 Carl W. Moucheron to Maj. Woodward C. Gardiner, 28th General Hospital, Liège, December 18, 1944, NA, RG-153, Case 6–24, Box 77.

16. Testimony of T/5 Carl R. Daub to Oliver Seth, December 18, 1944, 28th General Hospital, NA, RG-153, Case 6–24, Box 76.

17. Testimony of Theodore Flechsig, Company B, 285th FAOB, February 20, 1945, NA, RG-549, Case 6–24, Box 22. "After briefly searching a few of the captives, the rest were ordered into the field. An enemy halftrack which was pulled up at the side of the road, attempted to swing its mounted machine gun on the prisoners, however, its limited traverse made it impossible for them to use it. A German Lieutenant, directing the proceedings was standing in a half-track. Our medic, asking permission from the captors was permitted to administer first aid to a couple of wounded soldiers. The German Lieutenant, without any provocation, drew his pistol and shot through the forehead, a defenseless soldier who made no effort to escape. He then proceeded to do the same to another captive. This was the signal for several other German soldiers to fire upon the rest of the captives. There was definitely no attempt at escape or violence by any of the captives who had their hands clasped over their heads." On the collar of the SS lieutenant beside his bars were lightning bolts. Flechsig recalled a white rectangular marking or insignia. Unfortunately, within the Waffen SS insignia, this could have been the bars for an SS sergeant, so this could just as easily have been SS-Sgt. Max Beutner. However, a clear demarcation comes from the fact that a number of witnesses saw Rumpf armed with a pistol, but nearly all recalled that Beutner carried a machine pistol at the crossroads.

18. Theodore Flechsig statement, December 20, 1944, NA, RG-153, Case 6–24, Box 77. Flechsig was insistent that a German officer with a lieutenant's rank fired the first two shots. "I remember the lieutenant had something [special on his collar], I think that it was his bars. Q: "Was it a German officer who fired the initial two shots into the men?" A: "Yes sir, I was looking right at him when he did it, sir." Perhaps significantly, the most likely German officer with that rank at the crossroads that day was SS-1st Lieutenant Erich Rumpf, who showed up in a command car on the north end of the field. This other possibility is SS-2nd Lt. Hering under Rumpf.

19. Flechsig, ibid. According to the autopsy, Lt. Perry Reardon, who was shot through the knee, was later struck in the head leading to his death. Reardon (Tag #52) was in the front of the group at the north end of the field.

20. Testimony of Pvt. Donald W. Day to Col. Lamar Tooze, 77th Evacuation Hospital, December 17, 1944, NA, RG-153, Case 6–24, Box 76. Also see statement of Donald W. Day, 318th Station Hospital, April 15, 1945, NA, RG-549, Case 6–24, Box 22. Day had been among those unwounded who fell to the ground as soon as the machine guns began firing. However, as the Germans came through the field to kill those still living, one fired at Day with a

pistol, hitting him both in the right leg near the groin and in the helmet, although the latter wound only grazed his scalp. When all the others rose from
the tangle of bodies and ran, Day did as well, moving haltingly with Pvt.
Robert L. Smith who, although unwounded, was slowed by a nearly total loss
of feeling in his legs from lying awkwardly in the field for a long time. Smith
thought he and Day were among the last to escape in the large group that first
ran. Testimony of Pvt. Robert L. Smith to Col. Lamar Tooze, 77th Evacuation
Hospital, December 17, 1944, NA, RG-153, Case 6–24, Box 76. Although the
enemy fired at them as they ran, neither Day nor Smith was hit by this fire and
arrived in Malmédy at the railroad bridge there, where American guards
drove them in a jeep to the 77th Evacuation Hospital.

21. Affidavit of Pvt. Clarence M. Musgove, 158th U.S. General Hospital,
March 12, 1945, NA, RG-549, Case 6–24, Box 22.

22. Paluch likely saw Conrad, Graeff, and Garrett, who escaped before
the prisoners were assembled. In three separate testimonies in 1944 and
1945, Paluch insisted that the first shots had come from a command car
near the front of the group of prisoners and that had fired two shots—one
to the left and one to the right. Sworn statement of Theodore J. Paluch to
Hazen W. Cole, CIC Det #8, December 20, 1944, NA, RG-549, Case 6–24,
Box 23; Testimony of T/5 Theodore J. Paluch to Lt. Col. Alvin B. Welsch,
HQ First U.S. Army, December 25, 1944, NA, RG-153, Case 6–24, Box 77.
Also see testimony of Theodore J. Paluch, October 10, 1945, Wiesbaden,
Germany, Box 30.

23. estimony of Pvt. Robert L. Smith to Dwight Fanton, October 11, 1945,
Wiesbaden, NA, RG-549, Case 6–24, Box 30. The eight tanks that Smith saw
approaching while they were being searched were almost certainly those from
the 7th Panzer Company.

24. Paluch, October 10, 1945, op. cit.

25. Paluch statement, December 20, 1944, op. cit. Also see Paluch testimony, December 25, 1944, op. cit. Finally, author interview with Paluch, September 17, 1997, and December 15–18, 2007. Paluch was likely standing close
to Cpl. Raymond Lester, who was one of the two men hit by the German pistol
shots. "Every tank that would pass by would fire into the group."

26. T/5 William B. Summers to Capt. Oliver Seth, HQ U.S. Army, December 20, 1944, NA, RG-549, Case 6–24, Box 23. Also see testimony of T/5
William B. Summers to Lt. Col. Alvin B. Welsch, HQ U.S. Army, December
23, 1944, NA, RG-153, Case 6–24, Box 77. In Summer's deposition he was unsure whether the first pistol shots had come from a tank or armored car.

27. Author interview with William B. Summers, September 21, 1995.
Summer's original statement of December 23, 1944 (ibid.) was very clear,

however, that three German halftracks were across from them when firing began.

28. Testimony of Cpl. George L. Fox to Capt. Oliver Seth, December 18, 1944, 28th General Hospital, Liège, NA, RG-153, Case 6–24, Box 76.

29. Account prepared for author by Charles Reding, Houma, LA, March 28, 1996. "From the opposite side of the building I could hear pistol shots and machine gun fire. This lasted about 20 minutes. Then there was silence and the tanks started moving down the road again. I continued to hear German voices. In desperation some of the wounded attempted to escape—running in different directions—some trying to take shelter in the café. The Germans continued to shoot them, turning them over to see if they were still alive and shooting anyone who moaned." The man whom Reding threw himself onto the ground nearby may have been dead or was otherwise feigning death. Those shot near the café included Pfc. Charles E. Hall (Tag #69) or Pfc. Carl H. Rullman (Tag #62).

30. Interview with Col. John Ray, Natick, MA, May 15 and 18, 1998. "We drove for some distance, maybe ten miles and he simply turned me over to some larger echelon of prison control." Ray was taken to Ligneuville.

31. Kenneth F. Ahrens to Capt. Clyde L. Walker, E&E Report 2907, March 11, 1945, in Paris, NA, RG-549, Case 6–24, Box 22.

32. Testimony of Sgt. Kenneth F. Ahrens to Capt. Oliver Seth, December 18, 1944, 28th General Hospital, Liège, NA, RG-153, Case 6–24, Boxes 76 and 77.

33. Pvt. John R. Kailer to Capt. Oliver Seth, 28th General Hospital, Liège, December 22, 1944, NA, RG-153, Case 6–24, Box 76. Kailer told Oliver Seth that he was not paying close attention when the shooting began; he simply remembered a machine gun suddenly firing and everyone dropping to the ground. "They kept spraying us with machine gun fire . . . there was apparently small arms fire too because that is what I got hit with as we lay there. I was laying parallel to the road with my head pointing south. I was lying on my stomach and the bullet entered my chest, under my left arm and it ranged downwards toward my heart. . . . I believe most of the automatic fire came from this one vehicle parked along the road. It was slightly behind us and to the north. To be shot as I was, the bullet must have come from a point further south down the road. I was shot by a pistol or something similar, the x-ray man told me. . . . They continued to fire for a couple of minutes while we lay there. While laying, I heard another bunch of vehicles go up the road. We could hear they were tracked vehicles. After they had all gone up the road, we thought. After we could not hear any more motors for four or five minutes a number of fellows got up and ran for cover. There were about 30 in this group and I was one of them."

34. Testimony of Virgil Lary, June 1, 1949, MMIH, 1031. The officer asking for driving volunteers ("Chauffeur!") was most likely Werner Poetschke.

35. Statement of T/4 Robert P. Mearig, October 10, 1945, Wiesbaden, Germany, NA, RG-549, Case 6–24, Box 30. Also "A Malmédy Survivor Remembers," Robert P. Mearig, *The Lancaster Sunday News*, York, PA, December 16, 1973. "I finally ran across the road and pushed the door in with my rifle. Two elderly women were sitting inside crying fiercely. I asked in Pennsylvania Dutch, 'What's going on?' They just said in German, 'Go away—the Germans are here.' I ran back across the road." The building Mearig refers to is House #10, occupied by the families of Henri-Goffinet and Léonard Muller, right by the bend in the road to Ligneuville where Lary and the first vehicles were halted by enemy fire.

36. Mearig statement, ibid. It is important to note that in Mearig's recollections after the war (provided to the author) he appeared likely confused relative to the sequence of the events against those he clearly outlined in his earlier testimony at Wiesbaden. In 1945 Mearig first described how he made two initial attempts to get away, eventually culminating in his flight just before the shooting. However, after the war he came to believe that he, Stabulis, and Flack ran off from the group significantly before the main shooting occurred. For instance, in a letter to John Bauserman dated March 7, 1990, Mearig wrote that "The first tank was about twenty feet from us and I said to Stabulis, 'Let's run.' It was open field in back of us, but I took off and Stabulis was right behind me. We went about 30 feet or more and they were firing tracer bullets at us. Stabulis stopped and started to go back. I kept going. I don't know how far. Then I got scared and I turned around and went back part way and saw they were going up the road. I fell down and waited. Soon I saw more activity at the head. Next I hear several pistol shots. Then lots of machine gun bursts. . . . Then they started to shoot separately. I then got up and ran left towards a group of small trees." The author asked Mearig about the discrepancies of his early testimony and postwar recollections. "It's so hard to remember everything after some 50 years," he truthfully confessed in a letter to the author on October 30, 1996. Due to two facts, it seems much more likely that Mearig, Stabulis, and Flack fled just before the shooting: (1) At Wiesbaden, Mearig mentioned that there were two pistol shots just as he emerged from cover of the main mass of Americans in front of him in the field, which were the pistol shots just preceding the machine gunning of the Americans, and (2) The body of Donald Flack, whom Mearig said was running just behind him and Sgt. Stabulis, was found just to the rear of the group of dead in the field. Also, the Wiesbaden testimony fits neatly with one other fact: Mearig mentioned that he, Stabulis, Flack, and Charles Hall had at first attempted to slowly shuffle north toward the café, only

to turn around and return to the main body of prisoners, although Hall did not return.

37. Pfc. Charles Hall did not return to the group with his other three buddies, taking cover behind the hedgerow near the café and hiding in that building or in its shed. After the café was later set ablaze, Hall may have been killed after leaving his hideaway and shot at the front of the café, where his body (Tag #69) was later found. For "Stabulis said we better go back," Mearig letter to author, October 30, 1996.

38. All quotes from Mearig, October 30, 1996, op. cit.

39. Letter from Mearig to author, September 19, 1996.

40. The body of Sgt. Stabulis was removed to the Henri Chapelle Cemetery by Lt. Francois Desmedt of the Belgian interring service, who also located the bodies of Cpl. William H. Moore and T/5 Wilson Jones. Cpl. Robert Conrad had last seen Moore alive running in a westerly direction at the head of the column after he and several others hid in a ditch west of the main road after Werner Sternebeck's lead tank platoon passed by. "He was one of the men who ran this westerly direction about 40 yards over to this clump of trees. I didn't recognize him running across the field, but I later heard his voice from this clump of trees to the northwest of our ditch." Testimony of Cpl. Robert B. Conrad to Capt. Oliver Seth, U.S. First Army, December 29, 1944, NA, RG-153, Case 6–24, Box 76. It seems likely, after initially escaping from the German spearhead, that Moore returned to the road that led to Ligneuville, where he was later killed. Document describing Moore's fate courtesy John Bauserman. Moore's body was found crushed on the road to Ligneuville, while the bodies of Jones and Stabulis were found about a kilometer south of Baugnez, off the road and in the woods.

41. That the escape attempt of Dobyns, Mearig, and others could have precipitated the massacre events seems doubtful, as the Germans had already assembled the SPW vehicles and crews that would be used to fire on the Americans. Moreover, several testimonies revealed that the German SPW crews were preparing their weapons for several minutes before the shooting took place. Even so, after the war Georg Fleps of Panzer Nr. 731 cited running Americans as the reason he fired—at least in a leading question posed by Belgian researcher Gerd Cuppens in a telephone conversation on September 4, 1986. Gerd Cuppens, *Massacre a Malmédy?* (Bayeux, France: Editions Heimdal, 1989), 107. The American soldier Fleps referred to was Pvt. Samuel Dobyns, who admitted running, but only after the first pistol shot. This can be contrasted with Fleps's earliest confession of January 4, 1946: "I admit on 17 December 1944, in the vicinity of Engelsdorf [Ligneuville], to have fired the first round on the American prisoners of war. After that the machine gun

fired. When the machine gun had stopped, one American still stood alive in the field. I then finished him off with the pistol." William R. Perl Papers, George Washington University, Gelman Library, Box 4, Folder 24.

42. Merriken estimated that they stood in the field for only minutes before the first shots began, an estimate agreed upon by James Mattera. Others put the time at twenty minutes to half an hour—although that seemed to include the time when the group was being assembled at the intersection before they were marched across the fence into the field.

43. Ken Ahrens (March 11, 1945, op. cit.) remembered that several tanks and halftracks with a number of foot soldiers pulled up. "A young officer emerged from one of the tanks and stood in the turret. He pulled out his pistol, aimed at the group of prisoners and fired one round. Ten feet from Ahrens a man fell to the ground, shot through the head. The man fired another round and another man fell. Then, all the tanks, halftracks and infantry opened fire with machine guns." Cpl. Sciranko also remembered that the shooter was a man who stood up on a tank and fired two shots, one at each end of the assembled troops.

44. James P. Mattera, as told to C. M. Stephan Jr., "Murder at Malmédy," *Army*, December 1981.

45. Albert Valenzi interview, September 26, 1995. In Valenzi's original statement he clarified this episode: "I saw our medic—Cpl. Ralph Indelicato—try to bandage Carl Stevens and as he was bandaging him, they fired upon him. The medic was shot in the legs, I believe, with machine gun fire." Statement of T/5 Albert M. Valenzi to Capt. Oliver Seth, 28th General Hospital, Liège, December 18, 1944, NA, RG-153, Case 6–24, Box 77. In Valenzi's statement he was certain that the first shots had come from a soldier wielding a pistol on a tank that arrived after they had surrendered.

46. "I remember that the fourth or fifth tank stopped and those of us in the road who were being searched were told to shove our sleeves up on our arms so that they could see if we had any watches. . . . I also remember that while we were standing in the road, one German tank stopped in the intersection and fired a few rounds towards Malmédy." Paluch testimony, October 10, 1945, op. cit.

47. In his testimony S/Sgt. Henry Zach recalled that the men were not in formal ranks but were at least four deep, which he could see as he was at the rear of the group. Record of Evidence of S/Sgt. Henry R. Zach to Lt. Col. J. H. Boraston, March 7, 1945, in "Report of the Supreme Headquarters Allied Expeditionary Force Court of Inquiry re Shooting of Allied Prisoners of War by the German Armed Forces near Malmédy, Belgium, 17 December 1944," NA, RG-549, Case 6–24, Box 11.

48. Smith testimony, October 11, 1945, op. cit. The other man wearing a medical brassard that Smith saw with Indelicato was likely Pfc. Elmer Wald, a medic with the 200 FA Battalion who was shot to death immediately in front of Indelicato at the south end of the field.

49. Summers testimony, December 23, 1944, op. cit.

50. Angela J. Burrows, "Ligonier Man Survived Malmédy Massacre," *Greensburg Herald Review*, Pittsburgh, PA, no date but 1983 or 1984, clipping courtesy of Helen Skoda and John Bauserman. Skoda died in 1989.

51. In his testimony to SHAEF on December 22, Lary's account of what happened in the field varied slightly from the earlier one: "We stood there for about ten minutes in the group of 200 men, the Germans attempted to place an 88mm on the group, but were unable to do so. . . . Then two halftracks pulled up facing us, each with one machine gun stuck out on the side. Then one halftrack pulled in between the other two and a German officer with his pistol fired twice in the group, killing or wounding two men. At the second shot, both machine guns turned loose on the group. Those who were not immediately killed hit the ground. They continued to fire at us for 3-4 minutes. Then the Germans came into the group and shot men who were crying in pain. That went on for 15 minutes."

52. Testimony of Pvt. Peter C. Piscatelli to Oliver Seth, 47th Field Hospital, December 18, 1944, NA, RG-153, Case 6–24, Box 77. Piscatelli thought the first shots came from a tank: "We stayed there about 20 minutes until this tank showed up. This German officer pulled out his pistol and fired on the boys and hit one in the stomach." In his original statement of December 18, Werth (atatement of Pvt. Bobby Werth to Col. Lamar Tooze, 77th General Hospital, Verviers, December 17, 1944, NA, RG-153, Case 6–24, Box 77) said the first shot came from a "tanker who stood up on a halftrack and fired." In "The Massacre at Malmédy," *Field Artillery Journal* February 1946, Lt. Virgil P. Lary recalled it this way: "Just then a German officer in a command car stood up and fired two shots into our group, the first killing my personal driver [Cpl. Raymond Lester] who was standing next to me on my right. With the second shot, the machine guns opened fire at point blank range."

53. Statement of Pvt. Bobby Werth to Col. Lamar Tooze, 77th General Hospital, Verviers, December 17, 1944, NA, RG-153, Case 6–24, Box 77.

54. Ken Ahrens also saw a man shot in the forehead by one of the first two pistol rounds that were fired. Ahrens E&E Report, No. 2907, December 18, 1944, op. cit. "As they herded us into the field, our rear group medic, whose name was Ralph Indelicato, was bandaging up Carl Stevens who had been hit by mortar fire before the road. He didn't make a move out of the ordinary while giving aid to Stevens. As soon as he got through, the Germans shot

them both." Al Valenzi saw much the same as he related in his original deposi-
tions as well as his interview with the author. Moreover, Ted Flechsig, in his
testimony at the 28th General Hospital on December 20, 1944, related that a
medic was attending to a wounded American when a German soldier drove
up in an armored car. "He drew his pistol and he shot one boy between the
eyes, and he swung around to another boy." Machine gunfire came immediately thereafter. Flechsig estimated the machine gunfire went on for five minutes. Still another corroboration for this sequence of events comes from Pvt.
Donald Day, who stated on April 15, 1945 (NA, RG-549, Case 6–24, Box 22)
that an American medic was shot by pistol fire just before two armored vehicles opened up on the group with machine guns.

55. Piscatelli statement, op. cit.

56. Author interviews with William Merriken, July 4 and September 22,
1995. The man shouting "Standfast!" has been identified as Lt. John Munzinger. In his revisionist account Cuppens (*Massacre a Malmédy*, op. cit., 114)
made much of the fact that an American officer called out such an order. Why,
he reasoned, would Munzinger have to call out such an order if the Americans
were not already moving? Although the prisoners were moving *after* the shots
(see Zach testimony, op. cit., and Testimony of Pvt. Samuel Dobyns to Col.
Lamar Tooze, 77th Evacuation Hospital, Verviers, Belgium, December 17,
1944, NA, RG-153, Case 6–24, Box 76), the collective disquiet seems understandable given German preparations to fire.

57. Kenneth F. Ahrens to Capt. Clyde L. Walker, March 11, 1945, in Paris,
National Archives, copy of document provided to author by Henri Rogister.

58. Testimony of John O'Connell, December 17, 1944, op. cit.

59. Perpetuation of the testimony of John Anthony O'Connell to Donald
L. Crooks, Special Agent SIC, September 10, 1945, Kansas City, MO, NA, RG-
549, Case 6–24, Box 30. "The prisoners had become nervous as a result of the
[pistol] shooting and Lt. Munzinger, no doubt, issued the command in order
to prevent the Germans for having a reason for shooting us all."

60. Cpl. Michael T. Sciranko also saw Lester hit. He had watched while the
Germans guarding them had tried to train a large-caliber gun on them. "After
we had been standing in the field for about 20 minutes, one of the Tigers [sic]
stopped in the road and pointed his 88 at us. For a moment, we thought we
had had it. . . . They played around with the 88 for about five minutes and
then this tank started off down the road again. As it began to move, one
tanker stood up in the turret and with his pistol picked off two guys on each
end of the bunch. One of them was Cpl. Lester, a guy from my outfit. Right after that, the Germans on the same tank opened up on us with their machine
guns and we all hit the dirt. . . . After that, every tank that came down the road

opened up on us with machine guns. . . . They were laughing and yelling among themselves. It was just one big shooting gallery." Report of Cpl. Sciranko: E&E Report No 1.8.9 (WEA)/6/764/2669, no date, but 1945, Paris, NA, RG-549, Case 6–24, Box 42. That one of the first two pistol shots hit Lester is virtually certain, as there are multiple witnesses. The largest number of survivors describing those fateful moments thought Lester was shot first on the north end of the field and the medic, Indelicato, with the second shot on the south end (although Kingston and Mattera reversed the order and Paluch was unsure). In particular, Lt. Lary insisted that Lester, his driver, was hit first, falling immediately to his right. However, Lester was likely not killed by this wound and evidently was able to move away from the main group of bodies before collapsing. His body was not found until February 1945 at some distance from the crossroads by the N-23 to the south. When his body was disinterred on November 14, 1947, a postmortem examination decided he had been killed by a gunshot wound to the head.

61. Testimony of Skoda, May 28, 1945, op. cit.

62. "Just then a German officer in a command car stood up and fired two shots into our group, the first killing my personal driver who was standing right next to me on my right." Lt. Virgil P. Lary, "The Massacre at Malmédy," *Field Artillery Journal*, February 1946.

63. Testimony of T/5 Charles F. Appman, 285 FAOB, to Alvin B. Welsch, HQ U.S. First Army, December 18, 1944, NA, RG-549, Case 6–24, Box 23. "The man who fired the pistol seemed to take deliberate aim at a soldier in the crowd." Note the large degree of correspondence between Appman's statement and those made by Paluch regarding the appearance of the command car at the crossroads.

64. Sworn statement of Pvt. James P. Mattera to CIC Agent James G. Cox, December 20, 1944, NA, RG-549, Case 6–24, Box 23. "I lay there for about an hour sweating it out."

65. Mattera's sequence of who was hit by the first two shots is contradicted by other witnesses, who recalled that Cpl. Lester was hit first and then Cpl. Indelicato, the medic, by the second shot.

66. Using the map drawn by Kenneth Kingston and then including a detailed section showing where the various bodies were found, Mattera located the medical man shot first (he clearly saw his Red Cross brassard) at nearly the exact spot where the body of Cpl. Ralph Indelicato was found in the field. He indicated location No. 19, which was the location of the body of Elmer Wald. In fact, Indelicato's body (Tag No. 2) was immediately adjacent to that of Wald, and the autopsy clearly showed that the medical officer had been hit in the face by a pistol shot. Moreover, the autopsy revealed that his facial bullet wound

entered his left upper lip and exited the right side of his face. Thus, assuming that Indelicato was facing east when the shot was fired, the bullet would have had to come from the direction of the Café Bodarwe. This argues, too, for the pistol shots coming from Beutner or Rumpf. Testimony of T/5 James P. Mattera, October 11, 1945, Wiesbaden, NA, RG-549, Case 6–24, Box 30.

67. Affidavit of Sgt. Marvin J. Lewis, June 6, 1945, NA, RG-153, Case 6–24, Box 76.

68. Testimony of Edward Bojarski, December 19, 1944, NA, RG-153, Case 6–24, Box 76. In an illustration of the vagaries of memory, Bojarski not only thought the man with the pistol fired up to five shots (and from a command car), but he also thought that the vehicle that turned its gun on the Americans was a tank. Of course it is possible that there was more than one man firing pistol shots—the most likely ones being the always-mentioned Georg Fleps, but also Max Beutner and Erich Rumpf. Only grazed by a shot that went through his left sleeve, Bojarski would run with all the others when someone shouted encouragement. He and at least five other men, including Cpl. Wendt of his unit and John O'Connell, ran north until they came across an American captain in a medic's jeep and were taken to Malmédy.

69. Letter from Walter Wendt to author, December 21, 1998.

70. Letter of Walter Wendt, March 20, 1988. Courtesy John Bauserman.

71. "Appleton Corporal Survived Nazi Massacre of American Prisoners," April 14, 1945, *Appleton Post Cresent*, Appleton, WI. Wendt was interviewed while on furlough at his home after surviving Baugnez. He also claimed that, before the main massacre, an American medic was shot: "One of the fellows from the artillery outfit had been wounded in the arm and one of the American medics asked a German guard if he could take care of the guy. The guard apparently said OK and the medic bandaged up the wounded. After he finished, the guard just pulled up his gun and shot them both."

72. Ibid.

73. "*Da kriegt noch einer Luft*," Letter from Walter Wendt to author, December 5, 1998.

74. Reem statement, December 18, 1944, op. cit.

75. For years Jim Mattera—who became obsessed with December 17, 1944—claimed that just before the shooting he heard the Germans shout "*Machen alle kaputt!*" (Kill them all!) Mattera, "Murder at Malmédy," op. cit. Did Mattera really hear the Germans utter that command? Being Pennyslvania Dutch, Mattera had a basic understanding of the German language. It must be admitted, however, that near the end of Mattera's life, his embellishment of the Malmédy story reached fanciful proportions. This is seen in the versions Mattera was fond of repeating in the 1980s (e.g., Sepp Dietrich goose-

stepping by the prisoners at the crossroads), as used by Cuppens to discredit testimony of aging American survivors. See Cuppens, *Massacre a Malmédy*, op. cit., 90–91. As such, the author gave precedence to Mattera's three earlier accounts from December 1944 and October 1945. On this issue Mattera's statement of October 11, 1945, is illuminating: "I just saw a man pop up or stand up in this vehicle so that I could only see him from the waist up. *He yelled or shouted some words in a loud voice, none of which I understood* [italics mine], and almost immediately drew a pistol and fired two shots."

76. Testimony of Paul J. Martin, Private 1st Class to 1st Lt. Eugene H. Burris, JAG Department, Fort Oglethorpe, GA, August 24, 1945, NA, RG-153, Case 6–24, Box 76. "As the German vehicles passed along the road to St. Vith, they fired into us as we lay in the pasture. I was shot in the right leg. . . . After they stopped firing at us with a machine gun, several Germans walked among us and all the men who were wounded or making any noise at all were shot again. . . . I heard shots fired within eight or ten yards of where I lay." After the Germans left Martin fled helter-skelter with a score of those still living. Martin ran with T/5 Michael Skoda and Cpl. William Reem, but he dropped to the ground after the Germans fired wildly with machine guns. Undaunted, however, he and Skoda continued to crawl until they reached the Mathonet house about two hundred meters west of the crossroads on the road to Hédomont. Although Skoda was badly wounded and elected to stay at the home, Martin worried this place would not be safe and elected to take to the woods and fields. He worked his way to Malmédy, reaching a guard point just before sunset. Skoda, however, had little choice but to take refuge in the abandoned farmhouse, where he remained for five days before German regular army troops captured him (Skoda testimony, May 28, 1945, op. cit.).

77. Testimony of T Sgt. William H. Merriken to Ralph Shumacker, October 9, 1945, Wiesbaden, Germany, NA, RG-549, Case 6–24, Box 30.

78. The autopsy report of Capt. Kurcz found that Schwitzgold's first wound was likely a shot to the chest. However, the wound that killed him was a bullet that penetrated the victim's right eye, blasting away a section of his rear skull before continuing its grim trajectory. This was likely the round that lodged in Merriken's leg. NA, RG-549, Case 6–24, Box 23.

Chapter 7

1. Interviews with William Merriken, July 4 and September 22, 1995. In both interviews Merriken recalled after they had surrendered and were walking back to the crossroads a tall panzer officer calling out, "Chauffeur! Chauffeur!" and asking them to drive the abandoned trucks.

2. Author interview with Gerhard Walla, May 10, 1999, Aspach.

3. Testimony of Rolf Erhardt at Oberursel, October 30, 1946, RG 338, "English Summaries and Translations of German Documents Related to War Crimes," 290/59/18/2-5, Box 13. "While I was in captivity, I heard about the events in [near] Engelsdorf from SS-Cpl. Reinhard Meier that he had been present when Poetschke had answered the question of a messenger of what to do with the prisoners, with 'Kill them!'" Note that this testimony came after the trial.

4. Testimony of Josef Diefenthal, Wiesbaden, December 12, 1945, NA, RG-549, Case 6-24, Box 33, 7. This lengthy, early investigative interview by Dwight Fanton is the most important document dealing with Diefenthal in the Ardennes operations. After this interview, Diefenthal pointedly avoided any discussion of his and Peiper's movements at the crossroads.

5. BDC file for Erich Rumpf, NA, RG-242, A3343-SS0-055B, Frame 589.

6. Letter from Elly Rumpf to Parole Board, September 16, 1946, NA, RG-153, Case 6-24, Box 84. "In case he has done wrong and has done what he is accused of, [then] he acted under the pressure and terrible confusion of war and it really was a desperate situation at the time."

7. "The main care [sic, job] of the company leader was from the battalion Poetschke that all those soldiers were against his will, transferred to the 9th Company who had been punished in their former companies and were considered particularly undisciplined, for which reason they had to serve a special term of probation in the 9th Company. Almost all of them were soldiers of long service. . . . Rumpf referred to this order as an attempt of the battalion commanders to clear themselves of all soldiers that were inconvenient to them and difficult to deal with." Affidavit of Gunther Borchers, August 5, 1947, NA, RG-153, Case 6-24, Box 80.

8. Statement of Walter Fransee, March 21, 1946, NA, RG-549, Case 6-24, Box 33.

9. "*Kriegsverbrechen im Osten*," Statement of Walter Fransee, 1st Platoon, 9 Pz Pi. Bn, 1 SS Pz Rgt., handwritten statement and transcription and translation by Helmut Thiess, George Washington University, Gelman Library, William Perl Papers, Box 6, Folder 51.

10. In writing to American author John Toland in 1959, Peiper challenged these notions. "I regret that you do not write history," he wrote, "but prefer to still cling to the old and primitive pattern of the Nazi brutes slaughtering civilians and violating the laws of war and peace. . . . For a man with intelligence and reason, such a one-sided and biased story should be under his dignity. And above all: what is the good of it?" Letter from Jochen Peiper to John

Toland, February 22, 1959, LOC, John Toland Papers, Battle: Story of the Bulge, Box 108, Folder "P."

11. "Also, tell your men and impress on them so you don't experience failure, that no one must stay behind because every man and every vehicle are needed." Statement of Erich Rumpf, March 22, 1946. Handwritten and translated typescript is in NA, RG-549, Case 6–24, Box 7.

12. Letter from Jochen Peiper to Hedwig Potthast, March 24, 1943, NSDAP Hauptarchiv, Himmler Collection, Microfilm Roll #99, Hoover Institution, Stanford University. Originals at the Bundesarchiv Koblenz, "Nachlass Heinrich Himmler: Korrespondenz Hedwig Potthast," Bestand N 1126/37.

13. Testimony of Reinhard Maier, "Screening Results 24–29 November 1945," interrogated by Capt. Hoelzl, Ellis Papers.

14. According to Erich Rumpf's own testimony, his personal orderly and messenger was SS-Cpl. Richard Weck. No statements or testimony of Weck survives, although his driver, Karl Veil, is still living, but unwilling to communicate.

15. Reinhard Maier was in Room #24 of Barracks "D" at IC#78 and talked to SS-Cpl. Hubert Brückner with the 7th Panzer Company, who was prisoner there. "Peiper had nothing to do with it," Brückner remembered Maier saying, "He knows the whole story, that Poetschke gave the order and that when interrogated, he will tell all about it." "Screening Results 15–24 November 1945," witnesses interrogated by Capt. Shumacker, Ellis Papers.

16. Walla interview, May 10, 1999, op. cit. In the author's interview, over beer, Walla struggled with the story of what happened, claiming that he had seen the SPWs of the 9th Panzer Engineer Company fire into the prisoners brought on by someone firing at them. "The SPW of Hering had an MG-42 and while I was being pulled out, the SPW fired back. Can you imagine what happens to prisoners who are caught before firing like that? I cannot judge how many of the prisoners got hit in the firing and I was glad to get out of there under the cover of the SPW. . . . I began moving again after the intersection and got as far as Fischer's tank which had been shot down." In fact, according to testimony of Hering's radio operator, SS-Pvt. Walter Fransee, the main shooting had already taken place by the time that SS-2nd Lt. Günther Hering's 1st platoon SPW turned the corner at the crossroads, although Fransee did see Hering execute a wounded American in the massacre field who was pleading for his life. See "Statement of Walter Fransee," March 21, 1946, NA, RG-549, Case 6–24, Box 33 and associated detailed sketches. Fransee also testified similarly in the Malmédy trial (U.S. v. Bersin, May 27, 1946, 762–769) and in another undated statement in the William Perl Papers, George Washington University, Box 6, Folder 51. Significantly, Fransee never

repudiated his statements regarding the events at the crossroads. This would indicate that Gerhard Walla and Kurt Kramm, who was likely with him, may have been present at the crossroads when the massacre took place. In an interview with Mike Smeets, Walla told another version: "Suddenly, there was small arms fire coming from the woods north of the field, the SPW crews returning fire. As a result, the U.S. prisoners standing in the field panicked, and were running around like crazy. They were caught in this machine gun fire." Smeets to author, June 7, 2005. Adding to this likelihood is the statement of Rudolf Rayer: On December 24, 1944, the Americans took Rayer (who had a fractured pelvis and ribs and shrapnel wounds to his lungs) and other German wounded to a field hospital in Verviers. Under interrogation: "Did you talk to anyone about it, who saw American prisoners of war were killed?" "Yes." "By whom?" "Kurt Kramm." "What did he talk about?" "He told me that he saw how prisoners of war were shot at the crossing between Engelsdorf and Malmédy." Declaration of Rudolf Rayer, Dachau, April 26, 1947, and statement of Rudolf Rayer, October 27, 1947, NA, RG-549, Case 6–24, Boxes 28, 38.

17. Statement of Pvt. Heinz Kappermann, on February 26, 1946, after Kappermann was made captive on December 23, 1944, NA, RG-549, Case 6–24, Box 41. "About 700–800 meters after the road crossing our two vehicles had to stop since a combat action was in progress ahead of us." Kappermann, who was later told by an SS-Pvt. Fred Till (2nd squad, 1st platoon) on the night of December 18 that the prisoners had been shot, remarked to his interrogators that he likely did not distinguish the sound of the shooting that had happened behind him from the sounds of battle in Ligneuville just ahead. They were halted before Ligneuville for nearly an hour. "From my experience in the German army, I know that difficult unpleasant or painful assignments were given almost exclusively to the 'penal squads.'"

18. Maute did not know the identity of the officer in the panzer uniform standing by the other officer in the brown-yellow jacket, only that he did not believe it was Werner Poetschke.

19. Hering's SPW was driven by SS-Pvt. Paul Buth, with Pvt. Fritz Pupkulies as one of its machine gunners, Pvt. Spaeh as messenger, and Pvt. Walter Fransee its radio operator. The rest of the eight- to ten-man crew is unknown. Statement of Paul Buth, March 28, 1945, NA, RG-549, Case 6–24, Box 28.

20. Statement of Willi von Chamier, March 21, 1946. Handwritten statement with detailed map are in NA, RG-549, Case 6–24, Box 8. On the map von Chamier shows the locations of Rumpf and his own SPW. Lined up across the prisoners just before the shooting, according to his map, were three SPWs from another unit as well as four tanks.

21. Von Chamier statement, March 21, 1946, op. cit. The crew of the SPW consisted of SS-S/Sgt. Wedeleit (leader), SS-Sgt. Helmuth Haas (leader of 1st squad), SS-Cpl. Katcher (MG Gunner 1), SS-Sgt. Willi von Chamier (MG Gunner 2), SS-Sgt. Biotta (Rifle 1), SS-Pvt. Max Rieder (Rifle 2), and SS-Pvt. Corzieni (Rifle 3). A steelworker in Dortmund prior to the war, in April 1943, von Chamier was moved from his duty as a Luftwaffe flak gunner to the Waffen SS with SS Panzer Regiment 1. He was captured on December 20, 1944 and transferred from a POW camp in the United States to Dachau for the trial, arriving on March 20, 1946.

22. Twenty-six-page handwritten confession with detailed maps of Max Rieder, March 26, 1946, NA, RG-549, Case 6–24, Box 8. In a statement regarding the interrogation of Rieder, William Perl said, "We always knew that he shot at the crossroads, but could not prove it. . . . After von Chamier confessed, he confessed to Mr. Thon and gave a statement on the shooting at the crossroads." "Rieder, Max–#51," Box 38.

23. Rieder confession, March 26, 1946, op. cit. Rieder would later repudiate his statements on April 11, 1948, alleging abuse at Schwäbisch Hall such that he was "bodily and psychically in such a state that I wrote everything." In the statement Rieder incriminated himself and Erich Rumpf. Affidavit, 11.4.48, Landsberg/Lech, NA, RG-549, Case 6–24, Box 63. Perhaps most telling was Rieder's own post-trial plea for mercy at Dachau in July 1946: "Shortly before Christmas [1942] I took an oath to the Führer and the nation and the sanctity of orders. In the following year I was assigned the artillery regiment LSSAH. In this unit every order was demanded to be carried out, even if it meant death for myself." Rieder had fought long in Russia—a savage experience during which he was a member of the Straf, or penal platoon, of the 9th Panzer Engineer Company. "With the punishment platoon, I had to carry out every order as I did not wish to run the risk of being shot myself." *U.S. v. Bersin*, 3236–3237.

24. Roman Clotten, who was with one of the 7th Company tanks present during the massacre, claimed he saw Rumpf and another man with a machine pistol run back from the field just before the shooting started. From the crew weapons, this would likely have been SS-Sgt. Helmuth Haas, who was the only member with a machine pistol. Statement of Roman Clotten, January 22, 1946, NA, RG-549, Case 6–24, Box 7. "I distinctly remember that two people who immediately after the first shots had been fired had fallen to the ground or had thrown themselves to the ground walked towards the road from the direction of the prisoners. . . . This younger, blonde man who was walking on the right, I saw here in prison, and recognized him again and found out that

he is SS-1st Lt. Rumpf. . . . The older man was carrying a machine pistol. As these two were walking towards our tank, we had halted already."

25. Statement of Paul Buth, March 28, 1946, NA, RG-549, Case 6–24, Box 28. "I don't know if SS-2nd Lt. Hering also shot at the kneeling man. It is possible because I only rode about 10 meters behind Haas's SPW. SS-2nd Lt. Hering was at that time in my SPW and it is easily possible that he too shot at the kneeling American."

26. Statement of Walter Fransee, March 21, 1946, NA, RG-549, Case 6–24, Box 33. Two sketches showed the locations of men Hering shot as their SPW passed the crossroads.

27. Statement of Erich Maute, January 22, 1946, NA, RG-549, Case 6–24, Box 32. Maute claimed he did not shoot any American prisoners at the crossroads and described how all were still standing in the field when he departed the scene. Indeed, he did not notice the sounds of shooting, as there was shooting all over as the battle group seized Ligneuville. He was informed about it from others in the town later that afternoon. Though not admitting wrongdoing in the Ardennes, Maute did tell his interrogators of having shot a dozen Russian prisoners on March 5, 1945, in Hungary on the orders of Rumpf.

28. Many recalled seeing Rumpf at the crossroads: In statements both Rieder and von Chamier claimed to have seen Rumpf himself fire into the prisoners with a pistol after calling for Rieder and von Chamier to fire as well. Dörr claimed to crewmate Kappermann that Rumpf had told him to order the tanks present to fire into the prisoners, but Dörr protested. The medic in the same SPW, Erich Maute, corroborated this account. Also, machine gunner SS-Pvt. Fritz Pupkulies, in screening in the fall of 1945 before Schwäbisch Hall, said that his commander, Rumpf, should know about the massacre, as he was already there waiting when they arrived and saw the bodies lying in the field. "Screening Results 24–29 November 1945," interrogations by Capt. Hoelzl at IC#1, Ellis Papers. SS man Bernhardt Dietz went AWOL from training in Westphalia and was sent to the penal platoon of the 9th Panzer Engineer Company in the Ardennes. "When they were camped near Engelsdorf on the 19th or 20th of December, a man by the name of Jansen told him about the murder at the crossroads and said that Rumpf had given orders that anyone who talked about this murder would be shot. . . . Rumpf was very unpopular with the *Straf* platoon." "Screening Results 15–24 November 1945," interrogations by Morris Ellowitz at IC#1, Ellis Papers. Note that these interrogations were done prior to Schwäbisch Hall. Finally, members of Franz Siever's 3rd Panzer Engineer Company—Joachim Hoffmann, Gustav Neve, Siegfried

Jaeckel, and Gustav Sprenger—who were implicated in the massacre, all told of seeing SS-1st Lt. Rumpf at the scene when it took place.

29. Because both Rehagel and Rumpf were present—and both were in need of alibis excusing them from culpability at Baugnez—the possibility emerges that the SS officer members of Panzer Nr. 711 saw speaking to Rehagel near the crossroads was not Christ but Rumpf himself!

30. "When I came up, I saw the prisoners. So far, they have been standing already in the field. Some tanks and SPWs took over and my SPWs closed up there. On the road to the left, there was a Mk IV. Hering went to this tank and talked with the tank commander. At this time, I saw [Gerhard] Schumacher walking to the direction of the tank where some soldiers in black uniform were standing. One was wearing a machine pistol and so he belonged not to the crew of this tank. Also, men of my SPW were running across the fields to this point. Schumacher, I saw a second time passing my SPW in a slow way and drove by with his SPW to the crossroads. At this street corner, two officers in black uniforms were standing there. I went there and we said hello. . . . Krause said he wanted to go on and had orders with him and would be expected. . . . At this time, a Panther, in one of them Hennecke, passed and one of the Panthers stopped at the crossroads. I went behind the house, because I didn't want to see the shooting. I heard the first bursts of fire. It was machine gun and MP fire. When the shooting was over, I ordered everyone back on the truck and went back to my SPW and started. When I was on top of the vehicle, I saw in the field on the right side all the dead prisoners. One of the Panzer IVs stood with its turret towards the prisoners. Around the tank there were about 8–10 in a gray uniform and some in a black uniform. Some were with weapons and some were without. At this moment, there was no longer any shootings. When I was around a 100 meters away, the tank again shot and I heard single shots from other weapons." Handwritten statement of Erich Rumpf, no date, NA, RG-549, Case 6–24, Box 32.

31. Differing from Rumpf's earlier claim, the weight of evidence suggests Hennecke's tank showed up right after the massacre had taken place. Statement of Hans Hennecke, January 17, 1946, NA, RG-549, Case 6–24, Box 8. Indeed, Hennecke's tank sideswiped Rumpf's SPW on the right side of the road at the intersection, and this had elicited numerous curses. "I drove very slowly further, SS-Sgt. Richarts followed me. . . . As I was passing the house which lies on the right side of the street, I stood in the turret of my tank looking in the direction I was going. Ernst Rock, my loader, stood behind me. . . . Pvt. Rock called to me, 'SS-2nd Lt, there lie some men and they are all dead.' I turned around and saw 15 or 20 dead Americans lying to

my right on the field. I saw them lying in a heap, and from the manner in which they were lying, I could see that they had not fallen in combat. No weapons were with them." Hennecke remained with that version of the story, both in his first interrogation by Dwight Fanton on December 11, 1945, in Schwäbisch Hall (Box 23) and even in his later legal effort at exoneration from Landsberg Prison. Statement of April 11, 1948, NA, RG-549, Case 6–24, Box 55.

32. Rumpf statement, March 22, 1946, op. cit.

33. Statement of Joachim Hoffmann, March 6, 1946, *U.S. v. Bersin*, 645–667. Original is in NA, RG-549, Case 6–24, Box 6, with Hoffmann's detailed map of the crossroad incident. Even though Hoffmann would later repudiate his statement as did many others, it is significant that a typed transcript of an interrogation of Hoffmann regarding the crossroads incident survives from February 15, 1946 (RG-549, Case 6–24, Box 38):

Q: You passed Beutner's vehicle on the right?

A: Yes. When the SPWs of the 2nd platoon passed Beutner's SPW, he was still sitting on his SPW and shouted to every vehicle. "Go and bump them off—all of them." We stopped near the south end of the field. We stood parallel to the ditch.

Q: Before the first shot was fired, how long were you there?

A: One to two minutes. During this time, the entire crowd on all the vehicles started shouting, "Bump them off! Bump them off!" I remember that Bode, Beutner and some more people from other SPWs were among them. There was quite some excitement. The men took out their weapons. We only had one machine gun—the front gun mounted permanently and after we arrived Toedter alone mounted and fixed the rear machine gun. I took the machine pistol and left my driver's seat and posted myself in front of the right corner of my SPW. Shortly after I posted myself there . . . Witkowski said, "Well boys, let's go on and let them have it."

Q: Before Witkowski said that, did you hear any fire order or command from anyone else?

A: There was general shouting from all the vehicles. "We will bump them off. Bump them off."

Q: Do you remember any command from Beutner himself?

A: Beutner was one of those who shouted "Bump them off."

34. Interrogation of Gustav Neve, March 6, 1946, NA, RG-549, Case 6–24, Box 26. In the interrogation transcript Neve changed his story completely after being confronted with the statement of Gustav Sprenger while in captivity. Originally he said the Americans had already been shot when he arrived but so confronted then confessed to active participation in the shooting and provided detailed hand-drawn sketches. This exchange makes it clear, however, that an agreed upon tactic of the guilty in the crossroads shooting was to claim that the Americans were already shot when their vehicle arrived—or, conversely, that all the Americans were still standing there and unharmed.

35. Machine gunner Heinz Stickel in the same SPW recalled the preparations for the shooting as requiring only "a very short time": "I received the order from Witkowski to shoot the prisoners who were standing in the pasture." He claimed to have obeyed because SS-2nd Lt. Seitz had told them before the offensive that "You will not take any prisoners of war in this offensive." Statement of Heinz Stickel, April 18, 1946, NA, RG-549, Case 6–24, Box 7.

36. Statement of Joachim Hoffmann from March 20, 1946, NA, RG-549, Case 6–24, Box 6. Regarding the actions of Beutner: "He told Witkowski that they were going to shoot the prisoners and to move on down the road out of the way so that they would not be in the field of fire." Regarding Diefenthal: "In my affidavit dated 6 March 1946, I mentioned having seen an officer wearing a yellow jacket at the crossroads north of Ligneuville. . . . On this date I saw a man in Cell E-53 at the prison in Schwäbisch Hall. The man I saw in this cell is definitely the same man I saw in the yellow jacket. When I recognized him this morning, a guard opened the door of his cell and told him to state his name. He gave his name as Josef Diefenthal."

37. Neve interrogation, March 6, 1946, op. cit. "After we had come to a halt, I heard Beutner tell Witkowski that the weapons should be loaded and made ready so we could 'bump off' the American prisoners. . . . Finally Beutner gave the order to fire and everybody opened up with their weapons." Jaekel statement: U.S. v. Bersin, 681–692. Original statement and large detailed map are in NA, RG-549, Case 6–24, Box 7. Jaekel named Hans Toedter and Harry Ende as helping him load and fire the machine guns in his SPW, although both were never located or brought to trial. Statement of Heinz Stickel, April 18, 1946, U.S. v. Bersin, 705–706. That of Marcel Boltz: 711–715.

38. Not surprisingly, two other NCOs who were in Beutner's SPW— SS-Cpl. Ernst Goldschmidt and Max Hammerer, were evasive in their statements regarding the events at the crossroads. However, members of Hoffmann's and Sprenger's crews clearly placed them on the scene. Nonetheless, Hammerer did tersely admit that "at the crossing which leads to Engelsdorf . . . our SPW

came to a halt and I was present as American prisoners of war were shot." Statement of Max Hammerer, April 11, 1946, NA, RG-549, Case 6–24, Box 9. However, Goldschmidt insisted awkwardly at the Malmédy trial that the sixty Americans had already been shot when the 2nd Platoon SPW reached the crossroads—a fact five other witness statements dispute, thus placing him on the scene when the shooting took place. Trial testimony of Ernst Goldschmidt, *U.S. v. Bersin*, 2398–2434. Indeed, so perilous was Goldschmidt's nervous performance at the trial that Defense Counsel Everett sought to cut short his testimony. Interestingly, Hans Oettinger, who was working as a carpenter in Hedelfingen after the war, would emerge from silent hiding to testify on Max Hammerer's behalf (who was sentenced to die by hanging)—a considerable risk because Oettinger himself and the others in the SPW he drove at Baugnez participated in the shooting. Sworn statement of Hans Oettinger, Munich, December 19, 1947, NA, RG-153, Case 6–24, Box 80. There is a final postscript: In the summer of 2011, Hammerer, who was still living, responded to the author's request for a detailed personal confession about the proceedings at the crossroads. However, contrary to considerable evidence and his own handwritten statement from 1946, Hammerer denied any guilt, claiming the Americans were already dead in the field when the SPW, in which he rode with Beutner, passed the field on the afternoon of December 17. Letter, Hammerer to author, July 25, 2011.

39. Statement of Heinz Friedrichs, March 21, 1946, NA, RG-549, Box 9. Friedrichs was an eighteen-year-old SS grenadier in the SPW of SS-Sgt. Gerhard Schumacher. When they were preparing to fire on the prisoners—a mission that was aborted at the last moment, Friedrichs looked away. "I told him I could not stand it, whereupon he called me a coward." Unable to depress his cannon on the prisoners, an SS 1st lieutenant in a panzer engineer uniform who appeared to be in charge (likely Erich Rumpf of the 9th Panzer Engineer Company), ordered Schumacher to proceed to Ligneuville, as a tank was coming up that "would do the job."

40. Statement of Siegfried Jaekel, March 1, 1946, witnessed by Ralph Shumacher, NA, RG-549, CAse 6–24, Box 7. Original handwritten statements and detailed maps are in Box 7.

41. Trial testimony of Marcel Boltz, *U.S. v. Bersin*, 2464–2528.

42. Interrogation of Siegfried Jaekel on February 15, 1946, NA, RG-549, Case 6–24, Box 38.

43. Given his cooperation with the prosecution, on March 15, 1946, Ralph Shumacher escorted Sprenger around Schwäbisch Hall to examine thirty-five to forty men in their E-block prison cells. During the day he claimed to recognize SS-2nd Lt. Erich Muenkemer in E-56 as the dark-haired panzer officer he had seen standing beside the tank with Erich Rumpf just

before the Americans were shot at Baugnez. "Gustav Adolf Sprenger, 15 March 1946," NA, RG-549, Case 6-24, Box 7.

44. Sprenger's provocatively detailed statement with a detailed—and important—map: NA, RG-549, Case 6-24, Box 7. After the initial shooting Sprenger claimed to see Beutner on the north edge of the field, taking something from one of the American prisoners. Also see affidavit of Marcel Boltz, March 21, 1946, same box location.

45. As with all the Malmédy men held captive at Landsberg Prison, Sprenger would later repudiate all his previous statements, claiming duress and even beatings. Affidavit of January 1948 and April 9, 1948, NA, RG-153, Case 6-24, Box 80.

46. After the Malmédy trial, Friedel Bode would personally plead for leniency in his trial sentence from "a difficult life." Relative to his accused crime, he claimed no recourse but to follow orders. He was wounded near Bourgoumont, Belgium and captured at La Gleize on December 24, 1944. *U.S. v. Bersin*, 3209-3210.

47. Statement of Friedel Kies, March 26, 1946, NA, RG-549, Case 6-24, Box 9.

48. The SPW was likely that of Max Beutner of the 3rd Panzer Engineer Company, which had bridging equipment rack-mounted on their *Sdkfz 251/7* halftrack. The 9th Pz. Engineer Company did not have such equipment. Thanks to Timm Haasler for his critical information. Siptrott statement, U.S. v. Bersin, op. cit., 561-562. "Several hundred meters further south we stopped because of a traffic jam. At that spot, Fleps left the tank. We stopped approximately five minutes and Fleps was absent." Author possesses a copy of Siptrott's original handwritten statement as well as the accompanying drawing. The diagram showed his Panzer Nr. 731, Pilarzek and Clotten's tank behind him, as well as the tanks of Dubbert and Koch behind those. However, in his recollection Siptrott was hazy on the exact march order and did not realize that Pilzarek's tank with Manfred Thorn as driver was likely up ahead of his own as well as two other tanks: 702 with Heinz Schraeder and 701 with company commander, Oskar Klingelhoefer. Author interview with Thorn (March 23, 1996, and May 11, 1999) and Siptrott (May 17, 1997).

49. Born in 1922, Georg Fleps was a native of Michelsburg, Rumania, where he was drafted into the Rumanian army in January 1943. In July of that year he was discharged into the Waffen SS as a *Volksdeutscher* recruit. From there he was sent to Arnhem, Holland, as a part of an SS infantry replacement battalion (12.SS T.I.R. 1) where "I was given a short, but very tough basic training." By January 1944 Fleps had been assigned to the panzer regiment of the Leibstandarte Adolf Hitler and fought with the division in Normandy the

following summer. The Canadian prisoners were shot by SS-Sgt. Josef Frank and SS-Cpl. Wesenberg on the order of SS-1st Lt. Werner Wolff in charge of the 7th Panzer Company. Beyond Fleps, also witnessing the event were Willi Boltz and Rolf Ehrhardt: Statement from Georg Fleps to Sgt. A. Salomons, 21 Army Group B.A.F.O., March 6, 1946, PRO: WO 309/256; statement from SS Unterscharführer Josef Frank to Sgt. A. Salomons of 21 Army Group Special Investigation Branch B.A.F.O, March 6, 1946; Deposition of Josef Frank to G. W. Low of Canadian War Crimes Investigation Team, February 17, 1947, PRO: WO 309/256; statement from Rolf Ehrhardt, SS Unterscharführer, Lodged at No. 2 Internee Prison, March 6, 1946, PRO: WO 309/256.

50. Given the author's reconstruction of the events at the crossroads, the "SPW commander" giving Siptrott and Fleps the order would have been SS-Sgt. Max Beutner in charge of the 2nd platoon of the 3rd Panzer Engineer Company, which several accounts place on the scene, with Beutner relaying orders from Werner Poetschke in a panzer present immediately before the events took place. In Fleps's original handwritten statement he says that Siptrott scornfully referred to the men in the SPW as "*dise Elende Hunde*" (sic, poor German for "these miserable dogs"). Statement of Georg Fleps, January 5, 1946, NA, RG-549, Case 6–24, Box 7. Fleps statement, March 6, 1946, op. cit. Fleps also said that after leaving the scene at the crossroads, "We stopped again by the first house on the left side of the road, i.e. the house indicated as No. 9 on my sketch (which is just 30 meters or so behind the massacre field), because the column had stopped and besides our track was slightly damaged. I left the tank to take booty. I took some cans of condensed milk and corned beef from an American truck. There I saw to the right of the street behind a fence, three Americans lying who were either dead or wounded. . . . I saw there three men from another vehicle of another company—I believe they belonged to the Mk V tank. Two were obviously dead . . . the third one gave the impression that he was still living. The people ahead of me, who I assume belonged to the Mk V, fired about two shots at the American and I shot once into his head. We were standing at his feet."

51. Interrogation of Roman Clotten by Dwight Fanton at Ebensee, October 1, 1945, NA, RG-549, Case 6–24, Box 31. Clotten ventured in this early statement that it was Poetschke who gave the original orders.

52. Clotten statement, January 22, 1946, op. cit. Clotten's statement included a detailed sketch that was similar to those from other members of his company as well as members of Rumpf's 9th Company and Siever's 3rd Company. Triangulation of these sources allowed a fairly accurate assessment of the positions of the vehicles at the time when the massacre took place. However, the diagram given in the map on page 144 is approximate and likely does not reflect the actual spacing of the vehicles at the time of the shooting.

53. Whether Dubbert's tank was on the scene when the shooting took place is one of the unresolved questions in the author's research to recreate a chronology of the event. Although Clotten's testimony and the sketch of Siptrott placed SS-Sgt. Dubbert on the scene and firing into the prisoners, neither he nor any of his tank crew (SS-Pvt. Anton Stephan, Hans Muling, Pvt. Menzel, and Cpl. Alfons Ziesemann) were called to testify at the trial. This may be because of testimony of Ziesemann. Prior to arriving at the crossroads he claimed to have heard a lot of shooting, which "he recognized as fire from machine guns. . . . As he passed the corner where the crime took place he saw many Americans dead and he knew from the way they were lying that they had been shot down." He claimed that SS-Sgt. Heinrich Burk commanded the tank ahead of him. Interrogation of Alfons Ziesemann, IC #1, Screening results from November 24–29, 1945, Ellis Papers. Georg Fleps in a statement dated March 4, 1946 (NA, RG-549, Case 6–24, Box 22) claimed to have spoken with SS-S/Sgt. Erich Dubbert on the night after the shooting in a farmhouse on the outskirts of Stavelot, where Dubbert said, "he had shot and killed four American prisoners of war who were still alive at the road crossing before Engelsdorf." The grim implication was that the main shooting had already happened and Dubbert had finished some off. Thus, it is possible that Clotten mistook Koch for Dubbert just behind him.

54. At Bliesheim on December 13, Clotten claimed Klingelhoefer told him that no quarter would be given in the upcoming operation. "We should revenge our women and children who have been killed by airplanes and said 'No prisoners will be taken.'" And on the eve of the offensive his platoon leader addressed them, saying that they would "fight in the old SS spirit and should not show any mercy to the enemy." "I would have hindered Bock in this shooting," Clotten later said, "had I myself not been incited by the speeches of our Company commander, SS-2nd Lt. Klingelhoefer and our platoon leader, SS-2nd Lt. Muenkemer." Statement of Roman Clotten, April 2, 1946, NA, RG-549, Case 6–24, Box 7. It is noteworthy that whereas others repudiated their statement, Clotten never denied that Bock shot at the crossroads but instead said he had only joined in after others started the shooting. "I have always expressed my opinion disapproving of the shooting. . . . At that time I had a gunner, who was a very young man and a soldier with no combat experience at all and at the time of the incident at the crossroads had the first direct touch with the enemy." "Appeal for Review: Roman Clotten," Landsberg/Lech, November 7, 1947, NA, RG-549, Case 6–24, Box 49. Clotten had been a driver at Hitler's headquarters since 1940, but he was transferred to the Leibstandarte in May 1944.

55. The originals of these very significant sketches of the events at the crossroads can be seen in NA, RG-549, Case 6–24, Box 7, "Statement of

Roman Clotten." In the author's assessment the Schwäbisch Hall sketches of Clotten, Siptrott, Joachim Hoffman, Siegfried Jaeckel, and Gustav Neve, when taken together, provide a cohesive picture of the events at the crossroads on December 17, 1944. Clotten reckons that Heinrich Burk's Panzer Nr. 714 was ahead of Siptrott's, although he was uncertain in his recollection. In fact, the panzer ahead of Siptrott was likely Nr. 734 of Pilzarek, with driver Manfred Thorn, who had managed to take the lead of the entire 7th Company given the trouble with mud that Siptrott and the others had encountered. Unlike many other statements made at Schwäbisch Hall, that of Roman Clotten was never retracted. In Landsberg Prison, in an appeal on November 7, 1947, for review of his sentence of ten-year imprisonment, Clotten charged that William Perl had abused him, but "I admitted to him [the investigation officer] that the gunner of my tank had fired once as a reaction after the general turmoil had started. . . . I had a gunner who was a very young man and a soldier with no combat experience at all, and at the time of the incident at the crossroads he had his first direct touch with the enemy. . . . I had nothing to do with the shooting. The fact that my gunner fired once as a nervous reaction, when the general firing had started, can certainly not be interpreted as a violation of any written law." Also Kurt Mai, who had also been with the 7th Company, said in a statement on October 21, 1947, that he had a conversation with Clotten later in the war: "I remembered that he spoke once in the presence of myself and some comrades about the happenings at the crossing of Engelsdorf during the Eifel Offensive. He said at this time that this was a very dirty mess [grosse Schweinerei]." NA, RG-549, Case 6–24, Box 49.

56. Clotten interrogation, October 1, 1945, op. cit.

57. Werner Löhmann and Werner Reicke testimony at the Malmédy trial, U.S. v. Bersin, 548–558.

58. This was almost certainly medic Cpl. Ralph Indelicato of the 285th Field Artillery Observation Battalion, who was tending to the arm of Pfc. Carl Stevens, who had been wounded when Sternebeck's Spitze first fired on the American column.

59. Reicke: "Shortly before we were about to move out again and were just about to start our motor, I heard somebody behind us say, 'Why don't you throw them some hand grenades in there.'" Reicke testimony, U.S. v. Bersin, op. cit., 553.

60. Statement of Werner Reicke, February 12, 1946, NA, RG-549, Case 6–24, Box 25. Reicke's statement (including a detailed sketch) was similar to the testimony given at the trial.

61. Contrast Reicke's recollection of Fleps's attitude with his postwar lament to Belgian researcher Gerd Cuppens in 1986: "I have in myself a

permanent feeling of regret since 17 December 1944." Gerd Cuppens, *Massacre a Malmédy*? (Bayeux, France: Editions Heimdal, 1989), 107–114. Even with Fleps's continued confession and Siptrott's corroboration, Cuppens harbored to doubt over Fleps's personal admission of guilt. He claimed that Fleps had been convinced to confess at Schwäbisch Hall in return for his freedom. However, no evidence of such a claim can be found in the records. Indeed, in Fleps's claim of duress at Schwäbisch Hall of January 23, 1948 (NA, RG-549, Case 6–24, Box 52), he complained of physical abuse at the hands of William Perl and Harry Thon, but his alibi says nothing of false promises from his captors. Also persuasive was his plea for mercy at the end of the Malmédy trial, in which Fleps looked to atone for his deeds: "I was instructed that all orders had to be carried out without asking questions, even if the orders are connected with death," he said aloud to the court. "I never received any instruction on the Geneva Convention." *U.S. v. Bersin*, appeals for mitigation of sentences on the afternoon of July 11, 1946, 3209–3217.

62. Trial testimony of Hans Joachim Piper, *U.S. v. Bersin*, 578–586.

63. Statement of Heinz Rehagel, March 8, 1946, *U.S. v. Bersin*, 589–591. This provides strong reason to doubt Rehagel's and Rumpf's contentions that Friedrich Christ was at the crossroads just before the shootings. Although Piper saw Rehagel speak with a superior officer before the shooting, he testified to the defense counsel at the trial that he was not sure if it was Christ. "Defense Interrogations: Piper, Hans Joachim," no date, but June or July 1946, NA, RG-549, Case 6–24, Box 32. One possible motive for the subterfuge was Christ's wildly unpopular conduct in the regiment; another may have been a keen desire to shift responsibility away to superior officers. Multiple witnesses established that both Rumpf and Rehagel were present at the crossroads at the time of the shootings.

64. Interrogation of Günther Feuchner (sic: Flächsner), Camp Dachau, November 21, 1946, NA, RG-549, Case 6–24, Box 44. Flächsner was the driver in Rehagel's tank.

65. Peiper testified that Rehagel and the gunner of his tank, Willi Brandt, fired at the prisoners.

66. Siptrott interview, May 17, 1997, op. cit.

67. Affidavit of Otto Arnold, January 7, 1948, NA, RG-153, Case 6–24, Box 81.

68. Siptrott interview, May 17, 1997, op. cit. It is noteworthy in Cuppens's "reconstruction" of the Baugnez proceedings that he cited an anonymous German officer interviewed on August 1, 1988, who had been at Baugnez. Although Siptrott was an NCO, the quotes Cuppens used (and the fact that he was in frequent communication with Siptrott that year) makes it likely the

description of the deadly moment came from Siptrott himself: "in such a [tense] situation, a small event is enough to set off a disaster. It is enough that the nerves of single idiot cracked up so that he presses on the trigger of a machine gun." Cuppens, *Massacre a Malmédy*? op. cit., 113.

69. John Bauserman, The *Malmédy Massacre* (Shippensburg, PA: White Mane, 1995), 23.

70. This psychological phenomenon has much in common with the varied perceptions victims have in car crashes. Some details, those on which attention is focused, will be recalled in great detail, but many other circumstances that hardly register in memory at all are distorted and filled in by the brain. Similarly, witnesses to a crime scene will have notoriously different perceptions of the same event—a reason why multiple witnesses are so important to every investigation.

71. Löhmann testimony at the Malmédy trial, *U.S. v. Bersin*, op. cit., 548–50. Löhmann was the gunner with Horst Pilarzek's Panzer Nr. 734 of the 3rd platoon, 7th Panzer Company. He made a virtually identical statement at Schwäbisch Hall on March 7, 1946, NA, RG-549, Case 6–24, Box 32. However, there he recalled the briefing Hans Siptrott gave to the platoon just before the attack: "The enemy must learn to fear us again. Therefore, we will fight in the old SS spirit. There is a new order that no prisoners of war will be taken."

72. Hoffmann's statement of March 6, 1946 (op. cit.): "As far as I can remember, the first shots were from Beutner's SPW." Jaekel's statement of March 1, 1946 (op. cit.): "My recollection is that the first fire I heard was pistol fire from Beutner's SPW." Neve's statement (March 6, 1946, op. cit.): "I heard Beutner tell Witkowski that the weapons should be loaded and made ready so we could bump off the American prisoners. . . . Finally Beutner gave the order to fire and everybody opened up with their weapons."

73. "I am quite sure that I saw him fire." Rieder confession, March 26, 1946, op. cit.

74. Jaekel statement, March 1, 1946, op. cit. Jaekel named many of those he saw shooting at the crossroads, both in his SPW and those of Beutner, Bode, and Sprenger. Oettinger's SPW also showed up just as the shooting started and participated in the "mercy shootings" that followed. Years later, members of the 9th Panzer Engineer Company would attempt to provide some cover for Erich Rumpf. An example is the affidavit of Joachim Braunroth of Michelstadt on April 19, 1948 (NA, RG-153, Case 6–24, Box 81) claiming that "Rumpf did not give any order for the shooting," but then later he wrote that "After a short stop in front of the crossroads, which lasted about 5–10 minutes, the column proceeded and we drove pass the crossing in the direction of Engelsdorf. At the crossroads, we saw about 40–50 dead Americans

which we passed. At the crossing at that time was standing one officer in tank uniform and some German soldiers in gray uniforms. Vehicles standing there were a German tank, an SPW and 10–15 American lorries."

75. Statement of Gustav Sprenger, February 27, 1946, NA, RG-549, Case 6–24, Box 7. Sprenger was one of the few witnesses who claimed to have seen SS-1st Lt. Sievers at the crossroads—something denied by his other comrades. All agreed, however, that SS-1st Lt. Erich Rumpf was on the scene.

76. Sprenger's plea for mitigation of his sentence: "I was continuously taught that every order had to be carried out and that refusal to obey an order would be punished extremely, even with death. . . . From November 1943 up until I was wounded, I participated in the Russian Campaign with the LSSAH. Fighting in Russia was very hard and ruthless. The nameless cruelties the German prisoners of war who were taken by the Russians had to suffer, shocked me deeply."

77. Statement of Willi Schaefer, April 8, 1946, NA, RG-549, Case 6–24, Box 9, and of Hoffmann statement and Neve interrogation, March 6, 1946, op. cit., and of Siegfried statement, March 1, 1946, op. cit. Beyond themselves, those named as having shot the Americans in the field included SS-Sgt. Beutner and Ernst Goldschmidt, Cpl. Max Hammerer, Sgt. Sepp Witkowski, and Sgt. Edgar Dieckmann, as well as Pvt. Oskar Tratt and Willi Taut, Hans Toedter, Josef Aistleitner, Friedel Bode, Walter Schulte, Jirassek, and Losenki.

78. Testimony of Walter Fransee and Paul Buth, U.S. v. Bersin, May 27, 1946, 762–779.

79. Those implicating Hubert Huber in administering "mercy shots" to those in the field were numerous: Testimonies of Kurt Plohmann, Horst Kiefer, Walter Landfried, Rudolf Zimmermann, Adolf Weiss, and Kurt Dethlefs, May 27–28 1946, U.S. v. Bersin, 792–835. As will be seen in chapter 9, the likely soldier whom Huber forced to get up and then shot in the head was 2nd Lt. Lloyd Iames as witnessed by S/Sgt. Henry Zach. Indeed, Huber himself admitted to the shooting, describing its particulars in gruesome detail: "I fired the final shot directly into the center of his forehead. During my years in the German Army, I have seen many dead soldiers, both enemy and our own, and there is absolutely no question that this soldier was dead after I fired these shots at him." Huber drew a detailed diagram showing his movements in the field on a map showing where the American bodies had been found (see p. 158). He estimated that the man he had shot at point-blank range was the body tagged as #38—1st Lt. Thomas McDermott. (In autopsy McDermott was found to have been shot in the left forehead at such a close range that there were powder burns.) Huber described how members of his own crew, Panzer Nr. 625, participated in shooting at the prisoners in the

field with the tank machine gun. He named SS-Pvt. Martin Grischatz as the gunner, SS Pvt. Karl-Heinz Schroeder (loader), and SS Pvt. Schreier (the radio operator), all three of whom eventually also came into the field with pistols along with SS-Sgt. Rudi Storm and another man of Briesemeiseter's Panzer Nr. 114. Affidavit of Hubert Huber, February 16, 1946, NA, RG-549, Case 6–24, Box 9.

80. One of the most bizarre stories concerns Huber's tank gun loader—a young enlisted Waffen SS man, Karl Heinz-Schroeder. In the fighting Schroeder was wounded during the offensive and taken prisoner near La Gleize. After capture Schroeder was first sent to the United States to Ft. Eustis, where he met Afrika Korps veterans who still thought Germany might win the war. He then spent a brief time at Ft. Pickett in Virginia and was repatriated to Germany through Belgium, where he was held for six months for war crimes investigations. Amazingly, Schroeder later returned to the United States to settle in Hanover, Virginia, where he would become the city attorney! In 1994 the local newspaper interviewed him for the fiftieth anniversary of the Battle of the Bulge, and he acknowledged that he had been at Baugnez: "About the second or third day of the attack, his column popped over a small hill and saw an American convoy passing through a crossroads. The Germans immediately attacked the convoy and within a matter of minutes had captured several hundred American soldiers. Schroeder and the other men in the lead vehicles were holding up the drive as they prepared to round up and disarm the Americans. He and the others barely had gotten off their vehicles when they were ordered to get back on and keep going. . . . Schroeder never heard what happened to the captured Americans until much later." Story of Karl-Heinz Schroeder, "Christmas 1944: The Battle of the Bulge," The *Crewe-Burkeville Journal*, Crewe, VA, December 22, 1994. This can be readily contrasted with Hubert Huber's account in which Schroeder went into the field to assist with the final executions, with Huber drawing his path among the bodies where he fired. After the article appeared in the local newspaper, Schroeder came to public attention and made a hasty departure to Germany.

81. Although Huber of the 6th Panzer Company and members of the 3rd Panzer Engineer Company were apprehended, it remains curious that more than half of the named individuals implicated in shooting the Americans lying in the field were missing and unavailable at the Malmédy trial. Huber, however, was the last of the Malmédy men released from Landsberg Prison—a month after Jochen Peiper himself.

82. "Look at these bodies," SS-Pvt. Hans Knospe remark to his squad leader with the 9th Company of the III Panzer Grenadier Battalion. "There

was some dirty work here." "Screening Results 15–24 November 1945," Ellis Papers. Interrogated by Lt. Schweitzer.

83. Interview with SS veteran at the Hotel Sonnenhof, Aspach, May 1997. Name withheld.

84. Several American survivors put the time interval between Peiper's departure and the main shooting as minutes at most. This is possible because many of the forty-odd American survivors saw Diefenthal in his easily recognized tan leather jacket along with Peiper in his vehicle, and they related the timing of the events after the departure of their command SPW.

85. Here Peiper accurately describes the escape of Schmidt, Graeff, Conrad, and Bower near the head of the column where the forest covering Houyire Hill came close down to the road.

86. Letter from Peiper to John Toland, February 22, 1959, LOC, John Toland Papers, Battle: Story of the Bulge, Box 108, Folder "P." The letter was written after an extensive discussion between Otto Skorzeny and Peiper. Was it worthwhile to communicate with Toland, who was writing an account of the events at Malmédy? Peiper's opinion: no advantage.

Chapter 8

1. Author interview with Bobby Werth, September 21, 1995.

2. The autopsy by Maj. Giacento Morrone (NA, RG-549, Case 6–24, Box 23) determined the round that Charles Haines took had passed all the way through his chest. He was later shot in the forehead with a gunshot that left powder burns.

3. James P. Mattera, as told to C. M. Stephan Jr., "Murder at Malmédy," *Army*, December 1981.

4. Author interviews with Ted Paluch, December 17–20, 2007.

5. Virgil P. Lary "The Massacre at Malmédy," *Field Artillery Journal*, February 1946. Ken Ahrens also remembered the maniacal Waffen SS mood during their execution detail. "They were having a hell of a good time laughing and joking," Ahrens recalled in his trial testimony, "while our boys were praying." *U.S. v. Bersin*, 474–497.

6. Author interview with William B. Summers, September 21, 1995.

7. In a letter to Charles MacDonald (January 20, 1983), Al Valenzi stated that he saw Ralph Indelicato hit by one of the first pistol shots. USa.m.HI, Charles B. MacDonald Papers, Box 7. "I noticed a tank trying to maneuver into position to guard us, I thought. The Germans were barking orders and the next thing I know, I saw this German level his pistol at the driver in our group [Cpl. Lester] and fire. Then, he picked off another man; he killed them both. The medic they shot was Ralph Indelicato. . . . Everyone hit the ground

then. I figured we were all goners when the Germans started firing indiscriminately into our group. I was hit in both legs."

8. Mattera, "Murder at Malmédy," op. cit.

9. Report of Cpl. Sciranko: E&E Report No 1.8.9 (WEA)/6/764/2669, no date, but 1945, Paris, NA, RG-549, Case 6–24, Box 42.

10. Official statement of Harry C. Horn, April 10, 1945, NA, RG-549, Case 6–24, Box 22.

11. Statement of William F. Reem to Capt. Alvin B. Welsch, December 18, 1944, NA, RG-549, Case 6–24, Box 23.

12. Account prepared for the author, "The Malmédy Massacre as Remembered by Charles F. Appman," March 30, 1996. Appman escaped with others from the field to be rescued by the 291st Engineer Combat Battalion. "Medics found holes in my clothing, but my body was unscathed. The wounds I received that day will never be seen—but the pain is felt every day."

13. Ralph S. Rainey, "The Boy Played Possum at Malmédy," newspaper clipping, no date or edition, Charles Hammer Papers, 285th FAOB, USAMHI, Box Battery Rosters.

14. Testimony of Pfc. Aubrey J. Hardiman to Maj. Woodward C. Gardiner, December 18, 1944, 28th General Hospital, Liège, NA, RG-153, Case 6–24, Box 76. Hardiman's foot was under the body of Genthner, and after one of the shots Hardiman was wounded. The autopsy report revealed that Genthner was killed by a gunshot wound to his right temple.

15. "Boy Played Possum at Malmédy," op. cit.

16. Statement of Pfc. Mario Butera, 91st General Hospital, March 16, 1945, NA, RG-549, Case 6–24, Box 22.

17. Statement of Harold Billow, 185th U.S. General Hospital, undated but early 1945, NA, RG-549, Case 6–24, Boxes 30 and 41.

18. Testimony of Sgt. Kenneth F. Ahrens to Capt. Oliver Seth, December 18, 1944, 28th General Hospital, Liège, NA, RG-153, Case 6–24, Box 77.

19. In his testimony Ken Ahrens (March 11, 1945, Paris, NA, RG-549, Case 6–24, Box 22) indicated Indelicato was working on Stevens in the field when the prisoners were assembled there, but then the first pistol shot hit the medic. The autopsy report on the men found that Stevens had been given first aid to his upper left arm before he was shot in the head. Based on the author's evaluation, Indelicato was the first man shot by German pistol fire. The autopsy revealed a pistol gunshot wound to the lower face, with hands raised as if in autonomic response. Moreover, the testimony of James Mattera almost precisely located the body of Indelicato at the south end of the field from a diagram of the scene, without having any prior knowledge as to identify to the numbered bodies. (Testimony of James Mattera, October 11, 1945, Wiesbaden,

NA, RG-549, Case 6–24, Box 30). In postwar accounts Michael Skoda also recalled seeing Indelicato as the first American shot at the crossroads. "Malmédy Survivor Upholds Army Probe," no date, but 1949, USa.m.HI, Charles Hammer Papers, Box Battery Rosters. In addition to the original gunshot to the face, Indelicato likely died from many hits from large-caliber machine-gun bullets: left shoulder, neck, left arm, and wrist. His eyes had been removed, but this grizzly mutilation appears to have come from birds picking at bodies rather than enemy intention. This, in contrast to sensational speculation in autopsy reports of Capt. Joseph A. Kurcz and Maj. Giacento C. Morrone, Medical Corps, 44th Evacuation Hospital, January 22, 1945, NA, RG-549, Case 6–24, Box 23. See Michael Reynolds, "The Malmédy Massacre" in *The Devil's Adjutant: Jochen Peiper, Panzer Leader* (Sarpedon, NY: Pen and Sword, 1995), 92–93, 194, and note on 67.

20. "One of the medical aid men, slightly wounded, bandaged the wounds of a man. When he finished a German approached him and asked if he was through, then shot and killed both the medic and his patient." "Details of Atrocities: Pfc. Peter A. Piscatelli," War Crimes Office, March 23, 1945, NA, RG-153, Case 6–24, Box 71.

21. Interview of Robert L. Smith at Wiesbaden on October 11, 1945, NA, RG-549, Case 6-24, Box 30. "The fellows that made the break before me, they all run [sic] ahead. By the time I got out of the field, they were out of sight. My legs were frozen from cold weather, and I had to go through barbed wire to a little dirt road and across the dirt road, and through a hedge and through another barbed wire fence, and I heard someone holler behind me. It was Pvt. Donald Day, so I waited for him. By that time, they started shooting machine guns from a tank about the fork in the road. We were trying to run and doing the best we could . . . and we made our way down through the woods to Malmédy." Day and Smith entered Malmédy along the railroad where a Belgian boy who told them where they could find some Americans up ahead. Reaching friendly lines, the two men were sent back from Malmédy to the 77th Evacuation Hospital in Verviers by jeep. "When we got there, they put Day in the operating room and they put me upstairs."

22. Letter from Al Valenzi to author, November 23, 1995.

23. Statement of Homer D. Ford to Alvin D. Welsch, U.S. First Army, December 17, 1944, NA, RG-153, Case 6–24, Box 76.

24. See Appendix I for the dispositions of the Malmédy survivors. A total of forty-three victims of the massacre incident ran from the field and managed eventually to reach American lines. However, the number who ran initially was even larger, as a number were shot attempting to escape. Their bodies were found well beyond the massacre field. It is also certain that another group of

soldiers—particularly those with worse wounds—waited until dark to make their escape. Thus, it seems likely that the first group to run when Mattera rallied them was about thirty men—a tally similar to the estimates Piscatelli and Kailer made.

25. Lary, "Massacre at Malmédy," op. cit. "After it got dark, I decided I had better try to make my get away. I slipped out to the hedge which ran beside the road leading westward. . . . I hobbled along in the protection of the hedge for a while. . . . I turned toward the right and navigated across the dark fields, taking my bearings or azimuth from buzz bombs which every few minutes passed overhead, apparently aimed at Liège. . . . I walked on that [one] foot for about two and a half miles before having to get down and crawl on for about another mile until I reached a small settlement [Floriheid on a steep hill above Hédomont]. Here I found a friendly old Belgian [Monsieur Louis Martin] and his small granddaughter carrying a note to the hospital commandant asking that an ambulance or other vehicle be sent for me."

26. "About twelve of the men ran into a house nearby and myself and two other soldiers took off over the open field. They fired at us with machine guns, but by luck we made it to the woods where we hid until dark. The house where the twelve men ran into was burned down by the Germans. Anyone that tried to escape from the fire were shot by machine gun fire." However, in a clarifying statement on Christmas Day, Mattera admitted that he had not seen the Americans being shot as they left the burning building, but "heard them hollering for help." Testimony of Pfc. James P. Mattera, December 25, 1944, U.S. First Army, NA, RG-153, Case 6–24, Box 76. That Americans had first hid in the café is corroborated in numerous early statements: Harold Billow, Ralph Law, and Ted Paluch on December 18, and later by Charles Reding, who was hiding in the immediate vicinity. Although no American bodies were found in the burned-out remains of the café, a number of Americans were found shot just outside: Pfc. Hall, Cpl. Rullman, Sgt. Kinsman, and Pfc. Klukavy.

27. Statement of Henri Lejoly-Jacob (age fifty) to Lt. Col. Alvin B. Welsch, January 6, 1945. Also see statements of Johanna and Madeleine Lejoly on, January 4, 1945, NA, RG-549, Case 6–24, Box 23. Lejoly-Jacob was a cousin of Henri Lejoly-Quirin, living just north of the crossroads. Interview with Madeline Lejoly, Malmédy, February 10, 2008. On the night of December 17, ten German soldiers joined the fearful Lejoly family in their cellar, and they did not leave until the following day.

28. This was likely the same Waffen SS trooper who shot Pfc. Carl Frey, Pvt. Samuel Hallman, and likely Pfc. Robert McKinney as they escaped. The same SS man also attempted to shoot Pvt. John Kailer.

29. Testimony of T Sgt. William H. Merriken to Ralph Shumacker, October 9, 1945, Wiesbaden, Germany, NA, RG-549, Case 6–24, Box 30.

30. Author interview with Ken Ahrens, March 11, 1945. Also, interview with Kenneth Ahrens, Toland Papers, *Battle: Story of the Bulge*, LOC, Box 37.

31. Statement of Sciranko, no date, op. cit. "Five of us jumped up and got out of there as fast as we could. . . . As we were running across the field, a machine gun opened up on us from across the road. No one got hit. We ran like hell for about a mile and a half across fields, hedgerows and barbed wire. Then we came up to the Malmédy road and just after we crossed it, a jeep came along from Malmédy with an ordnance captain in it. He picked us up and took us to an aid station in Malmédy." In fact, the five men (including one member of the 3rd Armored Division—likely Cpl. Edward Bojarski) had been rescued up by Lt. Col. David Pergrin and Sgt. Crickenberger of the 291st Combat Engineer Battalion.

32. Author interview with Al Valenzi, September 26, 1995. With Valenzi was Ken Ahrens, Michael Sciranko, Paul Gartska, and possibly Edward Bojarski. "They didn't believe us at first," Valenzi recalled, "we were talking out of our heads."

33. Walter Wendt to John Bauserman, March 20, 1988. "We went and sat by the road and we were picked up by the Red Cross and taken to a hospital. I was given two morphine shots. Later that night, I was taken to Liège."

34. In a letter to Gerd Cuppens on January 24, 1981, Skoda said the man speaking to him while he lay in the field was Pvt. William Reem. Gerd Cuppens, *Massacre a Malmédy?* (Bayeux, France: Editions Heimdal, 1989), 98. Cuppens made much of the fact that Skoda claimed to have run with Paul Martin in one letter and William Reem in another. However, as seen in the original deposition Skoda gave in 1945, it is clear that he ran with both men, but he was so weak from loss of blood that, upon reaching the Mathonet household, he could not go on.

35. Skoka to Cuppens, op. cit.

36. "We crawled directly west inside the pasture about 200 yards into a house where Skoda wanted to stay. I said we were under observation and that it was not safe to stay in the house. . . . I left him there and crawled back to the fence and the road and continued crawling across a field until I was out of observation, about a mile from the crossroads." Testimony of Paul J. Martin, Private 1st Class to 1st Lt. Eugene H. Burris, JAG Department, Fort Oglethorpe, GA, August 24, 1945, NA, RG-153, Case 6–24, Box 76.

37. Testimony of T/5 Michael J. Skoda to 1st Lt. Vincent P. Clarke, RAMP Camp No. 1, Lucky Strike Area, Normandy Base Section, France, May 28, 1945, NA, RG-549, Case 6–24 (specific box unknown). Also see Angela J. Burrows,

"Ligonier Man survived Malmédy Massacre," *Greensburg Herald Review*, Pittsburgh, PA, no date, but 1983 or 1984, clipping courtesy Helen Skoda and John Bauserman. The wounded private whom Skoda saw was almost certainly Pvt. Elwood Thomas, who remains missing to this date. The location of the barn where Thomas was located is uncertain. From Skoda's description it was close to the massacre field, perhaps near Thirimont, as the paratroopers took him by that place again to reach Thomas. That Skoda stayed at the farmhouse of Joseph Mathonet was verified by an interview by Henri Rogister with Maria Mathonet-Meyer. Communication with Henri Rogister, October 20, 2007. The German paratroopers soon evacuated Skoda from the Ardennes and moved him to a prison hospital in Rheinbach, Germany. There, on December 27, a surgeon operated on him to remove the bullets from his shoulder. Upon recovery, in early 1945, Skoda was moved to Stalag 3A in Luckenwalde near the Polish border. Later, as the Russians approached in May 1945, he was moved once more to Stalag 3B near Fürstenberg; he and his comrades cheered the Russians when they took the camp under fire. But after the Germans took off, Skoda was "captured," this time by the Russians, who had learned that the American son of Russian immigrants could speak their language. Detaining Skoda as an interpreter, the Russian liberators gave him no choice but to stay. Then on Sunday, May 6, 1945, as Skoda was outside the Russian-held camp on an assigned errand, he spotted an American jeep. Quickly explaining his plight, he hitched a ride out of the Russian zone. He not only escaped from the Germans but then from Russians!

38. Summers interview, September 21, 1995, op. cit. During his escape Summers ran with O'Connell (who was shot in the face), Butera (who was shot in the foot), and Bobby Werth.

39. "We returned to Battalion headquarters to give the men a change of clothing and a chance to clean up as they and their clothes were drenched in muddy water as a result of the time they had spent in the drainage ditch. After these men calmed down, they were able to give us the details of the massacre." Letters of Thomas Stack to Janine Holt Giles, January (undated) and February 11, 2969, Janice Holt Giles Papers: *Damned Engineers*, Western Kentucky University.

40. Summers interview, September 21, 1995, op. cit.; "Yanks, Crying in Rage, Tell How Nazis Killed Wounded," *Stars and Stripes*, December 19, 1944.

41. Werth interview, op. cit. "On Christmas day, I was moved to a hospital across the English Channel. Later we moved back to England. I stayed there a long time. I never went back to the unit; I stayed and worked at the hospital. I think I stayed there because of my nerves. After the war I was bothered by dreams. I would wake up in a cold sweat and there was someone who was try-

ing to drive over me in a tank. At first it was about every night and then it got to be less. I didn't talk much about it to people. We had a large family and I never talked to my kids about it. I would have moods where I didn't get along with people. I wouldn't talk to my wife. . . . My daughter knew something was wrong; we never talked. I finally talked to them all. It had a big effect on me—it was bad. I think it reduced my trust in people. . . . Every December 17th I think about it, but I think of it as a lucky day. Still, December is a hard time for me; I don't enjoy Christmas."

42. "Boy Played Possum at Malmédy," op. cit.

43. Although unwounded in the first volley, Flechsig was hit in the right arm, the left calf, and in the fingers on the right hand as machine guns swept the bodies lying on the muddy ground. "One of the Germans came over and looked at me, but he must have thought that I was dead because he didn't shoot me again. He did shoot the boy next to me."

44. Author interview with George Fox, January 18, 2010.

45. "How Ted and I Met the Xhurdubises," prepared by George Fox along with map and provided to author.

46. Kenneth Ahrens, "Escape in Belgium," E&E Report No. 2907, prepared by PW & X, MIS, 1945, NA, RG-549, Case 6–24, Box 22. One of those physically unable to leave in the field may have been T/5 Carl H. Blouch, who had been terribly wounded in both knees by machine gunfire in the middle of those standing in the field, but he was otherwise unscathed. The autopsy of Capt. Joseph Kurcz determined that Blouch slowly bled to death, having survived over others in the field next to him (i.e., Cpl. Lawrence Martin and T/5 James E. Luers) being executed by shots to the head.

47. Testimony of T/5 Theodore J. Paluch to Lt. Col. Alvin B. Welsch, HQ First U.S. Army, December 25, 1944, NA, RG-153, Case 6–24, Box 77. Also see testimony of Theodore J. Paluch, October 10, 1945, Wiesbaden, Germany. Madeleine Lejoly, in an interview on February 10, 2008, said she observed the Germans setting the café on fire, which was burning by 4 P.M., and verified that the farmhouse had a watering trough outside.

48. When Paluch arrived to the safety of the Malmédy medical detachment that night, he began to shake uncontrollably. "I was really scared then." The attendant wanted to give him a shot of morphine, but he refused, pointing to a mere scratch on his right hand. At 5 P.M., while Paluch was being treated, combat engineers hauled Pvt. John H. Cobbler inside. Even though he spoke to Paluch, Cobbler was in pain and bleeding terribly. He died just hours later. Author interview with Ted Paluch, September 17, 1997.

49. Testimony of Pvt. Peter C. Piscatelli to Oliver Seth, 47th Field Hospital, December 18, 1944, NA, RG-153, Case 6–24, Box 77. If this little-known,

episode is true and Piscatelli was given temporary refuge in the café with the Germans becoming aware of such, this may have sealed the fate of Madame Adele Bodarwe.

50. Piscatelli statement, March 23, 1945, op. cit.

51. Mattera, "Murder at Malmédy," op. cit., 34.

52. Pvt. John R. Kailer to Capt. Oliver Seth, 28th General Hospital, Liège, December 22, 1944, NA, RG-153, Case 6-24, Box 76. John Kailer lay by the hedgerow until dusk when they Germans set the café on fire. When he looked back he could see the scattered pile of American bodies in the field illuminated by the flames, but none seemed to be moving. He then fled across the road and made his way north toward Malmédy to be rescued by an American ambulance. The bodies of Frey (Tag #59) and Hallman (#58) were found right by the hedge along the Hédomont road where Kailer saw them executed. Frey had been shot in the head and Hallman had been shot multiple times in the stomach and chest. Within a few feet was also the body of T/5 John McKinney (#61). The men who Kailer saw the Germans shooting further beyond the road were likely S/Sgt. John D. Osborne (Tag #1, killed by a blow to the head), Pvt. Stanley F. Piasecki (Tag #67, shot in the head), Pvt. Keston E. Mullen (Tag #66, shot in the head), and Pvt. Paul L. Paden (Tag #68, shot in the back of the head, with powder burns).

53. See statement of Kurt Briesemeister, April 4, 1946, NA, RG-549, Case 6-24, Box 8.

54. Testimony of Pfc. Ralph W. Law, February 19, 1945, 52nd U.S. General Hospital, NA, RG-549, Case 6-24, Box 22.

55. "44th Evacuation Hospital," NA, RG-407, MDEH44-0.1 thru 0.7. Under Lt. Col. Lodomell the semimobile hospital unit trained in Elkins, West Virginia, then Camp Atterbury, Indiana, before shipping to Europe.

56. Official statement of Harry C. Horn, April 10, 1945, NA, RG-549, Case 6-24, Box 22. Members of "Task Force Hansen"—the 99th Norwegian Battalion—picked up Horn on December 22, 1944. The family with whom Horn took refuge is unknown, but they were likely in the vicinity of Hédomont. "Action Against Enemy, December 44," AAR 99th Infantry Battalion (Separate), January 9, 1945, NA, RG-407, INBN-99-0.3.

57. Testimony of T/5 John A. O'Connell to Col. Lamar Tooze, 77th Evacuation Hospital, December 17, 1944, NA, RG-153, Case 6-24, Box 77.

58. Letter from Dwane Londagin to John Bauserman, January 1990.

59. Their vehicle was hit three hundred yards from the lead American jeep in the 285th FAOB column. Map drawn for Bauserman by Londagin, December 18, 1991.

60. Londagin to Bauserman, January 1990, op. cit.

61. Author interview with Lacy Thomasson, August 26, 1995.

62. AAR 86 Engineer (HP) Battalion, December 1944, NA, RG-407, ENBN-86-0.3. The After Action Report shows that John J. Clymire was taken captive on December 17 along with five empty pontoon tractors and trailers, although five men escaped. One, Pvt. Vestal McKinney, was wounded. McKinney's story related by his surviving widow, Joyce, on August 16, 2007. "We were close to the front line. In December 1944, I came awful close to being captured. We ran into the enemy at morning and left our trucks on the road trying to get away. I was shot running from them. Even though they winged me, I dragged myself in a ditch by the road around a curve until the Germans couldn't see me. I eventually came to some American guards who took me to a field hospital."

63. Clymire was taken prisoner when the Germans came down the road in a halftrack. He ended up in the field with the other dead at Baugnez.

Chapter 9

1. AAR Report for the 200th Field Artillery Battalion, December 1944, NA, RG-407, FABN-200-0.3. Pfc. Elmer Wald died in the field so suddenly that his body was frozen with his hands over his head in surrender. His body (Tag #19) was found at the southern end of the field in the front row, next to the corpse of Cpl. Indelicato. Capt. Kurcz determined in his medical autopsy on January 22, 1945, that Wald died when a large-caliber shell struck his right hand after machine-gun bullets penetrated his left armpit and the right side of his head (NA, RG-549, Case 6–24, Box 23).

2. Statement of T/4 Russell T. Carr, February 20, 1945, NA, RG-549, Case 6–24, Box 22.

3. When they decided the SS men were gone, Johnson ran with the others to escape, hiding in a barn until dark. Testimony of S/Sgt. Herman Johnson to Captain Oliver Seth, 28th General Hospital, December 18, 1944, and additional statement by Johnson two days later to Maj. Woodward C. Gardiner, December 20, 1944, NA, RG-153, Case 6–24, Box 76.

4. Letter from Dwane Londagin to John Bauserman, January 1990.

5. The two men of the 552nd AAA AW Bn were AWOL by the time they returned to Verviers.

6. Corp. Bernard Koenig, "Account of Malmédy," 1st Squad, 3rd Platoon, 291st Engineers, November 25, 1968, Damned Engineers Papers, Western Kentucky University.

7. Sgt. Ed Cunningham, "Road Out of Town," Yank, January 1945.

8. For the sequence of events here, I have examined all the extant original sources and added details from my own interviews. Also, John Bauserman, *The Malmédy Massacre* (Shippensburg, PA: White Mane, 1995), op. cit 55–57.

9. Testimony of Pvt. Samuel Dobyns, 77th Evacuation Hospital, Verviers, Belgium, December 17, 1944, NA, RG-153, Case 6–24, Box 76.

10. Dobyns testimony, December 17, 1944, op. cit.

11. Within his testimony immediately after the shooting on December 17, 1944 (op. cit.) and at the Malmédy trial on May 22, 1946 (*U.S. v. Bersin*, Dobyns witness testimony, 507–522). Samuel Dobyns admitted that he ran to the rear of the group in the field after the first pistol shots were fired, and just before the machine gunfire began.

12. For the order of the vehicles in the American convoy, I supplemented the work of Henri Rogister with my own. Henri Rogister, *Sur Les Traces Sanglantes des Troupes de Joachim Peiper, 16–24 Décembre 1944* (Liège, Belgium: privately printed, May 1994), 25–29.

13. Testimony of Stephen J. Domitrovich, 575th Ambulance Company, 28th General Hospital in Liège, December 18, 1944, NA, RG-153, Case 6–24, Box 76.

14. Testimony of Pfc. James M. McKinney, 575th Ambulance Company, at the 28th General Hospital in Liège, December 18, 1944, NA, RG-153, Case 6–24, Box 76.

15. Testimony of Roy B. Anderson at the 28th General Hospital, 575th Ambulance Company, December 18, 1944, NA, RG-153, Case 6–24, Box 76. "We went into the field where the others were," Anderson related. "They searched us and took watches and stuff like that. They opened fire on us with a machine gun. Everybody hit the ground. They continued to fire at us on the ground." Anderson said his Red Cross armband seemed of no help when the Germans later entered the field. "They walked down where we were and would just shoot." Lucky to survive, Anderson had been shot in the stomach and lay in the field for what seemed like hours; he escaped with the others when the survivors ran.

16. Testimony of Stephen Domitrovich, December 18, 1944, NA, RG-153, Case 6–24, Box 77.

17. Statement of Stephen Domitrovich, July 10, 1945 at the office of War Crimes Team #6834 at Reims, France," NA, RG-549, Case 6–24, Box 41.

18. Trudy Gray, "For Some Reason He Didn't Die," *Beaver County Times*, November 11, 1982. "When you come so close to death," said Domitrovich, "you appreciate life much more."

19. McKinney testimony, December 18, 1944, op. cit. Unwounded, McKinney estimated that his break from the field came after lying with the dead

and wounded for over an hour. "I'd say around twenty men were in the bunch that were with us. They were scattered out, and as we got up to run, they would shoot at us too from the vehicles that was [sic] parked at the intersection. I wouldn't say whether it was a tank or halftrack, but machine gun fire was pouring at us." McKinney ran with at least three others—Stephen Domitrovich, Roy Anderson, and Samuel Dobyns.

20. Affidavit of Sgt. Marvin J. Lewis, June 6, 1945, NA, RG-153, Case 6–24, Box 76.

21. "Record of Evidence of S/Sgt. Henry R. Zach to Lt. Col. J. H. Boraston," March 7, 1945, in "Report of the Supreme Headquarters Allied Expeditionary Force Court of Inquiry re Shooting of Allied Prisoners of War by the German Armed Forces near Malmédy, Belgium, 17 December 1944," NA, RG-549, Case 6–24, Box 11.

22. After the war Zach examined photographs of German armored vehicles and concluded that the vehicles that did the machine gunning of the Americans in the field were firing from *Sdkfz-251* SPW halftracks. Letter from Zach to John Bauserman, February 24, 1994.

23. Oral history interview with Henry R. Zach, Wisconsin Veterans Museum Research Center, 1999. Thanks to Don Patton for assistance in obtaining this helpful source.

24. Sworn statement of S/Sgt. Henry R. Zach to Robert C. Howley, 116th U.S. General Hospital, January 23, 1945, NA, RG-549, Case 6–24, Box 42.

25. Zach oral history, op. cit.

26. Letters from Zach to John Bauserman, February 27, 1989, and May 23, 1993. "When I die, everything will be gone. I think I was the last living person to leave that field of dead. People will forget what was done there with such joy and ruthless pleasure. . . . I do not hate the Germans, only the sickness to cause a person to do such a thing."

27. 1st Lt. Thomas McDermott (Tag #38) was likely killed just in front of Zach. Capt. Kurcz's autopsy revealed that a machine gun round pierced his right thigh, after which he fell to the ground with his hands over his head. However, the wound that killed him came from a close-range gunshot wound to the left forehead, which left powder burns. Similarly, Lt. Lloyd Iames (Tag #63) was hit in the stomach but was killed by a gunshot to the forehead.

28. The civilians included Henri Lejoly-Jacob and his brother Henri Lejoly-Quirin, as revealed by their respective testimony. Capt. Edward W. Schenck could not understand the Belgian men who likely tried to tell of another American located in the shed behind the home of Lejoly-Jacob.

29. When Zach reached the hospital he was near death from loss of blood. The surgeon, Capt. Raymond K. Minge at the 44th Evacuation Hospital, noted

that Zach's left leg had been nearly sheared off by a high-caliber shell. Minge gave him two units of plasma as quickly as it could be administered. Recovering, Zach wanted to know about his leg—would he keep it? Would he be able to fight again? "Son, for you the war is over," Minge told him, not bothering to mention to him how close he had come to death. Returning from Europe to the United States with nearly endless medical procedures to follow, Zach was never again able to use his left leg. He died in Wisconsin in 2002.

Chapter 10

1. Author interviews with William Merriken, July 4 and September 22, 1995, and correspondence dated June 5, 1996. All quotations are from this interview unless otherwise noted. Statement of William H. Merriken, February 1, 1945, NA, RG-549, Case 6–24, Box 42. Also see "My Personal Story, by Bill Merriken," Charles B. MacDonald Papers, USa.m.HI, Box 7.

2. Merriken interview with Charles Reding, June 10, 1991. Author interview of Reding, March 3, 1996, and Reding account of his experiences prepared for author, March 28, 1996. Also see Reding interrogation by Oliver Seth at MP station in Malmédy on December 19, 1944. Letter, Charles Reding to his mother, January 17, 1945.

3. Information on Anna Blaise: courtesy of Henri Rogister and Henri Dannemark. The two-story masonry house where Charles Reding and Bill Merriken took refuge is today Restaurant San Remo. The author and a host of others visited the building with Bill Merriken in 1999.

4. Story of Emile Jamar is taken from "How the Bigger Part of My Day of 19 December 1944 was Spent," interview with Andre Dejardin, April 9, 1999, courtesy of Henri Rogister.

5. The officer was likely Capt. Alvin B. Welsch with the U.S. First Army.

Chapter 11

1. For Col. Benjamin Dickson's view of the complex situation in Belgium: "Counterintelligence in Belgium: G-2 Estimate No. 25," September 11, 1944, U.S. First Army, NA, RG-407, U.S. First Army G-2, 301–2.2, Records of U.S. First Infantry Division, Box 5058.

2. In the late 1930s a group of young fanatics organized along SS lines in the Belgian Ardennes and Eifel. They were the *Bogenschuetzen Verein* in St. Vith, along with an even larger group in Eupen. They were thoroughly indoctrinated with Hitler's ideology, and they trained under strict quasi-military discipline, performing night marches, terrain exercises, and the like. In 1939 handpicked members of the organizations were taken secretly into Germany for further training. In May 1940 these operatives were used during the inva-

sion of Belgium within "Special Battalion 800." This clandestine military formation operated in civilian clothes ahead of the panzer divisions, securing bridges, guiding German columns, and carrying out Fifth Column activities. So dedicated were the Belgian youths that many were later absorbed into the Waffen SS and fought for Germany. "The Pro-German Movement in the Eupen-Malmédy Region of Belgium 1920–1940," U.S. First Army, Annex No. 2, December 11, 1944, NA, RG-407, 1st Infantry Division, 301–2.2, G-2 Records, Box 5071.

3. Born in January 1887, Count Louis d'Oultremont, the head of a noble family known for participating with the Belgian resistance, was murdered on the grounds of his five-turreted castle at Ham-sur-Heure ten kilometers south of Charleroi on August 12, 1944, by two carloads of Rexist thugs. The killers of d'Oultremont and his forty-year-old governess, Mme. Schmidt, were apprehended after the war and executed. At the time Louis's son, Lt. Edouard Count d'Oultremont, was a commando leader on the three-man "Team Andrew" that parachuted behind German lines near Charleville in August 1944. Their objective—right out of a Hollywood thriller—was to sow mayhem behind German lines and link up with the French Maquis as the Americans approached. Roger J. Spiller, "Jedburgh Team Operations in Support of the 12th Army Group," Combat Studies Institute, U.S. Dept. of Defense, October 1991. Thanks to Howard Anglin and Henri Rogister for uncovering details of this little-known episode.

4. For the story of Marie Maraite Mathonet (House #2): Henri Rogister, "*La vie des civils aux carrefours de Baugnez et de Bagatelle, avant, pendant, et après la massacre du 17 Décembre 1944*," privately printed, Liège, 2009.

5. Author interview with Peter Lentz, March 22, 1996, Amel, Belgium. Also, "Shooting of American Prisoners in Malmédy: Belgian Interrogation of Peter de Hepscheid Lentz," January 17, 1945, NA, RG-549, Case 6–24, Box 22.

6. Identifying the two shot Americans is possible by their unique location relative to the other massacre victims. On the numbered map from the trial these are bodies #70 and #71 (Raymond Heitmann and Cecil Cash), which were about three hundred feet east of the Henri Lejoly farmhouse. This fact was first identified by Henri Rogister, *Sur Les Traces Sanglantes des Troupes de Joachim Peiper* (privately printed, May 1994).

7. "In mid January after the German counter offensive had been liquidated, the bodies of the two men were found in the snow beside the road near Malmédy." "After Action Report 197 AAA AW Battalion: December 1944," NA, RG-407, CABN-197-0.3.

8. All quotations are from Lentz interview, March 22, 1996, op. cit.

9. Because Peter Lentz was clear that the man who shot Heitmann and Cash had a bolt-action rifle, this seems to establish that the perpetrators were members of the SPW (halftrack) of SS-Cpl. Karl Ohlrogge. It is important to keep in mind that as they approached the Bagatelle, Sternebeck's *Panzerspitze* was now down to two tanks—the Mk IVs of Werner Sternebeck and August Tonk—and Karl Ohlrogge's lone SPW. Because the panzer crews did not have rifles but rather submachine guns and pistols, this most likely indicates that the killer was not from Sternebeck's or Tonk's tanks but instead the SPW crew. Although Lentz claimed a tank confronted him, it seems likely that a Belgian farm boy of fifteen would not distinguish between a panzer and a heavily armed halftrack, particularly in a very frightening confrontation. Information from detailed summary on 9th Panzer Engineer Company written by Timm Haasler, e-mail on March 25, 2009. The known crew of the SPW was as follows: SS-Cpl. Karl Ohlrogge, SPW commander; SS-Pvts. Herman Büttner, driver; Till, machine gunner; Süsse and Lüssen, medics.

10. The time that SS-1st Lt. Sternebeck's lead tank platoon (*Spitze*) was ahead of Peiper's main column has been long debated among SS veterans, as a long interval was used to advance the theory that the approach of the main column, mistaking the American prisoners for armed soldiers, resulted in the men being shot in the field. The testimony of Peter Lentz provides a critical clue on the time between the departure of Sternebeck's original encounter with the 285th FAOB and that of the later approach of the 7th Panzer Company at Baugnez—the time it would take for a young boy to walk 150 feet from just after the Bagatelle to the entrance to the house of Henri Lejoly, where he was forced to take cover from renewed gunfire. At a typical walking speed of three miles per hour, it would take less than a minute to cover the distance. This suggests that the last of Sternebeck's trio of spearhead vehicles were likely only one to three minutes ahead of the main panzer vanguard.

11. Author interview with Robert Pfeiffer, March 21, 1996, Waimes.

12. Leaving the Lejoly house, the first people Peter Lentz ran into on the afternoon of December 17 were Americans, and they asked him how far the Germans were away. He said two kilometers. Lentz interview, op. cit.

13. To prevent it from falling into enemy hands, the Americans had detonated Ammunition Supply Point #126 not far from Malmédy that afternoon. It exploded with a deafening roar—so powerful that fourteen soldiers and nearly two hundred civilians in Waimes were injured from shattered glass.

14. Pfeiffer interview, March 21, 1996, op. cit. One of three civilians who saw the Malmédy massacre, Pfeiffer is one of the most important witnesses to the event, although he was never called to the Malmédy trial because of his young age.

15. Author interviews with Robert Pfeiffer, March 21, 1996, and May 24, 1997. "The day after the shooting we went out into the field and took a look at them. They had no weapons; they were all dead in heaps." Pfeiffer described how the body of a dead American soldier lying in the road just east of the café was flattened to nothing by German tanks driving down the road. This was the body of Pfc. Charles E. Hall (Tag #69), whose body was so crushed that the autopsy could not determine the cause of death.

16. Robert Pfeiffer was briefly interviewed early in the Malmédy investigation. "Interview with Robert Pfeiffer," "Evacuees from Bagatelle, Atrocity Committed Against American Prisoners in Baugnez," 2nd Lt. George L. Sears, January 6, 1945, NA, RG-549, Case 6–24, Box 23. Corroborating the 4 P.M. timing for the burning of the café: Testimony of Ted Paluch on December 17, 1944, with map, dated December 20, 1944, at HQ U.S. First Army, NA, RG-153, Case 6–24, Box 77. He said the Germans set the café ablaze immediately after he and the other twenty at the crossroads jumped up and ran.

17. Like many young men of eastern Belgium, Louis Bodarwe had been drafted into the German Wehrmacht. Fighting in Russia, Bodarwe was wounded for the last time at Stalingrad with the 11th Panzer Division. He did not return home to Belgium until the summer of 1945.

18. After having been captured at the crossroads, Charles Appman remembered, "We stood on the road near a house, and I noticed two elderly people coming out onto their front steps. A German soldier walked up to them and shot one in the head. I watched as they fell down the steps. . . . No one else mentioned the one person I saw get shot at the house—which was a café. I got letters from the lady's daughter stating that they found the man [Henri Lejoly], but not the lady. . . . It is still a mystery." Author's interview with Charles Appman, March 30, 1996.

19. "Narrative: Investigation into the Géromont area," Henrick Veigh, U.S. WD Civilian Investigator, no date. In July 1945 Lt. Francois Desmedt disinterred three bodies found in the area between Géromont and Ligneuville away from the massacre field. These were later identified as Cpl. William H. Moore, Sgt. Alphonse J. Stabulis, and T/5 Wilson M. Jones.

20. Statement of Henri Lejoly to Lt. Col. Alvin B. Welsch, January 6, 1945, NA, RG-549, Case 6–24, Box 23, and statement of Henri Lejoly to U.S. Army investigator Harold Olian, September 29, 1945, NA, RG-549, Case 6–24, Box 30. Finally, the interviews of Gerd Cuppens, *Massacre a Malmédy?* (Bayeux, France: Editions Heimdal, 1989), 17–18. Lejoly's story slowly changed over the years, with fewer details and without mention of his sympathetic attitude toward the Germans. In his first interviews in 1945, Lejoly claimed to have seen thirty to thirty-five American prisoners assembled in front of the café,

and in 1959 he told Georges Francy that "150 American prisoners were assembled in the nearby field," but in a 1978 interview with Gerd Cuppens, twenty-five became the number of men in the field. As with other witness testimony, precedence is given to earlier accounts. Human memory has shown a strong predilection to a reconstructive nature of traumatic events, potentially incorporating postevent details or suggestions that were not the witness's direct experience. See E. F. Loftus, "The Malleability of Human Memory," *American Scientist* 67, no. 3 (May–June 1979): 312–320.

21. There is some doubt about the story. The source is the interview of Henri Lejoly in John Toland Papers, LOC, Manuscript Division, *Battle: Story of the Bulge*, Box 37. In the interview notes Lejoly claimed that just before the 285th FAOB was fired on, a jeep parked near the café and three men entered. "Vielsalm?" the first asked, pointing south, at which point Madame Bodarwe nodded. "*Avez-vous vû des Allemands?*" Madame Bodarwe said no, but Lejoly was silent. "Krauts!" someone yelled outside, at which point the firing picked up. When the author interviewed local historian Kurt Fagnoul on March 25, 1996, he learned Lejoly had told Fagnoul repeatedly over the years that Americans had first entered the café to ask directions.

22. Video interview with Henri Lejoly, Peter Batty, *Battle of the Bulge* (documentary film), 1985.

23. Charles B. MacDonald, *A Time for Trumpets: The Untold Story of the Battle of the Bulge* (New York: William Morrow, 1984), 218. That Lejoly waved to the Germans is certain, as several American witnesses mentioned it, including Ted Paluch and Homer Ford.

24. Statement of Ralph W. Law, February 19, 1945, NA, RG-549, Case 6–24, Box 23. Those hiding behind the Café Bodarwe were from the tail end of the 285th FAOB column, including Sgt. Alfred Kinsman in Law's truck and members of the kitchen crew: T/4 Selmer Leu, S/Sgt. John Osborne, T/5 Charles Breon, Pvt. Andrew Profanchick, Pfc. Howard E. Desch, and T/5 John O'Connell. Joining them in that temporary refuge were T/5 Charles Haines, T/5 Harold Billow, and T/5 Charles Reding, who was driving a weapons carrier behind the kitchen truck. Pfc. Homer D. Ford, the MP at the crossroads, also ran to join them. See statements of Law, Ford, O'Connell, Billow, and Reding, NA, RG-153, Case 6–24, Boxes 76 and 77. Somehow Reding managed to hide himself in the shed such that he was not discovered, and he stayed there until the café was set on fire, forcing him to leave in the late afternoon by crawling into the ditch on the north side of the house under cover of smoke and darkness. "I heard firing, so I dismounted and ran to a nearby shed by the side of a house. I hid there under some things and could see nothing of what was going on. . . . A German soldier

came into the shed and started to disarm me, but he was fired upon and left. I went back and hid again in the shed until the house caught fire. This forced me to leave my hiding place so I got down into a ditch along the road by the house and stayed there in the water, not moving. . . . I heard machine gun fire most of the time I was there." Statement of Charles E. Reding, December 19, 1944, NA, RG-549, Case 6–24, Box 23.

25. Statement of Homer D. Ford, December 17, 1944, NA, RG-153, Case 6–24, Box 76.

26. Statement of Joseph Bodarwe to 2nd Lt. George F. Sears, "Evacuees from Bagatelle, Atrocity Committed Against American Prisoners in Baugnez," January 6, 1945, NA, RG-549, Case 6–24, Box 23.

27. "When the German car appeared to break down, some of the last ranks of the Americans clearly showed that they had the intention of taking flight. At that instant a German fired his pistol." This is from the Cuppens interview with Lejoly, Cuppens, *Massacre a Malmédy?*, op. cit., 17–18. What Lejoly saw was not actually the breakdown of a German SPW but rather one that attempted to train its cannon on the prisoners in the field—a fact attested to by nearly half of the American survivors.

28. "After that, several SS went into the field to finish the work and kill off those who were not dead. I don't think they were too keen to go into the field to finish off the dead. Later that evening I saw people moving through the field and disappearing into the distance across country." Georges Francy, "Interview with Henri Lejoly," *Le Soir Illustre*, December 24, 1959.

29. The handwritten compensatory note from SS-Sgt. Briesemeister to Henri Lejoly can be found at the National Archives, RG-549, Case 6–24, Box 42.

30. *U.S. v. Bersin*, 3209–3211.

31. Statement of Kurt Briesemeister, April 4, 1946, NA, RG-549, Case 6–24, Box 8.

32. "My men—which ones I don't know—set the barn on fire which borders directly the field with the [shot] prisoners and belongs to the larger house next to it. I didn't know yet at that time that American prisoners of war from the field had fled into the house to be smoked out in this manner. Only when I saw unarmed American soldiers run out of the house, I knew that prisoners had kept themselves hidden in this barn. There were six to seven in my estimation. They ran towards the woods and I now shot at the American prisoners who were running away with the machine gun which I laid on the shoulder of SS-Pvt. Nüchter." Statement of Kurt Briesemeister, April 4, 1946, NA, RG-549, Case 6–24, Box 8. Only one survivor admitted escaping from the café and its shed: Pete Piscatelli. Given the position of the bodies, it seems possible that four men were shot after running from the café as their bodies

were found immediately adjacent to the building—Pfc. Hall, Pvt. Piasecki, Pvt. Mullen, and Pvt. Paden.

33. Even though he always affirmed that the Americans at Baugnez were shot in cold blood after surrendering, Henri Lejoly would not appear at the Malmédy trial, as the Belgians sentenced him to death in 1945 for spying for the Germans—an accusation based on his assisting a man disguised as an American during the Ardennes offensive. The man was a member of the Belgian resistance who entrapped Lejoly into assisting him to go over to American lines. He was held in prison at Verviers and Huy for thirty-three months, and his sentence was eventually commuted. He long maintained that if he had testified at Dachau, Kurt Briesemeister would not have been found guilty, seeing as he had saved Lejoly's life that day. Born at Baugnez on June 1, 1900, Lejoly died on June 4, 1982. See Kurt Fagnoul, *"Baugnez: Henri Lejoly— einziger ziviler Augenzeuge," Der Verhängnisvolle Irrtum* (Eupen: Grenz-Echo Verlag, December 1984), 213–284.

34. Briesemeister statement, April 4, 1946, op. cit. This statement is reinforced substantially by a detailed nineteen-page interrogation done prior to Schwäbisch Hall and completed in Pocking, Germany on September 26, 1945, by Dwight Fanton, in which SS-Sgt. Briesemeister identified his loader, SS-Pvt. Günther Nüchter, as the member of his crew who claimed to have shot the woman in the café. The other members of Panzer 114 were SS-Sgt. Rudi Storm (driver), SS-Pvt. Hans Tielecke (gunner), and SS-Cpl. Joseph Heß (radio operator). Even as late as April 5, 1948, Briesemeister was still claiming that Nüchter had related to him that he had found arms and ammunition hidden under the straw in the back of the shed at the café as his justification for shooting the woman. His driver Storm and Heß then came back to fetch a can of petrol, which was used to set the shed and house on fire. "Kurt Briesemeister to Defense Counsel," April 5, 1948, NA, RG-153, Case 6–24, Box 81. Finally, in the Malmédy trial itself, after the proceedings were completed, Briesemeister, in making a plea for clemency, stated, "I have never denied what I had done and if responsible should answer for it."

35. The liberation for them was such a joyous occasion. "It was as if the sky had opened! You can't know." It was a great weight off their shoulders. The liberation church bells rang, but some people doubted it would last. "We were all so happy."

36. Author interview with Marthe Martin, October 19, 1995, assisted by Will Cavanagh.

37. Marthe Marx stayed with the family, having been evacuated with others from Elsenborn during the Allied advance in the fall.

38. Letter from Virgil Lary, May 12, 1965, Janice Holt Giles Papers, *Damned Engineers*, Western Kentucky University, Box 31.

39. After the war Virgil Lary located the Martin sisters and established occasional correspondence. In 1980 Lary returned from Florida to Belgium and Malmédy, but he was not able to locate Mme. Martin, who had moved.

40. The man who died in Henri Lejoly-Jacob's shed was S/Sgt. John Osborne; the other man whom the Germans evacuated was likely Pvt. Elwood Thomas, who is still missing. Lejoly-Jacob saw Osborne and the other American crawling to the watering trough on Monday, December18. The fifty-year-old farmer went down to the shed and provided some food to the men, who were both badly wounded and unable to walk. Osborne died on Tuesday, December 19, before Lejoly-Jacob and his family fled to the home of Josef Mathonet down the road. Author interview with Madeleine Lejoly, February 10, 2008, Malmédy.

41. Toland interview with Henri Lejoly, no date, but 1958. Toland Papers, *Battle: Story of the Bulge*, LOC, Box 37.

42. Louis Bodarwe: "There were thousands of Belgians for whom the tragedy of war did not end and were treated like traitors by their own people when they returned." Returning from the war, Bodarwe found his home wrecked and his mother missing; no one knew what had happened to her after Sunday, December 17, 1944. Neither Robert Pfeiffer nor Henri Lejoly had seen her after that day. However, in excavating the rubble of the charred ruins of the café to rebuild it, Louis located a severed leg bone in the ashes that was then later identified as that of a woman. Lacking current-day DNA forensics, to identify this as belonging to Mme. Bodarwe was impossible. In 1953 a Maria Themann from the village of Auw responded to a search notice in the *Grenz Echo* newspaper of Eupen, telling of having buried a fifty-five-year-old Belgian woman with a severe leg wound who had died at a nearby German aid station in Vershneid in early 1945. However, when Louis Bodarwe approached the community, the woman had already been buried in a communal grave and authorities refused to allow the body to be exhumed for identification. Mr. Bodarwe related this story to Will Cavanagh in the 1970s; other details can be found in Cuppens's *Massacre a Malmédy*, op. cit., 118.

Chapter 12

1. Interview with David Pergrin, December 15, 1982, Charles B. MacDonald Papers, USa.m.HI, Box 6, 291st Engineer Combat Battalion Folder.

2. David Pergin, *First Across the Rhine* (St. Paul, MN: Zenith Press, 1989), 89–90.

3. Author interview with Al Valenzi, September 26, 1995.

4. Pergrin interview, December 15, 1982, op. cit. In the AAR of the 291st Combat Engineer Battalion, Pergrin and Crickenberger are mentioned as having returned with the prisoners at 1430 hours ("After Action Report 291st Engineer Combat Battalion, December 1944, NA, RG-407, ENGB-291-0.3). However, this time almost certainly is incorrect, as Al Valenzi (whom Pergrin rescued in the first group with Ken Ahrens) clearly mentioned that when he and other prisoners rose to run from the Baugnez field, dusk was approaching (interview with author, February 10, 2008). As sunset at Malmédy, Belgium, came at 4:37 P.M. on December 17, Pergrin and Crickenberger must have returned fully an hour later than stated—3:30 P.M. Moreover, because Pergrin did not signal the U.S. First Army about the massacre until 4:30 P.M. (see Janice Holt Giles, *The Damned Engineers* [New York: Houghton Mifflin, 1970], 181), waiting for two hours to share the shocking news of the massacre with higher headquarters would have been very strange. Moreover, Valenzi told the author that he and the others rescued by the jeep were given first aid, provided with warm clothes, and questioned. That process lasted only for about a half hour before they were evacuated, and it was dark by the time they reached Malmédy. During the late afternoon Pergrin made two reconnaissance sorties toward Baugnez, picking up prisoners each time. However, Pergrin was certain that Ahrens (and, therefore, Valenzi, Sciranko, and Gartska) were in the first group he brought back.

5. "Unit Journal: 1111 Engineer Combat Group," entry for 1640, December 17, 1944, NA, RG-407, ENGP-1111-0.3-3.17. After being signaled by Pergrin, Anderson passed the information onto the U.S. First Army. Also, letter of Lt. John Scanlan, July 25, 1968, Janice Holt Giles Papers, Western Kentucky University.

6. Corp. Bernard Koenig, "Account of Malmédy," 1st Squad, 3rd Platoon, 291st Engineers, November 25, 1968, *Damned Engineers* Papers, Western Kentucky University. "We were disturbed by the continuing departure of men and material from the town. By early evening we were completely alone . . . and freezing. [The next day] we returned to our 3rd platoon CP. Evidence of the panic and haste with which the outfits had left Malmédy was all around. Vast amounts of equipment were strewn about. What was left would have been enough to supply a sizeable South American revolution."

7. Transcript of interview with David Pergrin, March 20, 1965, Janice Holt Giles Papers, Western Kentucky University, Box 30.

8. Baron Friedrich August Von der Heydte's parachute operation was to land at the Mont Rigi crossroads on the Hohes Venn. According to plan, it was

to be relieved on the first day by a reinforced panzergrenadier battalion of the 12th SS Panzer Division. The town of Malmédy that Pergrin defended was, in fact, on *Panzer Rollbahn C*, which was assigned to Kampfgruppe Kuhlmann— the tank regiment of the 12th SS named for SS-Maj. Herbert Kuhlmann and Peiper's tank leader competition in the 6th Panzer Army. At noon on December 17, the 12th SS Panzer Division had not even gotten off the starting line, never piercing the hotly contested frontline positions of the U.S. 99th and 2nd Infantry Divisions near Rocherath. Von der Heydte's parachute operation proved disastrous. Winds widely scattered the hundred Junkers-52 transports, and a number were shot down by friendly fire. Of the thousand men sent off, the Baron was shocked to find only twenty of his men at the target crossroads, and over a period of days he was only able to gather about three hundred of his paratroopers, who had hidden deep in the forest. Von der Heydte and his unsupplied paratroopers eventually made their way back toward German lines, but many were captured. "Kampfgruppe von der Heydte," MS B-823, NA, RG-238, Foreign Military Studies.

9. Author interview with Marthe Maria Martin, October 19, 1995.

10. Testimony of Lt. Col. Alvin B. Welsch to 1st Lt. Raymond D. Czapko, September 10, 1945, Ft. Jackson, SC, NA, RG-549, Case 6–24, Box 30.

11. Paluch (Testimony of Theodore J. Paluch, October 10, 1945, Wiesbaden, Germany) also mentioned that he believed that approximately ten German tanks had passed by before the shooting began.

12. Ford testimony from *U.S. v. Bersin*, Dachau, May 22, 1946. "The men were all laying around and moaning and praying. . . . Then they came along with pistols and rifles and shot some who were breathing and hit others in the head with rifle butts. . . . They were moaning and taking on something terrible. . . . We lay there for approximately two hours."

13. From his description of his wounded comrades, Ford likely ran with Dobyns, Werth, and O'Connell in his escape.

14. Interview with Al Valenzi, December 13, 2007. For his entire adult life, Al treasured the tricolor ribbon given to him by Yolanda Huby on the morning of December 17, 1944.

15. Testimony of Capt. Leon T. Scarborough to Capt. Oliver Seth, December 28, 1944. At the end of 1944 Sgt. Garrett would receive the Bronze Star for remaining behind to help Conrad, Graeff, and Bower to escape before the massacre.

16. The After Action Report for the 285th FAOB (NA, RG 407, FAOB-285-0.3) reveals that Gene Garrett, Conrad, Bower, and Graeff, who managed to escape before the massacre, returned to the battery on the night of

December 17 after being collected by a vehicle sent to Werbomont, Belgium. Most of the rest surviving, other than T/5s Kenneth Kingston and Ted Paluch, needed medical attention: Lt. Virgil P. Lary and twelve others were hospitalized. Six other enlisted men (Appman, Daub, Reding, Profanchick, Reem, and Smith) were so badly shaken by their experience—classified with "battle exhaustion"—that they were lost to the battalion for the month. Harold Billow was so deeply disturbed that he never returned. One man was still lost after escape: after wandering the frozen Ardennes for days, "Sketch" Mearig returned on December 20, 1944. However, it was not until January, when the graves registration teams unearthed the victims in the field, that the battalion could conclude that two officers and fifty-three men of Battery B had been killed, with many others still missing. There were also nine enlisted men who had previously been reported as missing but were now known to have been hospitalized. Flechsig, Valenzi, Gartska, Sciranko, Hardiman, Law, and Day were so badly wounded that their service to the battalion was done; Moucheron and Fox healed to return in January.

17. Ernest W. Bechtel, "Into the Mists of Malmédy," papers of Charles Hammer, 285th FAOB, WWII-5959, USAMHI, Box: Battery Rosters etc.

18. Ernest W. Bechtel, "The Untold Story of Battery B," 1982, USAMHI, Charles B. MacDonald Papers, Box 7. In the autopsy it was discovered that T/5 Swartz, standing at the south end of the field, had been wounded in the knee by a bullet but then was later executed by a close-range pistol shot to the left forehead with powder burns. Ernest Bechtel wrote to Supreme Headquarters and volunteered to "personally execute all the Nazi bastards for murdering my disarmed buddies and my closest friend." The letter was published in *Stars and Stripes*. Five men from Lancaster County were killed at the massacre: Pfc. Carl Frey, T5 Charles Haines, T4 Sylvester Herchelroth, T5 Luke Swartz, and T4 George Steffy.

19. Testimony of T/5 John A. O'Connell to Col. Lamar Tooze, 77th Evacuation Hospital, December 17, 1944, NA, RG-153, Case 6–24, Box 77. "Kansas City Soldier Escapes Murdering," Public Relations Office, 184th General Hospital, January 18, 1945, NA, RG-549, Case 6–24, Box 42, and "Perpetuation of the Testimony of John Anthony O'Connell to Donald L. Crooks," Special Agent SIC, September 10, 1945, Kansas City, MO, NA, RG-549, Case 6–24, Box 30.

20. A machinegun bullet had shattered Breon's left arm, and this may have caused him to fall to the ground to attempt to feign death once more. However, Capt. Kurz's autopsy determined that Breon was killed when his head was struck by a blunt object.

Epilogue

1. Francis Edwards to author, August 1995, Petersburg.

2. The night before, on December 30, a small "Combat patrol of Cupboard (120 Inf. Regt) reached Baugnez crossroads at midnight, but captured no enemy. Returned at 0030." The following evening Pulver would attack with a large combat team. RG-407, 330–2.2 G-2 Records 30th Infantry Division, Box 7595.

3. "History of the 120th Infantry Regiment," *Infantry Journal Press*, Washington, DC, 1947, 137.

4. Quotes from soldiers of the 30th Infantry recapturing Baugnez: Hal Boyle, "50 of Massacred U.S. Captives Are Dug from Snow in Belgium," Associated Press, January 15, 1945. Inspector General's initial report: "Information to Establish Prima Facie Case Required by SHAEF Court of Inquiry, Reference Number IG-101," January 27, 1945, NA, RG-153, Case 6–24, Box 70.

5. January 12: "Company L of the 120th Regt reports reaching Baugnez at 830 a.m. on the 12th. Left on the edge of town. Snow was 15 inches deep. 37 buzz bombs flew over during the 24 hours period." January 13: "To the East in the sector of the 120th Infantry, the 3rd Battalion advanced against mortar, artillery and small arms fire at 0830 when it passed through Géromont and seized the crossroads at Baugnez. Three PWs were taken in Baugnez, 2 from the 3rd Company of the 293rd VGR," RG-407, 330–2.2 G-2 Records 30th Infantry Division, Box 7597.

6. Hit by machine-gun bullets, T/4 Sylvester Herchelroth (Tag #7) had fallen with his hands over his head and froze in this position.

7. See Testimony of T/3 Richard A. Taylor to Dwight Fanton, 165th Signal Photo Company, Paris, July 1945, NA, RG-549, Case 6–24, Box 23. Taylor and Pfc. John Boretsky took 162 photographs of the American bodies as they were uncovered from the snow on January 13 and 14, 1945. (The photos themselves are contained in RG-549, Box 7, and RG-153, Box 72.) Lt. Col. Alvin Welsch had assigned Taylor to the case on January 12 while they waited for the 30th Infantry Division to recapture the massacre field. Pfc. Boretsky, who first arrived with Welsch, was later killed on February 25, 1945, while continuing to photograph the war.

8. Testimony of Lt. Col. Alvin B. Welsch to 1st Lt. Raymond D. Czapko, September 10, 1945, Ft. Jackson, SC, NA, RG-549, Case 6–24, Box 30.

9. Francis Miner to John Bauserman, January 1, 1997. Miner was with the 3060 Graves Registration Company that processed the bodies in January 1945.

10. Maj. Scott T. Glass, "Mortuary Affairs Operations at Malmédy— Lessons Learned from a Historic Tragedy," *Quartermaster Professional Bulletin*,

U.S. Army, Autumn 1997. The recovery operations on January 14 and 15, 1945, were conducted in the cold and under periodic German shellfire. With the deep snow, the operations did not find all victims; over the next four months some twelve additional corpses were recovered in the surrounding area.

11. Welsch testimony, September 10, 1945, op. cit.

12. Francis Miner to John Bauserman, January 1, 1997.

13. Autopsies outlining the cause of death of each crossroads victim are given in three large documents composed by the doctors involved: Testimony of Capt. John A. Snyder, Capt. Joseph A. Kurz, and Maj. Giacento C. Morrone, 44th Evacuation Hospital, January 22, 1945, NA, RG-549, Case 6–24, Box 23.

14. Henri-Chapelle eventually became a permanent U.S. Army cemetery for nearly eight thousand American dead. Although many families of the Malmédy victims chose to bring their dead home for interment, twenty-one of those killed at the crossroads still rest there.

15. Another twenty victims had small-caliber gunshot wounds to the head without powder burns, typically suggesting execution at close range by pistol.

16. Seven others died with their hands still raised over their heads: John Clymire, Sylvester Herchelroth, Richard Walker, Thomas McDermott, Benjamin Lindt, Paul Carr, and John Klukavy. See Testimony of Joseph A. Kurz, January 22, 1945, op. cit.

17. *"Die haben 'n ganze Menge auf der Kreuzung umgelegt."* Charles Whiting, *Massacre at Malmédy: The Story of Jochen Peiper's Battle Group, Ardennes, December, 1944* (London: Leo Cooper, 1971), 96. Peiper's corrections to Whiting's book as submitted to Ernst Klink did not contradict this remark. Jochen Peiper, *"Kommentar zum Buch Massacre at Malmédy von Charles Whiting,"* September 1971.

18. SS-Maj. Ralf Tiemann saw Peiper walking into Wanne with Josef Diefenthal on Christmas Eve morning. Both were wet, covered in mud and exhausted. Peiper's right hand—wounded during the escape across the Salm River—was bandaged by the regimental surgeon. Peiper threw back a cognac, complaining he had not slept in nine days and disappeared from view. Interview with Ralf Tiemann, Untergruppenbach, October 21, 1995.

19. "Nazis Massacre Captive Yanks in Belgium, Survivors Report," *Washington Post*, December 18, 1944, and "Nazi Slaying of 100 Yanks Is Confirmed," *Washington Post*, December 21, 1944. Hal Boyle, "German Tank Force Pours Fire into 150 Unarmed Americans," *Washington Evening Star*, December 18, 1944.

20. The earliest description of the shooting to call it the *Malmédy Massacre* came in an article by Sgt. Ed Cunningham ("Massacre at Malmédy"), which appeared in *Yank* on January 14, 1945. Several other articles took

Cunningham's lead. "Murder Beyond Denial," *New York Times*, January 17, 1945. "What happened near Malmédy, and probably elsewhere, was an outburst of savagery on the part of particular Nazi officers and their units. In as far as the guilty ones can be identified, their punishment will be certain." Bruce Summers escaped with a gashed hand, but his story was repeated from one wire service to the next. Hal Boyle rode with Jack Belden from *Time* magazine and interviewed Summers, who sobbed when Summers told them, "They opened up on us from their armored cars with machine guns. We didn't try to run away or anything. We were just standing there with our hands up and they tried to murder us all." Their reportage ended up in *Time* on Christmas Day 1944 (19). *Newsweek* ran a story, "Murder in the Field" on January 8, 1945. So disturbing were the images of the frozen American bodies found in the Baugnez field that *Life* magazine, on February 5, 1945, graced its cover with Florida beach beauty Amelia Crossland rather than shock those at home with grizzly airbrushed images of "Murder in the Snow," seen inside the magazine on page 27.

21. Hal Boyle, "German Tank Force Pours Fire into 150 Unarmed Americans," *Washington Evening Star*, December 18, 1944. Boyle also interviewed William F. Reem ("They were cutting us down like guinea pigs . . . "), Charles Appman ("We just hoped and prayed while we lay there listening to them shoot every man that moved . . . "), and Harold Billow, who described how they lay for nearly an hour until there was only a single German tank nearby: "It wasn't more than 100 yards away, but we decided we had to make a break for it then or never. We jumped up and scattered for the woods. The tank opened up on us, but I don't think they got many that time."

22. Author interview with Madeleine Lejoly, February 10, 2008, Malmédy.

23. John Wilhelm, "Germans Shooting Prisoners," *Washington Evening Star*, December 19, 1944. "According to eyewitness accounts, German tank columns engaged in the offensive are ruthlessly shooting groups of helpless American prisoners with machine guns which seems to suggest that to expedite their push, they may not be taking prisoners."

24. "Nazis Massacre Captive Yanks in Belgium, Survivors Report," *Washington Post*, December 18, 1944.

25. Peiper's direct testimony at the Malmédy trial on June 22, 1946, told of a conversation with his Tiger battalion commander, Heinz von Westernhagen just outside Trois-Ponts on December 18, 1944: "he told me in this conference that a 'mix-up' had happened at Ligneuville and that a rather large number of prisoners had been shot there. He did not know any details nor who had given the order to do that." NA, RG-153, Case 6–24, Entry 143, *U.S. v. Bersin*, Roll 3, Frame 000160, 1939 of courtroom proceedings.

26. "I immediately reported any news of that kind to the Führer and no one could have stopped me from doing so. As an example, SS-Gen. [Hermann] Fegelein told the Chief of the General Staff, Colonel Guderian and Gen. Jodl of atrocities committed by the *SS Brigade Kaminski* in Warsaw. . . . Ten minutes later, I reported this fact to the Führer and he immediately ordered the dissolution of this brigade." "Testimony of Alfred Jodl," Trial of Major War Criminals, International War Tribunal, Nuremberg, 1948, Vol. XV, 298.

27. "Screening Results 15–24 November 1945," SS-Cpl. Gerhard Ellhof, 2nd Company Panzer Signals Battalion, LAH, Ellis Papers.

28. BDC File on Joachim Peiper, NA, RG-242, A 3343-SSO-348A. "Vorschlag Nr. 1 für die Verleihung der Schwerter zum Eichenlaub des Ritterkreuzes des E.K," December 26, 1945.

29. "Fernschrift, 11 January 1945," BDC File on Joachim Peiper, op. cit. Message signaled from Hitler's headquarters by Waffan SS adjutant, Johannes Göhler at 2:25 a.m. and signed by Hitler. The press release was dated February 6, 1945.

30. Conrad Black, *Franklin Delano Roosevelt: Champion of Freedom* (New York: Public Affairs, 2003), 1032. Recently declassified documents reveal that top American intelligence was worried that Hitler had developed a "dirty" radioactive bomb that, though not of immense destructive power, would still be capable of rendering a large part of London uninhabitable.

31. For an evenhanded evaluation of the Malmédy trial and its aftermath, see James Weingartner *Crossroads of Death: The Story of the Malmédy Massacre and Trial* (Berkeley: University of California Press, 1979).

32. "Malmédy Survivor Upholds Army Probe," *Pittsburgh Post Gazzette*, April 22, 1949.

33. Many potential suspects were never apprehended or questioned, despite leads (see Appendix 3). In an undated memo to a Col. Derrick with the War Crimes Division: "Mr. Miller, Intelligence Division informs me that one Guenther A. Hering lives in constant dread that he will be picked up for his part in the Malmédy Massacre, . . . [Do we wish] the suspect picked up and questioned?" The handwritten note simply had "No action taken—JHD" scrawled across the top. "Malmédy Suspect?" NA, RG-549, Case 6–24, Box 13. Hering had been an SS-2nd Lt. leading the SPW immediately behind Erich Rumpf's SPW at the crossroads and was named in shootings there as well as in Ligneuville with Paul Ochmann. Additional SS men the prosecution identified as supposedly guilty at the crossroads, but not apprehended (spelling and titles are not complete, reflecting limitations of the trial closing statement): Herbert Losenski, Wolfgang Altkrueger, Stmn. Kissewitz, Sepp Witkowski, Harry

Ende, Gerhard Walkowiski, Hans Toedter, Ernst Rock, Werner Pedersen, Za-ckel, Skotz, Joseph Hess, Rudi Storm, Erich Dubbert, Strmn. Bock. Corzieni, Katcher, Piotta, Haas, Max Beutner, Josef Aistleitner, Bertel Schultze, Werner Jirassek, Manfred Mueller, George Deibert, Gerhardt Schlingmann, Willi Bil-loschetzsky, Hannes Martens, Johannes Oettinger, Günther Hering. *U.S. v. Bersin*, 3020–3031.

34. For more details of this period, see Jens Westemeier, *Joachim Peiper: A Biography of Himmler's SS Commander* (Atglen, PA: Schiffer Publications, 2007).

35. Author interview with Hans Siptrott, May 17, 1997.

36. Fleps never denied that he fired shots from Panzer Nr. 731 at the crossroads. However, he did tell Gerd Cuppens on September 14, 1986 he had fired due to the attempted escape of the Americans. "That is really the reason for the shooting. . . . That matter will be my obsession for the rest of my life," he wrote. Cuppens, *Massacre a Malmédy?* (Bayeux, France: Editions Heimdal, 1989), 107. Charles Whiting spoke to Fleps in 1969. "I asked him if he fired the shots at the crossroads. He said 'Yes.' I asked him 'Why?' but he changed the subject." Author's interview with Whiting, August 20, 2001, York.

After the war one Waffan SS panzer man (who, though interviewed, remains anonymous) refused to go to reunions if Georg Fleps would be present. He told the author that, when he was at the POW enclosure at Ebensee, Austria, beginning in August 1945, he was surprised to hear men of the 7th Panzer Company in Camp 18 "bragging of having shot the American prisoners." That the anonymous veteran and Fleps and Siptrott were held together at Ebensee is verified. (Screening of SS PWs at Camp No. 1, Ebensee, September 1945, NA, RG-549, Case 6–24, Box 31.) At first he did not know what they were discussing, but later this became clear. He found Georg Fleps to be "a thoroughly distasteful person" who nearly beat a comrade to death in captivity at Zuffenhausen in 1945. "He was a sadist." E-mails to the author on March 16 and 17, 2010, from Dr. Wolfgang Quatember, of KZ-Gedenkstätte und Zeitgeschichte Museum Ebensee, re-vealed that while at an internment center, fifty-eight SS men had died of illness and other unknown causes at Ebensee in 1945 and that there had been fighting over food, which was short at the camp at that time. In his interview with the author (March 14, 2010) Melvin Bielawski also men-tioned knowledge of altercations between SS men at Zuffenhausen while he was there working for the in-house U.S. Army hospital in late 1944 and early 1945.

37. "When we arrived at the crossroad, the American soldiers were al-ready lying in the field and we moved on without stopping. . . . We did not fire

there, and Beutner did not give an order to fire." Letter from Max Hammerer to author, July 25, 2011.

38. Letter from Robert Mearig to author, September 19, 1996. Mearig died in August 2007.

39. Author interview with Harold Billow, April 10, 2011. "I still have bad feelings about the Germans. It was a terrible thing they did. They machine gunned us. And then they shot anyone that was still alive and kicked everybody to see who still was."

40. Author interview with Stephen Domitrovich, April 11, 2011. Like Domitrovich, many Malmédy survivors never wished to return to the site of their brush with death. Daub, Ahrens, Kingston, Lary, Dobyns, and Ford returned to testify in the Malmédy trial. Others who later returned to Baugnez: Al Valenzi, George Fox, Ted Flechsig, Ted Paluch, and Bill Merriken.

41. Author interview with George Fox, January 10, 2010.

42. See John Bauserman, *The Malmédy Massacre* (Shippensburg, PA: White Mane, 1995), 118, and "*Baugnez: recapés de'enfer, les deux GI ont enfin retrouvé leurs anges gardiens!*" unknown Belgian newspaper clipping, October 3, 1990.

43. Author interview with Kenneth Ahrens, November 2, 1998.

44. Author interview with Catherine Lyon, January 6, 1997.

45. Michael Reynolds, "The Malmédy Massacre," in *The Devil's Adjutant* (New York: Sarpedon, 1995), 263.

46. Susan Ruiz, "Hunt Intensifies for Murder Suspect," *The Morning Call*, October 11, 1993, and Letter, Mrs. Kenneth Kingston to Charles Hammer, 1993, Charles Hammer Papers, USAMHI, Box Miscellaneous. For the resolution of Carl Daub affair: "DNA Shows Skeletal Remains Belong to 1988 Murder Suspect" *Times Leader*, Wilkes-Barre, PA, December 27, 2003.

47. When doctors examined Richard Walker, his arms were still frozen over his head, killed instantly when his heart was pierced by a machine-gun bullet. Report of Capt. Joseph A. Kurcz, 44th EVAC Hospital, January 14–16, 1945, NA, RG-549, Case 6–24, Box 23.

48. Reding letter to his mother, January 17, 1945.

49. For "nervous condition" and "I was pleased . . . ": Reding account of March 28, 1996, op. cit. Researcher John Bauserman reunited the two men in 1988, some forty-four years after their encounter.

50. Interviews with Al Valenzi on September 26, 1995, and January 13, 2008.

51. Much of the information on Al Valenzi after the war was kindly provided by George Gaadt.

52. "Local Soldier Feigns Death," Corapolis, PA, newspaper clipping, no publication and no date, but 1945.

53. Valenzi interview, September 26, 1995, op. cit.

54. Author interview with Ted Paluch, December 15, 2007.

Appendix IV

1. William Faulkner, *Requiem for a Nun*, Act 1, Scene III.

2. Madame Bodarwe was likely shot by a member of Kurt Briesemeister's tank at the crossroads—SS-Pvt. Günther Nüchter.

3. Gerd Cuppens, *Massacre a Malmédy?* (Bayeux, France: Editions Heimdal, 1989), 108–110.

4. "Report of the Supreme Headquarters Allied Expeditionary Force Court of Inquiry re Shooting of Allied Prisoners of War near Malmédy, Belgium, 17 December 1944," Na, RG-331, Entry 56, Box 127.

5. Most of these men were found within a kilometer of the crossroads, with their death tied to the events at Baugnez. The following men's bodies were discovered in 1945 after the snows melted: Frederick Clark, Warren Davis, Solomon Goffman, Wilson Jones, Raymond Lester, William Moore, David Murray, Walter Perkowski, John Rupp, Alphonse Stabulis, Elwood Thomas, and Louis Vario. Louis Vario was found dead at Neuhof, Germany, some eighteen kilometers east of Malmédy with no idea of how he reached that place after the massacre. Elwood Thomas, seen badly wounded in a barn near Thirimont by Michael Skoda on December 21 or 22, is still listed as MIA and presumed dead. His remains have never been located.

6. See Cuppens, *Massacre a Malmédy?*, op. cit., 109.

7. In Cuppens's "Reconstruction" (*Massacre a Malmédy?*, op. cit., 111–114), he claims that when Sternebeck approached that "Most of them [the Americans] defend themselves against the tanks that approach. Several American soldiers are killed during the German attack." As a source for this notion, Cuppens vaguely sources American, German, and Belgian testimonies. In truth, only a very few of the Americans in the 285th FAOB returned the German approach fire, with only two wounded (Al Valenzi and Carl Stevens).

In fact, no Germans were seen killed in any of the ninety American testimonies from the survivors (many had multiple interviews and affidavits) that the author reviewed. Moreover, the approach of enemy tanks was the reason for most of the Americans to put down arms and give up. Clearly, as Lt. Lary judged in calling for surrender as the tanks approached, to attempt to resist with no more than rifles would have been absurd.

Cuppens subscribed to the popular Waffen SS alibi that the vanguard opened fire on the Americans when they approached after Sternebeck—causing more casualties. Again, although numerous American recollections agreed that there was a short minute interval between the first tanks and halftracks and the main German armored column, with additional shellfire on the 285th, none of these accounts describe additional casualties from the approaching vanguard. Even more importantly, all the American eyewitness testimonies are clear that the main shooting came from stationary German vehicles lined up on the road in front of the assembled American prisoners. Mistaking the unarmed men with raised hands for combat soldiers can be conclusively eliminated as a possibility.

Cuppens then used the described escape attempt of Dobyns (who ran after the first shots were fired) to excuse the shooting of those assembled at the crossroads. Although this certainly happened (and Mearig, Stabulis, and Flack also attempted to escape), these men only sought to get away *after* the Germans were already siting machine guns on the group and trying to use the howitzer on a passing SPW to help execute the prisoners.

8. Details on those killed are summarized in Appendix I, Table A.1.

9. Those volunteering to drive for the Germans: T/5 Thomas Bacon, Sgt. Eugene Lacey, T/5 Ralph Logan, Sgt. Vernon Anderson, T/5 David Lucas, Pvt. William Barron, and Cpl. John Cummings.

10. For details see Appendix I, Table A.2.

11. Charles Whiting, *Massacre at Malmédy: The Story of Jochen Peiper's Battle Group, Ardennes, December, 1944* (London: Leo Cooper, 1971).

12. Paul Hausser, *Waffen SS in Einsatz* (Göttingen: Plesse Verlag, 1953).

13. Dietrich Ziemssen, *Der Malmédy Prozess* (Munich: Deschler, 1952).

14. Ibid., 16. Also Ralf Tiemann, *The Leibstandarte*, vol. IV/2 (Winnipeg, Canada: J. J. Fedorowicz, 1998), 47. Source is given as 1st Panzer Regiment Combat Report prepared in April 1947 by Hans Gruhle. The language used to describe the incident is precisely that used by Ziemssen in 1952.

15. Ralf Tiemann, *Der Malmédy Prozess: Ein Ringen um Gerechtigkeit* (Osnabrück: Munin Verlag, 1990).

16. James Weingartner, *Crossroads of Death: The Story of the Malmédy Massacre and Trial* (Berkeley: University of California Press, 1977), 240–244.

17. Ibid. "It is reasonable to conjecture that on that December afternoon at the crossroads Pringel [Weingartner's pseudonym for Poetschke] concluded that one hundred or so American prisoners were too many to be conveniently dealt with by a unit needing every ounce of manpower and second of time to gain its objectives."

18. "Testimony of Friedrich Christ," Wiesbaden, October 1945, NA, RG-549, Case 6–24, Box 28.

19. Klaus Hammel, "Der Fall Malmédy: Deutsche Kriegsverbrechen in der Ardennenoffensive?" *Das Ritterkreuz*, Ordensgemeinschaft der Ritterkreuzträger, 51 Jahrgang, Nr. September 3, 2005, 4–14. This publication uses the same sources

(Ziemssen, Tiemann, and Agte) to cast doubt on the guilt of Kampfgruppe Peiper.

20. Cuppens, *Massacre a Malmédy?*, op. cit., 111–115.

21. Claudia J. Stanny and Thomas C. Johnson, "Effects of Stress Induced by a Simulated Shooting on Recall by Police and Citizen Witnesses," *American Journal of Psychology* 113, no. 3 (Fall 2000): 359–386.

22. John C. Yuille, "A Critical Examination of the Psychological and Practical Implications of Eyewitness Research," *Law and Human Behavior* 4, no. 4 (1980): 335–345.

23. Patrick Agte, *Jochen Peiper: Commander Panzerregiment Leibstandarte* (Winnipeg: J. J. Fedorowicz, 1999), 483.

24. Ibid.

25. Michael Reynolds, "Massacre at Malmédy during the Battle of the Bulge," *World War II Magazine*, February 2003.

26. Michael Reynolds, "The Malmédy Massacre," in *The Devil's Adjutant: Jochen Peiper, Panzer Leader* (New York: Sarpedon, 1995).

27. "Kampfgruppe Peiper: 15–26 December 1944," MS C-004, Historical Division European Command, no date, but 1945 or 1946. Although the authorship of this document is not given, it likely comes from Hans Gruhle (USa.m.HI, D739.F6713, C-004). A similar account but one differing in details is given in Tiemann, *Der Malmédy Prozess*, op. cit., 46–47, and is cited as having come from a report prepared by Hans Gruhle in April 1947.

28. Trevor N. Dupuy, "Malmédy Massacre and Trial," Appendix G, in *Hitler's Last Gamble* (New York: Harper Collins, 1994). In 1993 Dr. Franz-Uhle-Wettler composed a long essay, "Malmédy Massacre and Trial: A View from Germany," which formed the basis for the questionable appendix in Dupuy's book on the Battle of the Bulge. This piece brought out the same tired SS apologists previously utilized: Most of the American dead at the crossroads had come from casualties in the first meeting engagement with Sternebeck's *Spitze* and then from a later meeting engagement with the succeeding elements of the Kampfgruppe Peiper. Uhle-Wettler even subscribed to the altogether fantastic idea that after the German armored vanguard had passed by, the Americans had taken up arms to confront the armor to follow. Yet in a letter to the author on May 14, 1995, Uhle-Wettler admitted that the ratio of dead to wounded in the crossroads engagement did indicate that "some of those found dead at the crossroads have been murdered."

29. The cannon-mounting SPW was under command of SS Sgt. Gerhard Schumacher of the 11th Panzer Grenadier Company. Statement of Heinz Friedrichs, March 21, 1946, NA, RG-549, Case 6–24, Box 9. Friedrichs was a Grenadier in the SPW of Schumacher.

30. Those attempting to escape at the first shots were Robert Mearig, Donald Flack, Alphonse Stabulis, and Samuel Dobyns. Mearig and Dobyns survived. Flack fell at the rear of the group, but autopsy revealed that the cause of his death was a close-range shot to the head. Mortally wounded in the escape, Alphonse Stabulis was found in the woods one kilometer south of the crossroads. His body was not discovered until spring 1945.

31. Less than an hour later another eight American prisoners of the 9th Armored Division, captured in Ligneuville, were shot as well: T/5 John Borcina, S/Sgt. Joseph F. Collins, T/4 Casper S. Johnson, Pvt. Clifford H. Pitts, Pfc. Michael B. Penny, S/Sgt. Lincoln Abraham, Pvt. Gerald R. Carter, and Pvt. Nick G. Sullivan. All were shot in the back of the head or in the face. Today a simple monument just before the Hotel du Moulin denotes the shooting, which occurred just before the entrance to the town.

32. Paul Zwigart, who was driving Diefenthal's SPW at the crossroads, spoke to SS medic Josef Frank while both were held in captivity in the fall of 1945. "Zwigart driver of the vehicle in which Peiper and Diefenthal were driving at the time of the shooting at the crossroad, told Frank, Schlachter, Moosbrugge and others that Peiper gave the order at the crossroads." Dwight Fanton's Personality Card Index File, NA, RG-549, Case 6–24, Index to Defendants in the Malmédy Case, Reference Witness Statements, 290/59/18/5, Card for SS-Sgt. Josef Frank, 7th Panzer Company. Zwigart's later confession at Schwäbisch Hall of February 11, 1946, is in NA, RG-549, Case 6–24, Box 9. However, in that confession Zwigart deliberately avoided saying anything about what happened at the crossroads—a key omission. "Till now, I have concealed all that could become a charge against my former commanders—in the naive belief that nothing could happen to me, as a simple soldier. . . . Further, I expected that our former idolized commanders would at least stand up to their orders and responsibility. . . . But as today, our former officers mainly pass off their previously given orders and their responsibility to subordinates, I feel obliged to conceal nothing more. On the crossroads near Malmédy, it was there that my former commander, in his yellow jacket, left my SPW. If Diefenthal had a good conscience, he would not need to deny that and to refute it with perjuries and declarations." Declaration of Paul Zwigart, Landsberg-Lech, August 26, 1948, NA, RG-549, Case 6–24, Box 14.

33. Letter from Manfred Thorn to author, October 2, 2010.

34. Author interview with Manfred Thorn, May 11, 1999.

35. Peiper to Toland, April 5, 1959. LOC, Toland Papers, Box 108.

36. Jochen Peiper to James Weingartner, February 19, 1976.

37. The prisoners at Chenogne were likely from Otto Remer's Führer Begleit Brigade. Martin K. Sorge, *The Other Price of Hitler's War: German Mili-*

tary and Civilian Losses Resulting from World War II (New York: Greenwood Press, 1986), 147. For the orders from the 328th Regiment, see Hugh M. Cole, *The Ardennes: Battle of the Bulge*, The U.S. Army in World War II (Washington, DC: U.S. Government Printing Office, 1965), 264. There were several other incidents of a mass shooting of their enemy by American soldiers in World War II. During the invasion of Sicily, involving the capture of the Biscari airfield on July 14, 1943, American forces of the green 45th Infantry Division were subjected to devastating sniper fire while pinned down. Raging for revenge, troops of the 180th Infantry Regiment killed seventy-one Italian and two German POWs in two incidents on the same day. When told of the massacre, Gen. Omar Bradley passed word along to Gen. George S. Patton that U.S. soldiers had murdered some fifty to seventy prisoners in cold blood. As he would later do with the Chenogne incident, Patton schemed in his diary:

> I told Bradley that it was probably an exaggeration, but in any case to tell the Officer to certify that the dead men were snipers or had attempted to escape or something, as it would make a stink in the press and also would make the civilians mad. Anyhow, they are dead, so nothing can be done about it.

Bradley refused Patton's cover-up, and the two Americans responsible were faced with courts martial. One, Capt. John T. Compton, used the defense of following superior orders and was acquitted, only to die later in fighting in November 1943. Meanwhile, Sgt. Horace B. West, admitting his role in machine gunning thirty-five Italians and two Germans, was found guilty. He was sentenced to life in prison but was given a shortened sentence and a dishonorable discharge. See James Weingartner, "Massacre at Biscari: Patton and an American War Crime," *The Historian* (1989): 24–39.

In the closing days for the war, on April 29, 1945, the 222nd Infantry Regiment engaged several dozen Waffen SS men still fighting at the tiny farm hamlet of Webling some ten kilometers northeast of Dachau. One American was gunned down as they approached the village at a time when GIs in Europe were sharply focused on surviving the last week of the war. The incident so angered the Americans capturing the first SS contingent that the seventeen surrendering were lined up against an earthen bank at the Furtmayer Farm and shot down in cold blood. Another group was killed nearby. In all, forty-one Waffen SS men were killed. "The Webling Incident," *After the Battle*, no. 27 (1980): 30–33.

38. Pierre Boissier, "Martial Law and Military Order," in *De Solférino à Tsushima* (Geneva, Switzerland: Histoire du CICR, 1953), 109.

INDEX